The
Illustrated Encyclopedia of
TREES
Timbers and Forests of the World

A group of foxgloves (Digitalis purpurea)
*thrive in a clearing in a mixed European broadleaved
forest. Many kinds of wild flowers
flourish in such forests where light
and space allow.*

*An acacia tree silhouetted
against the evening sky beside a lake in Amboseli
National Park, Kenya. The
gaunt, characteristically flat-topped
outline of acacia trees has become a symbol
of the African savannah.*

The
Illustrated Encyclopedia of
TREES
Timbers and Forests of the World

Herbert Edlin · Maurice Nimmo et al.

Consultants:
Dr. Eric A. Bourdo Jr. Dean, School of Forestry and Wood Products,
Michigan Technological University
Hugh Fraser Editor of WORLD WOOD magazine

Illustrated by Ian Garrard, Olivia Beasley and David Nockels

CORGI BOOKS
A DIVISION OF TRANSWORLD PUBLISHERS LTD

The AUTHORS

*All the rich and subtle range
of autumn's splendid palette can be seen at a
glance in these fallen sugar maple leaves,
shed each year to prevent the
tree drying out as soil moisture becomes
frozen during the winter.*

Herbert Edlin MBE
The author of many books on trees and other plants, Herbert Edlin was responsible, perhaps more than any other person, for encouraging the public to develop a deeper understanding and love of trees. Until his death, he was Publications Officer of the Forestry Commission.

Maurice Nimmo
Formerly a Forest Research District Officer with the Forestry Commission, Maurice Nimmo is now a photographer and writer on temperate trees. He has worked with Herbert Edlin on many books.

Allen Paterson
After spending four years at Cambridge University Botanic Gardens, Allen Paterson moved to the Royal Botanic Gardens, Kew, and then taught environmental studies in schools and colleges before taking up his present position as Curator of the Chelsea Physic Garden, London.

Dr. Pat Morris
A lecturer in Zoology at London University, Pat Morris has travelled widely in pursuit of his natural history interests. He is a frequent contributor to nature radio programmes.

Dr. Mary J. Burgis
An ecologist and lecturer in Biology at the City of London Polytechnic, Mary Burgis spent three years in Uganda contributing to the International Biological Programme and has also travelled in America and Europe.

Dr. John Mason
At present Dr. Mason is Deputy Regional Officer of the Nature Conservancy Council in Berkshire, England. He gained his doctorate with a thesis on the ecology of woodland beetles.

John Pitt
A Rhodes scholar in 1929, John Pitt joined the Colonial Forest Service and remained with it until the outbreak of war. He is now Editor/ Secretary of the Commonwealth Forestry Association in Oxford.

John R. Palmer
A timber expert working for a large forest plantation scheme in eastern Amazonia, John Palmer's speciality is the study of tree growth rates in the rain forest and in plantations.

Robert Andrew Paterson
Mr. Paterson studied horticulture in Dublin and at Kew and has collected plants for Kew in the forests of Indonesia and Zaire. He is now working as a horticulturalist for Tate and Lyle, mainly in Ghana.

F. Nigel Hepper
Mr. Hepper is Assistant Keeper in the Herbarium, Kew and has taken part in several botanical expeditions. He is Editor of the Revised Flora of West Tropical Africa.

Dr. John Dransfield
A Senior Research Fellow at Kew, Dr. Dransfield has a special interest in palms and has visited South America, Africa and Southeast Asia to study them.

Dr. Ronald Melville
Formerly a Senior Principal Scientific Officer at Kew, Dr. Melville has made a lifelong study of Australasian plants.

THE ILLUSTRATED ENCYCLOPEDIA OF TREES, TIMBERS AND FORESTS OF THE WORLD
A CORGI BOOK 0 552 98205 9

Originally published in Great Britain by Salamander Books Ltd.

PRINTING HISTORY
Salamander edition published 1978
Corgi edition published 1981

Colour reproduction:
Culver Graphics Limited, Buckinghamshire, United Kingdom
Positive Colour Limited, Essex, United Kingdom
Filmset:
SX Composing Limited
Essex, United Kingdom

This book is set in Century Schoolbook

Corgi Books are published by Transworld Publishers Ltd., Century House, 61-63 Uxbridge Road, Ealing, London, W5 5SA

Made and printed in Belgium by Henri Proost & Cie.

CREDITS
Editor: Geoff Rogers
Designers: Carol Collins, Roger Hyde
Illustrations: Ian Garrard, Olivia Beasley, David Nockels

The CONTENTS

Colonies of moss growing
on a fallen oak log epitomize the constant cycle
of decay and renewal that
keeps the forest alive; nutrients released
by the death of one plant are
essential food for others.

The FOREWORD

*Even in the darkest corners
of a tropical forest, the unrelieved monotony
of its foliage is occasionally
enlivened by sudden splashes of
vivid colour, as exemplified
by this striking view of Mucuna warburgii, a
native creeping vine of New Guinea.*

For many of us a tree is our most familiar symbol of the natural world. It represents freedom, a chance to escape from our increasingly hostile environment. Perhaps we feel at one with trees because the forest was man's ancestral home and a deep-seated yearning draws us back. Perhaps we are simply in awe of the sheer size and majesty of that dwindling band of arboreal giants that are disappearing from our landscape. Or perhaps it is because unconsciously we match our moods with the changing forms and colours of the forest as the seasons pass from the sombre reality of winter to the promise of spring.

Whatever our underlying reasons, we all benefit from the therapeutic influence of trees, whether we simply enjoy the dappled calm of a forest glade or rejoice in the life and colour that a single tree can bring to a bleak city street. It is only logical, therefore, that this identification with trees leads us to become curious about the type of species that grow near to us, so that enjoyment and study become one pursuit.

But the forest yields a dual satisfaction, for at the heart of a tree's beauty lies the strength of wood, as welcome and valuable a construction material today as it has always been. In the home wood emanates a friendly warmth, its texture a comforting reminder of its natural origins. But the cry has always been: 'Will there be enough to go round?' The answer is a paradox, for wood is both the most vulnerable and yet potentially the most permanent of the world's natural resources. A tree is easily felled, but a forest, properly managed, can be a self-renewing process for generations to come.

Thus our fundamental love of trees and our communal realization that wood is a valuable resource are two inseparable themes. It is to foster understanding of both that this book has been prepared.

The World of TREES & TIMBERS

*The tall stately trunks of beech
trees represent a living resource that for centuries
has provided man with a rich supply
of warm, dark wood, used even in ancient times
for beds, chests and tables,
and other household objects.*

*I*n most parts of the world, trees are the largest elements of the
living landscape. Yet many people take them for granted, like
hills or clouds, forgetting that each tree is a living entity and
food or home to a multitude of other plants and animals.

Trees—conifers at least—have towered above their fellow
land plants for 200 million years. They are ten times more
ancient than the grasses and were already a venerable group
when the first dinosaurs appeared. Trees still dominate huge
areas, but they are now slaves and raw materials for that modern
evolutionary upstart, man.

For trees are largely made of wood. This strong, solid, yet
flexible material evolved perfectly adapted for supporting leaves
against wind and rain. Leaves in turn sustain the tree. They
pluck gases from air and energy from sunlight and draw in
dissolved minerals taken up by the roots from soil. With these
ingredients leaves make more foliage, more wood.

Wood not only meets the needs of trees, it helps perform a
thousand human tasks as well. Hardwoods served as levers
and cogs long before machines were made of metals. Springy
woods made bows, traps, baskets—and still do, even in the age
of plastics. Wood supports our houses; inside the furniture
is of solid wood or compacted wood chips, often with a decorative
wood veneer. Then, too, man chemically dismantles softwood and
reconstitutes its cellulose as paper, cardboard and explosives.
Wood carbon forms charcoal filters for air and water.

Besides wood, certain trees yield special products—rubbers,
gums, medicines, spices, oils, resins, cork, fibres; to say nothing
of fruits, seeds and nuts.

Perhaps trees serve man in more ways than any other living
group of objects. Yet, for some of us, the fascination of these
living factories is their sheer beauty and variety of form.

The Guardian Forest

Since the dawn of man's awareness he has known and feared the forest. It was the home of his remote ancestors and he walks the world today with a physique and brain that could only have developed amidst an environment of growing trees. His grasping hand had evolved to hold branches long before he learnt to use sticks for his first simple tools, and so set out on his long career of advancement beyond all other animals. His keen forward-looking eyes, ideal for judging distance, are a legacy from remote ancestors who moved with confidence from branch to branch. More important still, the poise and balance developed through tree-climbing enabled man eventually to walk erect on his feet alone, freeing his hands, eyes and brain for all the important tasks that contribute to his present well-being.

So equipped, man learnt to live away from the woods and the trees, to become a hunter or fisherman, a herdsman or a tiller of the soil, or eventually a city dweller. From his forest upbringing he gained the power to destroy the forest, something that no other creature can do. As the centuries rolled on the people of successive cultures, in various regions of the world, swept away vast expanses of woodland with fire and axe, then farmed the land so thoroughly that the trees never came back.

A precious resource

In a timber-hungry world there seems something wicked about burning up a resource that has taken 250 years to grow, but every time and place has its own scheme of values. Today we think more and more of safeguarding each heritage from the past for the benefit of the future. Forest is, paradoxically, at once the most durable and the most fragile of such resources. Given the right care, it can endure for centuries, but a single act of folly—a fire or an ill-planned felling—can destroy it within weeks or even hours, and it will take a century to return.

Today we find that forests have survived only over the poorest or

least accessible regions of the world, though they still occupy around one quarter of the earth's land surface. They persist mainly on steep hillsides with poor or thin soils, too unrewarding to clear, or they are sited too remotely from centres of trade and industry for their exploitation to be, so far, worth while.

In a finite world, any limited resource acquires a value as soon as it becomes scarce. At this eleventh hour, most countries have realized that their remaining forests demand conservation as unique assets. Besides their value as timber producers, they have a unique part to play as protectors of mountain soils, controllers of rivers and water supplies, reserves for many kinds of wild plants, beasts, birds and insects, and providers of landscapes that, at every season of the year, delight the eye. Through their vast extent and natural, untamed character they present a challenge to the wanderer, who may need all his skills to follow a forest trail, whether afoot or on horseback. To the forest manager they offer an even greater challenge, for he must conserve and where possible improve a complex of living organisms—trees, plants,

Above: A modern-day forester trimming branches from a pine trunk. A tape attached to his belt measures the bole as he moves along and ear muffs deaden the sound of the chainsaw. On occasion, especially in confined spaces, it is more practicable to cut down trees manually than to use expensive modern machinery.

Below: The great grey owl (*Strix nebulosa*) a nocturnal predator of the world's northern coniferous forests.

beasts, birds, and small invertebrate creatures—over a fixed terrain but subject to variable circumstances of soil and ever-changing weather. To the scientific approach of a geologist, meteorologist, and biologist, the forest manager must add the practical know-how of an engineer, building roads and manipulating machines to take his timber speedily and cheaply to the right markets. As a businessman he must know what and where those markets are, and understand the marvellous technical properties of wood that fit it for a multitude of everyday uses, from the production of the frame of a sea-going boat to the manufacture of newsprint. At the same time he must remain a husbandman, able to make trees grow from seed and seedling to maturity.

The perpetual forest

The keywords for the care of the perpetual forest are simple ones: *sustained yield*. In their most obvious sense they involve maintaining a sustained yield of timber, which means that fresh young trees must spring up, or be planted, to replace those cut down for sale and use. But sustained yield has other important implications. Other outputs from the forest should be sustained indefinitely too. A major one is water, which should flow in clear streams from a catchment protected by woodland foliage and leaf litter, which check the erosion of the soil. Game of all kinds, and even fish, should find in the well-managed forest a perpetual home in which they can maintain breeding stocks yet still yield annual surpluses for sportsmen and anglers to shoot or catch. Continuing forest cover will also ensure that songbirds, squirrels, butterflies, wild flowers and all the other attractive creatures that delight the naturalist can find their places (though not always the same places on the map) in an environment that may change in detail, but not in overall character. Recreational and scenic values are also conserved by the perpetual sustained-yield forest. Individual views will alter from time to time, but each should be replaced by an alternative that leaves the total resource undiminished or even improved.

Today the greatest threat to the continued existence of the world's forests is not fire, nor timber felling nor even clearance for farming—for most of the surviving tall woods stand on lands too poor for anyone to farm at a profit. The greatest danger is the indifference of the people who control them, or claim to do so. Every nation today makes a show of its conservation laws and plans, yet few succeed in implementing them on the ground with real concern for the evolutionary growth that has brought into being the present-day complex of living soil, tree, plant, and animal life. Too often the forest is seen as something that is merely there, rather than something that has slowly evolved through a varying pattern of ecological change; and there is a temptation to stop the clock, to say that any particular wood or tree must cease to change or evolve as the years go by. With this attitude there is, of course, no true concern for the future. Things will stay as they are, so why plan?

The changing forest

In fact we can but step into the forest at a particular moment of time. If we come this way again a few hours, days, months or years later, we will never find it the same. Within one day the angle of the sun, the strength of the wind, the moisture of the air will vary—all factors of life that are as vital to the trees as they are fascinating to the observer. At certain hours of the day some leaves will be sunlit, others shaded; the pattern can

Above: Fallow deer bucks (*Dama dama*) at home in European open woodland. Deer are leaf browsers and thus among the many animals to disappear as forests are cleared.

never be the same for two hours together. At times the leaves and branches will be in violent motion, stirred by strong winds, at others deathly still, each leaf disposed in the peculiar fashion of its kind. Dawn may see tree crowns and branches shrouded in mist, which vanishes during the heat of the day, to be followed by the torrential rain of a thunderstorm, leaving foliage, stems and soil soaking wet.

A succession of days may see leaves unfold, flowers open, seeds ripen, and foliage fade, with different stages shown at the same time by various trees, or even by different branches on the same tree. The changing patterns of the seasons embrace, in a woodland of broadleaved trees, the stark bare branches of winter outlined by clinging snow, the bright green, tender, unfolding leaves of spring, the full majesty of dark green summer foliage, often enlivened by blossoms, and the glorious golden and orange shades displayed when the leaves fade in the autumn.

The changes that come with the passing of a whole year are clearer to the forester, whose job it is to assess them, than to the ordinary onlooker. Trees never stand still at some finite point of growth. Either they flourish and become larger, or else they decline and diminish in size. Over a twelve-month span, the seedlings in one corner of a wood will grow larger, perhaps by only a few centimetres in height. Elsewhere a sapling may shoot up by a metre or more.

Above: A longhorn beetle (*Rhagium mordax*), one of a great variety of plant-feeding woodland insects. The larvae of this particular beetle feed on dead wood.

Farther on a vigorous middle-aged tree expands its huge crown by both outward spread and upward height; at the same time its sturdy trunk, the eventual source of wealth to mankind when it yields timber, will have expanded measurably in diameter. At other points in the forest, mature trees may have been felled, or else, after invasion by the fungi that cause the decay of their heartwood, have fallen before a winter gale.

All other forms of wild life must change their situations and status to fit into the altered framework of tree growth. Flowering plants will diminish where the more vigorous tree seedlings, capable of growth to greater sizes than theirs, crowd them out. Flowers may disappear completely where tall trees close up their leafy canopies and shade out all lesser plants. To balance this, the felling or natural fall of mature trees will leave sunlit clearings where new flowering

Above: An ancient oak that was pollarded (literally 'cropped') over 300 years ago. This was done to encourage the growth of branches for timber and foliage for fodder.

plant seedlings can spring up, to flourish for several years ahead. Beasts, birds, and insects may move to fresh haunts as the forest cover changes. The loss of a hollow oak, for example, will cause hole-nesting woodpeckers and squirrels to find fresh homes, possibly in the same wood, maybe further afield, perhaps far away from the forest.

Forests in peril

This pattern of change can only be maintained, amid the impact of modern societies, where there is an effective overall plan to safeguard the forest far into the future. This need not and should not mean the preservation of everything in some static, passive way. Instead, the forest should be managed actively, to yield benefits, whether they be tangible things like timber or water, or intangible impressions like the sun or snow-clad firs or the exciting glimpse of a fleeing roe deer, for all future time.

Inevitably, the plan itself must be flexible, though its aims may remain constant throughout.

Where there is no such purposeful direction but only vague goodwill, the forest is doomed. It becomes the plaything of well-wishers having different aims at different times. It disappears gradually but inevitably, by a timber felling here, a farming clearance there and the reservation of land for a dozen different kinds of 'essential public needs' elsewhere. Water must be stored in enlarged reservoirs, troops need training grounds. Playgrounds for the multitude obviously attract public support, and grazing for cattle, sheep or horses can be provided all too easily, at no cost except the incalculable one of destroying forest cover. Fires take their toll, and as the timber diminishes in value through overcutting and overgrazing, the authorities become less and less concerned about putting them out.

The final result is inevitable. The forest ends its life, in poetic terms:

'Not with a bang but a whimper.'

When such an end approaches, there is rarely any great conflagration or massive cutting down, for in the final decades there is little left to fell or burn. Instead, a few veteran pines or oaks, scorched by past grass fires and left standing only out of some feeling for history or tradition, finally totter down, their hearts already rotted away by insidious fungi. They leave no viable descendants, for by now the land around them is too closely grazed, or too frequently burned, for any seedlings to survive. Then the forest becomes no more than a name on old maps, and a legend linked with wolves and outlaws.

Restoring the forest

Because man's capacity for forest destruction has long exceeded the forest's power to heal its wounds unaided, he has had to develop the science called *silviculture*. Just as *agriculture* implies the tending of fields to raise crops or nourish livestock, silviculture means the tending of woods to yield timber and all the other benefits that the forest can provide. But there are great differences in the time-scales involved in the two types of husbandry. The farmer sees a succession of grain crops, and many succeeding generations of cattle or sheep, during his lifetime. But the forester may tend only one continuing crop of trees, which grows to maturity at much the same rate as he does himself! Happily, he usually has in his care a range of crops of varied ages, so that he will see the start of a young plantation here, the felling of a mature timber stand there, and the steady progress of younger stands through advancing age-groups elsewhere. In the course of a single year's work he will create, tend, protect and fell woodlands, wherever and whenever these necessary tasks fall due. He plants, weeds, thins out, and finally cuts down tree crops, but always with the aim of maintaining the wealth and health of the forest as a whole.

Where nature fails to replenish clearings as fast as he would wish, the forester replants the ground himself. He is also likely, in most countries, to be engaged on the afforestation of waste lands or abandoned farms and grazings. He must therefore be skilled in collecting seeds, raising young trees in nurseries, and establishing them successfully under the difficult conditions of bare ground. He may plough, fence, drain, and fertilize large tracts of land, and at the same time build roads and bridges to ensure access. He must know the ways of wild life, for deer, rabbits, and even field mice all threaten his crops and may require control. The threat of fire, seldom absent for long from any conifer or eucalyptus forest, compels him to be a resourceful fire fighter, quick to react to any kind of emergency.

World forest types

In response to the varied climates of different regions of the world, forests of markedly different types have developed. The most familiar one, which civilized man likes best but has destroyed most ruthlessly to win farm land, is the *deciduous broadleaved forest*. Typically, this is made up of oaks, beeches, ash trees, birches, alders and maples, in pure or mixed stands, associated with other valued timber trees in lesser numbers. It flourishes over regions with ample summer warmth and rainfall, even where winters are distinctly cold. These broadleaved trees survive through winter by the simple mechanism

15

of shedding their leaves each autumn. This causes the circulation of sap to stop, though contrary to long established folk-lore, deeply ingrained in every countryman's heart, the sap does not 'go down' in winter. It simply stays where it is in the wood, but just stops moving. No tree can draw water from the soil when temperatures fall below about 5°C (40°F). If, therefore, these trees retained their thirsty, thin-skinned, broad-bladed leaves through winter they would all die of drought, through the transpiration of water that they could not replace. So, in a blaze of splendid gold, orange and scarlet colours, they let their leaves fade and fall.

Next spring comes the bright green outburst of fresh foliage, which will function with remarkable vigour and efficiency through the long, bright summer days, to build up the tree's tissues. The *hardwood* timber so formed is remarkable for its strength and diversity, and before man mastered metals, concrete and plastics he used it for an amazing range of important products, from tool handles to warships. In today's highly technological world, hardwood timber is in less urgent demand for many such products, which means that it commands correspondingly lower prices in the world's markets—a hard fact that saddens every traditionalist and lover of broadleaved trees.

The northern broadleaved forests form a broad belt stretching across the temperate zones of Europe, Asia and America, broken only by high mountain ranges or arid prairies. Their counterparts in the southern hemisphere are less significant, consisting of scattered woodlands on the slopes of the Andes and the mountains of Australia and New Zealand.

North of the great broadleaved forests, or high up the mountains where these range south, comes the *evergreen conifer forest* or *taiga*. This stretches in a broad belt right round the polar regions, from Scotland and Scandinavia across Russia and Siberia to the Pacific Ocean, thence from Alaska across Canada and the northern United States to Newfoundland. The cone-bearing trees of this vast region survive the winters, often intensely cold, by restricting water loss through their narrow, needle-shaped, tough, waxy-surfaced leaves. They yield, in huge quantities, the simple timbers called

Above: Pollarded beeches (*Fagus sylvatica*) in spring; one of the many and varied faces displayed by temperate broadleaved forests which inhabit the world's temperate zones.

softwoods, which show relatively little variation from one kind to another. For that reason, and also because they are easily worked at every stage, they enjoy a tremendous demand for use in today's technical manufactures, geared to the mass-production of standard goods like paper and building boards from standard materials. For paper-making, in particular, the long flexible fibres of the coniferous trees give them an inherent advantage over the broadleaved ones.

The subtropics, and the Mediterranean-climate zones of Europe, California, South Africa, and Australia, have their own characteristic forest types, designed this time to resist summer drought rather than winter cold. Long annual dry seasons oblige their broadleaved trees to conserve their limited water supplies in tough, thick, leathery textured and waxy-surfaced leaves, that are often spiny to resist browsing beasts. The conifers, especially the 'southern pines' of the United States, de-

velop exceptionally long, thick, tough needles, often with peculiar blue waxy surfaces. Here, again, the broadleaved trees now have little value, but the conifers, easily handled in bulk by specially adapted techniques, are a major economic resource.

Finally, over relatively small zones of year-round heat and constant rainfall, we find the *tropical rain forest*. This flourishes in Central and South America, West and Central Africa, parts of India and Burma, and Indonesia. Almost entirely broadleaved, but with many palms, it is evergreen. Its trees need no special adaptations to resist drought or cold, for they never encounter either. Both rainfall and heat are adequate the whole year round, and in consequence the trees grow almost continuously, though most have a rhythm of long active growth spells broken by brief resting pauses. The outcome is a multi-storeyed forest dominated by mature giants such as mahogany, with lower layers filled by adolescent major trees on their way up, plus a great variety of lesser trees that never aspire to the maximum size of the leaders. Below this

Above: Blanketed in snow, this stand of European larch (*Larix decidua*) and hemlock (*Tsuga* sp) assumes the classic 'Christmas card' appearance of northern coniferous forests in winter.

Left: This scene of woodland in New Zealand shows the dense, multilayered growth and variety of trees typical of tropical and subtropical forests.

again comes a shrub layer, while even at ground level flowering plants, adapted to shade, clothe the soil. Climbing plants called *lianas* weave their woody stems high into the crowns of the tallest trees. Epiphytes, that is, plants that grow on other plants rather than from the ground, flourish on rain-drenched stems, drawing their nourishment from falling debris.

Though this fascinating wealth of plant life makes the rain forest a store of wonders for the botanist, it is a poor resource for the timber producer. Its trees differ greatly in size, form, and the character of their wood. In practice the timber man can only profitably fell and haul out a few exceptionally strong or attractive timbers that attain

large sizes and meet established international demands. These include strong and durable teak, lustrous and adaptable mahogany, and light-weight balsa. Others meet only the local needs of a necessarily sparse population, for the rain forests yield little food and attract few settlers.

Pressures on the world's forests

Overall, the world forest area is estimated to be about 4,200 million hectares—say 42 million square kilometres or 16.2 million square miles. But this vast expanse of land has to be considered in relation to the demands made upon it.

In 1974 Dr Andras Madas, Chairman of the Timber Committee of the European Economic Commission, forecast that by the year AD 2000 the whole forest area of the world will have to be exploited to meet man's growing needs. He concluded, after an exhaustive study of works by renowned forestry economists, that only a harmonious combination of the various functions of forests can lead to their optimum utilization. Even if the consumption of wood and wood-based products on a per capita basis could be held steady, the

forecast increase in the world's population would double the annual demand for timber harvest; but in fact, consumption per capita soars rapidly as rising living standards call for better housing, safer packaging, and more newsprint to convey ideas.

Within the foreseeable future mankind will no longer be able to afford the luxury of vast virgin forest reserves, dedicated perhaps to the preservation of only a few rare birds, beasts, bugs or flowers. Timber production from man-made, man-managed forests is so much more efficient than that from unplanned natural regrowth that our successors will have to rely on it, just as we already rely on cultivated crops and domestic animals for our food. Centuries, even thousands of years ago, most human societies abandoned the idea of maintaining themselves by hunting flesh or gathering wild plant foods. Within a few decades we must forgo the cheap and easy business of gathering natural timber and place in its stead the business of growing wood as a crop. It is a renewable resource essential to civilization as we know it, and its perpetual supply, demanding long-term planning, must take a leading place in every country's economic programme.

International statistics on world wood supplies are staggering but confusing. A Canadian citizen, for example, has fifty times as much wood available within his own frontiers as does an Englishman; but he only uses twice as much, because the Englishman imports most of his needs, whereas the Canadian exports a substantial surplus. In general, the higher the standard of living the more wood each citizen uses. Within the present century, consumption of paper has multiplied twenty-fold in all developing countries, a trend that has offset every reduction in the use of wood for other purposes.

Ultimately, all the wood and paper we use perishes. It is burnt or rots, and the carbon it holds returns to the air as carbon dioxide gas. Carbon recycling is achieved through the life processes of forest trees, which use the energy of the sun to draw the carbon from the air and rebuild wood in the familiar form that serves man's needs. If man is to continue to base his economy on the resources he draws from the guardian forest, then he must become its dedicated protector.

The Living Tree

In the context of the guardian forest each single tree is a growing organism whose significance changes with the passing of time. Typically, it begins life as a seedling on the forest floor, one of thousands that sprout in the same spring from seeds shed the previous autumn by the parent trees around and above them. Only a minute proportion of these competing treelets can ever grow to full stature, and every few years there will be another heavy seed crop that launches still more seedlings on what is, for most of them, a sadly brief career. But the survivors of the intense struggle for existence, those whose leaves gain most light or whose roots strike the most fertile available soil, emerge from low thickets as saplings, ahead of their less fortunate fellows. Growing taller and spreading their branches wider each year, they eventually find a place in the upper canopy of the forest, filling a gap left by some felled or windblown tree. It is then their turn to flower and ripen seed, to provide for another succeeding generation. In nature, the forest is self-renewing. As with a human population, each generation provides for its eventual replacement.

With occasional exceptions (in which several trees spring as offshoots from a common root system), each tree is an isolated unit of life. We treat it physically as such when we plant it to form a unit in a timber plantation or to ornament a garden. In the same way we can mentally isolate the individual tree to study its vital processes, and the simplest way to do so is to start with a seed.

The seed is the dispersal unit in the life cycle of the tree. Its parent is fixed, rooted to the soil, but seeds can travel over long or short distances in a variety of ways. Some, with broad-bladed wings or tufts of hairs, get wafted on the wing. Others, more substantial nuts such as acorns, are carried by birds or four-footed animals that intend to eat them, but lose them accidentally.

A high proportion end up in situations where successful growth is impossible. They may alight on hard rocky surfaces or thick turf, in pastures grazed by sheep or fields regularly tilled with the plough. The lucky ones strike good soil that is not clothed with thick grass or weeds, where few animals graze and no ploughman turns a furrow. Most lie dormant through one or two winters, though a few kinds, such as willows, sprout in the summer of ripening.

Roots descend

As a first stage in germination, each dry seed draws in water from the adjacent soil, and its tissues soften and swell. A few days later a tiny root initially grows, by cell division, into a visible root that emerges through the seed coat, bends downward under the influence of gravity, and enters the soil. By so doing it makes a contact with ground that may endure for centuries or even thousands of years. The tree will remain fixed at that same point, no matter how huge it becomes. The root next develops root-hairs, small and individually short-lived structures that enter into intimate contact with the grains of soil around them. Through these root-hairs the tiny tree takes in all the water it needs for growth, but it is never pure water. Dissolved in the soil water there are always minute amounts of mineral soils composed of elements essential for plant life. These include nitrogen, phosphorus and potassium, in significant

amounts, and the abundance or scarcity of one or another of these is often critical for good growth. In lesser amounts come iron, magnesium, calcium, sodium, sulphur, and several other of these 'trace elements', normally present in sufficient amounts. The water itself provides two major constituents of plant tissue, hydrogen and oxygen, while the third, carbon, is won from the air, as will be explained later.

Within a few weeks the first root develops branch roots, and these in turn will later grow stouter and throw off more branches, until a whole root system ramifies out

Germination of Beech

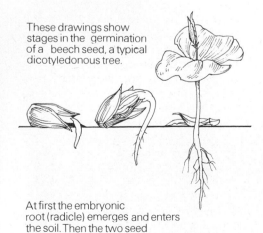

These drawings show stages in the germination of a beech seed, a typical dicotyledonous tree.

At first the embryonic root (radicle) emerges and enters the soil. Then the two seed leaves (cotyledons) withdraw and expand.

Left: A Scots pine seedling (*Pinus sylvestris*). Seeds that land on suitable ground develop fine roots and send up delicate leaves. The plant then relies for its energy on the outside world.

Below: The trees whose leaves gain most light and whose roots exploit the most fertile earth win the competition for life and provide the seeds for the next generation of trees.

through the soil. It may eventually extend as far from the base as the tree grows tall—there is no simple limit or yardstick. It will always remain surprisingly shallow. Deep tap roots are rare, for roots fulfil their functions best in the soil's surface layers. These are, in brief, to anchor the tree to the ground securely even in the face of the wildest winds, to win water, and to gather in as large a quantity of mineral salts as they can.

Shoots ascend

In a matter of days after the first tiny root has gone down into the soil to gain a firm attachment and take in water, the tree seed expands its first tiny shoot. All tree seeds contain one or more seed-leaves, also known as *cotyledons*. Palms have only one, broadleaved trees always two, and conifers from two to twenty or so, depending on species. In some tree seeds, such as the acorn of the oak, the seed-leaves serve only as storage organs; they remain within the husk, and the first shoot grows out from a bud between them. With other trees, such as most maples and all pines, the seed-leaves are raised into the air on an expanding stalk, while the husk that enclosed them falls away.

Germination in Three Seeds

In a dicotyledon such as beech (1) seed and adult leaves differ greatly.

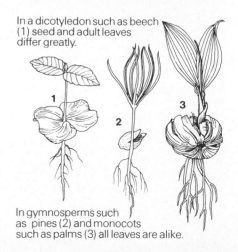

In gymnosperms such as pines (2) and monocots such as palms (3) all leaves are alike.

Once exposed to sun and air, these seed-leaves function as true leaves do, but only during the first year of the tree's life. They then fade and fall away.

Meanwhile, a shoot has emerged at the centre which bears the tree's first true leaves. These early or juvenile leaves often differ in form from the tree's later or adult leaves. An ash tree, for example, bears simple, individual juvenile leaves, but compound adult leaves, with many leaflets appear a year or so later.

The upward growth of the tree's first small shoot continues during the summer, then ends with the formation of a winter resting bud at its tip. This is accompanied by side buds. Next spring, upward and outward growth begin again with the breaking of these resting buds, and the expansion of fresh shoots from within them. In this way the tree's aerial parts will expand year by year until it has formed a great dome of leafy branches, possibly 50m (164ft) high and one third of that distance across or of even considerably greater dimensions.

Green leaves nourish

The increase in size and substance of both aerial shoots and underground roots that this growth implies is maintained through the nourishing function of the tree's green leaves. The key process is called *photosynthesis* and when this is translated from its Greek form to read, in plain English, 'building up with the aid of light', its object becomes clear. Every leaf is a complex chemical workshop, whereby the tree wins from the air around it the vital chemical, carbon, that it needs to create all its new tissues. This process absorbs energy, which is provided by sunlight; so trees, and in fact all other green plants, can only thrive where adequate light is available. If their leaves are overshaded, they perish.

Ample water must be present, and so must the mineral salts that serve as catalysts in the complicated chemical reactions that occur. The main chemical reagent involved is called *chlorophyll*, another bit of botanical Greek that means 'green of the leaf'. This tells us little except that only the green parts of any plant, mainly the leaves, carry out photosynthesis.

To put it all very simply, the leaves filter a constant stream of air through their tissues, which are open-textured with many air

passages. Air consists of about four parts of nitrogen to one of oxygen, plus a tiny but significant fraction of carbon dioxide—only 0.03 per cent of the whole. The chlorophyll, powered by sunlight, extracts the carbon dioxide from the air, and combines it with water to make chemicals called carbohydrates, of which the most familiar kind is sugar. Obviously large volumes of air must flow through the leaves, and as they depart they carry away with them large quantities of water. This process, known as *transpiration*, explains why trees require a large and constant water supply to support their life and growth.

The chemical process involved in photosynthesis can be expressed by the simplified chemical equation shown below.

$$6CO_2 + 12H_2O + \text{Light}$$
Carbon   Water   Energy →
dioxide

$$C_6H_{12}O_6 + 6O_2 + 6H_2O$$
Glucose   Oxygen   Water

The great gain to the tree is the production of glucose sugar, a soluble carbohydrate that can flow freely through the leaf veins and other conductive tissues to nourish every kind of growth and also supply energy for every vital process. It is the simple chemical 'brick' from which every tissue is built up—leaves, shoots, roots, the woody stem, flowers and finally the fruits and seeds.

Above: Soluble carbohydrates flow to all parts of the tree, especially to the ends of twigs with growing flowers or terminal buds. These male oak flowers need energy for the developing stamens to produce pollen for fertilization.

Sap flow

To enable the carbohydrate solution to reach all parts of the living tree there must be conductive channels. In the leaves themselves these take the form of visible veins. In the leaf-stalks and the youngest green shoots of the tree they are called *vascular bundles*, hidden within the tissues. Both veins and vascular bundles are two-way channels. Each strand includes elements called *xylem*, that carry

Leaf Structure

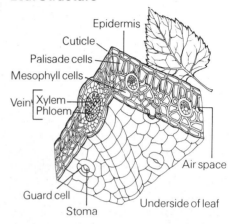

Below: Green leaves are the chemical factory of the tree. Using sunlight they combine carbon dioxide from the air with water, taken up by the roots, into soluble carbohydrates which are used to nourish the plant's growth.

Above: Conifers often live in severe climates, so need to restrict large loss of water by transpiration in drought or cold conditions. They achieve this through needle-like leaves with a thick cuticle and a waxy surface.

the root sap up from the ground, set beside other elements called *phloem*, that carry the sugar-rich leaf sap in the opposite direction. Similar bundles occur in the finer roots also.

In the main trunk and all the woody parts of the tree, however, the disposition of sap flow follows another pattern. The root sap, bearing its dissolved mineral salts, ascends through an inner part of each trunk or branch, through xylem tissues known simply as wood. The sugar sap descends, or moves on occasion sideways or upwards, through outer phloem tissues called *bast*. The change-over from the bundle or two-way pipe pattern to the scheme of concentric cylinders takes place very early in the life of each woody stem. It becomes established by the start of its second year of growth, sometimes earlier. The mechanism concerned is the formation of a *cambium ring or sheath*, which unites neighbouring bundles.

Cambium creates wood

Between the two elements of sap flow, in every woody stem, lies this very thin but enormously important layer of cells called the *cambium*. It forms a continuous sheath around all the woody parts of the tree, and is, from its situation,

21

constantly supplied with both root-sap and leaf-sap. The function of this cambium is to create, by repeated cell division, fresh wood tissues on its inner surface, and fresh bast tissues on its outer surface. In so doing it makes each woody stem thicker. It also, inevitably, forces itself outwards, and likewise obliges the outer bast and bark tissues to move outwards too. Cambium is active all through the growing season, but rests through the cold winter or during long dry spells.

Bark protects

It will be seen that two vital sap streams are constantly running, during the active growing season, in opposing directions just below the surface of each tree trunk. Sandwiched between them, as we have seen, lies that other essential layer, the thin, delicate cambium. To protect all three from sundry perils, the tree develops the protective coating of cork cells that we call *bark*. It is waterproof, so the tissues below it do not dry out; indeed it is almost airproof, and has to be provided with pores called *lenticels* to admit air needed for the life of the stem. Being unpalatable, it shields the bast beneath it against most, though not all, attacks by biting and gnawing beasts, and many insects. It is also a barrier to fungal spores that carry disease. Bark provides a buffer to sudden changes of temperature too, shielding the bast from blazing sun or sharp frost.

As each stem ages and expands, more bark is needed to surround it. Growth is effected by a special layer, called the *bark cambium*, that lies just below it. Changes in character that result from the splitting of old bark and the formation of new, provide a handy means of identifying trees, for each follows its own pattern.

Wood structure

The wood laid down by the cambium each year is a highly complex material. Remarkably, every kind of tree has its own plan, and any piece of wood, cut thin and placed

Top right: The swamp cypress (*Taxodium distichum*) often has some roots growing under water. To supply the tree with air, aerial root systems develop above ground.

Right: Bark protects the inner layers of the tree. In this oak, struck by lightning, the tissues are exposed to damage by sun, frost, insects and a variety of disease organisms.

under the microscope, will reveal to the wood anatomist the identity of the tree that produced it.

Basically, most wood substance consists of long narrow cells, called *tracheids* or *fibres*, that run vertically up the stem and serve to convey sap upwards. This sap passes from one tracheid to another, which carries it higher, through narrow openings called *bordered pits*. In the broadleaved trees, sap transport also takes place through larger pores or *vessels*, which are tube-like groups of cells, and these woods are strengthened by special *structural fibres* that serve only for support.

Wood, formed in the spring or the beginning of the growing season, when there is a great demand for sap to supply the expanding leaves, has large tracheids with thin walls, and in broadleaved trees, large vessels. This relatively open, light coloured, light weight and soft tissue is called *springwood*, or in technical circles *earlywood*. It is succeeded later by smaller tracheids with thicker walls, accompanied in most broadleaved trees by smaller vessels. This closer, generally darker, heavier, stronger and harder tissue is called *summerwood* or *latewood*, as it is often not formed until late in the season. It is this later-formed wood which gives the main strength or structural support needed by the growing tree.

Each year, therefore, in temperate climates, a tree forms in its trunk two concentric bands of tissues, with differences easily seen by the naked eye on any cross section. These two bands taken together are termed an *annual ring*. These rings accurately record the age of each stem, and make possible the 'dating' of individuals up to 4,000 years or more. The oldest living tree is a bristlecone pine—4,900 years—at Snake Range in eastern California.

In subtropical and tropical countries, where there is less difference between the seasons and where there may be two wet and two dry seasons a year, more than one ring may be formed each year; the term *growth ring* is therefore used and these are of little help in determining the age of the tree. Fast overall growth involves fast outward expansion of the trunk, creating broad rings, with bands having a combined width of up to 12mm (½in). Slow overall growth results in narrow rings only a few millimetres across.

Running at right angles to the trend of the tracheids and other tissues that convey sap upwards lie the *rays*. These are narrow bands of cells that run inwards from the cambium towards the centre of the tree, and look rather like the rays of the sun. Their function is to transport nutrients horizontally, and also to store reserves. All timbers hold such rays, but they are visible in relatively few, such as the oak.

At different times in its long life, and even in different parts of its stem during the same year, a tree may form some broad rings, some narrow ones. Ring width, therefore, tells us nothing about the identity of a tree, but it does indicate a great deal about its rate of growth—at particular times and to parts of its structure.

Sapwood and heartwood

The main function of all wood is to convey sap upwards and outwards from the roots to the branches and leaves. In young stems all the wood present is *sapwood*. But in older and larger stems only the outer zones function in this way and therefore retain their original 'sapwood' name. The inner zones undergo a gradual change to become *heartwood*, which no longer carries sap. Yet most trees depend for support on the continued pressure of heartwood, though a few, including picturesque old oaks, somehow remain erect after heartwood has decayed, supported only on an outer cylinder of sapwood.

As a rule, however, if heartwood decays, the tree blows over. Academic botanists—who don't have

The Anatomy of a Tree Stem

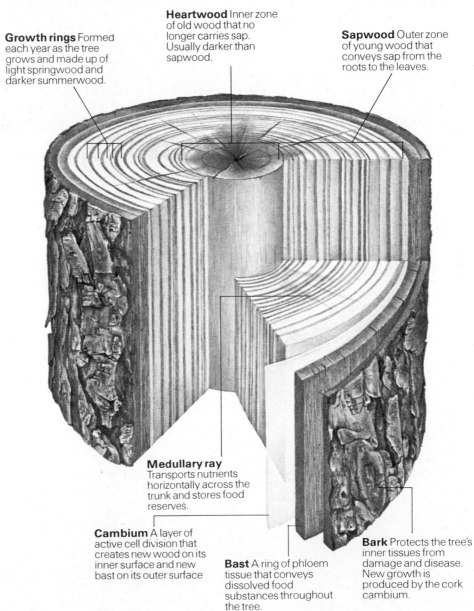

Growth rings Formed each year as the tree grows and made up of light springwood and darker summerwood.

Heartwood Inner zone of old wood that no longer carries sap. Usually darker than sapwood.

Sapwood Outer zone of young wood that conveys sap from the roots to the leaves.

Medullary ray Transports nutrients horizontally across the trunk and stores food reserves.

Cambium A layer of active cell division that creates new wood on its inner surface and new bast on its outer surface

Bast A ring of phloem tissue that conveys dissolved food substances throughout the tree.

Bark Protects the tree's inner tissues from damage and disease. New growth is produced by the cork cambium.

The Living Tree

Above: The purple flowers of lasiandra (*Tibouchina semidecandra*) burst from pink-red buds to attract pollinating insects in the steamy gloom of the Amazon rain forest.

to keep trees standing to earn their living—delight in calling heartwood 'dead'. To the forester, dealing with the living tree in the woodlands and not with a dry specimen on a laboratory bench, it is very much part of a living tree, as well as the most valuable portion of his marketable log.

The forester is also acutely aware that wood is a structural support tissue as well as a conductive one. It holds erect the great weight of the tree's crown of branches, leaves, flowers and fruit, often totalling many tons. Further, it resists the enormous sideways thrusts of high winds, bending before them, yet springing back promptly to regain its original position.

Heartwood is commonly visibly darker and somewhat harder and heavier than the sapwood from which it was formed. In softwoods or coniferous trees it holds *resins*, and in hardwoods or broadleaved trees *tannins*. These substances make certain heartwoods, though not all, resistant to decay, though only when their timber is finally converted for use. Examples are oak, sweet chestnut, yew and cypresses. During the lifetime of the tree, however, the sapwood usually shows better resistance to the particular fungi which, at that stage, rot the heartwood.

Breathing and upward sap transport
The life processes of the tree demand energy, and this is obtained by *breathing*. As with animal breathing, the result of a tree's breathing is to burn up, or oxidize, carbon compounds. In the course of breathing, these compounds are united at low temperatures,

Above: The flowering patterns of trees follow the forms of smaller plants. Insect-pollinated flowers, such as these wild cherry blossoms, have bright petals, whereas wind-pollinated ones usually lack them.

with the oxygen of the air. Breathing goes on in all parts of the living tree, by night as well as by day, all year round. But it is a low-key process, and uses up only a small fraction of the carbon compounds that the tree wins, during daylight only, from the surrounding air.

The upward transport of large volumes of sap, from ground level to heights that can reach, in the giant sequoias of California, as much as 117m (384ft), also requires energy. It was for long believed that physical forces—the 'push' of the roots and the 'pull' of the transpiring foliage — sufficed to move enormous weights of water upwards, against the pull of gravity. Now it is believed that the wood cells need the aid of minute protoplasmic strands to pump the sap from one cell to another. Dead stems carry no sap. Sap circulation is, therefore, a living process that needs the input of energy for its fulfilment.

Reproduction
An individual tree may endure for centuries, but eventually it will fall victim to physical failure, aided as a rule by inner fungal decay. Trees ensure the survival of their race by producing fantastic quantities of seeds, reckoned by thousands annually, and millions in the course of a lifetime.

The flowering and fruiting patterns of many trees follow the familiar form found in related smaller plants. A cherry, for example, bears flowers resembling those of a rose or a strawberry. Each flower has protective green sepals, white petals, a scent that attracts pollinating bees, and nectaries that yield nectar to reward them. These insects brush against male stamens that dust them with pollen, which they convey, more or less accidentally, to the female pistils of the next flower they visit. Cross-pollination is followed by the ripening of seed within the fruit—in this case the stone within the cherry—which is spread by the birds that pluck the fruit to eat

Above right: Star fruit or carambola—only one or two seeds need to germinate and reach maturity to ensure the continuity of the species, yet many thousands of seeds are produced annually.

Above: Female flowers of the date palm (*Phoenix dactylifera*); male flowers are on separate trees. Some tree species have male and female parts on one tree, or in one flower.

its soft flesh. Next spring, or maybe a year later, a seedling sprouts on the forest floor, and subsequent growth completes the cherry's life cycle.

Many other trees rely on the wind to carry pollen from male stamens to female pistils. In such cases the flowers lack attractive petals and have neither nectaries nor scent. They take instead the form of rather drab catkins, usually of a single sex. Male catkins, commonly long, hanging, tassel-shaped clusters of flowers, are devices for releasing clouds of pollen. Female catkins, bud-shaped, have exposed stigmas to collect it. The development of fruit and seed follows the usual plan, and many catkin-bearers yield large nuts or, with the conifers, big woody cones that contain numerous winged seeds.

Most trees postpone flowering until they have reached a fair size. There are no fixed ages, but pines, for example, rarely flower before they are ten years old and beeches may postpone flowering until they are twenty-five years old, sometimes much older.

Another characteristic feature of reproduction in certain trees is *periodicity*. In some years all the oaks and beeches in one district will bear a heavy seed crop, in the next year none at all! Heavy seed crops are linked to hot summers, not in the immediate past, but over a year before they ripen. A tree then builds up food reserves that result in abundant flowering the next spring, followed by heavy seed production next autumn. This exhausts, for the time being, its food reserves. The Anglo-Saxons, who fattened their swine on acorns in oakwoods, called such bumper seasons 'mast years', from an old Scandinavian word, *mat*, meaning food or animal fodder. Hence beech nuts and acorns are known as *mast* to this day.

In a mast year, there are more seeds than all the predators can possibly eat. Pigeons, pheasants, jays, squirrels, deer, mice, and possibly pigs all take their share, yet a surplus still remains to sprout next spring. Over-abundance of fruiting is therefore an effective practical means of securing the survival of the tree's race.

Trees in Time and Space

The age to which a single tree can endure may be measured by tens, hundreds and even thousands of years. Bristlecone pines, of the kind recently renamed *Pinus longeava* that grow in the White Mountains of California, have been found by actual counts of annual rings to have approached a life of 5,000 years, as long a span as is covered by the whole history of human civilization. But it was only the core of these rugged trees that was laid down at some time around 3000 BC. The rest of the wood has been added, in one thin layer after another, in each successive spring. The outermost rings, where active sap transport goes on, are recent additions of the last few years, and even as you read this page these pines may be laying down fresh wood cells, as new as today. Just how this is done is described in the previous chapter.

For all parts of the tree, life depends on *recent* growth—the newly formed shoot, leaf, flower seed and wood layer. Most of these are discarded as soon as they have served their purpose, to be replaced by successors next spring. The leaves of even so-called evergreens are replaced after one or two years. But the wood, which cannot be discarded because it forms the inner core of the tree, persists as an essential support. It matures gracefully from sapwood to heartwood, and once it reaches a workable thickness it attracts the lumberman seeking a structural material for man's needs. Strength for light weight, durability and ease of working are the qualities that people find desirable in timber. After a log has supported an oak for 500 years it may be required to hold up a cathedral roof for a further 500. But a cathedral roof is a relatively recent addition to man's need for timber.

Man's relationship with trees and forests

Since earliest times, it would seem, man has entertained a continuous and curious relationship with trees which can only be described as a love–hate one. Forests have been at the same time the source of his food and his building materials and the holders of danger, mystery and the eerie. It is hardly surprising that woodland groves, or particularly distinctive individual trees, were considered to be the habitation of spirits, gods or other supernatural beings. Indeed, in some cultures the tree *was* the god, to whom veneration in the form of offerings or blood sacrifices was naturally due. The Druids of northern Europe held oak trees in especial awe—and a not dissimilar aura clung to these trees when they were the basis of naval strength for several centuries. In Buddhist cultures, to the present day, the banyan tree.is considered sacred because of its association with the founder of the religion.

Man's first relationships with trees, however, greatly predate such formal considerations. We see him emerging from his sub-human beginnings first as a gatherer of fruits and seeds and then as

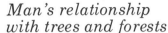

Left: In the White Mountains of California grows *Pinus longaeva*, the oldest tree species in the world. It belongs to the 'bristlecone' group.
Right: A vast raft of logs on Lake Superior—a sobering reminder of how readily man can reduce a generation of tree growth to inanimate raw material.

Left: A polished section of a fossilized tree, several million years old. Although now literally stone, it shows the annual rings as clearly as if the tree were still alive. Perhaps even more interesting is the fact that changes in climatic conditions are permanently preserved in fossilized tree rings. Specimens of timber remains or artefacts found at archaeological sites can be cross-matched with cores from fossil trunks to accurately date the finds.

a hunter. Later, in the development of relatively organized cultures, he started to cultivate the food plants that he had hitherto searched for in the wild. He also began to domesticate grazing animals for their meat, skins, and later, milk. Here, then, are the origins of the man–tree antagonism which, perhaps, most clearly manifests itself in the alarming speed with which natural forests are being cleared.

Both arable farming and stock-raising require land, and often the simplest way of winning more land for them seems to be by the mass felling of trees—despite mankind's ever-increasing need for wood and wood products. As a result, the depletion of forests, in many areas of the world, has reached a point of no return—a point all too easily reached in an age when one man with a powered chain-saw can cut down in minutes what has taken centuries, or in some cases even thousands of years, to grow.

When the chain-saw has done its work, more happens than the crash of the falling tree echoing through the forest. The tree, an integral part of the habitat, now destroyed, was not only a living organism itself; it was also host to countless other organisms—plants, insects, birds and animals whose whole evolutionary development had fitted them for that particular habitat and no other. If only one tree is felled, they may move to another one. But what if man clears the whole forest, as he frequently has done, and still does in his efforts to provide more land for agriculture? The simple answer is that all too often, because of its exposure to the weather, the soil that first made the forest possible and was then enriched and kept in good heart by it is washed away. So far from being capable of yielding good food crops, the

cleared land then yields virtually nothing, and a clamour arises for further deforestation to provide growing land to support the ever-increasing human population.

Above: Tropical forest in Tanzania being cleared for the cultivation of cash crops. Removing the protective canopy of trees could eventually lead to soil erosion.

The evolution of trees

If the speed at which a tree can be destroyed is in sharp contrast with how long it took to grow, it is in even sharper contrast with the immense period of time that trees require for their evolution. All plants, like all animals, are at the mercy of external influences over which they have no control, such as the profound changes of climate that our earth has witnessed over and over again in its long history. Whole species must either *adapt* to changes or die out, and in the course of geological time many have, indeed, died out, and virtually all that have survived have done so only because they did adapt. It necessarily follows that the plants of our modern world, including the trees, are by no means the same as those that first clothed our once-lifeless planet.

Primitive trees Although our earth has been in existence for some 4,750 million years, no fossil records exist of vascular plants—that is those with well-differentiated conducting tissues in their bodies—before the beginning of the Paleozoic era, some 600 million years ago. Plant life, like animal life, before that time is likely to have been of a type such as marine algae, whose structure leaves little trace in fossil-bearing rock strata.

Above: The impressions left by this fossil of tree-fern fronds are clear enough for them to be named and compared with their living descendants.

But during this era (which makes up 30 per cent of geological time) a vast tree flora developed. They were not trees as we know them but species of horsetails, club-mosses and seed-ferns (or pteridosperms) which reacted to the free availability of the essential requirements for plant growth—air, light, water, warmth and soil minerals. Competition was intense and size became a factor in success.

In the hot, swampy lowlands, untold generations of these primitive trees grew, died and decayed to form ultimately the coal and oil measures — the fossil fuels — on which man has recently based so much of his economy. These carbon-rich fuels give their name to the upper and lower Carboniferous periods which span some 60 million years of the Paleozoic era.

In parallel with the dominant fern or fern-ally trees of the carboniferous periods (which are now entirely extinct), evolved the first gymnosperms. The most important section of this group, the conifers, thus have a family tree (the pun is unavoidable) stretching back some 200 million years; and what is even more remarkable, they have maintained a very notable position in the forests of the world ever since.

Survivors from the past Extraordinarily, although most living gymnosperms are developments from extinct fossil species, a couple of species seem to have come down to us unchanged over this humanly inconceivable period of time. One of them is the maidenhair tree, *Ginkgo biloba*, which is the sole surviving representative of a group which was widespread in the Jurassic and Cretaceous periods (up to 180 million years ago). Most of the group was overwhelmed by more efficient and typical conifers and the developing angiosperms (the higher flowering plants). But the maidenhair tree hung on to become a revered tree in monastery gardens in China and Japan, from whence it was brought to Europe by travellers in the eighteenth century. *Ginkgo* has never, with any certainty, been found wild; even the biggest groups now growing in China seem likely to have been planted.

Even more strange is the story of the second survivor, *Metasequoia glyptostroboides*. Indeed, the story of this tree rivals that of the famous fossil fish, coelocanth, the discovery of whose living specimens in the Indian Ocean a few years ago took ichthyologists by storm. *Metasequoia*, or as it has since been called, dawn redwood, was first described and named by the Japanese botanist Miki in 1941. The material from which he worked was 20 million years old— fossils from rock strata laid down in the Lower Pliocene period. In the same year living representatives of this new genus were found growing wild in China, on the borders of western Hupeh and north-eastern Szechwan. When material was finally collected three years later any doubt of its identification was settled beyond doubt and another 'living fossil' tree,

Above: The ancestors of our modern trees grew, decayed and died in hot, steamy swamps possibly very similar to this one at Fakahatchee in Florida.

Left: *Gingko biloba* is the sole survivor of a group of trees which grew 160 million years ago. Although related to the conifers it has plum-like fruits.

Above: The seed-bearing organs of a female *Cycas*. The cycads are the last remaining members of a once large group related to the conifers.

comparable to *Ginkgo*, became known to botanists.

Seeds were collected in the autumn of 1947 and sent to the Arnold Arboretum in Boston, from whence they were distributed to a wide range of gardens in America and Europe the following year. Specimens of this lovely deciduous conifer in cultivation have already attained over 20m (65½ft) in height and are to be seen in many parks and gardens in the temperate world.

It was very fitting that *Metasequoia* should go first to America, because the western States are the remaining home of two of the most dramatic living trees in the world, which are also close relations to the dawn redwood. The family name of this group is Taxodiaceae (a name coined under the rules for botanical nomenclature from one of the genera in it—in this case *Taxodium* or bald cypress). Included here are the big tree or giant sequoia, *Sequoiadendron giganteum*, and the coast redwood, *Sequoia sempervirens*. The former, growing in scattered groves on the west-facing slopes of the Sierra Nevada in California and Oregon, reaches heights of 100m (328ft) with trunk diameters measured well above the ground attaining 10m (33ft). Redwoods, from the moister coastal strip, become even taller though with a less bulky trunk .

Altogether this family of redwoods and their relations comprises only 15 living species. Such a small number, coupled with the frequency of their fossil records, indicates that they are the remains of a very large, now mainly extinct group of trees.

The emergence of modern trees
From the end of the Paleozoic era in what geologists refer to as the Permian period (something well over 200 million years ago) to the

Miocene (only 12 million years ago) conifers ruled the forest scene. Some groups, such as the cycads and the redwoods, gradually declined in importance; others, more able to adapt to a range of changing conditions, took over the positions of any that were unable to keep up the pace. Amongst the most successful were the pine family which still has over 200 different species strewn about the world, including firs, spruces, larches, hemlocks, cedars and, of course, the true pines which comprise almost half the total.

Throughout these vast periods of geological time upheavals of the earth's crust, the making and breaking of continents and changes in climate combined to ensure that species of animals and plants continued to adapt or failed and became extinct. The age of dinosaurs came and went. These mighty reptiles were gradually replaced by the more successful mammalian groups. In the world of plants this development is paralleled by the replacement of coniferous domi-nance by that of the angiosperms— the higher flowering plants.

There is definite proof of the existence of flowering plants way back to the Cretaceous period— perhaps 100 million years ago—a time in which mammals have their earliest origins. But it took some 90 million years for both flowering plants and mammals to achieve the predominant positions they hold today. Plants and animals can, in fact, be seen moving in tandem over evolutionary time.

Throughout, as now, animals depend upon plants for food, shelter and (utterly basically) upon the oxygen of earth's atmosphere. Higher plants use animals to ensure pollination of their flowers and to assist in the dispersal of their seeds.

Man and the evolution of forests

Changes in conditions on the earth obviously, then, affect both animals and plants. A long period of drier climate, promoted by geologi-

Above: Flower of the African tulip tree (*Spathodea campanulata*), a fine example of a plant at the summit of its evolutionary line. It is pollinated by birds or bats.

cal uplifts, discouraged forest trees. Savannah and prairies took their place and a complementary change in animal species became apparent—notably in the fact that browsing species adapted into grazing ones. This pattern, on scales both great and small, affecting whole continents and whole

Above: The immense height of the giant sequoia (*Sequoiadendron giganteum*), 100m (328ft), makes it impossible for a photograph to indicate its true scale. These trees may be 1,000 years old.

Above: Goats feeding on olive trees in southern Spain. Their remorseless browsing has had a disastrous effect on forests right across the entire Mediterranean region.

groups of organisms as well as individual species inhabiting small areas, is seen throughout the development of life on this planet. Now man, a newcomer on the stage of life, is the most important biotic factor of all. The speed at which he is able to affect other organisms—especially trees whose time-span is so extended—does not permit adaptational changes which are dependent upon the emergence of worthwhile mutants or generic changes. The time-scale has changed.

When we remember the old hymn with the lines:

'A thousand ages in Thy sight
Are like an evening gone'

we obtain not only a deist view of time-scales but also the evolutionary one. At this point these two philosophies, so often regarded as being mutually antagonistic, clearly coincide. A good way of demonstrating this is to represent the time on earth—some 600 million years, since the oldest Cambrian rocks—as a clock-face. Each 'hour' then represents 50 million years, and as the hands of the clock turn we can follow the emergence and decline of different groups of plants and animals. The shock comes home to us when we realize that man appears at about one minute to midnight! Yet, as

has already been emphasized above, this upstart creature has had more effect—often harmful—upon the other organisms with which he shares his planet than any other.

The Mediterranean forest As far as forests are concerned the out-

standing example of climax, decline and fall is in the area to which, in a more literary context, we attach the epithet 'classical'. These are the lands of the Mediterranean. Western man's development from nomad to sophisticated city-dweller, with all the organized use of natural products that this implies, began to the east of the 'Middle Sea', in the fertile crescent of Mesopotamia. The pattern moved westward with the founding of the early civilizations of Egypt, Greece and Rome.

This area had avoided the most recent glaciation which, only 10,000 years ago, left much of the northern hemisphere as inhospitable tundra. Sheltered areas had maintained plants left over from Tertiary times, which began close on 70 million years ago, and as the climate became warmer again the Mediterranean floras went into swift acceleration. The weather pattern of, very simply, warm moist winters and hot dry summers encouraged a climatic-climax of evergreen forest. The shiny,

Left: Mixed coniferous forest in the Rocky Mountains. Here in Canada's Banff National Park, conifers are dominant to the tree-line. As may be seen this reaches to higher altitudes on southern slopes.

Right: 5,000 years of depredation by man and his animals has produced this typical barren Mediterranean scene. The rocky terrain, once covered in luxuriant forest, can now support only a few sparse shrubs.

thick-cuticled leaves of pines, oaks and other species, perfectly designed to prevent excessive water loss in times of summer drought, were ideally adapted to the prevailing conditions. Hence, before ranean littoral and its myriad islands were thick with forest. In the east cypress, aleppo pine and kermes oak (and the famed Cedars of Lebanon) were dominant, while in the west their counterparts were maritime pine, stone pine and holm and cork oaks. Above these forests, at altitudes of around 1,000 to 2,000m (3,280 to 6,560ft), grew a band of deciduous woodland, and higher still coniferous forests of cold-accepting species extended to the tree-line. This was the idyllic arboreal setting of Mediterranean lands that Odysseus might have seen in his wanderings.

Such a pattern of forest develops in response to climate and soil. Beneath the all-pervading tree canopy grow—in order of decreasing size—small-leaved evergreen shrubs, herbaceous plants (often bulbous), and finally ferns and bryophytes (liverworts and mosses). All, by supporting the climate and enriching the soil by their fallen leaves, combine to be mutually interdependent. However, when man hews down the evergreen forest canopy and permits the free grazing of sheep and goats, this hard-won balance is drastically disturbed. And that is precisely what has happened in Mediterranean lands throughout much of recorded history. As a result, in various parts at various

Above: The location of a series of scientific experiments carried out since 1882 in the now-famous Broadbalk field at the Rothamsted Experimental Station, in southern England, to observe what would happen to a wheatfield when it reverts to its wild state. Far left: wheat plots, which from 1843 extended across the whole area shown. Right foreground: recolonization by herbaceous wild plants (encouraged by removal of trees and shrub seedlings every winter). Right centre: the effect of sheep-grazing on vegetation originally similar to that in the foreground. Right background: trees allowed to develop unhindered since 1882.

times, the forest has degenerated first to maquis then to garigue, and finally to steppe conditions, where a few spiny or grey-leaved shrubs shelter deep-growing bulbs. A modern-day Odysseus therefore sees little more than sun-baked barren hillsides. And although regeneration to forest again is still possible, provided over-extensive cultivation and grazing are stopped, the soil itself has frequently become so impoverished that it will need to be built up again from scratch—which is a slow and laborious process.

Forests returning The degeneration pattern in the Mediterranean and other areas of the world where man's impact on natural vegetation has been exerted gradually and over several thousand years, allows time for at least parts of the flora to adapt to the changing conditions. Thus wherever man's impact makes itself felt gradually, provided that the human population also increases only slowly, man himself remains more a part

Above: Trees fight back. Here in Cambodia the ruins of a Khmer palace subside under the strangling growth of the jungle. In conditions of heat and high humidity recolonization of once cleared forest can be rapid.

of the ecosystem, less of a monstrous parasite. But where modern man, with his immense power sources, suddenly rushes into and exploits a hitherto human-free forest, as he has done into many areas of tropical forest, there is simply no time at all for a new and lasting balance of flora to be built up. Then the damage is all but irreparable.

Yet it is comforting to realize that here and there plants, and especially trees, are ready to return to places from which they have been deposed. One example has been scientifically well shown at the Rothamsted Experimental Station in Hertfordshire, England. Now a national institution, Rothamsted began as the private estate of J. B. Lawes who was a prime initiator of serious research into agriculture and the economics of plant growth. Continuous experiments are recorded at Rothamsted from the early years of Queen Victoria's reign to the present day. One of them began in

1882 when Lawes spoke as follows to his wheat crop at the top end of the now renowned field known as Broadbalk: 'I am going to withdraw all protection from you, and you must for the future make your own seedbed and defend yourself in the best way you can against the natives, who will do everything in their power to exterminate you.'

They did indeed. Four years later, in 1886, only two or three miserable plants, barely recognizable as cultivated wheat, were found in the whole of the neglected half acre. From then on no more of the wheat was seen. The native flora permitted by the 30cm (12in) of calcareous loam overlying clay in the centre of southern England had taken over.

Initially common bent-grass (*Agrostis vulgaris*) was the dominant plant. Forty plant species had come in by 1886, forty-nine in 1894 and fifty-seven wild plants made up the community twenty-one years after the wheat monoculture was told to look after itself.

To begin with—and this shows how any piece of ground behaves now or would have behaved at the dawn of plants' conquest of dry land 500 million years ago—the plants were all herbaceous. Many

were annuals, typical cornfield weeds. But these cannot take competition and were transient visitors, having to move on when they were not suited. A survey in 1913 showed that seventeen species recorded before had been eliminated and comparisons showed that the dominant plants changed as the permanent plant community built itself up.

Near the existing hedge, woody plants were recorded thirteen years after enclosure: oak, ash, hazel, rose and hawthorn began the development of climax woodland. By 1915 they composed a dense thicket, mainly of oak and hazel, blackberry and an ivy carpet. Stratification was already beginning. Thirty years later field maple, blackthorn, holly, cherry and ash were there. And, inevitably perhaps in Britain now, sycamore. This tree, *Acer pseudoplatanus*, is an exotic. Introduced, it seems, in the late Middle Ages it has, within this very short period (in terms of plant species colonization) become a dominant tree in many areas. Its seed germination is phenomenal and ability to withstand exposure remarkable; fortunately, too, in maturity it is a very beautiful tree.

Above: Sometimes man finds ways to coexist with mature natural woodland. Here, in a park in the environs of Vancouver, British Columbia, an unobtrusive suspension bridge provides people with a forest walk.

The Broadbalk copse, then, is in miniature a documented example of plant colonization, succession and woodland climax.

In New England, too, areas of forest cleared by the early settlers are reverting to forest. But one of the most dramatic examples of the natural resurgence of forest is to be found in tropical Mexico, where, many centuries ago, the Maya people cleared vast areas of land to grow their crops, build their cities and erect the mighty stone temples which were among the most impressive hallmarks of their great civilization. Today, visitors to the long-deserted Mayan cities find that forest trees have not only crept back to the very fringe of the temples but are even flourishing within them. And the same thing has happened to Angkor Wat in Cambodia.

Left alone, so long as the canopy has not been too much opened up and the soil completely lost, forests *can* regenerate, given time. But will they be given the time?

The Forest Ecosystem

It is estimated that in prehistoric times forest covered nearly two thirds of the earth's surface. Today, largely due to the activities of man, the original area of forest has been halved. Nevertheless, natural forests still cover more land than is used for agriculture, though in some countries relatively little of the natural forest remains.

A forest ecosystem is dominated by the trees and, although details of species composition vary enormously with local conditions of soil and climate, three major forest types can be distinguished. In the higher latitudes conifers are predominant; in temperate latitudes broadleaved trees are most common: to the north they are deciduous and further south they are evergreen. A third type of forest, found in the equatorial regions, is dominated by different families of trees in different parts of the tropics.

The structure of a forest

The growth form of trees gives the forest as a whole a structure that can be divided into several horizontal layers. The most obvious of these are the canopy layer, made up of the crowns of the largest trees, which may be 30 to 40m (98 to 131ft) above the forest floor; the shrub layer, in which shorter trees and bushes grow among the trunks of the great trees; and the ground layer of plants that grow close to the surface of the soil. There is also, of course, a root layer beneath the surface of the soil—a layer that is not so obvious to the casual observer but is nevertheless extremely important. Within the forest there is thus a complex, three-dimensional environment available for colonization by numerous plants and animals and a great variety of ecological niches for them to fill. The forest also provides a physical environment for its component and associated species distinct from that outside it. Within the forest humidity is high, there is shelter from extremes of temperature, and the soil surface is protected from desiccation. The power of the wind is also dimi-

nished in this sheltered environment, as can be clearly seen in conifer plantations where slim trees grow tall and straight. If standing alone they would be easily bent and broken by winter gales but in the forest each is protected by all its neighbours.

The forest energy cycle

Like all green plants, trees are food-producing organisms (primary producers). As explained in Chapter 2, they trap energy from the sun and use it to transform carbon dioxide from the air and water and nutrients from the soil into food substances like starches and sugars, through the process of photosynthesis. These foods are stored in the form of fruits, nuts, seeds, nectar and, above all, in the wood. The forest is thus an energy bank, trapping energy from sunlight and storing it in the form of a multitude of biochemical products. Each tree continues to accumulate capital as it grows, drawing nutrients from the soil and incorporating them into its tissues. Ultimately it dies, falls to the ground and there decomposes. Its stored energy is then released by the activity of the decomposer organisms that break down its tissues and return its nutrient 'capital' to the soil. The nutrients can then be recycled through the forest system.

It is in the way this cycle operates that we see one of the most fundamental differences between tropical and deciduous temperate

Above: Avenue of lime trees (*Tilia* × *europaea*). Energy reaches the forest in the form of sunlight. It is trapped by the leaves and used to fuel their photosynthesis. This builds up food (carbohydrates) and plant tissue.
Below: Cycle of energy and nutrients in the forest.

The Forest Ecosystem

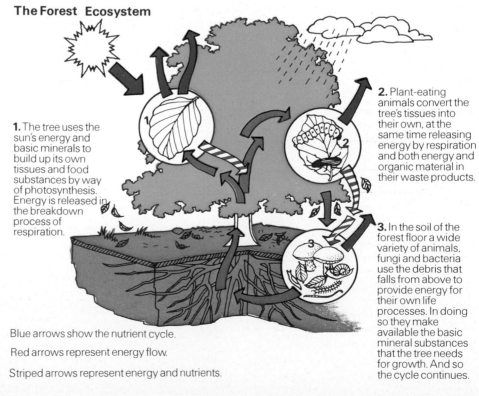

1. The tree uses the sun's energy and basic minerals to build up its own tissues and food substances by way of photosynthesis. Energy is released in the breakdown process of respiration.

2. Plant-eating animals convert the tree's tissues into their own, at the same time releasing energy by respiration and both energy and organic material in their waste products.

3. In the soil of the forest floor a wide variety of animals, fungi and bacteria use the debris that falls from above to provide energy for their own life processes. In doing so they make available the basic mineral substances that the tree needs for growth. And so the cycle continues.

Blue arrows show the nutrient cycle.

Red arrows represent energy flow.

Striped arrows represent energy and nutrients.

forests. In the latter, leaves, which typically fall at one time of year, are broken down relatively slowly and their nutrients are returned to the soil only over a long period of time. In these forests, therefore, a thick layer of humus accumulates under the trees, constituting a nutrient bank which supports an extensive flora and fauna of its own. In a tropical forest leaf fall is often irregular, and leaves are very rapidly broken down by the myriads of decomposer organisms on the forest floor which carry out their work very rapidly at the much higher temperatures. Very little of the forest's nutrient capital therefore remains for any length of time on the ground; instead, it is swiftly drawn up into the living trees once again. Consequently there is stiff competition for what little nutrients are available on the floor of the tropical forest. So, it is clear that if such a forest is cut down, not only is the energy stored in the wood removed but also most of the nutrient capital of the system. This leaves a poor soil which can support agriculture for only a very short time, because the harvesting of the first few crops removes the remaining nutrients and render it utterly useless. This is why the idea that a lush growth of crops can be obtained from the same ground that supported a lush forest is fallacious, particularly in the tropics.

Forest clearance may also have other, equally disastrous, results. For example, removal of the trees exposes the surface of the land to the full force of wind and rain. Soil is then washed away and, in the absence of trees, may only regenerate naturally at a rate of about 1cm (less than ½ in per year). In many places erosion occurs ten times more rapidly once the trees are removed. Irreparable degradation of the land and its top soil may result. Soil erosion is particularly bad on hillsides, where heavy rain sweeps soil downhill to choke rivers. Tree felling may not be the only cause of such erosion: in New Zealand serious problems have resulted from the introduction of alien animals such as red deer, which browse the vegetation. There are no native land mammals in New Zealand, so growth patterns of the trees and other plants are not adapted to compensate for browsing damage. Vegetation cover is thus removed and large quantities of precious top soil have been washed away from the hill-

sides and carried out to sea by the fast flowing rivers.

In natural forest the tree roots bind the soil and also hold much water. Indeed, up to 90 per cent of the rain falling on temperate forests is retained either in the humus or in the plant tissues. The forest thus acts as a giant sponge which plans a crucial role in the hydrological cycle. Rain is soaked up during storms and gradually released over the days and weeks that follow, and may continue to feed streams and rivers even during dry seasons. Hence the importance of retaining forest cover in upland catchment areas as an alternative to flooding lowland valleys to make artificial reservoirs.

When a tree dies naturally within the forest, its fall leaves a gap in the canopy through which more light than usual can reach the lower layers. Very quickly new

The Structure of a Tropical Forest

Above: The forest canopy is three-dimensional to ensure that the sun's energy is efficiently trapped and utilized. Occasional 'emergent' trees thrust up beyond the canopy and so enhance their chances to prosper.

species take advantage of this change in conditions and may swamp the usual shade-loving ground flora. These early colonizers are gradually replaced by others, including species of shrubs and trees that need light, and all the time the saplings of the dominant forest trees are gaining height and strength. After many years they overshadow and crowd out the light-loving species and the climax of the succession is approached. The gap in the canopy is filled and shade-loving plants once more regain their predominance in the other layers of the forest.

Thus a forest is not a static thing but a dynamic ecosystem in which

Above: Tropical forests characteristically have an enormous diversity of tree species. In the small area of this photograph taken in a tropical rain forest of Malaysia, at least 15 different species are present.

there is a great deal of interdependence between all the components. These components include not only the trees and plants which grow beneath them but also the plants which grow on them (epiphytes), as well as a great variety of animals that are adapted to take advantage of the abundant resources of the forest.

Tropical forests

In a belt around the equator, high temperatures and high annual rainfall combine to encourage a dense growth of lush forest whose greatest areas are in the Amazon basin, Central Africa and Southeast Asia. Characteristically these

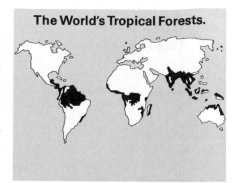

Above: Map of the world showing major areas of tropical forest; in a great many places such forests have been reduced to isolated patches and have very often disappeared completely.

light falling on the top of the canopy above.

Curiously, despite the similarity of physical conditions in the major areas of tropical forest, and the superficial resemblance of the trees of one area to those of another, each major region has its own specialities. For example, the dipterocarps are the dominant forest trees of lowland tropical Asia, from India through to New Guinea. Hundreds of species, of great diversity, are found there and nowhere else. In Africa and South America their place in the forest ecosystem is taken by trees of other families.

The tropical forest is warm throughout the year and has a high annual rainfall. If this is evenly distributed through the year, which is not always so, then seasonal effects, so characteristic of the temperate regions, are very muted: leaf fall, for example. Curiously, rubber trees, which originally came from the Amazon region, regularly cast their leaves in Southeast Asia. Whole plantations of bare trees may be seen but, although regular, this is not a seasonal event, and different groups of trees lose their leaves at different times. In the tropical forest, leaf fall is usually continuous, and flowering and fruiting show no seasonality either. Each species, or sometimes each tree, follows its own cycle, not necessarily in step with others, so that within the forest as a whole there are always fruits and flowers available. Such a regime makes it possible for a large number of animal species to survive as specialized nectar or pollen feeders, whereas they would not be able to live throughout the year in the seasonal temperate forests.

The nectar-feeding hummingbirds of the New World are ecologically replaced in Africa by the

Right: Epiphytes (such as this bromeliad, a relative of the pineapple) grow profusely on trees, but are not true parasites. They obtain the majority of their essential nutrients from the humid atmosphere.

forests are composed of an extraordinary variety of trees—hundreds of different species to the square kilometre. Nevertheless the forests as a whole all look superficially similar; the trees are commonly very tall, often 30m (98ft) or more high and sometimes 20m (65½ft) before the first branches are reached, and they are often heavily festooned with climbing plants struggling upwards to get at the light. Some very tall trees, known as emergents, project above the main canopy and may reach 50m (164ft) or more in height. The forest floor is necessarily dark under the dense canopy, being reached by only 0.3 per cent of the sunbirds, and in tropical Asia by yet other flower feeders such as the babblers and lorikeets. When these birds sleep at night the 'night-shift' takes over, in the form of nocturnal nectar-feeding bats. In tropical America these are members of the family Phyllostomidae and in tropical Asia there is a special flower-feeding subfamily of the fruit bat (flying-fox) family, called the Macroglossinae. Both these groups of bats have independently evolved the same adaptations, such as long, brush-tipped tongues, for feeding at flowers.

Plants lose nectar and pollen to these marauders but in return their flowers are pollinated as the animals move from plant to plant. We normally think of the wind and insects as being the most important agents of pollination but in the tropical forests many of the most important trees are, in fact, pollinated by bats. Indeed, some of the trees are specially adapted to ensure that they can only be pollinated in this way. For example, the flowers may open only at night and they often produce a strong, sickly smell which is very attractive to bats but not at all so to birds.

All these flowers have developed structures enabling them to be pollinated by animals which, in turn, are specially adapted for feeding efficiently from the flowers. Trees and animals have therefore evolved together in precise harmony over many thousands, perhaps millions, of years.

When fruits form on the trees, there must be some mechanism for ensuring dispersal of the seeds they contain, and again many tropical trees rely on animal partners, particularly birds. The fruits are often brightly coloured to attract the birds' attention but some grow in such a way that only hovering bats can eat them. The pips or seeds are swallowed by bat or bird and voided with its faeces far from the parent plant, which can thus establish its progeny over a wide area. This partnership would be useless if the bats fed and then hung up and slept inside caves, where it is too dark for seeds to grow into mature plants. However, most of the fruit-eating bats roost out in the open, since they lack the necessary adaptations for living in caves.

Some forest trees, such as the mango, have huge seeds which are much too large for a bat or bird to swallow. When such a fruit is carried away it does not go far before

the hard kernel slips from the soft, splitting fruit and falls to the ground, but it is still carried away from the parent plant.

Studies of the fruit-feeding behaviour of birds in the Caribbean and Latin American forests suggest that the fruiting cycles of the forest trees are staggered. Thus when birds have finished eating the crop of fruit from one species, that of another species ripens and is ready to be eaten. In this way birds are provided with food throughout the year and the dispersal of the seeds from all the tree species is ensured. This would not, of course, be possible if all the trees fruited simultaneously at one season. The annual cycle of the plants have evolved, as have the structures of both plants and animals, to ensure the efficient exploitation of these partnerships.

Temperate forests

There are large areas of forest in the cooler regions of the world, particularly in the northern hemisphere, and with increasing latitude, species diversity within them

Above: The tropical forest is often called 'rain forest' because it is so wet, but certain temperate regions receive enough moisture to grow a cool rain forest, as with this grove of eucalypts.

Right: Frosted oak leaves on the forest floor; deciduous trees shed their leaves to avoid risking frost damage to living tissue during the winter.

Below: The foxglove (*Digitalis*) takes advantage of a forest clearing.

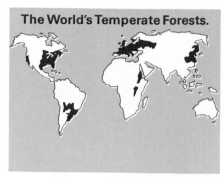

The World's Temperate Forests.

Above: Distribution of the world's temperate forests. (Some mountains in hot regions may support a kind of temperate forest on their cool slopes.)

Above: Squirrels, such as this grey squirrel (*Sciurus carolinensis*), are characteristic forest animals; they are highly adapted to life in the trees.

Above: Young leaves on beech trees. To trap all the light they can, deciduous trees deploy vast canopies of broad-leaved boughs on branches at all levels.

decreases. Whereas in a tropical forest one may see several scores of tree species in a single hectare, there may be no more than ten species in a similar area of mixed English woodland, and perhaps only one or two in Scandinavia.

Trees are very efficiently organized for trapping sunlight, as we have seen: hence the gloom within the tropical forest. In temperate regions sunlight may be less strong and often diminished by cloud. The trees therefore need to be especially efficient at trapping all the light they can, particularly where the growing season is short, and one factor that helps make them so is the sheer area of foliage many of them carry. Their many leaves, widely spread, are held out on branches at all levels. On a typical beech tree there may be up to 8 square metres (86sqft) of leaf area above every square metre ($10\frac{3}{4}$sqft) of ground beneath the tree. The beech therefore traps much light, but as a result casts a very dense shade. This is a major reason why little ground vegetation is present in beech woods. Other species do not cast quite such a dense shade, and plants that are tolerant to reduced light intensity may grow in abundance on the forest floor beneath them.

However, the maintenance of broad leaves during the often cold winters of the temperate zone, when they cannot, in any case, function efficiently due to the great reduction in daylight hours, is biologically uneconomic. Furthermore, in cold winter weather the tree's sap ceases to move, and if leaves were still carried by the tree it would lose more water by transpiration than it could replace from the soil. So the trees shed their leaves each autumn, before frost and diminished daylight make them more of a liability than an asset. This annual leaf fall, together with the seasonal production of flowers, fruits and seeds, does much to dictáte the seasonal behaviour of many plants and animals which make up the rest of the forest ecosystem. There are also other seasonal changes in the life of the trees which, though less obvious, are nevertheless of great importance to the other forest wildlife. For example, the renewed movement of the sap in spring is the trigger for much extra insect activity; it also makes the succulent cambium layers of the trees especially attractive to such animals as squirrels, which at this time can do considerable damage.

The seasonal loss of leaves inevitably also removes a large source of food for leaf-eating animals such as insect larvae; but the life histories of such creatures are adapted to these cycles, and they either transfer to another food or become dormant, if they have not already metamorphosed into adults and flown away. Leaf fall also robs the forest of its main protection from the weather, and a deciduous forest can be an exposed and inhospitable place during winter whereas the evergreen coniferous forests to the north are relatively sheltered—even though they commonly grow in environments which, overall, are a great deal more harsh.

As the length of daylight increases and temperatures rise with the coming of spring, many plants on the floor of deciduous forests make haste to grow and flower before the trees regain their leaves and blot out the light. Bluebells are a spectacular example of these early developers: by the time the canopy is closed they have flowered and wilted.

Thus the quantity and type of food available to the forest animals change through the year, and none can afford to be too specialized. There is nevertheless a rich variety of animals in these forests. The thick layer of litter on the ground provides food and shelter for many small animals as well as for the fungi and bacteria that bring about the breakdown of the fallen leaves. Because rain usually falls in moderate amounts throughout the year the atmosphere within the forest is very humid, and mosses and ferns thrive and in turn provide shelter for many invertebrates, as do all the nooks and crannies in the bark of the trees.

The deciduous forests reach their geographical limit in the northern hemisphere at something less than 60°N latitude, and beyond this the great boreal forest encircles the world. This conifer-dominated forest is the most homogeneous forest of the three main types. Many of the same species of trees (pines, spruces and firs) and of animals are found almost continuously from Siberia, across northern Europe and Scandinavia and into Canada. These forests extend to within about 3,200km (2,000 miles) of the North Pole where their by-now stunted forms give way to the treeless tundra.

This zonation of forest from north to south across the earth is paralleled by a similar zonation on mountains, where the changes in climate result from increasing altitude rather than latitude. Ascending the western side of the Rocky Mountains in the USA, for example, one can travel from hot desert scrub (too dry for tropical forest) through broadleaved forest of various types, to coniferous forest and finally out above the trees into alpine tundra. Animals show a similar but (due to their mobility) less clearly defined zonation. The actual position of the tree-line (and the boundaries between different zones) shows considerable variation, both latitudinally and altitudinally, depending on the annual rate of rainfall, shelter, temperature and various other local factors.

Coniferous forests

Many conifers thrive in mild damp climates, such as that of southern British Columbia, where the great Douglas firs grow, or the eastern slopes of the Sierra Nevada in California, where the giant redwoods flourish. Some of these trees grow to enormous heights and girths and live for thousands of years. In harsher climates conifers of other species tend to grow more slowly, and in extreme situations at the edge of the tundra trees of great age are stunted in their growth and have only relatively small diameters. Not many species can tolerate the whole range of conditions under which conifers as a whole thrive. The Douglas fir is found from Mexico to Alaska but other species are more limited in their distribution. The characteristic thick, needle-like leaves of conifers enable many of them to withstand drought, and in the more northerly regions this is particularly important because much precipitation falls as snow and ground water may be frozen solid for a great part of every year. Free water is thus often very scarce and the problems of water loss are as severe as in a hot desert. The xerophytic (water conserving) conifers are thus well adapted to life in the frozen north, but the same features also enable other

Above: In pine forests, the canopy is so dense that few plants can grow in the deep shade below, thus creating a very open and uncluttered appearance.

The World's Coniferous Forests.

Above: Distribution of the world's major areas of coniferous forests. Of the three main types of forest, the coniferous is the most homogeneous.

conifer species to form forests in dry, *warm* areas, eg in the Mediterranean region and on limestone mountains.

The trees of the boreal coniferous forest grow closely together and cast a very dense shade. The floor of the forest is covered with a thick layer of needles that are very resistant to decay and break down to release their nutrients only slowly. The spaces between the trunks are criss-crossed with fallen branches that have died through lack of light, and this limits the free-flying movements of birds. The forest is therefore a quiet place, especially in winter, when everything is blanketed in snow. But under the trees there is still shelter, especially from the wind (because the trees retain their full dress) and the forest soil freezes less deeply than that outside.

Animals adapted to survive the winter in these conditions either hibernate or grow long dense winter coats that enable them to remain active. Those in the latter category commonly have other adaptations which enable them to move over the snow without sinking in. The permanent residents of the boreal coniferous forest are supplemented in summer by vast multitudes of migrants from the south, which move north to take advantage of the short growing season and temporary abundance of food there. Many birds come to nest and rear their young, attracted by the multitude

Below: Forest fires generally appear very destructive, but they can be essential for the recycling of nutrients and to permit new growth to occur.

Above: Conifer forests usually contain relatively few tree species, though as seen here in the Rocky Mountains of Alberta several may be found together.

Below: Pines are not confined to cold regions; many thrive in hot dry conditions, such as these stone pines (*Pinus pinea*) of the Mediterranean.

Above: Fungi, such as this *Mycena inclinata* on an oak trunk, play an important role in helping to break down the tissues of dead trees. This releases the nutrients for use by other plants.

Left: The cool beech forests of the southern hemisphere are often very damp, harbouring a prolific growth of mosses, as shown here.

of insects that thrive in the forest at this season; but all food chains are ultimately dependent on the vegetation, particularly the trees. These provide food in the form of bark, leaves, cones and seeds, and although much of this is available throughout the year there is a marked difference in seasonal levels of growth and activity.

Fire plays a very important role in the clearance and regeneration of natural forest, and this is particularly true of coniferous forests. Fire opens up new areas of ground to the light, and colonization by herbaceous plants then occurs very rapidly: species grow which could never have survived in the darkness of an established conifer forest. The ash that remains after a fire provides nutrient to the soil and since it is weakly alkaline it helps to reduce the acidity usually associated with the humus beneath conifers; this, too, favours the growth of many young trees. The giant redwoods of California are a good example of a conifer species whose seeds will only germinate after fire and whose saplings need light and clear ground in which to develop. Thus, although fire appears appallingly destructive at the time—and indeed is, when it occurs too frequently or on too wide a scale—it is in fact vital for the rebirth and long term survival of the conifer forest community.

Lesser lights among the forest plants

Although the primary structure of a forest ecosystem is determined by the trees which dominate it, many smaller members of the plant community whose lives are closely associated with the trees also have a distinctive role to play. Plants that actually grow attached to trees but otherwise lead an independent life are known as epiphytes. Those that draw nourishment from the trees and generally live at their expense are called parasites.

Many mosses and ferns grow as epiphytes on trees. Because they have no thick outer cuticle to their leaves they need to live in damp, shady places and the interior of a forest is often rich in species of these groups. Among the most spectacular examples are the nest ferns of the tropical Asian forests. These plants grow from spores that have lodged in the fork of a tree. As they spread out they catch the falling leaves of the parent tree. These leaves then rot down in the base of the fern and form humus which supplies the

Above: Ferns and clubmosses growing epiphytically, using a tree for support but drawing nutrients from the air and rain, not from their host.

Left: In the humid, oceanic climate of the Galapagos Islands, several plants flourish as tree-growing epiphytes, such as the peperomias and lichens shown here.

Above: Bracket fungi are perennials, in contrast to 'toadstools' (such as the sulphur tuft fungi shown here), which actually develop an entirely new aerial structure every year.

fern with nutrients. Some species have their own leaves curling inwards to supplement and support this compost heap; others have leaves that fold under for the same purpose. So nourished, the nest ferns continue to grow on the tree until their weight becomes too great and they crash to the forest floor. In the meantime they have released many millions of spores on to the wind to find resting places on other trees.

Fungi, lacking chlorophyll, cannot manufacture their own food, and many of them depend on rotting wood or draw their nourishment from decomposing leaf litter. Among the most important are those which form a mycorrhizal association with tree roots. This is the name given to the relationship between a fungus and the roots of a tree from which both organisms

appear to derive benefit. The fungus gains from the tree roots carbohydrates and other essential growth substances which it cannot make for itself, and in return it helps to break down organic matter in the soil around the roots, turning them into inorganic nutrients that are then available for the tree. Many forest trees have their rootlets closely covered by a sheath of fungal hyphae, and in others the fungi actually penetrate within and between the cells of the root, thus connecting them directly to the soil. Often the trees respond by lengthening their rootlets, thus improving their own efficiency. The trees could grow without the fungi, and in fact the fungi are often a considerable drain on the products of their photosynthetic activity; but in places where soil

nutrients are in short supply it seems that this drawback is more than compensated for by the advantages of the fungal presence, and the trees may grow much better with their mycorrhizal associates. Indeed, introduced forestry seedlings are sometimes innoculated with mycorrhizal fungi to reduce the need for artificial fertilizers to enrich the soil.

Clearly a forest ecosystem is a very complex one, both structurally and functionally. The trees are certainly its dominant feature, yet even they are dependent for their wellbeing not only on a multitude of other organisms, both plant and animal, but also on numerous external factors, such as climate and weather. In their turn, the trees are a major factor in creating the environment in which those other organisms flourish.

Animal Life and Forest Trees

If the forest provides the ideal environment for many plants and animals, so do the individual trees of which it is composed. Each one offers a host of opportunities for food, shelter and support. Many animals use trees in a purely casual way, as a bird does when it perches or nests in the safety of lofty branches. But others, particularly insects, have evolved complex mutually beneficial relationships that require special adaptations of both themselves and the tree. Among the best examples are the pollinators, many of which have developed long tongues that enable them to feed efficiently on the nectar and pollen of tree flowers. In return for providing them with food, the trees rely on them for pollination, and have developed colourful flowers, as well as a copious nectar supply, to attract them.

Trees as homes

Many of the larger animals that live in trees obviously require special adaptations for climbing, such as prehensile tails and strong fingers or claws, and whole groups, including monkeys and squirrels, have evolved as primarily arboreal creatures. In the case of tree frogs, claws are replaced by sucker-pads on fingers and feet to facilitate climbing, and even flying animals like bats and birds may find it more convenient to scramble rather than fly among the foliage. Parrots, especially, have powerful gripping feet (with two toes pointing forward and two back) that are used in conjunction with the beak to climb among the tree tops.

However, flight is also obviously useful to tree dwellers, so useful that some non-flying creatures have developed aerial adaptations that enable them to travel from tree to tree in a manner that comes very close to flight. In the Southeast Asian forests are found 'flying' lizards and snakes that use elongations of their ribs to spread out a sheet of skin from the side of the body to act as a parachute. The so-called flying lemur and the flying squirrels also have a gliding membrane along their flanks, often stretched between fore and hind limbs. Certain frogs have extended webbing between their toes which serves to break their fall as they leap from one tree to another. In each case, the adaptation is for gliding rather than true flight, but its value in arboreal life is obvious from the fact that it has evolved independently in similar form in several quite different animal groups. Flying squirrels are so successful that various types are found in the forests of four continents; and in Australia there are close equivalents among the marsupials. Indeed, the flying phalanger of Australasia is almost an exact evolutionary replica of the flying squirrel of North America: it has the same size, shape and colour and even the same black and white edge to the flight membrane. The two animals are quite unrelated, but they have come to resemble each other by virtue of being similarly adapted to a particular tree-dwelling life style.

Above: Flying squirrels have a web of skin extending from the forelimbs to the hind legs that enables them to parachute from tree-top to tree-top. In this way they are able to avoid both the danger and the effort of having to climb down to ground level to reach the next tree. For similar reasons the gliding frog is equipped with webbed limbs—enabling it to glide up to 15m (40ft) between trees.

Below: Tree frogs are equipped with finger and toe suckers which serve, instead of claws, to grip branches and tree trunks.

Left: Southeast Asian long-nosed tree snake (*Ahaetulla mycterizens*). Many species of snake inhabit the forest canopy, scouring the tree-tops for birds, frogs and invertebrates.

Below: The slow loris of Asia (*Nycticebus coucang*) searches among the highest branches for food at night. By day these haunts are the home of its diurnal primate relatives, the monkeys.

Animal Life and Forest Trees

Above: Hornbills nest in tree holes, but the male walls in the female to protect her and the fledglings from predators, such as snakes. The male is forced to feed the whole family for several weeks.

Some of the creatures that nest in trees import or manufacture their building materials; numerous insects, for example, use mud, while certain tree frogs produce froth to surround and protect their eggs. However, most tree-nesters use material provided by the tree itself. The nests of rooks are made of dead twigs, and some large birds of prey such as the bald eagle collect branches and twigs and, using the same nest site for several years, add to the structure annually until it reaches huge proportions. Tailor birds stitch biggish leaves together to form a nest. Squirrels may chew bark to line their dreys, and orang utans pull together branches and leaves to make a sleeping platform for the night. Some of the most complex nests are those made by wasps. They chew dead wood, mixing it with saliva to make a kind of paper pulp to serve as the building material. Different coloured woods add different colours to the construction which, when dry, is surprisingly weatherproof and, though perhaps 30cm (1ft) in diameter, is strong enough to remain suspended from the tree by a single point.

In leaf axils or in forked branches, water may accumulate, offering a home and breeding ground to mosquitoes and certain frogs—moisture-demanding animals that would otherwise have to live in the highly competitive environment of the forest floor. The accumulation of water means

Above: Painted storks nesting in acacia trees in Rajasthan bird sanctuary, India. This region is regularly inundated in the monsoon and it remains flooded during the summer, creating a lake and island.

Below: A large nest of mud and wood built by ants in Sierra Leone, West Africa. The ants construct the nest up in the tree to keep it clear of the wet forest floor.

Above right: The great spotted woodpecker (*Dendrocopos major*) has a long barbed tongue and powerful bill; both being used to extract larvae from their burrows in rotten wood.

Above: Weaver ants use silky threads (produced by their larvae) to sew leaves together to form a protective nest. They are common inhabitants of the forests of tropical Asia.

that parts of trees often rot and form cavities, especially at knot holes where old branches have broken off. These holes are much in demand as homes for birds, bats and insects, for they provide not only shelter but also protection from extremes of temperature. The inside of such a hole may be several degrees warmer or cooler than the air outside. Such cavities may be modified before use. The nuthatch, for example, uses mud to reduce the opening until it is small enough to keep out everything larger than its own slim body. In the tropics, several hornbill species nest in tree holes and the male uses mud to wall up his mate for the duration of the nesting season. He has to bring food for her while she incubates the eggs, and later he must feed the family as well; only when the young ones are ready to fly will they be liberated.

Woodpeckers, which form a family of their own, the Picidae, are without doubt the birds most highly specialized for tree life. They are found in forests in all the continents of the world, except Australia. Their claws are specially modified, with two on each foot facing forwards and two backwards—an adaptation which enables them to gain a secure grip on the rough bark of a vertical tree trunk. Their tails, like that of the nuthatch, are stiff and strong, serving as a support when pressed against the bark. Poised upright, the woodpecker hammers his beak against the trunk, aided by powerful neck muscles, to excavate a nest chamber which may involve digging out several litres of wood chips.

Woodpeckers normally attack wood that has already been weakened by fungi and has become the home of boring beetles. They rarely attack sound wood, for that holds few insects, and they are quite unable to use timber itself as food. Foresters might regard them as friends of the forest but for the fact that they appear only where decay is already advanced. A long sticky or spiked tongue enables the woodpecker to extract insect larvae from the wood, so

that the tree provides it with food as well as a home. Some species also 'drum' on the tree, rapidly beating a resonant piece of dead wood to produce a loud, staccato sound. This form of non-vocal communication, much used in the breeding season, is aided by the properties of the trees, dead, split hardwoods like oak providing the greatest amount of resonance and sound magnification.

Trees also play an important part in the social life of many animals. For instance, they serve as nurseries for huge breeding colonies of fruit bats; and some particularly colourful birds, notably certain birds of paradise, may use a special tree as a display perch for males to show off their finery. Often a communal display will take place, centred on one particular forest tree used for generations. In a similar way,

Above: This 'merveille du jour' moth (*Dichonia aprilina*) is highly camouflaged; enabling it to match very precisely the lichen-covered tree bark on which it rests.

certain butterflies use distinctive trees as meeting places at which to congregate, display and mate. Purple emperors, for example, use a particularly large oak as their focal point.

The most remarkable assemblies of butterflies on trees are those of the North American monarch or milkweed. This species undertakes long-distance migratory flights, moving north into Canada during the spring and summer and returning south to spend the winter in a few very restricted areas on the Californian coast and in the Sierra Madre Mountains of Mexico. In the latter area they accumulate in vast numbers on coniferous trees in the

Top right: Many insects, such as this African bush cricket, are bright green, thus disguising them against the background colour of the leafy vegetation on which they feed.

mountain forest, where they remain in hibernation until the coming of spring.

Life on the bark

Few large animals live on tree bark because of their vulnerability in such an open situation, but a great variety of forest insects and other invertebrates use the surface of tree trunks as a resting place during inactive periods. Species that habitually do so may be recognized by their cryptic colour patterns, which closely resemble bark. Moths such as the death's head hawk and the red underwing hide their brightly coloured hindwings behind dappled bark-coloured forewings that

trunk—a position in which their pattern matches the vertical lines or cracks in the bark. All these insects hold themselves close against the surface so as not to cast a shadow that might reveal their outline. Bark-inhabiting mantids, bush crickets, lizards and certain Southeast Asian spiders are also cryptically coloured, and often extremely flattened, in a way that helps to prevent detection by predators.

Aphid-like scale insects, which are common on tree trunks, are permanently protected by a scale-like waxy shell formed from a body secretion. One particular forest species found in Southeast Asia produces a resinous scale which is collected commercially to produce shellac.

Tree trunks provide many tiny crevices and other niches where insects can lay their eggs or where their larvae can hide. These insect young may remain dormant in such places for months during the cold temperate winter or the searing tropical dry season. The silver washed fritillary butterfly lays its eggs during the late summer on the bark of woodland trees. The eggs hatch before winter and the young larvae promptly hibernate in crevices in the bark until the following spring, when they migrate on to their larval food plant, the dog violet.

There is thus a wealth of microfauna tucked into the nooks and crannies of tree bark, providing a source of food exploited by tree creepers. These birds have a narrow curved beak adapted to probe for food, and their successful exploitation of this niche enables them to remain resident in northern latitudes throughout the year, whereas many other small insectivorous birds are forced to migrate south in winter to find food.

Below: Caterpillars also make use of camouflage devices. This peppered moth larva (*Biston betularia*) additionally holds itself out to simulate the appearance of a twig.

Above: The buff tip moth (*Phalera bucephala*) not only matches the tree bark on which it sits, but settles in such a way as to resemble a dead twig.

camouflage them very effectively when at rest on a tree trunk. Colour patterns are matched to a particular type of background so that species like the peppered moth that habitually sit on silver birch bark are coloured in such a way as to resemble that bark and no other. The bark of forest trees is not always clean: it may be covered with a green film of algae, or densely clothed with mosses or lichens. Insects such as the merveille du jour moth are so patterned as to be perfectly camouflaged on a lichen-covered trunk. Geometrid moths with dark and light streaked patterns running horizontally across their wings may be found resting sideways on a

Leaves as food

Many of the arboreal mammals feed largely on leaves, though most of the birds eat buds or fruits. Leaves are also taken by ground-dwelling mammals, which reach as high as they can to feed. All young leaves are then bitten off to this height to form a 'browse line' —a feature that is particularly evident on park trees where there is a high population of deer.

Foliage is also readily devoured by a great variety of defoliating insects. Butterflies and moths commonly feed on the leaves of forest trees during their larval stage. The caterpillars of some species are very specific in their food requirements, feeding on only one species of tree, while others are very catholic in their tastes. The caterpillars are usually thinly scattered and rely on green coloration and other camouflage devices to avoid detection by predators. Those of some of the large silk moths and the eyed hawk moth are apple green and blend perfectly with the foliage. Other species, such as the buff-tip moth which feeds an oak, birch, and other deciduous trees, have caterpillars that are protected by hairs. A few caterpillars live in large colonial 'nests' of silk. These may take the form of a huge silken tent which covers the foliage and within which the caterpillars can feed undisturbed, as is the case of the North American fall webworm; others form silk tubes, discreet retreats from which the caterpillars emerge to feed. The pine processionary moth caterpillar, which is brightly coloured and bears irritating hairs, rests in a large cocoon-like nest during the daytime and marches out, head-to-tail with its fellows, to feed at night.

It is relatively rare for defoliating insects to do catastrophic damage to forest trees, though a few species have become serious pests in different parts of the world, regularly and completely defoliating trees over large areas. The gypsy moth and the notorious larch sawfly are very destructive to forests in North America. Usually, insect leaf-eaters are the larvae (caterpillars) of species whose adults feed on something else, but in the New World tropics defoliation may be caused by an altogether different type of insect: the leaf-cutter ant. Here it is the *adult* that strips leaves from the trees. This ant may form enormous colonies of hundreds of thousands of individual workers. While foraging they clear broad swaths through the forest and strip forest trees of their leaves by snipping them off piece by piece. The ants are particularly remarkable in that they do not eat the foliage itself but use it for their own agricultural purposes. They return to their nest with the leaf material and add it to an underground mound of rotting vegetable matter on which they culture a fungus that provides their food requirements.

All these defoliating insects actually bite off portions of leaves

Top: Browsing animals such as deer bite off the lower foliage of trees (or ivy as in this case), leaving a characteristic 'browse line' in the forest.

Above: Most insect species take a heavy toll of tree foliage; the sawfly larvae shown here are being particularly destructive to this common sallow leaf.

(except for caterpillars at a very young stage, which, being unable to bite right through the leaf, merely rasp off the surface layers). However, there are some more specialized feeders that eat only the middle layers of leaf cells, leaving the upper and lower surface layers (the epidermis) intact. These creatures, called leaf-miners, are the larvae of tiny moths and sawflies. They are well protected during their larval life because they remain within the leaf, instead of feeding exposed on its surface.

Much of the leaf's structure is cellulose, a substance with little food value, so it is more efficient to feed only on the cell contents, or

better still, on the sugary sap of the plant. This requires special adaptations and is only really feasible for very small creatures, mostly insects. Many of these are bugs that have a long stylet which they insert into the plant to obtain the sap. The largest of these sap suckers are the adult cicadas, which may be found sitting on the trunks of trees in warm countries. There are many smaller related insects, such as leaf hoppers, tree hoppers and aphids, with similar habits. While cicadas feed from the larger branches of a tree, the tiny aphids usually suck sap from the leaves. Sap suckers may infest trees in enormous numbers, causing extensive damage to the leaves

Above: Leafcutter ants collecting pieces of green foliage, which they take to their underground nest to cultivate the fungi on which they feed.

Above: The track of a leaf miner in a bramble leaf, showing the site where the egg was laid (at left) to the place where the adult insect broke free from the leaf. Leaf mines are caused by larvae that tunnel through the tissue, eating out only the mesophyll cells and leaving the epidermal layers intact.

by making them curl up through lack of sap. Aphids excrete a sweet, sticky fluid called honeydew which rains down on the leaves and the ground below. Where it coats leaves it provides a medium on which moulds can grow. Both the moulds and the honeydew itself are eagerly devoured by other insects. Tiny plant lice called *Psocids* graze on the moulds, while butterflies and other insects' sip the sweet moisture of the honeydew. Ants are also particularly partial to the honeydew, and they protect and even culture suitable aphids on trees near their nests.

Wood as food

Few animals can survive on a diet of wood alone. This is partly because it has only a low nutritional value and partly because much of it is composed of materials that animals cannot digest, so that most of what they eat passes out undigested (and therefore wasted) in their faeces. Most wood eaters are insect larvae, and their poor diet is doubtless the reason why some have to serve an extraordinary long larval apprenticeship before becoming adult. In warm forests the soil-dwelling nymphal stages of the cicada chew away at the roots of trees, often for many years, before emerging as adults. The caterpillars of moths such as the goat moth, leopard moth and certain clearwing moths, tunnel through the solid wood of the trunk and roots. Like the cicada, they have a very long larval life. The length of larval life is almost legendary in the case of

certain wood-boring beetles, such as the brilliant metallic-coloured buprestids of the tropics. Cases have been reported of these spectacular adult beetles emerging from wood of tropical origin which has been incorporated for many years into furniture and other finished products. Goat moth caterpillars may infest a tree, eating away the bark and leaving holes from which a sticky mixture of dung and sawdust oozes. This smells strongly of billy goat— hence the name of the moth. The most destructive of the wood-boring insects, however, are termites. These creatures are small but very numerous, living in large colonies numbering many thousands of individuals. They tunnel through the soil to a suitable source of wood, or they may construct mud-covered runs over the surface of hard-baked ground. When they attack a tree they sometimes hollow out the heartwood for the entire length of a trunk. The termites are unable to digest the wood unaided, so they rely on micro-organisms (protozoa) which inhabit their guts and which assist by chemically breaking down the wood fragments.

The bark of a tree is not very

Above: Elephants in East Africa very often cause serious damage by stripping bark from acacia trees, apparently in search of nutrients.

Below: Termites (often called 'white ants') feed on dead wood. Though important in the forest cycle, they can be destructive to wood in buildings.

nutritious, as it consists largely of dead material that forms an outer protective layer for the trunk. There are, however, a number of bark beetles that tunnel into the bark to lay their eggs between the bark and the sapwood. The off-spring then devour the tissue of the inner layer of bark. In this way they may cause destruction out of all proportion to their small size. If there are enough beetles in a tree, they may succeed in severing the vital but very thin cambium and phloem layers of the trunk or branch, causing the death of the tree above that point. When the adult beetles emerge from the bark they leave on the surface a pattern of holes resembling shot holes. One or two species of these bark beetles have been responsible for the spread of the destructive American fungus disease known as Dutch elm disease, which has caused the widespread destruction of elm trees in European countries.

In East Africa elephants have taken to ripping the bark off acacia and baobab trees, but they are apparently seeking the nutritious underlying sapwood. A similar destructive activity is also practised on a small scale by many of the world's forest rodents, particularly squirrels. At certain times of the year they will chew into the bark, causing deformation of valuable timber trees. In extreme cases, where the chewed zone encircles the tree or branch, sap can no longer flow and the tree (or part of it) dies.

Even when they are dead, trees continue to provide food for insect life. Wood-boring beetles that specialize in feeding on dead branches during their larval life help to break down the dead material and return it to the forest floor. When a dead tree has broken up or has

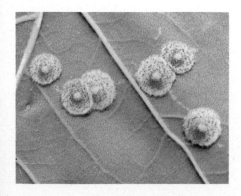

Above: Spangle galls on an oak leaf. These galls are caused by the gall wasp, which lays its eggs in the oak leaf tissue. Gall growths on leaves can be induced by various insect species.

been blown over, these creatures continue the process. As the wood becomes sodden and rotten it is attacked by the larvae of flies, which riddle the material and assist its attack by fungi and bacteria; what remains is then eaten by various decomposer organisms like woodlice and millipedes, which also clean up the annual accumulation of dead leaves. Ultimately most of the material is recycled through the soil, to be incorporated into new trees and other forest plants.

Some tree products, especially fruits and seeds, are commonly very nutritious and are eagerly devoured. Often the fruit has evolved to encourage this process, so that the seeds within it are scattered by the animals in the course of their feeding. The very specialized habit of crossbills in pulling apart pine cones is an example; some seeds go to feed the bird but a considerable proportion must be dropped. However, in some cases the tree gains little or nothing from animal attention. Weevils, for example, attack young hazel nuts or acorns. The female uses her long snout to bore a hole into the centre of the nut in which she lays an egg. The larva then feeds on the kernel until it is full grown—and until the seed is no longer of any use to the tree.

The most extraordinary feeders are those insects that cause galls and which feed on the gall tissue

Above: An adult male stag beetle with its ferocious-looking jaws (which are used only for sexual display). The stag beetle larvae spend most of their lives tunnelling inside wood.

produced by the tree, again with no apparent benefit to the latter. For example, the female gall wasp lays her eggs in the tissues of oak trees such as buds or leaves. The plant then produces an abnormal growth (called a gall) in response to the presence of the young larva of the gall wasp. The larva in turn devours the plant tissue in the gall. In the case of the oak apple gall there is an alternation of generations: the wasps that hatch from the oak apples lay their eggs in the roots of the oak tree, producing root galls from which hatch wasps that lay their eggs in the buds to produce more oak apples.

This kind of plant–animal association, though interesting, seems a little one-sided, but perhaps it is not always so. Certain acacia and other tropical trees develop on their stems swollen gall-like structures that are colonized by a particular kind of ant. Since these ants vigorously attack anything that disturbs the tree, it may be assumed that the tree benefits from the association. Indeed, it is tempting to believe that the gall-like structures are provided especially for occupation by the ants—the tree providing a barracks for an army that will defend it!

Reaping the Timber Harvest

After the trees have been grown and tended to maturity the forest manager has a vital part to play in deciding how they are to be harvested. Today, with so much emphasis on the amenity value of forests, the forester has not only to consider what is the best way to harvest the crop from a particular area (to avoid erosion of valuable soil following cutting and to obtain the best cost levels), but also what the impact of the operation may be on the general public.

Much of the total felling work over the life of a single forest crop takes place before the final harvest, though. Selective fellings, or thinnings, are not such 'sensitive' operations as final harvest, as only part of the crop is removed in each thinning cycle. For the final harvest, or clear felling, however, when the trees have reached the desired size, the forester must be much more careful. From the technical point of view, it is obviously more economical to fell a fairly large area so as to save frequent moves of men and machines; but in many parts of the world the general public do not like to see a sudden wholesale clearance of trees, and clear felling operations are kept to smaller areas. In the high Alps, for example, no Austrian forester will ever fell more than 2–3 hectares (5–7$\frac{1}{2}$ acres) at a time in one place—to check or reduce avalanches.

Another point which the forester must consider is the quantity to be felled, be it a thinning or a clear felling. The increase in the volume of timber that trees yield each season is called the *increment*; and it is the volume equal to this increment over a carefully calculated period of years which should be cut at the end of each thinning cycle. A good forester is like a good investor—he should not take more than the interest (increment) out of the business or he will reduce his capital; but here the parallel ends. If a business man reinvests some of his interest he increases his capital. For a time the forester, too, can leave his increment in the forest which is his business, but after a while the trees become too crowded and the rate of increment actually falls off. Hence the need for periodic thinning operations.

Harvesting

To some men, working in a forest has always been an attraction in itself, but it has always been hard work, often under difficult conditions, and it has always required considerable physical effort. Rural depopulation, which is continuing even now from its beginnings in the Middle Ages, has had ever more drastic effects on the availability of labour for forest work as well as in agriculture. Efforts to improve the lot of those who remain in rural employment has brought higher wage costs. These two factors, and the general industrialization of forest work, have favoured increased mechanization wherever possible over the last two decades. The steepest rises in labour costs have come during the 1970s and this has brought the need for mechanization into almost all forest operations and requires use of systems offering improved efficiency.

In bygone times, it used to be fairly easy to divide the operations that go to make up harvesting into four main phases—felling, extraction, loading and transport—with a fifth phase, simple processing, being done either before or after extraction. The first machines for harvesting were developed more than 15 years ago in North America with another breed of machine being developed in the early and late 1960s in Scandinavia. Now, machines developed from these, which often carry out more than one of the harvesting phases, are well established in Sweden, Finland, Canada and the southern USA, though by no means universally in the industrialized world. For obvious reasons, these complex, costly machines have no place in the developing countries, where the skills for operating and maintaining their complex electronic controls and hydraulic circuits are insufficiently developed.

In Europe, the Scandinavians have pioneered a generation of forest 'processors', 'feller-bunchers' and, most recently, 'harvesters' and these are used on about 20–25 per cent of the output of Sweden's forests. Other machines have been developed in North America and Australia, both of which regions make some use of these types of machine, but they are large and heavy, represent large investments and require forest areas with high wood volumes to be able to operate economically.

In Continental Europe, where foresters want lighter machines

No other raw material used by man offers constant yield in perpetuity, which the managed forest gives. Thus by the time one tree has matured and is being harvested (such as the Douglas fir shown below), three or more seedlings are ready in the nursery to replace it (left). So, with well managed forests, timber can become a renewable resource. Yet it needs to be handled with tremendous care if it is not to be irretrievably lost to mankind.

and where the unit of forest ownership is much smaller, the sophisticated Nordic and North American machines have yet to gain a foothold. Also, a different breed of much smaller, simpler machine appears to be emerging.

Felling

Felling used to be done with axes and saws, often two-handled saws for large trees, bow saws for smaller ones. In the 1950s, use of motorized chain saws rapidly became widespread, and machine design rapidly progressed to give the lighter, more powerful and much safer machines in general use today. Finally, there are the new 'feller-bunchers' and harvesters incorporating large shears or chain saws which can fell 50 or 60 average sized trees of 30 to 40cm (12 to 16in) diameter in about an hour.

To fell a tree by axe or saw a V-shaped cut is first made on the side to which the tree is to fall; this cut is called the *under-cut* and it should go in about a quarter or a third of the diameter. The back-cut is then made horizontally on the opposite side of the tree at the

Above: These drawings show a common method of tree-felling. First a V-shaped under-cut is made on the side of the tree facing the intended direction of fall, then a back-cut is made on the opposite side.

same level as the point of the 'V' or a centimetre or two higher.

Often, immediately after felling, the manual operator will trim off the branches, cut off the top and perhaps cut the trunk, or bole, into two or more lengths—an operation called cross-cutting. This operation is an example of simple processing. In softwood harvesting, when this processing is done 'at the stump', the method is known as the 'shortwood' system in contrast to the 'whole tree' system, longwood or tree length system. In the latter, the branches are left intact and are used to help 'skid' the stems in bundles, and ease the trunk's movement.

Extraction

The extraction phase, that is moving the bole, in one or more

pieces, from stump to roadside or ride (a track through a forest) may be done in any of several ways. In the case of small light pieces it is done by hand. Otherwise extraction usually entails the use of ordinary or modified farm tractors fitted with a winch, by a purpose-built rubber-tyred skidder (a special tractor); by crawler tractor, or, especially in Scandinavia, eastern Canada, southern USA and parts of Continental Europe, by 'forwarder'. These are three- or four-axle machines with large rubber-tyred wheels, 'hinge' steering in the chassis and a large bunk at the rear, loaded by a hydraulic grapple boom.

In the UK and other countries where forest output is largely on a modest scale, though, the modified farm tractor still predominates. The 'skidder' modifications normally consist of front wheel weights (to keep the wheels on the ground when pulling heavy loads), radiator, sump and valve guards, larger tyres, anchors and, of course, one or two winches. The winch cable may pass over a pulley on a small arch, and in this case there will be a butt plate to prevent the raised front end of the load from damaging the rear part of the tractor.

There are many other, more highly specialized, extraction systems used in particular conditions encountered around the world. River floating—which ceased to be used in North America and in Scandinavia in the early 1960s— is still the main system used in some parts of the tropics where the rivers are relatively slow flowing, though it is more a transport system. For extraction from the stump, the great array of winch and cable systems has to be mentioned. These can use 'towers' (still known as steel 'spar trees' even though use of natural, standing trees ceased at least 15 years ago); they can use up to three winches; they can use radio-controlled carriages running on the 'skyline'; or they can be small, nimble systems for the lighter loads in thinning work.

In some countries horses, often with part of the load on a sledge, were used before mechanization, and the work was done mainly in the winter. Today, as in so many other spheres of life, machines are

taking over more and more, though the elephant, and even manpower, is still used in some tropical countries.

With tractors and skidders, wheeled or tracked, the machine may go to the load, which is then fastened to it and dragged out. Sometimes a cable from the winch is pulled out by hand to the load; this is hard work, especially in hilly country, so there may be a second winch with a cable passing through a pulley which can be used to pull out the haul-in cable.

Today, the most popular machine for moving large quantities of small diameter timber where the terrain is not too steep is the *forwarder*. This is usually frame-steered—that is the front and rear parts are moved hydraulically about a central pivot—and there is a crane or grab built in near the middle to load the rear part. The rear wheels follow the tracks of the front when turning.

Processing

Some modern processing machines can go to the tree and not only fell it but also remove the branches and top either before or after felling. They may also cross-cut the bole into lengths. The produce may then be left on the ground for another machine to collect, or alternatively it may be collected in a cradle; and when the cradle is full the load may be wired and then dumped. This is the case with the Busche combine in which the felling (for pulpwood), processing and extraction phases are done by one machine.

Some processors are stationary at a depot, often referred to as a 'landing', to which the stems (bole lengths) or whole trees may be brought in by tractors, skidders or 'feller-bunchers'; with these last-mentioned machines the trees need never be felled to the ground, but are held up after cutting and loaded on to the back of the machine. When whole trees are brought out, they are fed to a processor in which the branches and tops are removed and the bole often cut into shorter lengths, with the larger and smaller sizes being off-loaded on separate sides. In some machines the stem is debarked and chipped, and the chips are blown into trailers which are then taken direct to pulp mills. If only bole lengths are extracted, the processor may just cut them into shorter lengths, or else actually debark and chip them as well.

Reaping the Timber Harvest

Loading

Except where the forest produce is chipped and blown into a trailer (rather like silage), it has to be loaded after the extraction phase. There are many different ways of doing the job, ranging from hand loading for small, light pieces to using large cranes or 'A frame' derricks for huge logs. Much of the small and medium sized produce is now loaded by hydraulic grabs; these may be on separate machines or fitted to the transporting vehicle. For the largest logs heel boom loaders can be used.

In less developed countries, or where only a few logs are to be loaded, there may be some device for pulling the logs up skids on to the lorry or trailer—but this is, inevitably, a slow process.

Transport

Most forest produce is taken by road to where it is to be converted or used. Much of it is loaded on to ordinary trucks, but usually without any sides; some of it is taken in trailers behind trucks and some—usually the large logs or large long poles—goes on to special bunks riding on a bogey towed by a tractor or a 'tug'. Again, several variations are possible. Bogies (log carriages) are sometimes lifted up for the return journey and carried on the back of the towing vehicle, pick-a-back fashion.

In the past, much forest produce was floated down rivers but the practice is now sharply on the decline, especially in temperate regions. This is for a variety of reasons: cost (trucks have become cheaper); large numbers of logs were inevitably lost; the work was one of the most hazardous occupations then practised; and, for the few companies still river driving at the outset of the 1970s there arose new legislation almost everywhere to outlaw the practice due to the fouling of river water that it caused. Labour shortages and hydroelectric schemes resulted in changes away from river driving.

Another disadvantage of river transport is that many streams are frozen in the winter, and the voracious pulp mills, which have increased in number and size, need large supplies all the year round, and can no longer tolerate long winter delays.

Cableways are still used in some mountainous regions, but their use too is decreasing. They are expensive to install and much less flexible than road transport. Forest railways have also given way to roads for the same reason.

Helicopters are occasionally used in particularly difficult terrain, but they are very costly to operate. Balloons are being developed on the mountainous west coast of North America to give the necessary lift to the cableways, though these are really employed more in the extraction than in the transport phase. Lastly, 'ground-effect' machines such as hovercraft can be used over flat swampy country or along rivers. As these machines are developed and their costs come down their use may become more common.

A French project undertaken in 1976 is to experiment with an interesting balloon-helicopter hybrid, the 'Helicostat'. It will use uplift from its two blimp-shaped envelopes to offset the deadweight of the machine. It will have a helicopter rotor to provide positive lift. The project is being undertaken to increase France's forest resource volumes by allowing the extraction of wood from previously inaccessible mountainous regions for the first time.

The harvesting of timber can be a very complicated operation with many possible alternatives. The headache for the poor forest manager is that he has not only to work out which of the many possibilities

in each phase is likely to give the most economic overall result—no one phase can be considered in isolation—but also how the amenities of the locality may be affected. For example, it may make good economic sense to cut a main forest road across a hillside, but how will local people react to the ugly 'gash' that may result? In less developed countries, the problems of erosion and the level of skills among the local workers must be taken into account when making a decision as to whether to introduce more sophisticated harvesting and processing machines.

Tree farming

The art of managing forests is thought to have begun centuries ago, probably in Germany, where the Black Forest has records dating back 400 years. The early foresters tried to help nature re-

Above: Balloon-logging uses cables hung from above to winch out logs from land where building roads could cause undue erosion of soil or would turn out to be too costly.

Below: Removing Douglas fir and red cedar logs from a forest in British Columbia. Transporting timber is very costly, so where possible the largest trucks are used.

create the forests with the same or a similar composition of trees and other plants as in the original forest, and this objective persisted in Europe wherever forestry was strongly supported.

Experiments with artificially created plantations of trees—all seeded or planted at the same time—began in the late nineteenth century. Three approaches were tried: plantations with a mixture of several species, with two or three species, and with a single species. The fear that pests and diseases would upset the health of these artificially created forests made some foresters reluctant to adopt plantation forestry on a large scale, but experience in the last 100 years has shown these problems to be less extensive than the pessimists had forecast. Plantation forests have gone ahead by great leaps and bounds in many regions throughout the world.

In fact, so common has plantation forestry become today, and so standardized the management practices for some plantations in several temperate, subtropical and tropical regions, that the word 'tree farming' has come into use.

Forests are perpetuated in two main ways, referred to as *natural* or *artificial* regeneration. Of course, there is often also a combination of the two. If a forest is left after exploitation, and protected from fire and browsing or grazing, it will regenerate of its own accord; but not necessarily with all the same species. If fire is allowed in there can be considerable change and grassland interspersed with groups of trees can soon develop; this is a particularly common occurrence throughout the subtropical area.

Natural regeneration

After felling in any area, whether in temperate, subtropical or tropical parts of the world, trees and other plants that require a lot of light are the first to become established. They may grow as seedlings or as regrowth from stumps, referred to as *coppice*, or sometimes as root suckers. The faster growing species soon outshadow the regeneration of the slower, shade tolerant ones, which are usually the ones that make more useful timber. It is at this stage that the manager has to decide what to do to favour the kinds of trees that he wants to form the new final crop.

Sometimes the more useful species, especially if needing light, such as the pines, hold their own over most of the area. If the regeneration is not adequate in parts of the area, it is here that artificial regeneration may be resorted to, to ensure a crop of desirable species.

In some cases the faster growing natural regrowth, or only some of it, is treated deliberately; this may be by cutting it back or poisoning it with a chemical. This is done so that other species will not be suppressed, though some species undesirable for the future crop may be retained for several years to give some protection to the more desirable ones in their earlier years. These desirable species may be part of the natural regrowth or they may be introduced artificially. Forests of natural origin are normally managed as even-aged or *uniform* stands or as uneven-aged, irregular or *selection* stands.

In the former case the stand is generally clear felled at one time, when the majority of the trees have reached the required size or age; sometimes, the canopy may have been opened up, to a greater or lesser extent, several years earlier to encourage natural seedling regeneration, and sometimes a few of the best trees are left for several years after the felling to provide more seed for the next crop.

In well managed forests, whether even-aged or uneven-aged, periodic measurements are made over small sample areas so that, with the aid of tables, the manager can know what quantity of timber to remove in any one thinning without seri-

Left: Tree nursery in Papua New Guinea. Forest management in the tropics is still in its infancy, but great strides have been made to improve native skills.

ously affecting the final yield.

There are several variations in the final felling of even-aged or uniform stands. Felling may be in large blocks, in several smaller scattered blocks, in wide or narrow strips, or in various forms such as triangles or circles.

In the case of uneven-aged stands, the manager aims at some form of a selection system to regenerate his crop. Ideally, trees of all ages and sizes are present in any one area; periodically the old ones are felled, and also some younger ones, so that there is more space for others to grow. Crops managed in this way are to be found mainly in mountainous areas where avalanches and landslides or perhaps erosion of the soil would occur if clear fellings were made on a considerable scale.

Artificial regeneration
The other way of regenerating forests, which is also used for creating new ones, is by artificial means. This is normally done by putting out young plants on ground which has been prepared to a greater extent, perhaps by partial or complete ploughing or, to a lesser extent, perhaps by just digging small holes. Sometimes, especially in tropical and subtropical areas, seed is sown direct.

In many countries, even where the original crop is uneven-aged, and perhaps composed of several species, the useful trees are felled and removed and then the others are felled and burnt and the area planted up; this planting is often done with different and faster growing species, or perhaps better varieties of the previous ones.

Conversion
There are now many different ways that a log can be processed into useful products and you can

be sure that there is going to be very little waste of wood fibre, so valuable has it become. Even sawdust is now a valuable by-product. Substantial rises in the price paid for roundwood since 1972 have markedly influenced the type of processing used and has encouraged accelerated development of a number of new or modified processing techniques which give improved 'recovery'. This is the industry term for the volume of marketable products produced from a unit volume of log raw material. For the actual harvest, this seldom exceeds 50 per cent, and for any one processing operation it seldom exceeds 55 per cent. Altogether, then, harvesting and one basic processing operation utilize little more than 25 per cent of the total 'biomass' in the forest.

The 'basic' processing operations are: sawmilling, where sawn wood or lumber is made, with subsequent grading, planing, moulding, seasoning, preservation treatment or other secondary process may be carried out; plywood manufacture, particleboard and fibreboard are other processes. The last two can be major users of residues from either of the first two operations, since they use the fibrous characteristics of wood and not the rigidity of solid wood.

Most of these processes using by-products can function better using bark-free wood, so debarking has become a more universal operation carried out even by sawmills so they can obtain the better price offered for bark-free chips produced in a chipper from their offcuts and 'edgings'.

Sawn wood For timber, the logs are taken to *sawmills* for conversion to pieces of wood of the required size. The first saw, called the 'head' or 'breakdown' saw,

generally cuts the log up into large pieces of timber for resawing by other machines (resaws) to smaller sizes. There are three main types of sawing machinery. Today by far the commonest is the 'band' saw, in which a long steel ribbon with teeth on one edge passes round two pulleys one above the other, and the log is moved into the saw on a carriage guided accurately by rails. The latest of these machines are worked by push button or lever control by a comfortably seated operator. Not only does his console control the thickness of the piece to be cut, but it can be 'programmed' by a small computer to carry out cuts in a sequence found in advance to give the best 'recovery' rate or economic return for a log of given diameter. No part of the log goes unused. The 'slab' (the outer piece with or

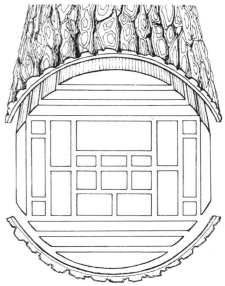

Above: A diagram showing how a softwood log might be sawn. Nordic and North American mills now use computers to select the pattern giving highest volume.

Below: Pit sawing allows a second man below to work a two-man had saw. First used in iron age times, it is still in use today in some primitive regions.

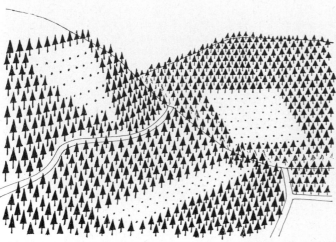

Felling Patterns
This diagram shows felling patterns used in even-aged temperate forests for planned, phased clear felling. On high slopes the trees are felled in inverted triangles up to 2 hectares (5 acres) in area. This pattern is designed to contain avalanches and prevent erosion and any retreat of the treeline. In flat situations various felling patterns are used, including square blocks and narrow strips about 25m (82 ft) wide. In uneven-aged stands circular felling patterns may be used.

without bark) can go along rollers or a conveyor belt to another part of the mill where smaller pieces of wood can be cut out of it. The planks, cut from the rest of the trunk, go to other resaws.

The next type of head, or breakdown, saw is the 'circular' saw, a steel disc or plate with teeth along the edge. These teeth may be cut directly into the plate or they may be separate pieces of metal, often hardened at the tip, which are fitted into portions of the plate.

The third type of head saw is a 'frame' saw or 'reciprocating' saw, where the blade is fixed in a frame moving up and down, or, as mainly in the past, from side to side. Usually there are several saws in the frame, hence the term 'gang' saw. Although these saws cut more slowly, their output can be quite high, as several pieces are cut at the same time. The spacing between the saw blades can be varied, depending on the thickness of the planks required.

The main points to be borne in mind when converting logs to sawn timber are:

1. To sort logs first according to species, sizes and perhaps quality. Different kinds may need different types of saw teeth.
2. To make as few cuts as possible by the head saw, which, because it is thicker than the resaws, takes out more sawdust.
3. To cut for quality or grade of timber required. The best comes from near the outside, where there are few or no 'knots'. (So long as a branch, whether alive or dead, is attached to the tree, new growth rings of the trunk continue to enclose those of the branch, in the form of 'knots'. To avoid this, pruning is carried out as the tree grows. However, the outer sapwood may have to be excluded, especially from hardwoods. For instance, oak furniture 'squares' must be all heartwood because the sapwood is susceptible to borers.

4. To cut into recognized standard thicknesses and widths.
5. To decide whether to cut to specialist sizes or to a wide range of sizes. The former is clearly more wasteful, but can command a higher price.
6. To consider size range of end products. Smaller sizes mean less waste, since more of the slabs can be used, but they necessitate more resawing.

The resaws, to which the pieces go from the head saw, may be either smaller band saws or circular saws. The pieces, if large and heavy, may go on to a carriage, and be pushed or driven past the saw. Most pieces, however, go on to the saw bench where there are ribbed rollers, either vertical or horizontal, which help to feed the piece to the saw. The bench has a fence which the operator can move, either mechanically or manually, closer to or farther away from the saw, depending on the width or thickness of the pieces required.

Some of the resaws are called 'edgers'. These are used for pieces from the log which have 'wane'— that part of a partly sawn piece of

Above left (Top): A hardwood log being cut with a standard bandsaw. (Bottom): The sawn log, stacked before edging and drying. Above: Sawn timber, stacked with spacers to assist drying, awaits shipment outside a small sawmill in British Columbia, Canada.

The Three Main Types of Saw

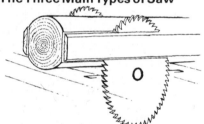

Circular saw This is a bench-type circular saw that is in common use in small sawmills.

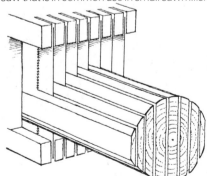

Frame or reciprocating saw Often used with bandsaws in large sawmills.

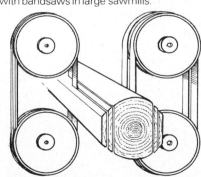

Bandsaw This one is a reducer bandsaw (quad) that gives two boards each side.

timber which has an uneven edge or edges along which there is or was a strip of bark—which must be removed, so as to give square or rectangular pieces of sawn wood. Some edgers have two saws, the space between which can be varied so that as wide a piece as possible can be cut free of wane. In some cases there is even a third saw, so that two narrower planks can be cut at the same time.

Finally, there will be one or more trimmer saws for cross-cutting, or 'docking', where the pieces are cut to specified lengths.

When the timber has been cut to the required sizes, it is usually carefully stacked with thin pieces of wood called 'stickers' between each layer, and allowed to dry out; if used green it will later shrink and warp. Many large mills have kilns to speed the drying process.

There are situations when being able to move an entire sawmill is a great advantage and for this there have been for many years portable and mobile sawmills. The advantage is greatest when the volume of resource around any single site for the mill is limited. These portable or mobile saw systems can be almost as complex as a normally installed sawmill, though usually they are much more basic. In some of these the log is fixed and the saw, mounted in a frame on wheels which move along on rails, is pushed through the log. In such cases, the blade is horizontal with

Below: A kraft paper production plant in Sweden. Paper products account for the largest volume of forest produce.

pulleys on each side of the frame.

Plywood Some large sized logs go to *plywood* mills. Here, after de-barking, the logs, which must be straight and of high quality, are usually steamed for a day or two. They are then put into a machine which holds them at each end and are rotated against a very sharp large knife, so that a veneer is peeled off. After these veneers, usually from 1 to 3mm ($\frac{1}{25}$ to $\frac{1}{8}$in) thick, are dried and clipped to size, glue is applied and sheets built up of a varying number of plies, each ply being laid so that its grain direction is at right angles to those above and below it.

Instead of being peeled, as for plywood veneers, high quality logs of some species are sawn lengthwise into a few sections and then very thin slices (about 0.25 to 0.5mm; $\frac{1}{100}$ to $\frac{1}{50}$in) are cut from them. These slices become the decorative veneers for use on panels and furniture. Wood in the round in smaller sizes from the forest may also go to other kinds of mills, producing pulp, particle (chip) board or fibreboard.

Paper and cardboard In *pulp mills* the wood is usually debarked and then ground to small pieces (for newsprint) or chipped to various sizes. The chips are then treated with chemicals, or 'cooked', to a greater or lesser degree to give individual fibres that are more or less free of lignin, the substance which turns newspaper yellow in sunlight. After various treatments, the pulp is dried, pressed into

sheets and packed for despatch, or it may be passed on in suspension (about 5 per cent solids) to an adjoining paper mill.

There are many different kinds of pulp, depending on how the fibres have been separated from the wood, and for nearly every kind of paper or cardboard there is some blending of pulps in the manufacturing process.

Particleboard At a *particleboard* mill the round wood is debarked, and chipped into much smaller pieces than at pulp mills. It is dried, thermal setting resin added in a fine spray and blended with the chips and the chips spread on a wide moving belt which transports the 'mat' past a cutoff saw and then into the hot press where it is pressed at high temperatures. The forming of the 'mat', as it is called, on the belt, is done in various ways, but nearly always to give finer chips on the surface and larger, coarser ones in the middle. This gives a stronger but lighter board than if all the particles were of one size. Many of these plants are highly automated and require very few people to operate them.

Particleboard has seen tremendous technical development over the last ten years and is an attractive product commercially: it makes good use of a relatively low cost form of wood. The range of types of particleboard has widened hugely, particularly in the 1970s, with research in the Federal Republic of Germany— where it was first produced experimentally during the last war—in

Sweden and, to a lesser extent, in the USA and Canada.

Some of these developments have resulted in special boards that use either a particularly large but thin wafer-like chip, or long strands of wood. The latter are now being 'oriented' in a single direction during forming and before pressing. This results in board as strong as plywood but with raw material costs less than a third that of plywood.

Other developments have centred around use of new types of resin and use of normal mineral cement powder as a binding agent instead of the synthetic resins normally used. This board is safe from termite attack, resistant to fire and has a great potential for making low-cost housing in the tropics, among other uses.

Other developments have given rise to 'hybrid' boards, which use a particle core but have veneers on each surface, giving the appearance of plywood. A new board made in Finland does a similar job but has ultra-fine fibreboard skins.

All this rapid development of new products has given rise to

the concept of 'wood fibre engineering', where the characteristics of the various basic ways of processing wood fibre are examined with a view to combining them in the best way for manufacture of a product with a given set of properties. The field is seeing intense research and development and a few more product types appear on certain markets each year.

Fibreboard At *fibreboard mills* using the conventional 'wet' process the wood is chipped, often without removing the bark, and the chips are then steamed under pressure and ground to give small bundles of only a few fibres; these go in suspension in water to the board-forming machines. Some adhesive, usually a resin, is added and the mixture is spread out to a uniform thickness on a wire gauze to drain. The board is then cut into lengths and the pieces go on metal plates or cauls into a press with up to 40 openings, one for each board. The kind of board produced depends on the temperature and pressure in the press.

Fibreboards vary from very light soft boards, such as are used for acoustic tiles on ceilings, through medium boards to much heavier hardboards and oil tempered

Particleboard is a high-value product made from low-grade roundwood (left) Conversion of logs to chips is the first stage (below left). Graded chips finely coated with resin (below) are then formed on a moving belt into a 'mat', which then advances into a hot press to produce a strong, rigid board (illustrated below right).

boards. There are, in fact, about a dozen different kinds of fibreboards.

If you look at a piece of hardboard, you will see that one side is smooth—the platten side—while the other side shows the marks of the gauze in the press. This gauze is necessary to let out the water and then the steam during the pressing and heating stages. If smooth plattens were used on both sides, the steam could not escape and the boards would burst.

'Dry' process fibreboard is made in a number of mills built for the purpose around the world. Most of them make yet another new product known as 'medium-density' fibreboard. This is the board type that showed the greatest annual growth in output worldwide of all wood-based panel products over the two years 1975 and 1976. A few dry process mills do make the long-established hardboard with which most people are familiar. A research-oriented mill in India claimed in 1975 to be making dry process fibreboard without the addition of a binder, but using the natural resins in the wood.

Much of the intake of particleboard mills in most countries consists of residues from sawmills and shavings from joinery works; fibreboard mills and pulp mills also use these residues. This use of residues from one type of mill by another type is an important contribution to the conservation of forest resources and a necessary response to the stark realities of raw material supply shortages and high roundwood prices.

Building with the Strength of Wood

Ever since man left his cave behind he has used wood in various forms for his dwellings in almost every part of the world. Even before leaving the cave he used wood outdoors for such things as bows and arrows, spears, axe handles and hammer handles and log bridges thrown across small streams.

Traditionally, wood has been the most widely used material for many outdoor structures, such as houses, farm buildings, some public buildings, bridges, fences and gates, poles, docksides and locks. The tradition, naturally, has been considerably stronger in regions where forests cover a relatively large proportion of the land, such as North America, Scandinavia, northern Russia, southern Ger-

many, Austria, France, Switzerland and many parts of the tropics. Like many other countries that are today regarded as developed, Britain destroyed most of its forests many centuries ago; in the developing countries similar wanton destruction is still in progress, as we saw in the first chapter.

Buildings

Today, in certain parts of Europe, very little wood is used on the outside of houses, though it is tending to come back. In houses and other buildings constructed a few centuries ago timber framing was quite common, and many fine examples are still preserved. Generally, in most modern timber-framed houses, the frame is usually covered over by some form

of *cladding*, commonly of timber or of tiles. Timber cladding, often referred to as *shiplap*, is normally in the form of horizontal planks with the piece above over-lapping the upper edge of the one below.

Wood can also be used for roofs, nearly always in the form of *shingles*. These may be hewn or split in less-developed areas, but in most countries they are usually sawn, with one end thinner than the other, so that the lower end does not project so much. Among the woods most widely used for shingles is western red cedar from Canada.

Why did the use of wood for the outside of buildings decrease, and why is it now coming back to some extent? One reason for the decreased use was that timber steadily

Above: A modern American house built with plywood cladding. Wood can have many advantages over other building materials; it can be relatively cheap and it allows fast erection.

Right: A subsistence farm in Canada. Here all the farm buildings are constructed from wood, supplies of which traditionally have been plentiful over the whole country.

Left: An early American wooden church, in Dakota. Renouncing the monumental style of European architecture, the American colonials built their churches like their framed houses, simply, with large windows and weatherboard cladding.

Below: Western red cedar shingles on the roof of a modern building. To avoid warping, shingled roofs must be steeply pitched to shed water quickly.

became scarcer in many places, while other materials, such as bricks and concrete, became more readily available. Another was that people grew more afraid of fire as towns and cities increased in size and density of population. Fire continues to be cited as an objection to wood, but, with fire retardants and good fire services, this prejudice is really unjustified today. In North America and Scandinavia the advantages of using wood for house building are clearly evident: it allows faster erection, better insulation and, when in good supply, it is often significantly cheaper. The main objection, however, was that most timber was liable to decay or attack by insects—as it still is if not properly treated.

Apart from the proximity to large supplies of timber, an important reason why wood has always been used for houses in northern temperate regions and in mountainous areas is that the far colder climate makes conditions much less favourable for wood-attacking fungi and insects.

We saw on page 23 that various changes take place in a tree as the sapwood becomes heartwood, resulting in the latter becoming considerably more durable. This is due partly to the removal of protein (food) material as the cells die, and partly to the deposition of substances such as tannin or one of the terpenes (oily hydrocarbons), which make oak or pine heartwood more resistant to fungal decay and insect attack.

For a number of years, with diminishing supplies of large-sized trees coming to the sawmills, the proportion of sapwood in the output of sawn timber undoubtedly increased, resulting in a higher ratio of less durable timber coming on to the market. The result was that many people decried the use of wood for building purposes on the grounds that it rots and decays, is attacked by various borers and burns easily.

However, because of the development and use of efficient preservatives properly applied, wood has in recent decades become much more resistant to destructive agents, including fire. Unfortunately, some woods such as sitka spruce, which is the most widely planted species in parts of northern Europe, are not only lacking in natural durability, but are also very difficult to impregnate with preservatives; such woods, therefore, should still not be used out of doors except for articles which, by their very nature, are carefully looked after, such as boats and oars.

On farms many of the buildings are still made of wood, though not as many as in the days when it was abundant and cheap. We have all seen wooden sheds of various sorts, pig sties, chicken coops and feeding troughs. In recent years some troughs have been made from plywood of an exterior grade or even of oil-tempered hardboard fixed to a wooden frame. It has been possible to use plywood because of the development of modern

Right: Wooden 'Zaanse' houses of northern Holland showing a merchant's house (at left) and a tradesman's house (right). They were built mainly in the mid-eighteenth century to traditional designs.

Above: A Japanese wooden pavilion, its elegance and simplicity characterizing the skill with which successive generations of Japanese craftsmen have worked with wood.

Left: A 'long house' of Sarawak. Construction is based on the use of local trees, which are roughly squared off and used as support pillars. The roof is composed of wood shingles or palm fibres, and the walls of plaited palm fibres, palm-wood or bamboo.

Right: The traditional multistorey house of Switzerland, with a masonry base to guard against the risk of fire.

adhesives, which are resistant to the weather, and of certain types of preservatives.

Where trees were plentiful and other building materials difficult to come by, log cabins were at one time common. Some are still built today, as weekend cottages in Scandinavia and North America, and in parts of Europe, to serve as mountain shelter huts or bases for hill walkers and climbing expeditions. The large poles are usually trimmed on two opposite sides so that they fit snugly, and are placed with the butts and tips alternately one above the other. To keep the wind out, packing of some sort—moss can be used—is placed between the logs. For the corners the logs must be deeply notched to fit securely. Virtually any species can be used so long as the boles are straight, but the more resistant ones are obviously better.

For public buildings, timber has been used rather less, although the writer has seen wooden churches in countries as far apart as Norway and Guyana, and has stayed in a variety of wooden hotels in both countries.

Bridges

Timber, both in the round and sawn, has long and frequently been used for bridges. Notable among wooden bridges were the quite elaborate structures built in North America during the early days of railroads. Today, the forest engineer frequently uses timber for the bridges needed to open up country where large areas of trees are to be felled or new plantations made. The type of timber he uses depends very much on how long he needs the bridge to last. If the harvesting or planting operation is to last for only a season or two,

Building with the Strength of Wood

the wood will usually be in the round, and not necessarily of a very durable species; if the operation is to extend over a prolonged period, the bridge will be built of durable or suitably preserved sawn timbers.

In recent years, thanks to the development of adhesives that are weather resistant, a new type of timber construction has evolved for bridges. This consists of building up a large bearer or girder by gluing together a number of smaller pieces. One advantage of this technique is that, because thinner planks are used, they can be bent and glued to give a most attractive arch. A number of examples of this 'glulam' technique can be seen in small bridges in parks and pleasure gardens.

'Glulam' has in recent years become a building technique in its own right. The size of wood used varies according to the final application but the following serves as an example. Strips about 1cm ($\frac{2}{5}$in) thick, 30cm (1ft) wide and between 2 and 5m ($6\frac{1}{2}$ and $16\frac{1}{2}$ft) long are joined together to make planks up to 30m (98ft) long. These are coated with time-setting resin on both sides and several 'layers' are clamped together in a special press so that the joins between individual pieces are staggered in the final beam. The beautiful curves so easily allowed by this technique and their aesthetic appeal have created considerable demand for this efficient use of wood. A 'prestressed' glulam technique, using tensioned steel cables internally,

Below: A modern wooden bridge constructed by the 'glulam' method. This involves the use of glued, laminated members, made from small-section boards which can be shaped to conform to any sort of arch or curve.

Above: Wire-supported wooden bridge over the river Balue in Long-Busang, central Sarawak. The bridge represents a kind of hybrid technology, for it uses wire braces as well as the more traditional wood slats and fibre ropes.

Below: A system of fencing used in Sweden. Split lengths of wood are lashed between sapling poles—thus giving the fence both strength and a measure of flexibility, enabling it to 'bend with the wind'.

has been developed in Austria recently and supports a 60m (197ft)-wide building in the city of Klagenfurt, Carinthia.

Fences

Long before man learned how to saw timber, he used wood in the round, or split, to make fences. Not only fixed fences, but also movable ones in the form of hurdles —usually made from chestnut, ash or hazel—have been used from time immemorial. Today, wooden fences come in many forms. In suburban gardens, sectional fencing is in common use, notably waney lap or wavy edge, often made from larch; and in the country, wood is used a great deal for post-and-rail fences. Both types owe their increasing popularity to the effectiveness of preservatives.

Along country stretches of main roads and highways there has been an enormous increase in the use of post-and-rail fences over recent years. This has been a great boon to both the forest grower and the sawmiller. Logs that would have been unsuitable for converting to pieces for constructional purposes—for, say, planks or joinery—can often yield pieces that meet the specifications for motorway fencing. The post-and-rail fence does not demand long pieces, so the individual logs do not have to be long, and bends can therefore be cut out; and because the timber does not have to be planed, there is a considerable saving of wood and the cost of processing time and equipment.

Here, too, the use of suitably applied preservatives has meant that many more kinds of wood can now be used than formerly. Oak and larch, and then only the heartwood, were at one time regarded as the species that must be used if a fence was required to last a long time, but now a wide range of species is accepted.

Gates and gate-posts are, of course, essential adjuncts of fences. Posts are cut from the centre of short logs, and usually from heavy durable species, but gates can now be made from almost any kind of tree.

Any discussion of fences would be incomplete without a mention of *chespaling*. This is a kind of movable fence, and is made from split pieces of wood held between pairs of twisted wires, usually at three levels—near the bottom, the middle and the top of the split stakes. The stakes themselves are not usually driven into the ground, but the strands of wire are fastened every so often to stronger stakes or posts that *are* in the ground. This old type of fencing has come into common use in recent years to form snow barriers along open stretches of road. The spaces between the stakes let the wind through, but its speed is reduced, and snow collects between the fence and the road. The term chespaling is used for this type of fence because the stakes, or *pales*, are usually made from chestnut—the sweet or Spanish kind, not the horse chestnut.

Other uses

Although mining underground is hardly an outdoor activity, it is certainly not an indoor one. With the increasing use of machines for cutting out the coal from the seams, there has been a sharp decline in demand for wooden pit props, though some are still used in places. Wood may still be used for sleepers or ties for lines along which the trucks for coal, or other materials, are moved. It is also used for chocks—pieces about 5cm (2in) square and 60cm (2ft) or so long—to build up cribs for temporary supports; another use is for wedges, which are needed to make various supports firm on uneven surfaces. Both chocks and wedges can be cut from short lengths of wood or from pieces that are not of sufficiently high quality for many other purposes.

Wood finds yet another important use in the construction of wharves, docks, canal locks, marinas and breakwaters. For marine works the poles—if we can use this word for what are usually called *piles*—have to be large, long and very straight, because they have to be driven down a considerable depth below the bed of the sea or river.

In the sea there are several animals that burrow into and live in wood under the water; the commonest of these are the teredo (or shipworm) and the gribble. Some trees produce wood that is naturally fairly resistant to these animals, and is therefore especially suitable for marine structures, one of the best known being greenheart *(Ocotea rodiaei)*, which comes from Guyana. But the use of certain preservatives, in higher concentrations than for most purposes, makes it also possible to use woods that would otherwise be

Building with the Strength of Wood

Above: The sturdy ribs of this fishing boat stand as a nostalgic reminder of the days when great beams of oak were used to build the keel, frame and sides of the hulls of the world's mighty sailing ships.

attacked, or to give longer life to the most resistant ones.

An increasing use for low-quality timber in short lengths is for *pallets* (low sturdy platforms for the handling and storage of goods). A pallet is so constructed that it can be handled by a fork-lift truck. The pieces are usually nailed together, sometimes with special twisted or 'ringed' nails, which do not come out as easily as ordinary wire nails. There are many different designs of pallets, but they may be grouped into one-way, two-way or four-way entry for the lifting forks.

Wood is not now much used for shipbuilding, except for fishing boats, larch being a favoured species for the frame and planks. The use of fibreglass for small boats is now almost universal, except when someone wants a 'one-off' boat. For decking, teak is the best wood, because its natural oil prevents corrosion when in contact with iron. Mahogany or teak is often used for other parts of the boat, such as hatches. Frequent coats of varnish are needed to keep the wood looking smart.

Poles—that is, wood in the round —have many uses out of doors. The commonest one is for transmission poles for electric or telephone wires. In both cases the poles are de-barked and must be straight and strong to withstand gales. Usually they are of softwoods, Scots pine

Above: Wooden sleepers, or ties, are still used by railways, particularly in such specialized roles as crossing ties under points, their more traditional use being replaced nowadays more and more by prestressed concrete.

being the most popular species in temperate regions and eucalypts being used in many warmer countries. The poles should always be treated with a preservative, unless their use is to be very temporary. In hopfields poles are used to support the wires from which strings hang down for the hop vines to climb. For this less demanding purpose larch poles are the most commonly used species.

Timber for scaffold boards has to be strong, but fairly light for handling on the scaffolding, often high above the ground. In some countries wooden poles are still used for the scaffolding itself; these, too, must be strong and light.

Above: Peeling the bark from a Douglas fir in southern England while preparing the trunk for use as a telegraph pole. The pole will then be treated with suitable preservatives to give all weather protection.

Another use for wood, though now a comparatively rare one, is for farm equipment and tools. These range from the waggon and hay wain to gigs, pony traps, small carts and trailers, and for such implements as hay rakes, wheelbarrows and tool handles. In the heyday of wooden farm vehicles, elm was the favourite species for the wheels of carts and ash for the wooden frames and shafts.

As a final example of the versatility of wood out of doors, it should be remembered that timber is used, though again on a diminishing scale, for railway sleepers or ties. In many industrial countries today, most of the main lines con-

Above: Spraying roof timbers to protect them against woodworm. Most wood needs to be treated with chemical preservatives if it is not to be susceptible to attack from insects, fungus, water or fire.

sist of welded rails laid on pre-stressed concrete sleepers, which have about double the life of even well-preserved wooden sleepers. The latter, however, are still used for crossing ties under the points, because mass production of concrete ties is less easy. And in many developing countries wooden sleepers are still the most common, especially where durable species are available; where such species are not easily available, less durable species are employed, having first been well impregnated with preservatives.

Preservatives

As we have seen, the continued or revived use of wood for many outdoor purposes is due to the development of modern preservatives and improved means of applying them. The main destructive agents against which they act as safe-guards are fungi and wood-boring insects.

The preservatives fall into three main groups: organic solvent preservatives, waterborne preservatives and tar oils. Fungicides and insecticides are added to the first two groups, but the tar oils (of which creosote is the best-known) have these properties inherent in them.

Many different chemicals are effective in varying degrees and no one preservative is effective in all cases. Some can be applied by simple methods such as brushing, spraying, deluging or soaking, but others have to be forced into the wood under pressure. Some of the waterborne ones can be leached out, so they are of little use under wet conditions (eg copper sulphate and salts of boron). Others are resistant to leaching, especially if the wood is impregnated under

pressure (eg a mixture of the salts of copper or zinc, chromium and arsenic, as used in some Celcure or Tanalith preservatives). Although applied in solution in water, these chemicals—especially under pressure—form complex insoluble substances when in contact with the cellulose of the cell walls, and are fixed firmly in the wood. In nearly every case, the wood must be dry and clean before being treated.

The preservatives best known to most of us are in the organic solvent group. Such chemicals as pentachlorphenol, copper and zinc napthenates, chlorinated hydrocarbons such as gamaxane, and tributyl tin oxide—all of which are insoluble in water—are used in such solvents as paraffin or mineral spirits. It should be stressed that most manufacturers of well-known brand-name preservatives also make a wide variety of others, each formulated for a specific purpose and to a specific chemical composition.

Finally we should mention the water-repellent preservative stains, in the organic solvent group. These also contain pigments—which leave a colour *in* the wood (not, like paint, on the surface)—and a water repellent that keeps the wood drier and so less liable to shrink or swell. They are much easier to apply, and to renew, than paint.

The Warmth of Wood Indoors

One of the biggest users of wood is the building industry. Some of this timber, as we saw on page 64, is used in a strictly out-of-doors fashion, as in the frames, cladding and sometimes the shingles of timber-framed houses. But far more is undoubtedly used indoors, concealed within the outer shells of houses and other buildings that we generally regard as brick-and-tile structures.

Roofs

A great deal of timber goes into roofs, usually in the form of *trusses*. The commonest form is the 'W' truss, so called from the arrangement of the four struts. The pieces (two rafters, four struts and a tie beam—the horizontal member) are cut to shape and assembled in a jig—a frame that holds them in place. Toothed plates are placed under and over the joints and the plates are then pressed hydraulically into the pieces, called truss members. There are various kinds of plates, but all serve the purpose of assembling all the members of the truss in one plane, thus producing a stronger truss than the earlier types, in which the members overlapped and were bolted together. The *pitch* (ie the slope) is varied according to the type of roofing material to be used.

Mass-production methods, involving the use of jigs and presses, are thoroughly justified, because one truss is required for every 45–60cm (1½–2ft) of wall length of every building. For 'one-off' jobs, plates with holes can be used, so that they can be fixed with nails.

Softwoods (conifers) or soft hardwoods must be used, otherwise the projections on the plates would not penetrate easily into the members they are intended to join together. The woods most commonly employed are redwood (Scots pine) and whitewood (spruce).

Long thin pieces of wood, called *battens*, are fastened horizontally across the upper edges of the rafters to take the tiles, slates or other roofing material. The spacing between the battens depends on the size of the roofing material. More wood is used on the underside of the eaves and also across the ends of the rafters, to keep out birds and bats. Where the house longhorn beetle occurs, it is legally necessary to impregnate the timber first with a preservative.

For the roofs of very large areas, glulam structures (see page 68) may be employed. The use of these, and of timber generally, may be important when considering a possible fire. Although wood burns, wooden structures—especially in large dimensions—are more durable in fires than steel or concrete ones: at high temperatures, steel softens and suddenly gives way, and concrete breaks up (especially when water is sprayed on it). A large wooden girder or column takes much longer to give way. The frames of some aircraft hangars are made of glulam members; if the hangar catches fire these

Above: This swimming pool has glulam support beams in the roof, which give the structure aesthetic appeal and strength, and reduce the risk of collapse in a fire.

comparatively fire-resistant frames allow the very expensive planes to be removed before the roof falls in.

One unusual type of wooden roof, named for its peculiar geometric shape, is the *hyperbolic parabaloid*. Seen from directly above, it appears to be square, but in fact two opposite corners turn down and the other two turn up. Normally, to produce such a roof, three layers of planks are nailed together and fastened to a glulam frame, and then covered with a suitable waterproof material.

Above: A timber staircase, making use of one of the lightest, strongest and most easily-worked building materials, yet one that suggests an atmosphere of airy space.

Several squares with only corner supports can be joined together to cover large areas.

Joinery

Next to roofs and roof trusses, the most important indoor use of wood in buildings is in *joinery*—windows, floors, stairs, built-in cupboards, shelves, skirting boards, and counters in banks, offices and shops.

Left: A set of 'W' trusses, the most common way of using timber in roof construction.

Below: A modern kitchen. The use of wood surfaces in kitchen furniture is an indication of how architects now consider exploiting wood's aesthetic qualities—its warmth and rich, grainy texture—rather than merely its strength and durability.

Until recent years, doors, usually panelled, were quite elaborate structures and had to be skilfully made. Today, with high wood costs, most doors are flush (that is, they consist of sheets usually of plywood or hardboard—fastened to both sides of a wooden frame). A decorated surface can be obtained by applying a sliced wood veneer, some form of plastic material or just paint. Where fire resistance is necessary, as for the door of a built-in garage, a layer of asbestos sheeting may also be included; a thin wooden board is naturally not resistant to fire for long unless specially treated.

Many windows and window frames are still made of wood, as, of course, are door frames. Impregnating the wooden members with an organic solvent preservative before assembly ensures that the wood is no longer liable to decay, thus countering one of the main arguments in favour of metal windows. Spruce and pine are the species normally used, but for the windowsills (which, in fact, exemplify an outdoor use of wood rather than an indoor use) a durable hardwood such as oak, or some tropical wood such as afzelia, should be used, or else a preservative-treated harder softwood. Even with a durable wood, it pays in the long run to apply a preservative before the sill is inserted—its life could be doubled at little extra cost.

Floors   Floors may be either suspended on *joists*—large pieces of timber with the edge uppermost—from wall to wall (on ground floors these are inserted above the damp-proof course), or laid on a

and, because the tree is slow-growing, it is being replaced (if at all) by much faster-growing trees. usually subtropical pines.

Furniture Modern wooden furniture may be either of solid wood or else of wood particle board, covered with a real wood veneer or with one of the plastic laminates. (Many people in the wood industry take it as a compliment that the most imitated pattern is the grain of wood.) Solid wood furniture can be divided into two groups: elegant and utility. Items in the elegant group are usually copies of classical designs. Some are made of mahogany, often by reshaping

Above: At one time, cabinets, wall units and other furniture were made of solid wood and intended to last, whereas today most are produced from veneered boards.

Above: Making a chair by hand. This man is putting the finishing touches to the wooden frame of a straight-backed chair, before it goes for upholstering, and polishing.

solid slab of concrete. For suspended floors, at least the ends of the joists should be treated with a suitable preservative, because no matter how carefully the building is done, moisture, leading to decay, may get on to these ends. The floor itself, if made of wood, may be of *tongued* and *grooved* pieces, the tongue or rib on the side of one piece fitting into the groove of the adjoining piece, or of strips or *parquet*—narrow short pieces generally arranged in small blocks with the adjoining blocks at right angles. Strips and parquet are laid on a sub-floor, which may consist of ordinary deal (pine or spruce) or occasionally large sheets of particle board. However, sub-floors are usually made up of a layer of bitumen over concrete.

Sometimes two, or more, different-coloured woods are used to give floors a very effective pattern. Marvellous examples can be seen in the Hermitage Museum in Leningrad; and some years ago it was fashionable in Portugal and Brazil to use a very dark wood (acapu or sucupira) and a pale yellow one (pau amarelo) to form various patterns.

A wood that has recently become popular for joinery is Parana pine, from Brazil. It is light-coloured but often has darker or pinkish streaks. It is not really a pine, though, but comes from the genus *Araucaria,* and is closely related to the monkey-puzzle. The tragedy, to the forester, is that the Parana pine forests are now being overcut,

pieces from larger, heavier, old and ugly items of furniture, while others are made from very carefully dried good-quality elm; oak and teak are also very popular. The slow-growing fine-grained mahogany (Spanish mahogany from Central America) that was used so much during the furniture-maker's classical era from 1700 to 1850 is now very rare.

In high-quality furniture, even the parts that are not seen—for example, the sides, back and bottom of a drawer—are made of the same timber. As good quality wood became more expensive, first other kinds were used, and then plywood, for the bottom of drawers and the back of such articles as sideboards, desks, chests of drawers and wardrobes. In the last few years, a new type of particleboard has been produced, only 2–3mm (up to $\frac{1}{8}$in) thick, and this can now be used instead of plywood.

For utility furniture—kitchen tables and chairs, benches, school desks and the frames of cupboards —less expensive woods are used, such as beech and pine. A new 'medium density' fibreboard is now making inroads with a number of major furniture makers — primarily in North America—who prefer its even texture to the rough edges common to particleboard.

A common item of furniture that

comes between the elegant and the utility class is the Windsor chair. The seat is made of elm, the legs are of beech and the back is of ash, or sometimes of beech. Elm is used for the seat because something fairly thick and sturdy is required, with some grain or pattern. Beech, which is a fairly fine-grained strong timber, can be turned on a machine to give smooth and nicely shaped legs. The back of the chair, which has to be bent in a curve to take the upright pieces, must not only be strong but also very slightly springy; ash is generally used, because it is a supple wood.

For bending, except for slight curves required in glulam structures, the wood needs to be steamed first and the whole process must be carefully controlled with special equipment to hold the bent piece of wood in shape until the bend is set. It is an interesting fact, which no one has yet been able to explain, that hardwoods from temperate regions, such as ash, beech and oak, can be bent more easily than either temperate softwoods or tropical hardwoods.

A recently developed technique that makes it easier to bend pieces of wood when cold, is first to steam them (at least the portion to be bent), then press them from the ends to make them shorter (by about 10 to 20 per cent) and let them cool and set; the pieces can then

be bent quite easily by hand to the required curve and incorporated in the article being made.

The uses of board products

On page 62 we mentioned what is collectively referred to as 'board' or 'panel' products: plywood, particleboard and fibreboard. Another panel product, also used in joinery, is called *blockboard,* because it is made up from short lengths of wood, 6–12mm ($\frac{1}{4}$–$\frac{1}{2}$in) or so thick and 2.5–5cm (1–2in) wide, which are laid close together to form a core which is then covered on both faces by gluing on rotary-peeled veneers which hold the whole board firmly together; the grain of the veneers being at right angles to the blocks. Blockboard is often used for long shelves because it bends less readily than particle board.

Thick sheets of plywood may be employed for flooring, while plywood with thin sliced veneers of decorative woods is now used a great deal for wall panels. Fibreboards, too, are widely used in buildings. Softboards in large sheets may be employed for ceilings, especially in outbuildings, where a little sagging does not matter; and in smaller sizes they are commonly found as 'acoustic' tiles on ceilings and walls as well as in open telephone booths.

Two other board or panel products that find widespread application in buildings are hardboards and particleboards, although the use of hardboards is to a certain extent restricted by the fact that they are not so rigid as other boards, and, being thinner, may buckle. Particleboards are used for flooring, partitions, short shelves, cupboards and stairs. Boards faced with sliced veneers are also used for decorative panels.

Wood in various forms is still sometimes used in vehicles. The floors and sides of trucks, for example, may be of wood, and a resilient wood such as ash may be used for the internal parts of the frames of some cars. The floors of shipping freight containers are also most often made of wood. The frames of caravans are usually of wood and the inside of hardboard or plywood; the latter is also used on the outside. In coaches and buses wood makes up the frames, and plywood or fibreboard the linings. The interiors of expensive cars are often embellished with wood, such as walnut.

Above: Furniture design is concerned with function and appearance. The Stettman chair, produced as a design exercise, successfully manages to combine both concepts.

Below: These two chairs were designed by students. They were striving to give form to the special qualities of wood: its strength, resilience, warm texture and attractive grain.

Craftwork in Wood

Above: Hurdle-making is a centuries-old art that involves the cleaving and interweaving of slender stems of willow or hazel to form a strong, living fence.

From the earliest human times craftsmen have worked with wood. With the advent of first the softer metals, then iron and steel, then concrete and plastics, and finally with the introduction of mass-production methods for many articles of wood, the craftsman in wood has gradually almost disappeared—at least in the more developed countries. Nevertheless, some articles are still made by craftsmen, though sometimes more as a hobby than as a means of earning a living.

Weaving with wood

One ancient craft that still survives is basket weaving from withies (young thin supple branches from pollarded willows —trees that are cut back every few years). In some parts of the world similar young shoots are used for making fish traps, bird traps, bird cages and the trugs in which gardeners collect weeds. Sometimes the wood is split before the hand weaving begins.

Not the least important of the various types of fence mentioned on page 69 are hurdles, which, because they are made in sections that are light as well as strong, can be easily moved and re-erected wherever they are needed. They have another traditional use, too. Long before athletics became a highly organized world sport, active young farmhands used to run races, jumping every ten yards or so over hurdles. A hurdle fence may, at first sight, look a trifle crude. but in fact the making of it calls for a good deal of skill, because the wood has to be very carefully split and assembled if the fence is to last.

Hand cleaving

Another craft, though one usually requiring less skill, is the making of handles for tools in places far from a turnery. In such places the handles may be shaped entirely by hand, though some may be turned at home on primitive lathes. In the same category of craft products are items such as tent pegs and the split clothes pegs made and sold by gypsies; for the former ash is generally used, and for the latter willow.

Several types of canoe used in various parts of the world are still

Left: Though it looks rather primitive, the dugout canoe is an efficient mode of native transportation in places where shallow-bottomed craft are required.

Below: A detail from the wood carvings adorning the front of a Dutch organ named 'The Schelm'. Built in 1905, its styling is characteristic of many cinema and street organs of Holland.

Above: A cooper shaping an oak stave to repair a wooden barrel. Cooperage is one of the oldest and most highly skilled of all the wood crafts.

the work of craftsmen. There are simple dug-out canoes, which must call for a great deal of patience, and the birch bark canoes of North America, which require considerable skill and experience. But perhaps the most interesting variety is the 'sewn' canoe of Lake Victoria Nyanza in Central Africa. To make it, thin planks, which can be shaped and curved a little, are fastened to the sides of a shallow hollowed-out keel by threading cord made from banana fibre through holes in the flanges of the keel and near the edges of the planks. Other planks are fastened in similar fashion to the lower ones and the whole is kept in shape by being fastened to a number of ribs. The overlapping planks are caulked with more fibre.

Wooden barrels or casks for wine and sherry are still craft products, though beer now comes in metal drums. The side pieces of a wooden barrel, called *staves*, are made from oak, and they have to be very carefully split and shaped so they can be held tightly in place with

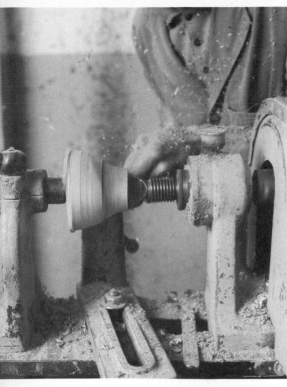

Above: The ancient craft of wood turning favours woods such as birch that would otherwise end up being burned by the forester.

metal hoops round the top and bottom discs. All the staves must fit together exactly, so that no liquid can leak out. Oak is grown to large sizes in France specifically to produce wood suitable for stave making. Today the economics of growing such large trees just for sawn timber are questionable. Veneer fetches better prices.

Some woods are more suitable than others for *turning*—a process in which a length of wood is put into a lathe and rotated while a tool is moved along it to make the wood round and give it a suitable and attractive shape, as for lamp stands or table legs. Because of their detailed structure, not all woods can be turned easily; sometimes bits chip off and it is difficult to get an even surface. Fortunately, some woods, not regarded as very suitable for use as timber, are ideal for turning. One of them is birch. In some forests the birch has been, and in some cases still is, regarded as a weed tree—one that the forester should get rid of; but in fact a turnery manager may buy it

and thus save it from being wasted. Several species are turned for tool handles, and for those where resistance to shock is important, as in the handles of hammers and picks, hickory from North America is ideal and ash also excellent. For other tool handles beech or birch is often used. Broom handles are made by turning short thick pieces of wood *(billets)* until they are round and then cutting them down the middle to produce two heads.

For carving, just as for turning, some woods are unsuitable. The best are often fine-grained ones, such as box and ebony. Ebony is really a group name: different black, or nearly black, woods from different parts of the world which are hard, heavy and fine-grained are called ebony. Most African ebonies are species of *Diospyros*; 'brown' ebony is *Brya ebenus*; East Indian ebony is *Diospyros ebenum*; Maracaibo (Venezuela) ebony is *Caesalpinia granadillo* and Mozambique or East African ebony is *Dalbergia melanoxylon*. In some cases, the souvenir black elephants that tourists buy along the East African coast are carved from other heavy woods and then stained black.

Sports goods

Several sports goods, too, call for the services of craftsmen. Articles such as tennis racquets are made from laminated sheets of wood glued together and bent to the required shape; the sheet is then sliced to give sections of the required thickness for several racquets and some pieces are next fastened on to give the handle the desired shape. It is not always possible to see all the different pieces because of the covering over the handle and the paint or other finish, but the different plies can normally be seen at the top of the racquet. The inner and outer plies are commonly of ash, with a ply or two—rather thin—of mahogany and one or two of beech. The earlier frames were solid ash, which, as we have seen, does bend easily, but with several thin plies the bending before the adhe-

Left: These humorous statuettes follow a tradition of hand-carving in Germany that began with the annual fairs of the Middle Ages.

Right: A modern-day craftsman making a lute. Several different woods are used to make this 16th century instrument, including cedar, walnut and sycamore.

Above: Cricket bats are made from special strains of light but resilient willow. The face always coincides with the radius of the tree trunk, making the bat warp-free.

Right: Golf clubs are now generally made of laminated maple (top). The heads are filled with different amounts of lead depending on the required weight of the club (bottom).

sive sets is done much more easily.

The heads of hockey sticks are usually made from two laminates of ash, which have been steamed, glued and bent in a tight curve. In the Indian sub-continent mulberry is used. There is an interesting story behind this. Some of the earlier irrigated plantations of forest trees were in the Punjab, and birds migrating from the foothills of the Himalayas rested in them. Mulberry seeds in the birds'

droppings germinated, and the young trees were at first regarded as weeds. However, in some areas, the mulberry more or less took over and today it supplies much of the wood for sports goods.

Sports quality ash often fetches a good price. It has to be fast grown, ensuring wide annual rings with a high proportion of early wood, so that it is more flexible than slowly grown timber with a much higher proportion of late wood.

The special very hard wood used for the heads of good croquet mallets, and sometimes for bowls, is known as 'lignum vitae' and is obtained from *Guaiacum officinale* from the West Indies and tropical America. Lignum vitae, which has a natural oil in it, is often also used for bearings, particularly for the propellor shafts of boats and ships. The words 'lignum vitae' mean, literally, 'wood of life' and imply the very long lasting characteristics of this timber.

Musical instruments

One indoor use of wood that is worthy of mention is for the making of musical instruments, mainly those with strings. A violin, for example, is traditionally made from a number of different woods, each favoured for its decorative, structural or acoustic properties. The back is made of European sycamore wood radially cut from selected trees to produce the well known 'fiddle-back' pattern. The front, or table, is fashioned from a piece of Swiss pine, which has the right qualities to make a good sounding board. The fingerboard and other fittings are usually made of ebony or rosewood and the bridge is cut from a pressure-resisting type of maple wood. The favoured material for violin bows is Brazilwood, while American oak is much used for bows in general.

Trees–the Universal Providers

The number of products that can be obtained from trees, though not necessarily from the wood only, is legion. Nearly every country produces some that are unique to itself, or to a very limited number of countries. For example, a French beverage—'tisane de tilleul' or just 'tilleul'—is made from an infusion of the dried flowers and flower stalks of the lime tree, *Tilia × europaea*, known as 'tilleul' in France.

Charcoal Perhaps the most important minor product (because it is used all over the world) is charcoal. This is partly-burnt wood which will no longer burst into flames, and is used mainly for cooking and sometimes for heating. Charcoal is sometimes made by dry distillation of wood, that is by heating wood in special metal retorts so that the by-products—gases and liquids—can be recovered. This, however, is an expensive process and the same gases and liquids can usually be obtained more easily from chemical works, although rises in petroleum prices are changing the cost situation in favour of wood-derived products, including distillation by-products.

The more common way of making charcoal is in a kiln. This may be either a metal one, rather like a very small gasholder, which can be moved from place to place, or the age-old earth kiln. In either case considerable skill and experience is required of the charcoal burner. The billets—short pieces of wood about 60 to 90cm (2 to 3ft) long—have to be carefully stacked and must fall within a certain thickness range, generally between about 7.5 and 15cm (3 and 6in). They can, of course, come from larger pieces that have been split. If the billets are too large they will be insufficiently burnt and so not suitable; if too small, they will burn away to ashes. During the stacking, a space is left in the middle to act as a chimney down which the kindling to start the fire may be dropped. When ready, the kiln is closed. In the case of a metal one a top is put on and carefully sealed. With an earth kiln the stack, shaped like a large beehive, is covered over with moss and earth, turves or sods of grass. A few openings are left round the bottom of the sides of an earth kiln to let in air during the early stage, and metal kilns may have doors or pipe manifolds that serve a similar purpose. A fire is then started in the kiln, from the top of the air vents, and it is left for many hours, perhaps even a day or so, depending on the size. After a time, when the flaming stage is over, the smoke gradually changes from black or dark grey to a more or less transparent blue. When this stage is reached, the 'chimney' and all the air vents are closed and the kiln is left for as long as two or three days for the fire to die out and the charcoal to cool down. Finally the kiln is opened up and the charcoal removed. Any oversize partly-burned billets may be used in the next charge or stack.

One of the advantages to the forest manager of charcoal burning is that it is one way he can make use of forest produce that would otherwise be wasted. All the branches except the smallest ones can be used as well as the smaller and otherwise almost valueless parts of stems. For some time sawmills in less developed parts of the world, and also, since the oil price rise in 1973, in highly advanced forest industry complexes, the residues or offcuts may also be used, generally in metal kilns, for charcoal making.

If the reader has a barbecue and wants to make his or her own charcoal on a small scale, this can easily be done by taking partly-burnt pieces (ie large coals) of wood from a wood fire, putting them in a bucket of cold water, draining off the water and drying out the suitable sizes of charcoal. This operation can even be done safely indoors, where there is a wood fire. Some steam is given off, which goes up the chimney, but little heat is generated in the bucket. A plastic bucket can safely be used and even if half-filled with large glowing 'coals' the water will still only become lukewarm.

Cork Cork is obtained from the bark of the cork oaks, *Quercus suber* and *Q. occidentalis*, which grow around parts of the Mediterranean. About every seven years cuts are made round the outer bark, but not into the cork cambium, and strips or sheets of bark are peeled off. As we saw on page 22, the bark has pores or lenticels which allow air to get through to the stem. If bottle stoppers were

Left: A vast number of valuable products are obtained from trees apart from wood. Here, the latex of the Pará rubber tree is being collected to make rubber.

Below: Charcoal, considered the most widely used minor wood product in the world, is usually made today in kilns. Even with modern technology at his disposal the charcoal burner still needs to be extremely experienced and skilful.

cut out radially—that is in the direction of the rays towards the centre of the tree—liquids or gases could leak out through the lenticels; corks are therefore cut from strips in a vertical or tangential direction—that is at right angles to the direction of the rays. Large pieces of cork are used for floats, and small pieces for the manufacture of such products as linoleum and the inside of 'crown' corks.

Rubber Rubber comes from the latex of a tree, *Hevea braziliensis* or Pará rubber, which is a native of the Amazon forests in the Brazilian states of Pará and Amazonas. The tree has since been planted on a large scale in several other tropical countries. Shallow cuts are made in the bark in a herring-bone pattern and the sap or latex collected in a sort of cup; fresh cuts are made every day or two. Several

other trees are tapped for their latex, the best-known ones being chicle *(Achras sapota)* and jelutong *(Dyera* sp.). The latex, in this case, is used in the manufacture of chewing gum.

Resins, syrups and gums Exudations from certain other trees are also of considerable importance. Pride of place must be given to *resin* and *turpentine*, obtained

Above and left: The cork oak (*Quercus suber*) is an evergreen tree that grows in the Mediterranean area. The thick bark is harvested for its cork and it regrows without the tree appearing to suffer any damage.

from species of pine in different parts of the world. Vertical grooves are cut in the bark and the resin is collected in special cups. The grooves, generally three or four, depending on the size of the stem, are gradually extended up the tree to a height of 2 or 3 metres (6½ to 10ft). The freshly exposed surface may be sprayed with dilute sulphuric acid, which has the effect of increasing yields. The maritime pine, *Pinus pinaster*, in the Landes (France) and Portugal, the Chir pine, *P. longifolia,* in the Himalayas and the American pitch pines, *P. elliottii* and *P. palustris* in the southern United States, are amongst the main producing species.

Another valuable exudation, in this case in Canada and northern USA, is *maple syrup* from *Acer saccharum*. The sap from this tree yields not only the syrup, but also maple sugar, both of which are prized for culinary purposes. Waffles with maple syrup are a very popular breakfast dish.

Gums, such as gum arabic, are collected from various species of *Acacia*, eg *A. arabica* and *A. senegal,* from the drier subtropical zones of West Africa, the Sudan, Tanzania and India. In this case the trees are by no means always tapped; more often, large pieces of gum called 'tears', which have been exuded naturally, are simply collected by hand.

The difference between a resin and a gum is that a resin is soluble in alcohol but not in water, while, on the other hand, a gum is soluble in water but not in alcohol.

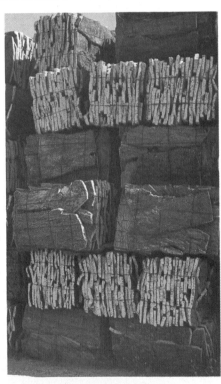

Above: Bundles of oak cork drying in the sun in Spain. Once dried, the cork is cut in vertical strips and used for floats, bottle stoppers and linoleum.

Tannin Tannin is yet another forest product, obtainable from the bark of several kinds of trees. This substance has always been in great demand for treating leather, but today much of it is produced synthetically in chemical works, though natural tannins are still used in many parts of the world. In Europe and North America tannin was obtained principally from the bark of oak and sweet chestnut; in South America it

came from the quebracho tree *Schinopsis* sp. When the quebracho was overcut plantations of other tannin-producing trees, such as the Australian wattle, *Acacia decurrens,* were widely established in other countries. In India, where the tannin is referred to as 'cutch', it is obtained from another species, *Acacia catechu*. Wattle does not reach a large size and is not regarded as a timber tree; it is usually felled and the bark stripped after a period of about eight to ten years.

New uses for tannin in the manufacture of natural resins are still developing. Resin costs, which represent 20 to 30 per cent of unit production costs for plywood and particleboard, have risen by up to 350 per cent with petroleum price increases. Natural sources of tannin-derived resins are therefore being looked at with increasing interest by major plywood and board producers.

Essential oils Trees also yield several essential oils. Perhaps the most widely known is eucalyptus oil, which is distilled from the leaves of *Eucalyptus citriodora*. Another one is sandalwood oil, much prized in India. The tree that yields this oil, *Santalum albidum,* cannot be grown by itself; it is a root parasite that occurs on other trees in various parts of India.

The commercial value of certain oil seeds is so high that the trees or palms producing them are grown in plantations. This is so with the oil palm, *Elaeis guineensis*, in West Africa, though much fruit is

Above: Tapping a tree for turpentine. Shallow vertical grooves are cut in in the bark of pine trees and the resin is then collected in special cups.

Above: Dried peelings of the inner bark of *Cinnamomum zeylanicum*, known more familiarly as cinnamon sticks.

also collected from wild palms in the forest. Most of the oil comes from the pericarp, the fleshy part round the nuts, but some is also obtained from the kernel after the nut has been cracked. Palm oil is so important that the holds of some ships are specially adapted for its transport, especially from Ghana. The oil is used in the manufacture of such commodities as margarine, soap and candles.

Another important oil seed is the brazil nut, also used for making margarine. The brazil nut tree, *Bertholletia excelsa*, could be described as the king, or certainly one of the great princes, of the forests of the Amazon. It has a beautifully straight stem going up as high as 30m (98ft), before forming a crown. The fruit is interesting; it is about the size and shape of a croquet ball and has a shell harder than a coconut, with some 25 to 30 seeds inside. These seeds are exported in ships' holds either just as they are or else decorticated (shelled).

Spices and drugs Several much-prized spices and drugs come from trees; the former include cloves and cinnamon.

The clove is the flower bud of *Eugenia caryophyllus* and is one of the two main exports of Zanzibar. The pleasant smell of cloves awaiting shipment from the quayside offsets the rather rancid one of copra, the white part of the coconut, which is the other main export. Cinnamon comes from the inner bark of *Cinnamomum zeylanicum*, a tree grown in the East Indies.

Amongst drugs, there is strychnine, from the fruit of *Strychnos nux-vomica*, and cortisone and strophanthin, from *Strophanthus hispidus*, a forest climber rather than a tree. Quinine, formerly of unique importance in the treatment of malaria, is obtained from the cinchona bark. *Cinchona ledgeriana, C. succirubra* and other species were once common in the forests of the Andes, but they were so overcut that supplies nearly ran out. As a precaution, the Dutch established plantations in Indonesia early this century, to ensure future supplies. Now, however, several other drugs, with less unpleasant side effects, have been developed; further, with the use of such insecticides as DDT sprayed from the air, the malarial mosquito has been vertically eliminated from a great many places where it once flourished.

A guide to CONIFERS

*A green mantle of conifers softens
the harsh features of these peaks in the Rocky
Mountains. Despite the uncompromising
nature of this environment,
coniferous trees are able to thrive and multiply there,
even on the bleakest slopes.*

Conifers go back geologically to the Carboniferous period, hundreds of millions of years before broadleaved trees appeared. They form part of that great class of primitive plants called Gymnosperms ('naked-seeded'); gymnosperm seeds are not concealed in an ovary but lie exposed on tiny scales.

Strictly speaking, conifers should include only trees of the order Coniferales. But yews and the maidenhair tree are usually called conifers although they have their own orders (Taxales and Gingkoales respectively). True conifers bear seeds in hard, woody structures called cones, and their leaves are narrow and needle like. Most species are evergreen and flourish in temperate climates. In the northern hemisphere, huge stands of a few species form some of the world's largest forests.

The timber is resinous. But the idea that it is all 'softwood' is misleading. Many conifers have harder timber than some of the 'hardwood' broadleaved trees.

Certain conifers form excellent pioneer crops on poor soil or extremely exposed sites. This helps to explain why half the world's timber derives from these trees.

With about 650 listed species, it is not surprising that conifers come in amazing variety. They include the world's largest living thing (a giant sequoia) and the oldest (a small, gnarled, bristlecone pine). To an already vast range of size, form and colour, nurserymen have added countless ornamental cultivars that are a major feature of parks and gardens all over the world.

The illustrations in this guide to conifers are intended to aid recognition of the main species of each group. The drawings are not to scale; details of tree and foliage sizes are listed in the accompanying text. In some groups the whole tree of one species has been drawn larger for emphasis.

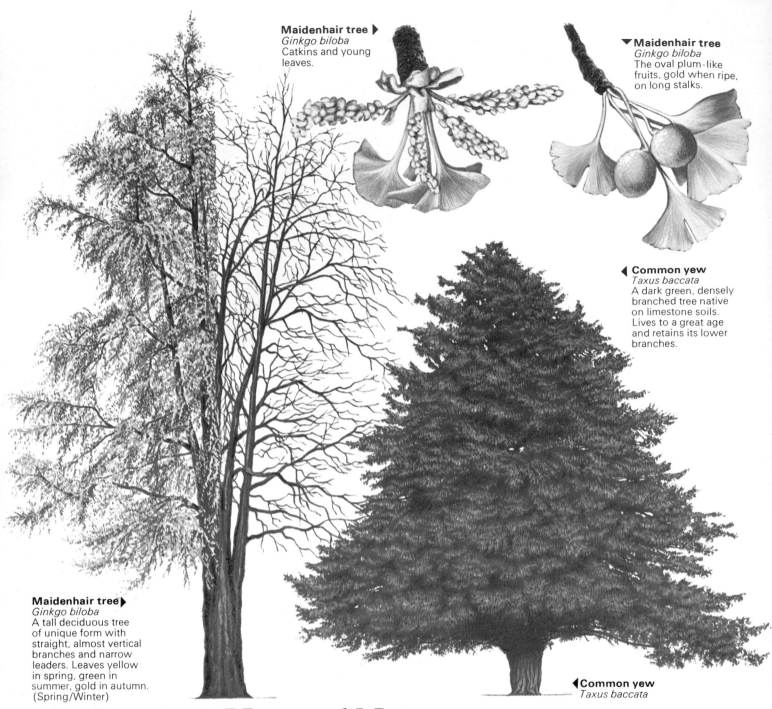

Maidenhair tree ▶
Ginkgo biloba
Catkins and young leaves.

▼Maidenhair tree
Ginkgo biloba
The oval plum-like fruits, gold when ripe, on long stalks.

◀ Common yew
Taxus baccata
A dark green, densely branched tree native on limestone soils. Lives to a great age and retains its lower branches.

Maidenhair tree ▶
Ginkgo biloba
A tall deciduous tree of unique form with straight, almost vertical branches and narrow leaders. Leaves yellow in spring, green in summer, gold in autumn. (Spring/Winter)

◀Common yew
Taxus baccata

Maidenhair, Yew and Nutmeg

The maidenhair tree is the sole survivor of an ancient family of trees—Ginkgoaceae—widely distributed in earlier geological times and well represented in fossils, forming a link between the ferns and higher plants.

Maidenhair Tree
(Ginkgo biloba)

Now native in the Chekiang Province of China, the maidenhair tree is widely planted in all temperate regions as an ornamental tree growing to 30m (98ft) tall. It is deciduous, the leaves turning to a wonderful gold before falling in the autumn; and in the winter the very slender rather gaunt tops of young trees, with their long bare leading shoots and short irregular side branches, are very distinctive, but with age they get broader with more rounded tops.

The foliage has a striking resemblance to the fronds of maidenhair fern—hence the common name of this tree, but in China it is often called 'ducks-foot tree', also on account of the shape of the leaves.

The red-brown buds are spirally ar-ranged on the twigs and, on emerging, the leaves are decidedly yellow but turn green as they flatten out, becoming leathery, fan-shaped, with a cleft at the top, and variable in size from 6–10 × 4–8cm (up to 4 × 3⅛in). They have conspicuous straight veins radiating from the base, stalks up to 4cm (1½in) long and are borne spirally on new shoots but in whorls or bunches on the stout spurs that grow on the older twigs.

Nearly all the trees are male and have yellowish catkins 5–7cm (2–2¾in) long, several together. On the very rare female trees the small green ovoid flowers, two-or three together but each on its own stalk 2–5cm (⅘–2in) long, develop into fleshy oval-globular fruits like small plums about 2–3.5cm (⅘–1⅜in) long, green at first but orange-yellow when ripe, and with a putrid smell as they rot. The seeds are edible and considered a delicacy in China when roasted; they are sold as 'Pai-Kwo'.

Maidenhair timber is yellowish, light, brittle and of no great value though used locally in China and Japan for small carvings. The trunks are often deeply fluted and the grey-fawn bark is rather corky with irregular wide fissures dividing rough plates. Burrs and bosses are common.

The yews (*Taxus*) comprise about half a dozen species, with many variations within each one, very widely distributed across the northern hemisphere and distinguished from true conifers by their single seeds being enclosed in a fleshy cup or 'aril'.

Common yew
(Taxus baccata)

This tree is one of the most common and best known hardy evergreens. It is native to Europe, Algeria, Asia Minor, Persia and the Himalayas, preferring limestone soils.

It is the species most widely planted in churchyards, hence it has acquired an unfair dismal image and to appreciate its real charm one should see it in its native chalk downland.

Yews live longer than any other tree in Europe and it is likely that a few may have reached almost 1,500 years and quite a number over 1,000 years but, as usual, there

◀ Common yew
Taxus baccata
Foliage and the yellow male flowers, which shed clouds of golden pollen in February.

Common yew ▶
Taxus baccata
Showing the bright red, hollow-ended fruits.

Irish yew ▼
Taxus baccata
'Fastigiata'
Typical form with multiple, vertical leading shoots.

California ▼ nutmeg
Torreya californica
Typical foliage and obovoid fruits, green at first, striped with purple later.

◀ Irish yew
Taxus baccata
'Fastigiata'

ever to be certain. Almost all the large yews are hollow—even those that still appear sound on the outside.

The strong, hard, tough timber is unusually elastic and was once used for archer's longbows; it has pinkish-brown heartwood contrasting sharply with the very thin layer of whitish sapwood and is very durable out of doors and therefore good for fences and gate-posts. Often it has very attractive grain suitable for high-grade furniture and turnery, while the burrs that sometimes occur are made into valuable veneers. The trunks are usually deeply fluted, often sprouting several side shoots, and the reddish-brown bark scales away leaving irregular patches of dark red and fawn. Buds of yew are often deformed by a midge-fly that causes small leafy 'artichoke galls'. Normal leaves are 2–4cm ($\frac{4}{5}$–1$\frac{1}{2}$in) long by 2–3mm ($\frac{1}{12}$–$\frac{1}{8}$in) wide, linear, abruptly narrowing to a point, very dark green above, matt dull green below, set spirally on erect shoots but in two flat ranks on side shoots. Masses of male flowers look like little beads; the females are usually on separate trees, small, green and pear shaped. The beautiful berries or 'arils', enclosing the dark poisonous seed, are bright red when ripe.

There are many cultivars of yew, examples being golden yew, silver yew, weeping yew and dwarf yew, but perhaps the best known one is Irish Yew, 'Fastigiata', a compact columnar tree with all branches almost erect and very dark green leaves set all round the shoots. This cultivar is always female and is very widely planted, especially in churchyards and gardens. It has a golden type called 'Aurea'.

Japanese yew
(Taxus cuspidata)
A broad bushy tree from Japan with hard spine-tipped leaves 2–4cm ($\frac{4}{5}$–1$\frac{1}{2}$in) long, turned sharply upwards, dark green above, brownish-yellow beneath. The berries are paler than those of common yew.

Chinese yew
(Taxus celebica)
Of very similar form to Japanese yew but with shorter, more slender pale green leaves arranged in two flat ranks.

The Californian and Canadian yews are probably not really separate species but just different forms of *Taxus baccata*.

Closely related to the yews, the nutmeg trees are so-called because of the shape and appearance of their fruits. They come from California and Japan.

California nutmeg or torreya
(Torreya californica)
This species grows up to 30m (98ft) tall and has a broadly conic form. The foliage is rather yew-like but has longer (4.5-6cm; 1$\frac{3}{4}$–2$\frac{1}{3}$in), narrower, stiffer, more pointed needles which have a strong smell when crushed. Its green plum-like fruits are about 3–4cm (1$\frac{1}{6}$–1$\frac{1}{2}$in) across and are striped with purple when ripe. The bark is shallowly and irregularly fissured. It is not a very hardy species but, like the yew, will grow on limestone soils.

Japanese nutmeg
(Torreya nucifera)
This smaller but hardier tree also likes alkaline soils. Compared to *Torreya californica*, it has shorter needles (2.5-3.5cm; 1–1$\frac{3}{8}$in), similar but rather smaller fruits and redder bark.

Above: Common yew (*Taxus baccata*). A sample of the distinctively reddish, close-grained timber.

has been much exaggeration, and caution is needed in accepting local figures quoted. The trunks reach quite large dimensions, many are between 2 and 4m (6$\frac{1}{2}$–13ft) in diameter, but great heights are not reached; one of the tallest, at Midhurst, southern England, is only 25m (82ft). The specimen at Fontingall in Scotland is probably the oldest living thing in Britain, estimated at 1,500 years, but too decayed

Above: Common yew (*Taxus baccata*). The bole of a mature tree, showing the characteristic fluting and the scaly bark, reddish in the fissures, grey brown on the ridges.

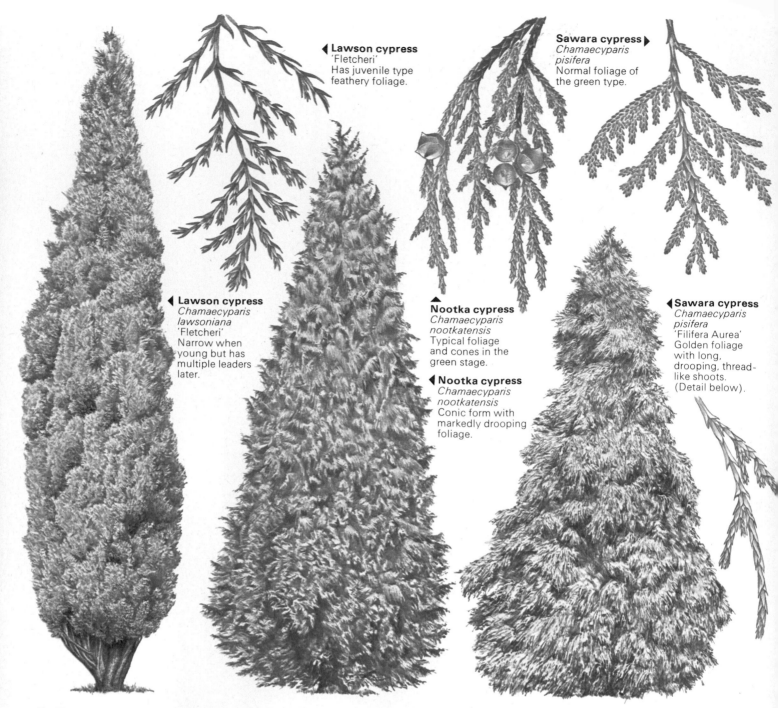

Lawson cypress
'Fletcheri'
Has juvenile type
feathery foliage.

Sawara cypress ▶
*Chamaecyparis
pisifera*
Normal foliage of
the green type.

◀ **Lawson cypress**
*Chamaecyparis
lawsoniana*
'Fletcheri'
Narrow when
young but has
multiple leaders
later.

▲ **Nootka cypress**
*Chamaecyparis
nootkatensis*
Typical foliage
and cones in the
green stage.

◀ **Nootka cypress**
*Chamaecyparis
nootkatensis*
Conic form with
markedly drooping
foliage.

◀ **Sawara cypress**
*Chamaecyparis
pisifera*
'Filifera Aurea'
Golden foliage
with long,
drooping, thread-
like shoots.
(Detail below).

Neo-Cypresses

This is a group of six species whose foliage is flattened so that each twiglet is broader than it is thick. In the 'true' cypresses the foliage is rounded or angular.

Port Orford cedar or lawson cypress
(Chamaecyparis lawsoniana)
This is an important timber tree in northwestern America, where it is well scattered through the forests of southwest Oregon and northwest California, but it is increasingly being planted in many other countries. It is also a very variable species which has given rise to an extraordinary number of cultivars covering a wide range of size, shape and colour. It will grow in almost any soil, is very hardy, transplants well, stands frequent clipping, is easy to propagate and is unusually free from pests and diseases.

It is a large tree, reaching a height of 60m (197ft) in its native forests with a diameter up to 3m (10ft) and brownish bark fissured into irregular vertical plates. The light yet strong, very durable timber varies in colour from yellowish to reddish brown, is fragrant, rather gummy and a little difficult to work. It is used for shipbuilding, joinery, furniture, roofing, and vats. The short scale-like leaves are dark green above and paler beneath, somewhat compressed, and strongly scented when crushed. Crimson male flowers 2–3mm ($\frac{1}{12}$–$\frac{1}{8}$in) long are abundant on the ends of small twigs; female flowers 5mm ($\frac{1}{5}$in) long are slate blue, turning green. The globular cones are 6–8mm (up to $\frac{5}{16}$in) in diameter and woody with wrinkled scales that turn from a glaucous green finally to brown.

Nootka cypress or Alaska cedar
(Chamaecyparis nootkatensis)
Native to a narrow coastal belt from Alaska to north Oregon, this large forest tree may grow to 53m (174ft) tall with a diameter extending to 2m (6½ft). It yields fragrant, yellow, close-grained, very durable timber used for boat-building, carpentry and cabinet work. It will succeed on poor soils and exposed sites and should be used in forestry more than it has been. The foliage is dull green without white markings and feels rough if rubbed the wrong way; it has a strong smell if crushed.

The flat twigs tend to be pendulous. The cones, blue-bloomed at first but brown later, are about 1cm ($\frac{2}{5}$in) in diameter with scales carrying curved-tipped short spines. The bark is fissured into long peeling strips. There is a very beautiful cultivar, 'Pendula', with yellowish green foliage and long pendulous shoots.

Hinoki cypress
(Chamaecyparis obtusa)
A Japanese species growing to 36m (118ft), this is much valued for durable, fragrant, straw-coloured timber that is used for high quality building construction, bridges, joinery and panelling.

The branchlets are flattened, with the tips drooping or turned back. The leaves are closely pressed, blunt tipped, with the lateral pairs longer than the others. They are shining green above, patterned with white lines below, and have a sweet resinous scent when crushed. The cones are about 1cm ($\frac{2}{5}$in) across, green turning to orange-brown in maturity, with a small ridge in the centre of each scale. The red-brown bark usually tends to peel away in

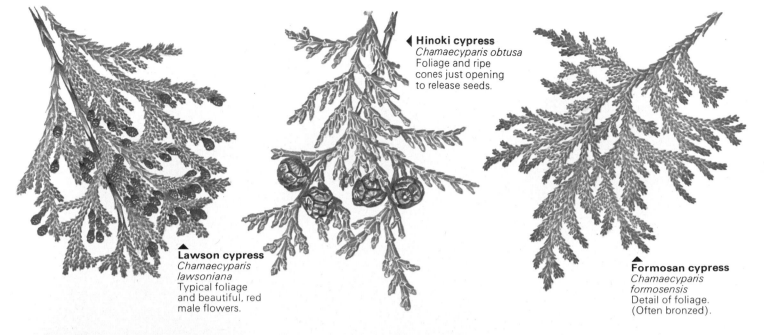

◀ **Hinoki cypress**
Chamaecyparis obtusa
Foliage and ripe
cones just opening
to release seeds.

▲ **Lawson cypress**
*Chamaecyparis
lawsoniana*
Typical foliage
and beautiful, red
male flowers.

▲ **Formosan cypress**
*Chamaecyparis
formosensis*
Detail of foliage.
(Often bronzed).

Above: Nootka cypress (*Chamaecyparis
nootkatensis*). A mature tree, showing the finely
fissured bark that peels off in thin strips. The
timber is durable and close-grained.

Right: Port Orford cedar or lawson cypress
(*Chamaecyparis lawsoniana*). The bark of a young
tree; mature bark has clear vertical ridges.

Common cultivars of *Chamaecyparis lawsoniana*

'**Allumii**' A narrowly conic tree with blue-grey foliage and vertical shoots.
'**Columnaris**' An even narrower form that does not widen out at the base, being more parallel sided. It has dense blue-grey foliage.
'**Ellwoodii**' A slow–growing type rather wider than 'Columnaris' with steely blue-grey foliage.
'**Erecta**' A much larger tree, up to 25m (82ft), with bright green foliage in vertical planes. Tends to broaden with age.
'**Fletcheri**' Blue-grey feathery juvenile foliage often with several leaders. Grows to 10m (33ft).
'**Lutea**' Columnar, conical at the top, with golden foliage. Rather a fast grower to 16m (52½ft).
'**Pottenii**' A narrow form tapering at both top and bottom with dense green foliage and vertical shoots.
'**Stewartii**' Another golden variety with older foliage green and small arching branches.
'**Wisselii**' A very distinct tree with little turrets of dark bluish-green foliage at the ends of the branches. Narrow form.

soft, stringy, rather long, shaggy strips.
One cultivar, 'Crippsii', has golden foliage and, after initial slow growth, reaches a height of about 15m (49ft). There are many other cultivars—two of the very slow growing ones are 'Filicoides' with fern-like pendulous branchlets, and 'Juniperoides', a rounded dwarf tree with cupped sprays of foliage on loose branches.

Sawara cypress
(*Chamaecyparis pisifera*)
This is another Japanese species growing to about the same size as hinoki cypress, but the timber is not of the same quality though still used locally. The crown is conic, but often broadened by multiple leaders, while the lower heavy branches sometimes layer at the base. The leaves are a bright shiny green above, marked with white patches below, and the small closely pressed leaf scales have fine incurved points. The male flowers are very small and pale brown; the female flowers are round, green and about 5mm ($\frac{1}{5}$in) in diameter. The round cones, about 7mm ($\frac{1}{4}$in) in diameter, are grey-green ripening to

brown, with small spines on the centre of each scale. The bark is reddish-brown, deeply fissured and peels off in long thin strips.
Again there are many cultivars, some of which are:
'Squarrosa' A very popular small to medium-sized tree with broadly conical outline and beautiful soft blue-green juvenile foliage with long, thin needles.
'Filifera' A broad, often many-stemmed tree with spreading branches and thin cord-like pendulous twigs with small bunches of scattered dark green side-shoots. A very distinctive tree.
'Aurea' A form with golden young shoots.
'Plumosa' A medium-sized tree with flatly pinnate plumose sprays of juvenile foliage with much shorter needles than those of 'Squarrosa'. It has a number of variations both of colour and form.

Formosan cypress
(*Chamaecyparis formosensis*)
This is a huge tree, which in its native forests reaches a height of 53m (174ft) with a diameter up to 2m (6½ft) and yielding good

durable timber, but in other countries it seldom grows to any great size and is usually only planted as an ornamental. Its foliage is dull green tinged with bronze, curved downwards at the tips of the shoots. It differs from sawara cypress in the colour and shape of foliage and in its elliptic rather than round cones.

White cypress
(*Chamaecyparis thyoides*)
This valuable timber tree grows to about 36m (118ft) and is native to the Gulf and Atlantic coasts of eastern North America where its fragrant, durable, reddish-brown wood is used for buildings, mining timbers, poles, and cooperage. It often has a rather wavering conical outline with foliage varying in colour from green to bluish-grey. The little bunches of short flattened branchlets bear scale-leaves with short pointed tips. The cones are 6–7mm ($\frac{1}{4}$in) in diameter, initially purplish but becoming brown in colour, with about six short-pointed scales. The bark is of a dark grey-brown colour, and tends to peel off in long, thin strips.

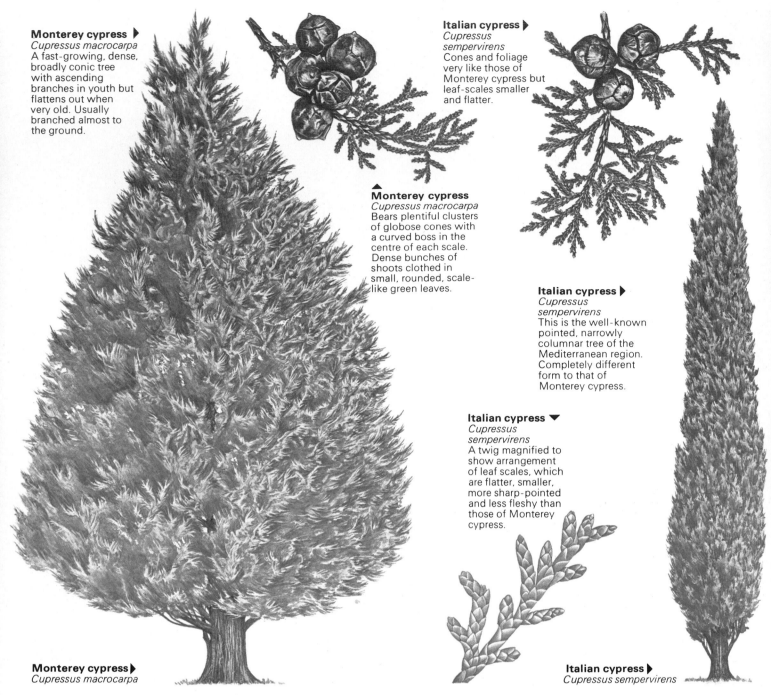

Monterey cypress ▶
Cupressus macrocarpa
A fast-growing, dense, broadly conic tree with ascending branches in youth but flattens out when very old. Usually branched almost to the ground.

Monterey cypress ▲
Cupressus macrocarpa
Bears plentiful clusters of globose cones with a curved boss in the centre of each scale. Dense bunches of shoots clothed in small, rounded, scale-like green leaves.

Italian cypress ▶
Cupressus sempervirens
Cones and foliage very like those of Monterey cypress but leaf-scales smaller and flatter.

Italian cypress ▶
Cupressus sempervirens
This is the well-known pointed, narrowly columnar tree of the Mediterranean region. Completely different form to that of Monterey cypress.

Italian cypress ▼
Cupressus sempervirens
A twig magnified to show arrangement of leaf scales, which are flatter, smaller, more sharp-pointed and less fleshy than those of Monterey cypress.

Monterey cypress ▶
Cupressus macrocarpa

Italian cypress ▶
Cupressus sempervirens

True Cypresses

This is a group of about twenty widely distributed species in which the foliage is arranged evenly round the twigs to give a rounded or angular section, rather than flattened as in the neo-cypresses.

Monterey cypress
(Cupressus macrocarpa)

Originating from very small sea-cliff areas at Point Lobos and Cypress Point near Monterey, California, this large, quickly growing cypress has been widely planted as an ornamental, shelter-belt or hedge tree in very many countries. However, it is subject to damage by severe winters or hard spring frosts and is rather unreliable when planted away from the sea. It will reach 30m (98ft) in 40 years but seldom exceeds about 37m (121ft). On windswept coasts it becomes gaunt and ragged but under more sheltered conditions is a fairly broad conic, or rather narrow columnar tree that finally flattens out at the top almost like a Lebanon cedar. The short scale-like leaves are closely pressed to the twigs in four rows, darkish green and lemon-scented when crushed. The nearly round cones are 2.5–4cm (1–1½in) long, with large scales with curved bosses in the centre of each. The seeds have small warts on the surface.

The trunk is large, often divided half way up; the bark is grey-brown, shallowly fissured into an irregular network of plates. Because of its tenderness it is unlikely to be used widely in forestry, but the fragrant, yellowish-brown timber might be quite useful and give high volumes on selected sites.

'Lutea' is a cultivar with dullish gold foliage—a fast grower, very resistant to salt winds. Two brighter gold ornamentals are 'Goldcrest' and 'Donard Gold'.

Leyland or hybrid cypress
(× Cupressocyparis leylandii)

A cross between *Cupressus macrocarpa* and *Chamaecyparis nootkatensis*, this very valuable addition to our trees is even faster-growing than *macrocarpa* (annual shoots of 1m (3¼ft) or more are common) and much more hardy. Its foliage is closer to *nootkatensis* but less pendulous. It has largely replaced *macrocarpa* as a hedging and screening tree and may prove to be useful in forest plantings.

A new form of Leyland cross has recently been produced — 'Castlewellan' — using golden foliaged parents. It exhibits even faster growth, excellent form and golden colour. This may be a very important tree.

Italian cypress
(Cupressus sempervirens)

This tree, the classic cypress of Mediterranean scenery, is without doubt the best known, with its slim, dark-green, pointed columns rising spire-like to as much as 50m (164ft), among associated trees and shrubs. It is too tender to withstand more northern climates and only succeeds in the milder parts of Britain. It is very close to *C. macrocarpa*, differing only in its narrower form, smaller, more closely pressed leaves, less strong scent and seeds with relatively few or no warts on them.

Arizona cypress
(Cupressus arizonica)

A very variable species both in form and colour, the original type was a medium sized tree up to 22m (72ft) tall, ovoid-conic

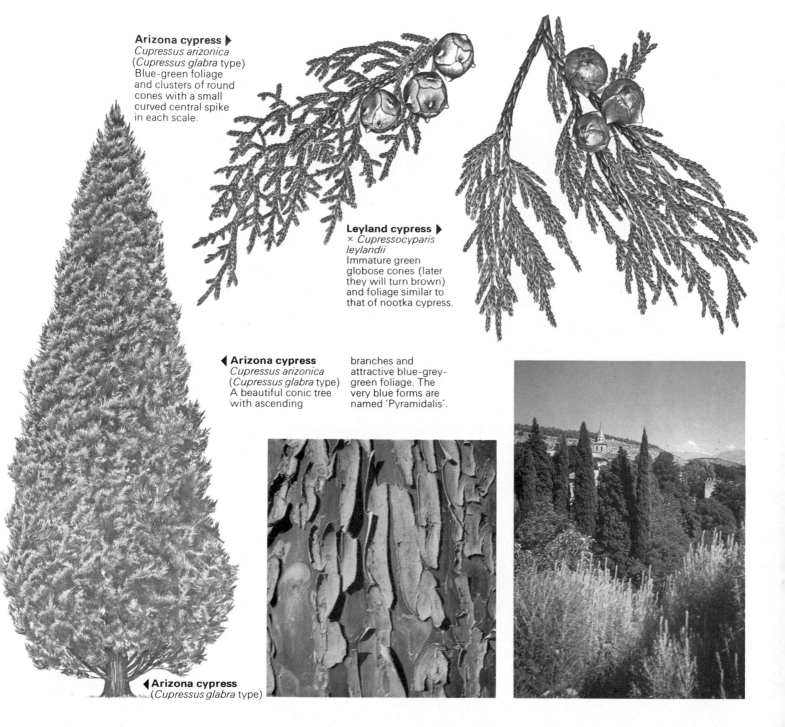

Arizona cypress ▶
Cupressus arizonica
(*Cupressus glabra* type)
Blue-green foliage
and clusters of round
cones with a small
curved central spike
in each scale.

Leyland cypress ▶
× *Cupressocyparis
leylandii*
Immature green
globose cones (later
they will turn brown)
and foliage similar to
that of nootka cypress.

◀ Arizona cypress
Cupressus arizonica
(*Cupressus glabra* type)
A beautiful conic tree
with ascending

branches and
attractive blue-grey-
green foliage. The
very blue forms are
named 'Pyramidalis'.

◀ Arizona cypress
(*Cupressus glabra* type)

in shape; this yields soft greyish-yellow, close-grained timber used locally for carpentry and fuel. The foliage is grey-green, and the finely fissured bark peels off in thin stringy plates. Botanists have now called the old cultivar 'Bonita' a separate species, *C. glabra*, which has blue-grey foliage and bark flaking off in roundish patches. 'Pyramidalis' is the best ornamental type with bright silver-blue upswept foliage with a white spot on every leaf and narrow conic form. The clustered cones of all this group are 1.5–2.5cm ($\frac{3}{5}$–1in) in diameter and are retained on the trees for many years.

Mexican cypress or cedar of Goa
(Cupressus lusitanica)
This is not a cedar and was never a native of Goa, but comes from Mexico and Guatemala where it grows to a height of 30m (98ft). It has rather pendulous twigs and a fairly wide conic form, usually with a single stem whose branches are more open than Monterey cypress. Its special feature is the conspicuously glaucous young cones about 1.5cm ($\frac{3}{5}$in) in diameter. The foliage is

dark greyish-green, the scale-like leaves having spreading acute tips. Its fragrant durable timber is much valued locally.

Bhutan cypress
(Cupressus torulosa)
This large tree grows to 45m (147$\frac{1}{2}$ft) in the Himalayas with a diameter up to 4m (13ft), yielding light yellow to brown very fragrant timber, which is exceptionally durable and used for building temples, houses, poles, sleepers, etc. The foliage is yellowish or deep green, the scale-like leaves closely pressed with uncurved points and slender, long, curved pendulous shoots. The small cones, 1.5cm ($\frac{3}{5}$in) in diameter, are reddish-brown when ripe with small uncurved spines on the scales. The bark tends to be spirally ridged, peeling off in curved strips. A very different tree which is included in the Cypress family is the incense cedar— *Libocedrus (or Calocedrus) decurrens* of western USA, from Oregon to southern California, where it reaches a height of 68m (223ft) and lives for more than 500 years. In its native forests it is of fairly narrow pyramidal form but in cultivation

Above: Italian cypress (*Cupressus sempervirens*). The dark green spires of this Mediterranean species here stand out on a heavily wooded hillside. Seen in isolation against a skyline they can be even more effective.

Above left: Arizona cypress (*Cupressus glabra* type). A close view of the trunk showing the bark flaking off in roundish patches.

in Europe and eastern USA it usually assumes an amazingly narrow parallel-sided column only about one eighth or one tenth as wide as high, with short upswept branches almost down to ground level. The soft, light brown, fragrant timber is used for a wide range of purposes but with age the trunks rapidly deteriorate, resulting in heavy losses on conversion.

The foliage is formed of long narrow overlapping scales grouped in fours, which are broader towards the tips and have a strong turpentine scent when crushed. The pendulous cones are most unusual, with two large fertile scales opening away from a central flat partition to give a trident effect. The bark is reddish-brown, fissured and peels off in irregular plates.

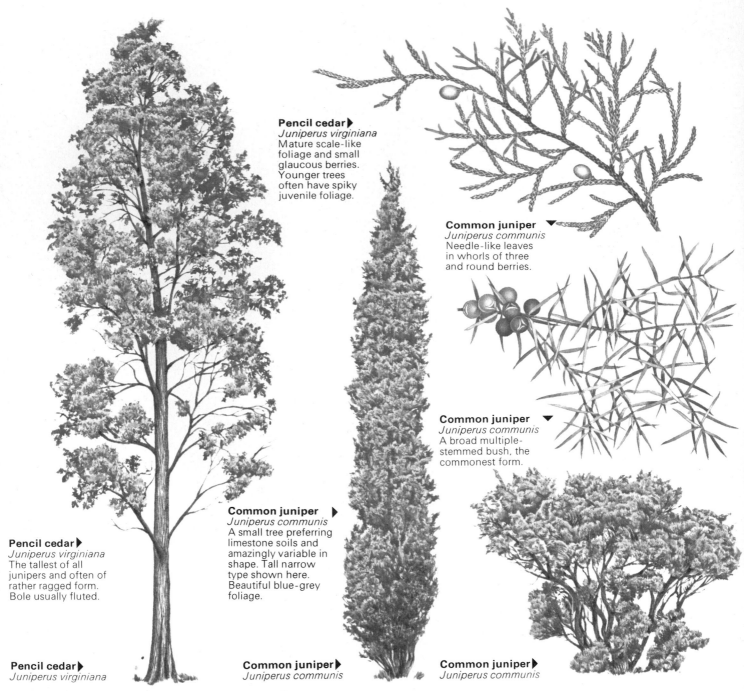

Pencil cedar▶
Juniperus virginiana
Mature scale-like
foliage and small
glaucous berries.
Younger trees
often have spiky
juvenile foliage.

Common juniper ▼
Juniperus communis
Needle-like leaves
in whorls of three
and round berries.

Common juniper ▼
Juniperus communis
A broad multiple-
stemmed bush, the
commonest form.

Pencil cedar▶
Juniperus virginiana
The tallest of all
junipers and often of
rather ragged form.
Bole usually fluted.

Common juniper ▶
Juniperus communis
A small tree preferring
limestone soils and
amazingly variable in
shape. Tall narrow
type shown here.
Beautiful blue-grey
foliage.

Pencil cedar▶
Juniperus virginiana

Common juniper▶
Juniperus communis

Common juniper▶
Juniperus communis

Junipers and Thujas

A genus with over fifty species, as well as
endless cultivated varieties, ranging
widely over the northern hemisphere from
the Arctic Circle to Mexico and from
Britain to the Himalayas, China and
Japan. Their special features include very
small round flowers, small berry-like
cones, leaves of two distinct types, some
needle-like, others with small overlapping
appressed scales (in some species both
types on the same twig), a pungent aromatic scent to the bruised foliage and a
remarkable ability to survive on both
alkaline and acid soils and either dry or wet
situations.

Unfortunately many junipers have been
wrongly called 'cedars'. Only a small
selection are dealt with here.

Pencil cedar
(Juniperus virginiana)
A native of Canada and eastern USA, this
is the tallest species, sometimes exceeding
30m (98ft), and the main timber tree of the
group, yielding a soft, reddish, straight-
grained timber particularly suitable for
pencil casings and 'cedar chest' linings. A

fragrant oil is distilled from the waste
wood. The trunk is usually fluted and the
reddish-brown bark peels off in narrow
strips. It is a narrowly conic tree with
mainly small scale-like leaves but juvenile
needle-type foliage may be found on the
ends of some twigs. The small berry-like
cones are green at first but develop a
silvery-blue bloom later.

Grecian juniper
(Juniperus excelsa)
This is another tall species, native to Asia
Minor, southeast Europe and the Caucasus. It grows to about 28m (92ft); it has
larger berries but smaller scale-like leaves
than those of *J. virginiana* and produces
juvenile foliage only rarely. The timber is
of good quality, very durable, with a wide
range of uses.

Chinese juniper
(Juniperus chinensis)
This is a smaller tree, up to 20m (65½ft) in
height, from China and Japan. It is very
similar in most respects to *J. virginiana* but
has slightly larger leaf scales and cones,
and juvenile leaves which tend to be near

the base of the shoots instead of at the tips.
There are many cultivars available, one
of the best of which is 'Aurea', a beautiful narrow-form golden tree.

Sacred juniper
(Juniperus religiosa)
Drooping juniper
(Juniperus recurva)
Black juniper
(Juniperus wallichiana)
The wood from all three of these Himalayan
trees is burnt as incense in the Buddhist
temples; a cultivar of *J. recurva* called
'Coxii' is sometimes known as coffin
juniper and is presumably used for that
purpose. *Juniperus recurva* has graceful
drooping twigs and needle-type foliage,
J. religiosa has scale-like foliage, and *J.
wallichiana* is a large tree, up to 20m (65½ft)
in height, with both scale-like and needle-
type foliage and berries that are black
when ripe, hence the name black juniper.

Phoenician juniper
(Juniperus phoenicea)
A Mediterranean species seldom more
than 12m (39ft) high but living to a great

Western red cedar ▶
Thuja plicata
A splendid tree of narrow conic form with dense shiny green foliage and reddish-brown bark.

◀ **Western red cedar**
Thuja plicata
Foliage deep green above, paler beneath with white streaks.

◀ **Western red cedar**
Thuja plicata

▲ **Chinese juniper**
Juniperus chinensis
Has mixed juvenile and mature foliage.

age—up to 1,000 years, this has pyramidal form, very small leaf-scales on curved rounded twigs and berries up to 1.5cm ($\frac{3}{5}$in) in diameter.

Utah juniper
(Juniperus osteosperma syn. J. utahensis)
This desert species with short, heavily gnarled trunks, is a conspicuous feature of arid regions from 1,500 to 2,500m (4,920 to 8,200ft) elevation between· the Sierra Nevada and the Rocky Mountains.

Western juniper
(Juniperus occidentalis)
This is closely allied to the Utah species but is much larger—up to 20m (65½ft).

Common juniper
(Juniperus communis)
This bush or small tree, seldom as tall as 5m (16½ft) though in rare cases up to 15m (49ft), has an amazingly wide distribution from northern Europe to Asia, the Himalayas, the Caucasus, Canada and North America. It is unusual as regards soils, favouring either the very alkaline soils, such as chalk downland, or the very acid soils, such as boggy heathland.

The sharply pointed acicular leaves, up to 1cm ($\frac{2}{5}$in) long, in whorls of three, are grey-green on the outer surface but with a broad white band on the inside.

Male flowers are tiny yellow globes, and occur on separate trees from equally small greenish female flowers. The globular berries, 6–9mm (up to $\frac{1}{3}$in), take as long as two years to ripen. They are green at first, then blue-bloomed and finally black. An aromatic oil used for medical purposes is distilled from the unripe berries, and the ripe ones are crushed for flavouring gin. The bark is greyish and flakes off in long fibrous strips. There are many cultivars available such as the blue-green tall slim columnar 'Hibernica' and the dwarf bushy 'Compressa'.

Savin
(Juniperus sabina)
This is another small tree from Europe, the Caucasus and North America, which attains a height of up to 5m (16½ft). Young trees have short juvenile needles, but the mature foliage is of very short, rather blunt, overlapping scale leaves. Again

there are many cultivars, and varieties, including *tamariscifolia*, a prostrate form, and 'Variegata', a dwarf form with patches of creamy white foliage.

Syrian juniper
(Juniperus drupacea)
A fine, quite distinct species from Greece, Asia Minor and Syria, narrowly conic or columnar in form and up to 17m (56ft) in height, this tree has the longest spiny sharp-pointed needles of any juniper, each 1.5–2.5cm ($\frac{3}{5}$–1in) long, shining green on the outer surface, with two silver bands on the inner side. The berry is the largest of the genus—up to 2.5cm (1in) in diameter.

Of the many trees known as cedars, the most important is western red cedar, once called giant arbor-vitae, from the West coast and northern Rocky Mountains of North America.

Western red cedar
(Thuja plicata)
This is a splendid tree up to 60m (197ft) tall whose timber is used for nearly all 'cedar-wood' houses for siding, and for the roofing 'shingles' so much in demand the world over. The soft, reddish-brown, exceptionally light, easily worked wood will last a lifetime out of doors without any chemical treatment and is very valuable; it is widely used for all sorts of jobs as well as building—such as ladders, poles, boats, weather-boarding and is much planted in the forestry programmes of many countries.

On old open-grown trees the lower branches sometimes tend to layer and form rings of vertical boles all around the mother trunk.

The overlapping scale-like leaves are strongly aromatic when bruised; shining dark-green above, whitish streaked beneath. Both male and female flowers are small, yellowish and inconspicuous. The cones are about 1.5×0.5cm ($\frac{3}{5} \times \frac{1}{5}$in), and have six large scales with tips spreading as small spines. The bark is reddish-brown, rather soft and lifting off in strips.

White cedar
(Thuja occidentalis)
This close relation to western red cedar occurs in eastern Canada and northeastern USA. It is a much smaller tree, growing only to about 20m (65½ft) in height. Its wood has properties similar to western red cedar but it is not available in such large sizes, is generally less valuable and is yellow in colour. The scale-like leaves are smaller, less shiny, more flattened, paler green and without the white marks on the lower surface that characterize *T. plicata*. Its cones, produced in great abundance, have only four large scales instead of six as in *T. plicata*. White cedar has a great many cultivars differing in colour, form and size.

Hiba cedar
(Thujopsis dolabrata)
This is a small tree, up to 15m (49ft), native to Japan, with beautiful frond-like foliage, which is bright, shining green above but with a specially attractive under-surface which is pure silver edged with green. The small almost spherical woody cones 1–2cm ($\frac{2}{5}$–$\frac{4}{5}$in) across have little hooks on the scales which open widely when ripe. It is an important forestry tree much used locally in Japan, yielding a light, soft yellowish, durable, non-resinous wood.

Coast redwood
Sequoia sempervirens
Foliage yew-like but
silver bands beneath.
Small, broadly ovate
cones.

Coast redwood
Sequoia sempervirens
The tallest tree
in the world.
Columnar form
with drooping
branches and
thick, red-brown
bark.

Dawn redwood
*Metasequoia
glyptostroboides*
Small fat cones with
a few large scales.
Next year's buds are
below last year's bud
scars.

Dawn redwood
*Metasequoia
glyptostroboides*
A deciduous conifer.
Narrowly conic with
delicate fern like
foliage.

Dawn redwood ▲
*Metasequoia
glyptostroboides*
Beautiful, feathery,
light-green foliage.

Coast redwood
Sequoia sempervirens

Dawn redwood
Metasequoia glyptostroboides
(Summer/Winter)

Redwoods

In the old days we could happily think of
the two magnificent *Sequoia* species together, but now, due to the ever-changing
fashions among botanists, they are as-
signed to separate genera, and the giant
sequoia now comes under another heading.

Coast redwood or Californian redwood
(Sequoia sempervirens)
The tallest living thing in the world at just
over 112m (367ft) and a girth of over 13m
(42½ft), is a tree of this species—the Howard
Libby Tree in California.

Unlike most conifers the redwood will
grow from new shoots round the edge of a
cut-over stump, thus regenerating itself
without seeds, but it is not so hardy as the
giant sequoia. It dislikes dry soils, cold
winds and low temperatures, but on deep
Californian soils where it is exposed to
cool, moisture-laden Pacific Ocean breezes,
it will live up to 2,000 years or more.

The native redwood groves are unique
because not only do they contain dense
stands of trees between 60 and 100m (197–
328ft) tall, with diameters often between
4 and 6m (13 and 20ft), but many of these

giants stand so close together that there
is only a narrow path between them.
One of their special features is their soft,
fibrous, rufous-red bark which may become 40cm (16in) thick on old trees and is
usually deeply fissured into rough-edged
intertwining ridges. The tree is highly
resistant to insects, fungi and fire. Its
foliage is very like that of yew, with linear,
sharp-pointed leaves 1.5–2cm (⅗–⅘in) long
by about 2.5–3mm (⅛in) wide and dark
green above but with two whitish bands
below that are missing in yew. Yellow male
flowers 2mm (1/12in) across, occur on the
ends of small shoots, while the female
flowers are oval, 1cm (⅖in) long, greenish
and formed of 14–20 bracts tipped with short
points. The cones are approximately 2cm
(⅘in) long, and grow on slender stalks. They
are initially oval-round with wrinkled
scales; green but turning brown or
brownish. The seeds are narrowly winged
and amazingly small, running at about
250,000 to the kg (over 100,000 per lb).

The soft, durable, easy to work timber is
very difficult to distinguish from that of the

giant sequoia but is a little stronger. (In
any event, the latter is no longer harvested.) In the past it was used for buildings and railways sleepers (cross-ties).
Tremendous volumes of redwood timber
are still marketed annually, but large
areas have recently been set aside in state
and federal parks.

There is an interesting cultivar of redwood called 'Adpressa' or 'Albospica'
which has creamy white new shoots,
shorter, more closely packed leaves with
whiter stomata bands beneath, and smaller
cones. It is a much smaller tree, only grow-
up to about 20m (65½ft).

Dawn redwood
(Metasequoia glyptostroboides)
This is a most interesting species, very like
swamp cypress, that was thought to be
extinct and only known as a fossil until
1941, when it was discovered in eastern
Szechwan and Hupeh provinces of southwest China. It is now widely planted in
many countries as an ornamental tree and
is of added interest because it is one of the
few deciduous conifers. (The only others

Above: Dawn redwood (*Metasequoia glyptostroboides*). A mature tree with typical furrowed trunk and reddish, peeling bark.

Above: Coast redwood (*Sequoia sempervirens*). A dense stand of these impressive trees in California, where they reach over 100m (328ft).

Right: Coast redwood (*Sequoia sempervirens*). The thick, red, spongy, fissured bark.

are in the genera *Larix* and *Taxodium*.)

Characterized by narrowly conic form, ascending branches and rapid early growth, it reaches a height of at least 35m (115ft), possibly much more on good sites. A curious unique feature is that the buds, which are opposite and not alternate as in swamp cypress, appear *below* the twigs, not in the axils, as is normal. Its beautiful green foliage has longer (2–4cm; $\frac{4}{5}$–1$\frac{1}{2}$in), softer leaves than those of swamp cypress.

The flowers are very small and similar to those of swamp cypress, while the cones, 1.5–2.5cm ($\frac{3}{5}$–1in) are long, round to ovoid with a short pointed tip, have only a few relatively large scales and are on long stalks. On older trees the trunk often becomes deeply fluted and buttressed and the bark comes away in stringy strips.

Little is yet known about the timber, which in any case would only be available in minute quantities. It would no doubt be similar to that of swamp cypress.

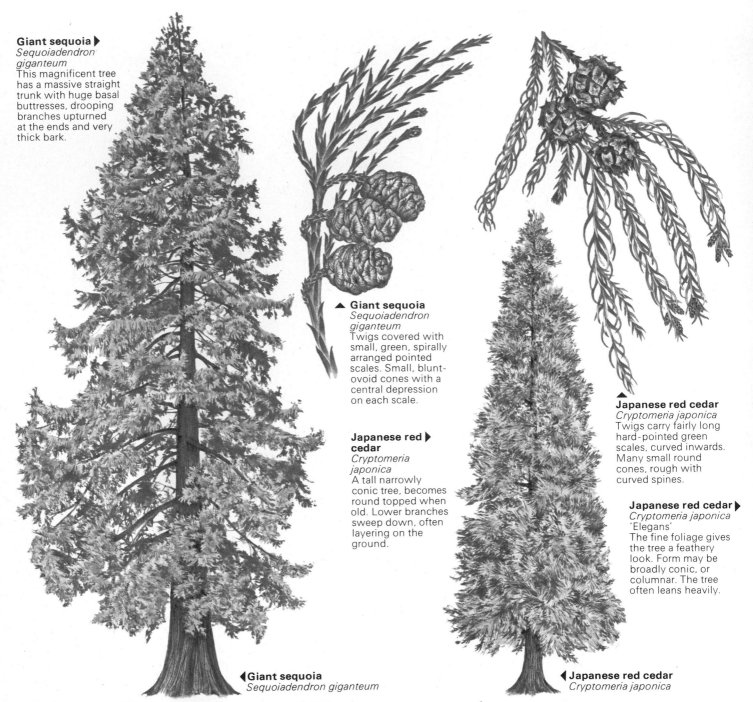

Giant sequoia ▶
Sequoiadendron giganteum
This magnificent tree has a massive straight trunk with huge basal buttresses, drooping branches upturned at the ends and very thick bark.

▲ Giant sequoia
Sequoiadendron giganteum
Twigs covered with small, green, spirally arranged pointed scales. Small, blunt-ovoid cones with a central depression on each scale.

Japanese red ▶ cedar
Cryptomeria japonica
A tall narrowly conic tree, becomes round topped when old. Lower branches sweep down, often layering on the ground.

▲ Japanese red cedar
Cryptomeria japonica
Twigs carry fairly long hard-pointed green scales, curved inwards. Many small round cones, rough with curved spines.

Japanese red cedar ▶
Cryptomeria japonica
'Elegans'
The fine foliage gives the tree a feathery look. Form may be broadly conic, or columnar. The tree often leans heavily.

◀ Giant sequoia
Sequoiadendron giganteum

◀ Japanese red cedar
Cryptomeria japonica

Giant Sequoia and Cryptomeria

As time passes and people become a little more thoughtful and imaginative there is hope that the common name of this magnificent tree will revert to 'giant sequoia' and that the use of the imposed name 'wellingtonia' (which is never used in the USA), will slowly fade. The Duke of Wellington had nothing whatever to do with it.

The next best alternative would be 'mammoth tree', which is indeed an apt name for the giant sequoia called 'General Sherman', the largest living thing on earth.

Giant sequoia

(Sequoiadendron giganteum)

It is difficult to realise just how immense this tree is, but it may help to know that the next largest form of life to great trees is the blue whale of which the largest ever caught was estimated at live weight of 174 tons, against 2,145 tons for the 'General Sherman'. Other figures for this giant tree are: height 83m (272ft); girth at 1.5m (5ft) above ground 24.1m (79ft); estimated contents in board feet of timber 600,000; estimated age over 3,500 years. (The 'General Grant' tree

is taller and almost as large.) Other giant sequoias have lived to 4,000 years and until recently were thought to be the oldest living things on earth as well as the biggest, but since 1963, however, it has been found that some of the bristlecone pines growing in the White Mountains of California, are at least 4,900 years old.

The giant sequoias do not quite reach the heights of the coast redwoods, but there are many between 60 and 90m (197–295ft), and they easily beat them on girth: specimens between 20 and 25m ($65\frac{1}{2}$–82ft) above the final basal sweep are not uncommon.

The foliage is completely different to that of the coast redwood and consists of spirally arranged scale-like needles each 4–7mm ($\frac{1}{6}$–$\frac{1}{4}$in), which are long and sharp pointed, grey-green at the base, deep green above. The twigs are upright at the branch ends, pendulous and out-turned elsewhere, while the heavy lower branches droop but are upswept again towards the tips. Male flowers occur as abundant little yellow beads, while the ovoid female flowers are erect and about 1cm ($\frac{2}{5}$in) tall on rather

Above: Giant sequoia (*Sequoiadendron giganteum*). The bole of a mature tree, showing the reddish brown, very thick bark that gives the tree protection against fire and other damage.

Japanese red ▶ cedar
Cryptomeria japonica
'Elegans'
Very attractive, with leaves both longer and thinner than in *Cryptomeria japonica*, bluish-green in summer but turning reddish-orange in winter.

◀ *Cryptomeria japonica* 'Elegans'

Above: Giant sequoia (*Sequoiadendron giganteum*). Heartwood and paler sapwood.

Above: Giant sequoia (*Sequoiadendron giganteum*). A giant tree starting life as a seedling on the forest floor.

Below: Japanese red cedar (*Cryptomeria japonica*). New cones and spiky foliage.

pinkish-yellow stalks 2cm (⅘in) long.

The green cones are up to 8×5cm (3⅛× 2in) but usually smaller, bluntly ovoid with flat, diamond-shaped scales each with a central depression. The tiny flat-winged seeds—though slightly larger than those of the coast redwood—are still amazingly small for the largest plant in the world and run at 200,000 per kg (over 90,000 per lb).

The bark is not quite such a bright red as that of the coast redwood, but is just as soft and even thicker—it can be 50cm (20in) on old trees and equally resistant to fires and other hazards. The trunk buttresses are both larger and wider.

Giant sequoia timber has pinkish-red heartwood and yellowish sapwood just like coastal redwood and was once used for the same purposes, though it is rather weaker and more brittle. In the past much of the wood was used for vineyard stakes. The wood is almost indestructible—trees which fell centuries ago still have sound hearts at least, while trees toppled only 100 or 200 years ago appear intact. The tree has been very widely used for orna-ment and avenues in parks and estates, and has considerable possibilities for forestry.

There is a freakish cultivar of the species called 'Pendulum' with upright stem but small weeping branches.

Japanese red cedar
(Cryptomeria japonica)
Native to China and Japan, this unusual tree, the only species of its genus, is narrowly conic with a slightly rounded apex but gets more parallel-sided with age and grows to a maximum height of about 54m (177ft). With red-brown heartwood and pale yellow sapwood, it is one of the great timber trees, yielding a strong, durable, fragrant, first class wood used for buildings, joinery, and furniture; many temples are also built with it. The Japanese call it 'sugi' and it is also known as 'peacock pine'. The thick, soft, fibrous, reddish-brown bark peels away in long strips and is used locally as a roofing material.

Cryptomeria is fast growing and would be a worthwhile tree in the forestry of many countries; its use is likely to increase. In Japan it is a favourite avenue tree and much used in temple grounds and large gardens, while in other countries its orna-mental value is becoming better known.

The foliage is much like that of a giant sequoia but the scale-like leaves are longer, more pointed and bend out from the stem more widely. The colour is a yellower green, the twigs longer, sparser and more pendulous and the branches fewer. Yellow male flowers 3mm (⅛in) in diameter grow in clusters; the females are small green rosettes. The globular cones are about 2cm (⅘in) in diameter, on short stalks, green turning to bright brown.

There is a very popular garden cultivar, 'Elegans', noted for the fact that its long, soft, juvenile type foliage turns bronze or purple in winter. It has a lax spreading habit and the lower branches sometimes layer, forming a ring of new trees. There is a smaller, more stable, slower growing cultivar 'Elegans Compacta' that is very suitable for smaller gardens.

Another cultivar, 'Lobbii', is of nar-rower form, with stiffer branches, uneven crown with the twigs tending to be in tufts.

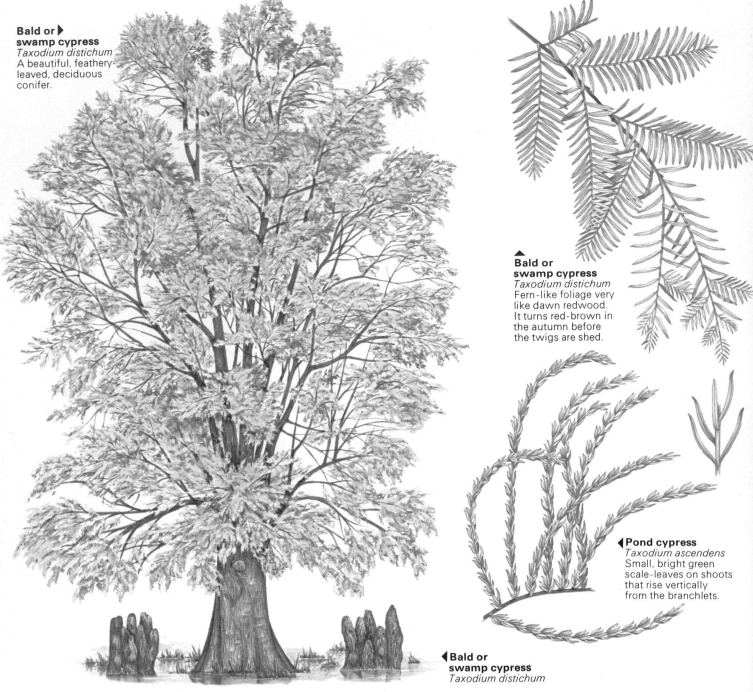

Bald or ▶ swamp cypress
Taxodium distichum
A beautiful, feathery-leaved, deciduous conifer.

▲ Bald or swamp cypress
Taxodium distichum
Fern-like foliage very like dawn redwood. It turns red-brown in the autumn before the twigs are shed.

◀ Pond cypress
Taxodium ascendens
Small, bright green scale-leaves on shoots that rise vertically from the branchlets.

◀ Bald or swamp cypress
Taxodium distichum

Deciduous Cypresses

There are three very closely allied deciduous or semideciduous conifers from southern USA and Mexico which instead of shedding individual leaves shed lateral twigs in autumn.

Bald or swamp cypress

(Taxodium distichum)

Native to swamp areas in southern USA, this remarkable species grows to 45m (147½ft) tall and provides a most unusual soft timber with a characteristic sour smell. Its dark red or almost black heartwood is extremely durable when wet and therefore especially good for cooperage, vats, water tanks, greenhouses, and fencing. On wet sites it produces knee-like upright growths from its roots, often in large numbers, properly called 'pneumatophores'. These assist in aerating waterlogged roots. One of the very few deciduous conifers, it is a fine ornamental species, very like *Metasequoia* in general appearance, whose reddish-brown autumn colouring is especially attractive in southern areas. The soft green foliage consists of fern-like sprays of slender linear leaves,

Above: Bald cypress (*Taxodium distichum*). The beautiful red-bronze autumn colour.

Left: Bald cypress (*Taxodium distichum*). An example of the extraordinary pneumatophores, or 'knee' roots, that develop on wet sites.

Above: Pond cypress (*Taxodium ascendens*).
The remarkable and characteristic erect shoots.

about $12 \times 2mm$ ($\frac{1}{2} \times \frac{1}{12}$in), set alternately on twigs that are themselves alternate on the branches. On lateral twigs the leaves are arranged in two flattened ranks and on terminal growing shoots they are set spirally; both flush very late in the spring. Male flowers are in the form of catkins, usually two or three together, 5–7cm (2–2$\frac{3}{4}$in) long and green at first, then lengthening to 8–12cm (3$\frac{1}{8}$–4$\frac{3}{4}$in) and turning purplish before shedding their pollen; the females are little green balls of bracts and scales. The cones are globular, 2–3cm ($\frac{4}{5}$–1$\frac{1}{6}$in) in diameter, with a few rather large scales with thickened edges, green ripening to purplish-brown. The bark is reddish-brown with many fissures and the trunk often has large buttresses.

Pond cypress
(Taxodium ascendens)
The remarkable feature of this tree is its tufts and lines of neat little *erect* new shoots all along its twigs and branches—a most striking sight in early summer. Native from Virginia to Alabama, it is a narrow form tree growing up to 25m (82ft) tall,

rather sparsely branched and open crowned, with the trunk swollen at the base. The scale-like leaves are only 4–8mm ($\frac{1}{6}$–$\frac{5}{16}$in) long, much shorter than those of swamp cypress. There is a cultivar 'Nutans' in which all the branch ends curve downwards, producing a beautiful effect.

Mexican or montezuma cypress
(Taxodium mucronatum)
The botanical features of this tree are almost identical to those of *T. distichum* and it may not really be a separate species, but in its native Mexican haunts it is not properly deciduous and retains its foliage until the new year's shoots are out.

There is an extraordinary specimen of this cypress at Santa Maria del Tule called 'El Giganti' with the amazing girth measurement, at 1.5m (5ft) above ground level, of over 34m (111$\frac{1}{2}$ft), undoubtedly one of the biggest in the world; it has a huge rounded crown, and is approximately 37m (121ft) high and probably an age of over 1,000 years, but, as usual, there are many wild exaggerations about the statistics for this and many other giant trees.

Above: *Taxodium mucronatum*. The trunk of the amazing 'El Giganti' Mexican cypress, which has an immense girth of over 34m (111$\frac{1}{2}$ft).

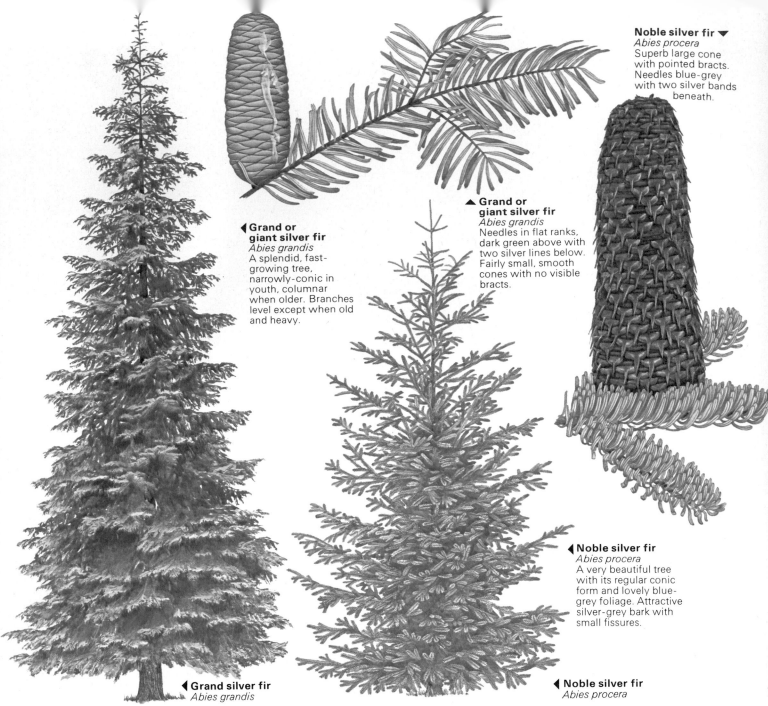

Noble silver fir ▼
Abies procera
Superb large cone
with pointed bracts.
Needles blue-grey
with two silver bands
beneath.

◀ **Grand or
giant silver fir**
Abies grandis
A splendid, fast-
growing tree,
narrowly-conic in
youth, columnar
when older. Branches
level except when old
and heavy.

▲ **Grand or
giant silver fir**
Abies grandis
Needles in flat ranks,
dark green above with
two silver lines below.
Fairly small, smooth
cones with no visible
bracts.

◀ **Noble silver fir**
Abies procera
A very beautiful tree
with its regular conic
form and lovely blue-
grey foliage. Attractive
silver-grey bark with
small fissures.

◀ **Grand silver fir**
Abies grandis

◀ **Noble silver fir**
Abies procera

Silver Firs

With about 50 species, all evergreen, the silver firs are one of the largest groups of conifers, widely distributed within the northern hemisphere, native to Europe, Asia, the Himalayas, North America and North Africa and much used in forestry. The characteristic general features of the *Abies* are as follows: upright cones that break up while still on the tree; short, leathery, usually flattish needles set singly, leaving circular scars when they fall, and if pulled off the shoots they do not tear away a splinter as occurs with the spruces. Most species have silver stomata lines on the lower surface of the needles—hence the name 'silver' firs. They have persistent vertical leading shoots resulting in very straight trunks and in many species the young bark is beset with resin blisters. In the space available we can only deal with a selection of the most important and interesting species.

Grand or giant silver fir
(Abies grandis)
This splendid species from Vancouver Island to the interior of southern British Columbia and south to California is of extraordinary vigour and speed of growth. Native trees have reached a height of 90m (295ft) and in Britain it is already the tallest tree, having topped 56m (183½ft), although only introduced in 1832. Some trees in Scotland have grown to 45m (147½ft) in 60 years and annual shoots of 1.5m (5ft) often occur. This very rapid growth produces rather brittle young stems and some Scottish foresters refer to *grandis* as 'arboreal celery'! But the wood strengthens as it matures and the light coloured timber can be used for much the same varied purposes as spruce; its early production of very high volumes makes it very attractive for forestry.

The flat leaves, 2–5cm (⅘–2in) long by 3mm (⅛in) broad, are dark shiny green above with two silvery bands below; arranged horizontally in an almost flat layer with shorter needles uppermost. They have a slight notch at the tip and are very aromatic when bruised. The small blunt buds are dark purple unless covered with white resin. Flowers occur only in the upper crown of mature trees; the males purplish and 3mm (⅛in) across, females upright 1.5cm (⅔in) tall, green and purplish. The cones are 6–9 × 3–4cm (up to 3½ × 1½in), green at first, reddish-brown when ripe; they often have white resin spots. Young bark has resin blisters, old bark is dark grey, cracking into small irregular plates.

Noble silver fir
(Abies procera syn. A. nobilis)
From Washington to northern California and northwest Oregon, this is another magnificent tree reaching to 80m (262ft) and living up to 700 years, but it is not so fast as *A. grandis*, annual shoots seldom reaching over 0.75m (2½ft). The soft creamy timber works well and is stronger than *grandis*. It is usually sold as 'white fir' and it is used for all sorts of carpentry, especially for boxes because it is odourless.

The small buds are hidden by little needles crowding all over the upper side of the twigs, pointing forward and upwards, and parted into two ranks on the lower side. Normal needles are bluish grey-green on both surfaces, bent at the

Colorado white fir►
Abies concolor
Long, upswept, blue-grey pointed needles. Fine rather tapering cones with broad scales and hidden bracts.

Pacific silver fir ▼
Abies amabilis
Another fine tree of very regular conic form with dense foliage and lower branches downswept, often touching the ground.

▼Pacific silver fir
Abies amabilis
Typical mature foliage, dark, glossy green above, two silver bands below. New needles glaucous all over.

◄Pacific silver fir
Abies amabilis

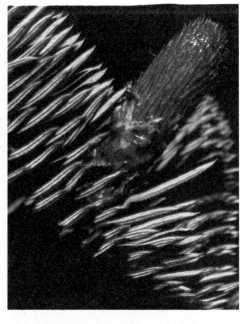

Above: Pacific silver fir (*Abies amabilis*). A close view of the female flowers, which will later develop into the barrel-shaped cones with overlapping scales and extruding bracts.

Below: Grand or giant silver fir (*Abies grandis*). A sample of the light-coloured, easily worked timber that, though not very strong, is used for a wide variety of general purposes.

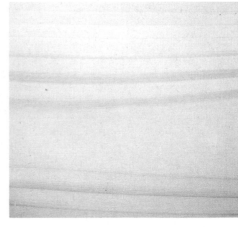

base with no notch at the tip. They are very different from *A. grandis* needles. The bright crimson male flowers are globular, 5mm ($\frac{1}{5}$in) across and crowded on the underside of the twigs; the females are upright, about 3cm ($1\frac{1}{6}$in) tall and yellowish-green. The cones, green and purple at first, turning brown later, are the finest of all the silver firs. Measuring 18–25cm (7–10in) tall by 7–9cm ($2\frac{3}{4}$–$3\frac{1}{2}$in) wide, with beautiful spirally arranged protruding bracts bent over against the scales, they are usually erect but sometimes bent over by their own weight. The beautiful mature bark is silvery-grey with fine fissures; young bark is marked with resin blisters. Noble silver fir makes a very handsome ornamental tree.

California red fir
(Abies magnifica)
Another species from California, Oregon and Sierra Nevada, it is very like *A. procera* except for the following points: It is not so large and is of narrower conic form; the bark is red-brown on old trees; the needles, longer and less densely set,

are more rounded in section. The cones are a little shorter and wider with more down on the scales and the bracts less flattened to the cone. The timber is a bit darker but otherwise very like *A. procera* wood.

Balsam fir
(Abies balsamea)
A small tree, seldom more than 22m (72ft) high, this has a wide native range especially in Canada and northeastern USA, but its timber is poor and it is not a particularly ornamental species. Its main fame is the production of Canadian balsam from its resin blisters; and for its dwarf cultivar, 'Hudsonia', only about 0.5 to 1m ($1\frac{1}{2}$–$3\frac{1}{4}$ft) high with very densely crowded small branches. Used both for wood and for chemical pulp. This is an important pulping species, but fetches a lower price than spruce.

Pacific silver fir or red fir
(Abies amabilis)
The Latin 'amabilis' means 'lovely fir' and it is indeed a beautiful tree, reaching 76m (249ft) in its native stands along the west coast of British Columbia and in the Cas-

cade mountains, with good, strong, pale-brown timber. It has beautiful curved spreading needles up to 3cm ($1\frac{1}{6}$in) long, glaucous-green at first, dark glossy-green later with two silver bands on the under surface and an orangy scent when crushed. The cones, 10–15cm (4–6in) long, are dark purple at first, brown later.

Colorado white fir
(Abies concolor)
An important forest tree in western USA and parts of Mexico, up to 60m (197ft) tall, *A. concolor* yields good, whitish, moderately strong timber, almost odourless and therefore favoured for boxes, and many other general uses. It has very long needles, up to 5cm (2in), blue-grey on both surfaces, all upswept, and there are many cultivars with especially blue or silver foliage. The cones are smooth, 10–15 × 3.5–4cm (up to 6 × $1\frac{1}{2}$in), green then light brown.

Low's white fir
(Abies lowiana)
This is a variety of *A. concolor* with needles less densely spaced and set at a wider angle to the stem.

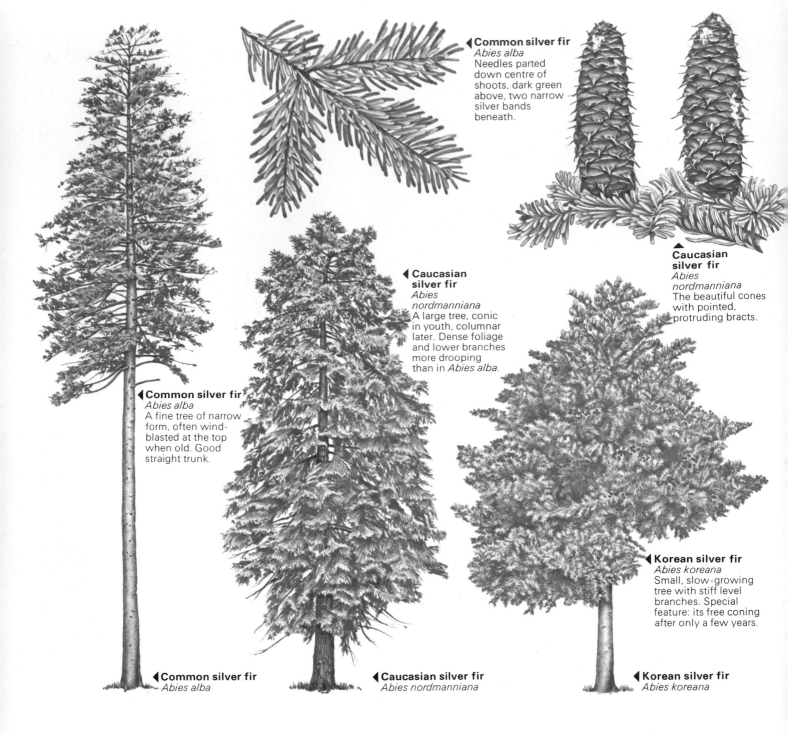

◄Common silver fir
Abies alba
Needles parted down centre of shoots, dark green above, two narrow silver bands beneath.

▲ Caucasian silver fir
Abies nordmanniana
The beautiful cones with pointed, protruding bracts.

◄ Caucasian silver fir
Abies nordmanniana
A large tree, conic in youth, columnar later. Dense foliage and lower branches more drooping than in *Abies alba*.

◄Common silver fir
Abies alba
A fine tree of narrow form, often wind-blasted at the top when old. Good straight trunk.

◄Korean silver fir
Abies koreana
Small, slow-growing tree with stiff level branches. Special feature: its free coning after only a few years.

◄Common silver fir
Abies alba

◄Caucasian silver fir
Abies nordmanniana

◄Korean silver fir
Abies koreana

Alpine fir

(Abies lasiocarpa)

This species has the widest distribution of any North American fir, right across from Alaska to New Mexico. On good sites it will reach 40m (131ft) and is of beautiful slender spire-like form with dense blue-green foliage. The cones are 11–15cm (4$\frac{1}{3}$–6in), barrel-shaped with pubescent scales, brown when ripe. The timber is unfortunately usually knotty and only used locally but it is a useful ornamental tree. There is a variety — *arizonica* — which is called cork fir owing to its thick soft bark.

Common silver fir

(Abies alba syn. A. pectinata)

Native to the mountains of central and southern Europe, the common silver fir is a major tree in the forestry of these regions, growing up to 55m (180ft) and yielding large volumes of whitish, soft, straight-grained timber with a very wide range of uses. Unfortunately it does not succeed well in Britain or America owing to severe aphid attacks. Its needles, 1–2.5cm ($\frac{2}{5}$–1in) long, are shallowly notched at the tip, arranged in two opposite sets, parted down the middle, dark green above, narrow white bands below. The cones, 10–15cm (4–6in) have turned down, pointed bracts.

Below: Common silver fir (*Abies alba*). The widely used, straight-grained timber.

Caucasian silver fir

(Abies nordmanniana)

Another giant, this time from the western Caucasus and north-east Turkey, soaring to 70m (229$\frac{1}{2}$ft) in height with fine lustrous dark green foliage; makes a splendid ornamental tree. The needles are dense, pointing forwards, with bright silver bands beneath and no parting on the upper side of the twig. The timber is much the same as that of common silver fir. The cones are 12–15 × 4–5cm (up to 6 × 2in) with protruding bracts bent down.

Greek fir

(Abies cephalonica)

This mountain tree of Greece grows up to 32m (105ft) tall, and is distinguished by its sharp pointed needles 2–3cm ($\frac{4}{5}$–1$\frac{1}{5}$in) long and radiating all round the shoot, upper surface shining green, lower side with two silver bands. The cones are 12–15 × 4–5cm (up to 6 × 2in) but the protruding bracts are smaller than in *A. nordmanniana*. The timber is only used locally.

Spanish or hedgehog fir

(Abies pinsapo)

Like Greek fir, the needles of this tree, from Ronda in southern Spain, radiate all round the shoot but they are shorter, 1–1.75cm ($\frac{2}{5}$–$\frac{2}{3}$in), thicker, stiffer, grey-blue colour all round and on older twigs tend to curve backwards. The cones are smaller—up to 10cm (4in) long with no protruding bracts. The timber is poor and not exported, but Spanish fir is unique in appearance and makes a most attractive ornamental tree.

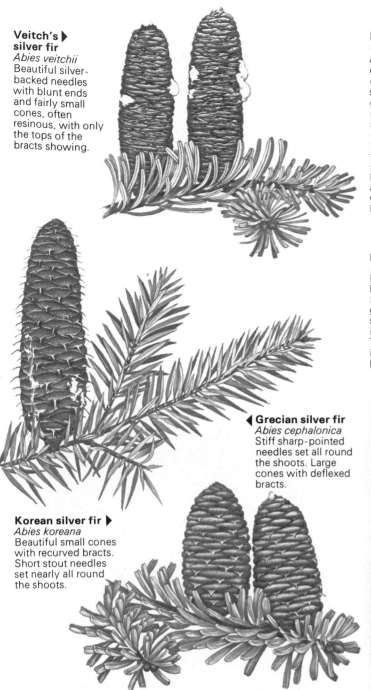

Veitch's ▶ silver fir
Abies veitchii
Beautiful silver-backed needles with blunt ends and fairly small cones, often resinous, with only the tops of the bracts showing.

◀ Grecian silver fir
Abies cephalonica
Stiff sharp-pointed needles set all round the shoots. Large cones with deflexed bracts.

Korean silver fir ▶
Abies koreana
Beautiful small cones with recurved bracts. Short stout needles set nearly all round the shoots.

Right: Spanish fir (*Abies pinsapo*). A remarkable and easily recognized conifer with thick, stiff, grey-green to grey-blue leathery needles radiating all round the twigs and stiff branches horizontal except near the tree top. It is sometimes aptly called hedgehog fir. There is a cultivar 'Glauca' with more pronounced blue-grey foliage.

Below: Greek fir (*Abies cephalonica*). Bole and bark of a very large old tree. The bark is fissured into a great number of rather short, very hard, irregular-sized plates. The trunk often divides into several heavy branches.

Veitch's silver fir
(Abies veitchii)
A medium-sized ornamental tree up to 22m (72ft) tall, this comes from the mountains of central Spain. Its attractive and unusual needles are truncated, being cut off at their broadest point, tapering towards the base, dark glossy green above, with broad silver bands below, densely set on the top of the shoots and pointing forwards and upwards. Cones appear on fairly young trees and are 6–8cm (2⅓–3⅛in) tall with smoothly wrinkled scales and the tips of the bracts only just visible. The timber is used locally.

Korean fir
(Abies koreana)
From the mountains of Quelpaert Island, this remarkable slow-growing little tree cones freely when only just over 1m (39in) high and is of broad, stiff conic form with short, blunt, notched needles radiating round the shoot, glossy green above with bright white stomata bands beneath. It is a really charming little tree, especially when flowering, the male flowers opening in bright yellow clusters and the upright

females 2–4cm (⅘–1½in) tall and light purple. The cones are small, 4–7cm (1½–2¾in) high, deep blue at first, brown later with recurved exserted bracts.

Delavay's silver fir
(Abies delavayi)
Common in south-west China where it grows to 30m (98ft) tall, this is valued for its soft, easily worked timber, and grown elsewhere, together with its varieties *georgii*, *forrestii*, *fabri*, *faxoniana*, etc, as ornamental trees loved for their dark shining green needles with bright silver bands on the underside, and their striking purple-blue cones, 7–12 × 4–5cm (up to 4¾ × 2in) with fine pointed, small, exserted bracts. Fairly young trees bear cones.

There are a few other species that should be mentioned, even if only briefly.

Himalayan fir
(Abies spectabilis syn. *A. webbiana* and very close to *A. pindrow)*
This tree is valued for its beautiful dark green foliage with brilliant silver bands on the underside and for the large grey-

blue cones 12–18cm × 5–7cm (up to 7 × 2¾in). In its native Himalayan home it grows to 60m (197ft) tall.

Santa Lucia fir
(Abies bracteata syn. *A. venusta)*
A large tree, up to 45m (147½ft) in California, this has distinctive very long (up to 5cm; 2in), sharply pointed needles, dark green above with bright silver bands below and very long (up to 5cm; 2in) protruding bracts to its cones which are 8–12cm (3⅛–4¾in) high.

Nikko fir
(Abies brachyphylla syn. *A. homolepis)*
Common in the mountains of central Japan, Nikko fir is a good ornamental tree because its needles tend to grow rather vertically, thus displaying their bright silver bands on the lower surfaces. Its timber is poor and is not exported.

Siberian fir
(Abies sibirica)
Of no great ornamental value, this species forms huge natural forests in Russia and Siberia where its timber is important and used for many purposes, including pulp.

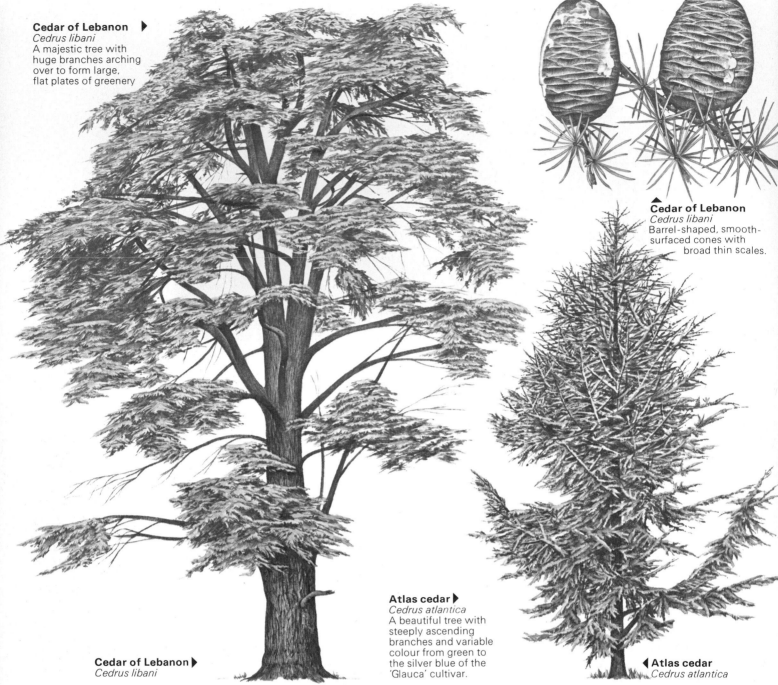

Cedar of Lebanon ▶
Cedrus libani
A majestic tree with huge branches arching over to form large, flat plates of greenery

Cedar of Lebanon
Cedrus libani
Barrel-shaped, smooth-surfaced cones with broad thin scales.

Cedar of Lebanon ▶
Cedrus libani

Atlas cedar ▶
Cedrus atlantica
A beautiful tree with steeply ascending branches and variable colour from green to the silver blue of the 'Glauca' cultivar.

◀ **Atlas cedar**
Cedrus atlantica

True Cedars

The name cedar should really only be used for members of the true cedar family, *Cedrus*, but unfortunately in various parts of the world all sorts of quite different species are known as cedars whereas in fact they may be junipers, cypresses, thujas, torreyas, cryptomerias, cedrela or libocedrus (now called calocedrus or austrocedrus). We shall consider here a closely related group of four *Cedrus* species from the Mediterranean and the Himalayas. These share the following features: the needles are arranged in two ways, just like larches, singly on the growing shoots but in tufts of 10–20 all together on older twigs but, unlike larches, they are evergreen. In contrast to most conifers, the true cedars flower in autumn. Their barrel-shaped cones are upright and disintegrate while still on the branches, producing winged seeds and leaving behind the central axis of the cone on the tree. The old saying about the tips of the branches is a useful guide to identification: Atlas—ascending, Deodar—drooping, Lebanon—level.

Cedar of Lebanon
(*Cedrus libani*)

King Solomon built his temple with timber from the cedars of Mount Lebanon and destroyed a great part of the once large cedar forest in the process. There are now only a few groves left, mainly at around 1,800m (5,904ft) elevation, but they contain some immense old trees up to 14m (46ft) in diameter. The age of these giants tends, as usual, to be grossly exaggerated, often quoted as being over 2,500 years, but this species is a fast grower and trees of only 150 years already assume an amazing air of timeless dignity, reaching up to 40m (131ft) high with huge boles and magnificent flat topped crowns over the massive lower branches. They tend to break up with age and it is unlikely that many reach even 1,000 years. Capability Brown, the great English landscape architect, made much use of Lebanon cedars in his garden layouts.

The needles, 2–3cm ($\frac{4}{5}$–1$\frac{1}{5}$in) long, vary in colour from dark green to a fairly blue green. The male flowers are erect, 3–5cm

Above: Cedar of Lebanon (*Cedrus libani*). The central stalks of the cones remaining on the tree after the scales fall off.

(1$\frac{1}{6}$–2in) tall and grey-green before they shed their yellow pollen, while the females, also erect, but only 1cm ($\frac{2}{5}$in) long, are green at first, turning purple when ripe. The barrel-shaped cones are 9–14cm × 6–7cm (up to 5$\frac{1}{2}$ × 2$\frac{3}{4}$in), the broad flat scales having purple edges and often being resinous. The seeds have broad wings. The dark grey bark fissures into short scaly

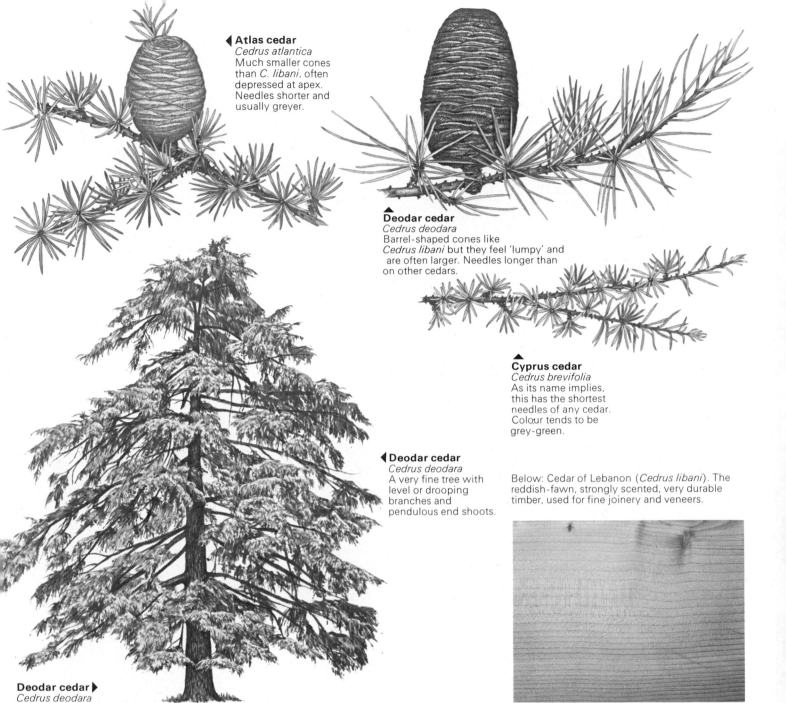

◄ Atlas cedar
Cedrus atlantica
Much smaller cones
than *C. libani*, often
depressed at apex.
Needles shorter and
usually greyer.

▲ Deodar cedar
Cedrus deodara
Barrel-shaped cones like
Cedrus libani but they feel 'lumpy' and
are often larger. Needles longer than
on other cedars.

▲ Cyprus cedar
Cedrus brevifolia
As its name implies,
this has the shortest
needles of any cedar.
Colour tends to be
grey-green.

◄ Deodar cedar
Cedrus deodara
A very fine tree with
level or drooping
branches and
pendulous end shoots.

Below: Cedar of Lebanon (*Cedrus libani*). The
reddish-fawn, strongly scented, very durable
timber, used for fine joinery and veneers.

Deodar cedar ▶
Cedrus deodara

Above: Cedar of Lebanon (*Cedrus libani*). The
massive bole of this stately tree, showing the
dark grey bark fissured into narrow ridges.

ridges and the rather oily, strongly scented
timber is brownish and very durable.

Atlas or Algerian cedar
(Cedrus atlantica)

From the Atlas Mountains of Algeria and
Morocco, this is a tree of narrower, more
upright habit, hardier than other true
cedars, with fairly short needles, 1–3cm
($\frac{2}{5}$–1$\frac{1}{6}$in), usually rather blue-green and in
the case of 'Glauca', very widely used in
parks and gardens, a wonderful silver blue
colour. The growing twigs tend to ascend
whereas Lebanon twigs are mainly level.
The male flowers are borne in great
number, about 4cm (1$\frac{1}{2}$in) high and pinkish
yellow when ripe; the female flowers are
less purple than those of Lebanon cedar.
The cones are smaller, 5–8cm (2–3$\frac{1}{8}$in) long,
and the timber is not unlike the Lebanon
wood. Atlas cedar will grow better on
alkaline soils than the other true cedars.

Deodar cedar
(Cedrus deodara)

This is a tall tree from the western Himalayas and Afghanistan at elevations from
1,200–3,000m (3,936–9,840ft), exceeding

60m (197ft) in height on the best sites, with
a girth up to 12m (39ft). Deodar cedar
yields good timber similar to that of
Lebanon cedar but more oily and with an
even stronger scent; cedar oil is extracted
from the wood. In form the deodar is
narrower and more conical than the
Lebanon but does not have the ascending
branches of the atlas. The growing shoots
droop gracefully and a young tree is indeed
a most beautiful sight. The green to silvery
green needles are long, 3–6cm (1$\frac{1}{6}$–2$\frac{1}{3}$in),
and narrow. The cones are less abundant
than on the other true cedars and larger,
up to 14cm (5$\frac{1}{2}$in) tall, with broad scales
more ridged than the others. It is a species
that could well be used in forestry more
than it has been in the past.

Cyprus cedar
(Cedrus brevifolia)

This much smaller tree from Cyprus,
seldom more than 18m (59ft) high, has level
branches and green or blue-green very
short needles, about 1cm ($\frac{2}{5}$in) long. The
cones, measuring about 7–10cm × 4–5cm
(up to 4 × 2in), are more tapered.

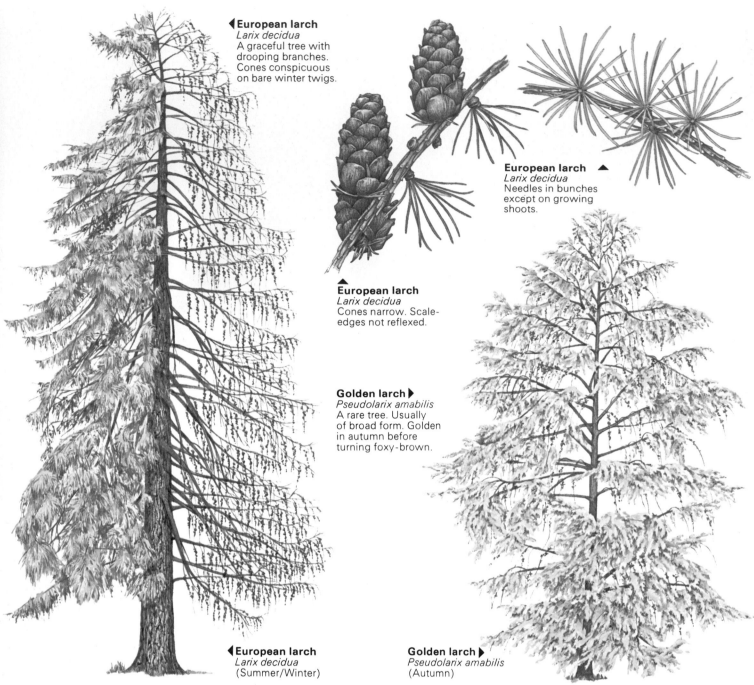

◀ European larch
Larix decidua
A graceful tree with
drooping branches.
Cones conspicuous
on bare winter twigs.

European larch ▲
Larix decidua
Needles in bunches
except on growing
shoots.

▲ European larch
Larix decidua
Cones narrow. Scale-
edges not reflexed.

Golden larch ▶
Pseudolarix amabilis
A rare tree. Usually
of broad form. Golden
in autumn before
turning foxy-brown.

◀ European larch
Larix decidua
(Summer/Winter)

Golden larch ▶
Pseudolarix amabilis
(Autumn)

Larches

The larches are a small family, only
about a dozen species, and are one of the
very few deciduous conifers. In spring they
burst into wonderfully vivid green earlier
than most trees; in autumn the leaves turn
gold; in winter the bare twigs, from pale
yellow to dark red-brown, according to
species, stand out from other trees.

With their straight trunks, rapid growth
and strong timber they are much used in
the forestry of many countries. A special
feature of the larches is the arrangement of
their needles—on long shoots they are set
singly, spirally all along the twig, but on the
short spur-like shoots, and on older woods,
they are borne in whorls, of from 15 to 40
in each tuft, as in cedars. The most important species are listed here.

European larch
(*Larix decidua* syn. *L. europaea*)
Native to south and central Europe, with
particularly straight and vigorous forms
in the Sudeten and the plains of Poland,
also in Russia and Siberia where it merges
into the species *L. sibirica*, this is a smaller
tree with slender needles that flush too

early when planted further south and get
caught by spring frosts. European larch is a
rapid grower, often having annual shoots
of 1m (39in) or more, and reaches up to 50m
(164ft) with diameters up to 2m (6½ft). The
fawn and reddish-brown timber is very
strong and durable, particularly when
used in the round, making it specially useful for farm and estate work such as fences,
rails, floors, and farm buildings, but also
for telegraph poles and pit-props.

The bright green needles are 2–4cm

Below: European larch (*Larix decidua*). A sample
of the reddish-brown, strong timber, which is
widely used for fences and other outdoor uses.

($\frac{4}{5}$–1½in) long, the winter twigs pale straw-
coloured or pinkish-fawn and the cones are
oblong-ovoid, narrower towards the top,
2.5–4cm (1–1½in) long by 2–2.5cm ($\frac{4}{5}$–1in)
broad, scales rounded and without any
curving back of the tips. Bark on old trunks
is quite deeply fissured.

Japanese larch
(*Larix kaempferi* syn. *L. leptolepis*)
This tree is similar to European larch but
has the following distinctions: winter
twigs much darker and usually reddish-
brown; needles longer, a little wider and of
more bluish green; leading shoots often
slightly wavy; cones, the most marked
feature, shorter (2–3cm; $\frac{4}{5}$–1$\frac{1}{6}$in), more
rounded and with strongly reflexed edges
to the scales; bark less deeply fissured;
timber very similar but not quite so strong.

On poor soils or very exposed sites this
species will succeed better than will
European larch.

Hybrid or Dunkeld larch
(*Larix × eurolepis*)
This is a cross between the European and
Japanese larches; it first occurred about

106

Golden larch
Pseudolarix amabilis
Needles in bunches except on growing shoots. Cones broad with large, triangular pointed scales.

Hybrid or Dunkeld larch
Larix × eurolepis
Cones with slightly reflexed scales. Needles greyer than on European larch.

Tamarack cones

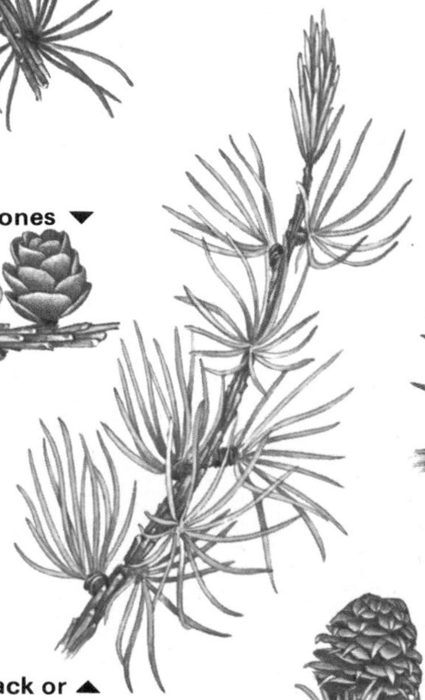

Tamarack or American larch
Larix laricina
Very small, square cones with broad, rounded scales. Needles in bunches except on growing shoots.

Tamarack or American larch
Larix laricina
A straight, narrow-crowned tree. Branches often twisting.

Japanese larch
Larix kaempferi
Needles longer and bluer than in European larch. Shorter, fatter cones with strongly reflexed scales.

Japanese larch
Larix kaempferi
Upright female flowers purple and green. Males like little golden buttons.

1897 at Dunkeld, Perthshire, and has characteristics intermediate between those of its parents. On good sites its growth is superior to either of them, often making leading shoots from 1–2m ($3\frac{1}{4}$–$6\frac{1}{2}$ft). This is an important tree for forestry, with very promising timber, and is now widely used in many countries.

Tamarack or American larch
(Larix laricina)
This remarkable and extremely hardy tree has the widest natural range of any American conifer, extending from the Yukon right along the northern limit of tree growth to Newfoundland and Labrador, with its southern boundary from British Columbia to Pennsylvania. It will tolerate extremely low temperature, swampy ground, low rainfall and elevations from sea level to 1,200m (3,936ft). On average it grows to about 22m (72ft) but on the best sites may reach 35m (115ft). The rather heavy timber has yellowish sapwood and reddish-brown heartwood and is used for transmission poles, railroad ties, fencing, ship building and construction work.

The needles are similar to European larch but rather smaller; cones are much smaller, about 1–2 × 1–1.5cm (up to $\frac{4}{5} \times \frac{3}{5}$in).

Western larch
(Larix occidentalis)
This is the other main larch in America, a much larger tree growing up to 60m (197ft) but with only a small native range in the upper Columbia River Basin. It lives to a great age—up to 900 years, and the timber is similar in appearance to European larch but of better quality, with a very wide range of uses. The needles are like those of European larch but the cones are larger, 3–6cm ($1\frac{1}{5}$–$2\frac{1}{3}$in) long, with curved, pointed projecting bracts.

Sikkim larch
(Larix griffithiana)
Native to east Nepal, Sikkim and Bhutan, this species is of no great commercial importance, nor does it grow very large (up to 20m; $65\frac{1}{2}$ft), but it is a valuable ornamental tree with beautiful weeping branches and the largest cones of any larch, 6–11cm ($2\frac{1}{3}$–$4\frac{1}{3}$in) long. Unfortunately it needs a mild climate to do well.

Golden larch
(Pseudolarix amabilis)
This tree from China is not a true larch but very close indeed, having the same sort of needle arrangement and being deciduous. But the cones are quite different, bluish-green at first, turning to light brown as they ripen, 3.5–4.5 × 3–4.5cm (up to $1\frac{3}{4} \times 1\frac{3}{4}$in) with large, triangular, acute-pointed leathery scales and whitish seeds with long (2.5–3cm; 1–$1\frac{1}{6}$in) pointed wings. Unlike true larches, golden larch cones fall off when ripe; they often only crop every second year.

The needles are long, 3–7cm ($1\frac{1}{6}$–$2\frac{3}{4}$in) and the bunches are borne on curved spurs, thickest at the tips. Because they turn golden in autumn the native name for the tree is *ching-sung*, meaning 'golden pine'. Male and female flowers are very small and borne on separate branches. The tree is broadly conic with long level branches and in China reaches to 40m (131ft) but is often dwarfed by pruning for ornamental effect. The wood is very good but the species is too rare to be cut for timber.

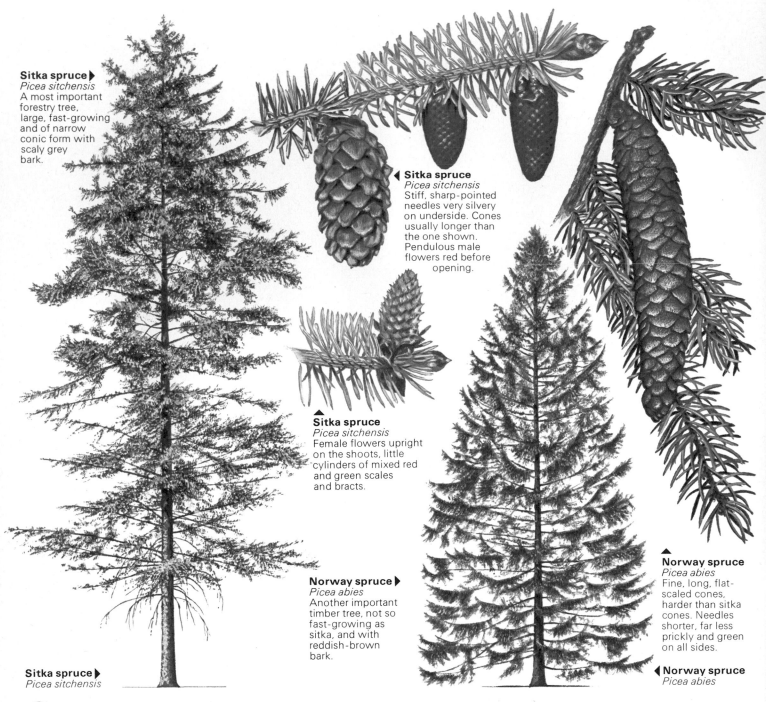

Sitka spruce▶
Picea sitchensis
A most important forestry tree, large, fast-growing and of narrow conic form with scaly grey bark.

◀ **Sitka spruce**
Picea sitchensis
Stiff, sharp-pointed needles very silvery on underside. Cones usually longer than the one shown. Pendulous male flowers red before opening.

▲ **Sitka spruce**
Picea sitchensis
Female flowers upright on the shoots, little cylinders of mixed red and green scales and bracts.

Norway spruce▶
Picea abies
Another important timber tree, not so fast-growing as sitka, and with reddish-brown bark.

▲ **Norway spruce**
Picea abies
Fine, long, flat-scaled cones, harder than sitka cones. Needles shorter, far less prickly and green on all sides.

Sitka spruce▶
Picea sitchensis

◀ **Norway spruce**
Picea abies

Spruces

This large group of around 50 species, including some important timber producers and many very beautiful trees, given time, may help to break down the widespread prejudice against all conifers. The broad characteristic of spruces are: single, needle-like leaves arranged spirally on the shoots, the lower ones often twisted at the base so that most of them are on the upper half of the twig; the needles are borne on little woody pegs which persist after the old needles fall, making the twigs very rough, and if a fresh needle is pulled off the twig part of the peg tears away leaving a little white splinter attached to the base of the needle; these features help to separate the spruces from the silver firs. The female flowers, upright at first, bend over later so that most spruce cones are pendulous and fall off the tree in one piece—unlike the upright cones of cedars and silver firs which break up while still on the branches.

Spruces have a very wide distribution in the northern hemisphere, coming from Europe, Siberia, Caucasus, China, Japan, the Himalayas, Canada and America.

A selection of the main species of spruce will now be considered individually.

Sitka spruce
(Picea sitchensis)

The wide use of this species in monoculture forestry has given it a bad name, which is very unfortunate because it is a magnificent tree, a giant of the forest, native of the Pacific coast from Alaska (it takes its name from the old capital town of Sitha) right down to California. It reaches 87m (285ft) with a diameter of up to 5m (16½ft) in its native forests, with huge basal buttresses.

Because of its rapid growth, annual shoots of 1.5m (5ft) are common, and its ability to grow on poor soils and exposed sites makes it a major tree in the forestry of many countries.

The creamy white and fawn timber, often called silver spruce, is light, strong, has good elasticity, works well, is obtainable in large sizes and is the most valuable of all the spruce woods. It was used to build the famous 'Mosquito' fighter planes and for countless more general purposes. The pale brown buds are ovoid; the stiff, sharply pointed needles, 2–3cm ($\frac{4}{5}$–1$\frac{1}{6}$in) long, are bright green above with beautiful bright silver lines below; the male flowers are drooping ovoids, red at first then yellow with pollen; female flowers little upright cylinders of green and red. Young shoots are pale buff, the cones (5–8cm; 2–3$\frac{1}{8}$in), cylindrical, green at first, pale brown later, with thin crinkled papery scales. The bark is grey-brown and flakes away in short, irregular, coarse scales.

Below: Sitka spruce (*Picea sitchensis*). A light-coloured, easily-worked timber of great value.

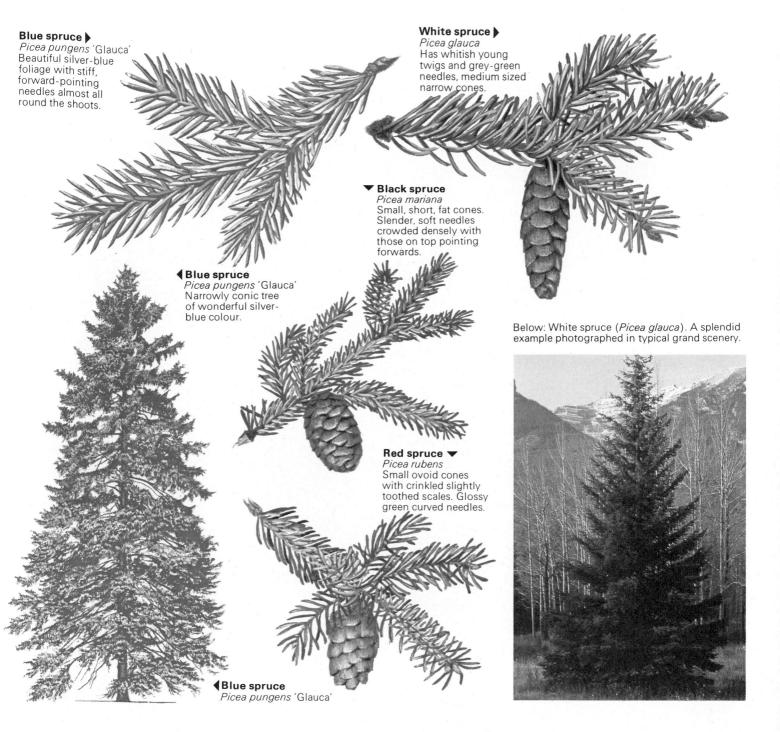

Blue spruce ▶
Picea pungens 'Glauca'
Beautiful silver-blue
foliage with stiff,
forward-pointing
needles almost all
round the shoots.

White spruce ▶
Picea glauca
Has whitish young
twigs and grey-green
needles, medium sized
narrow cones.

▼ Black spruce
Picea mariana
Small, short, fat cones.
Slender, soft needles
crowded densely with
those on top pointing
forwards.

◀ Blue spruce
Picea pungens 'Glauca'
Narrowly conic tree
of wonderful silver-
blue colour.

Red spruce ▼
Picea rubens
Small ovoid cones
with crinkled slightly
toothed scales. Glossy
green curved needles.

Below: White spruce (*Picea glauca*). A splendid
example photographed in typical grand scenery.

◀ Blue spruce
Picea pungens 'Glauca'

Norway spruce
(Picea abies syn. *P. excelsa)*
Another very important timber tree,
native to Europe from the Pyrenees and
Alps to Scandinavia and from the Balkans
to Russia, this is not so large or fast growing as sitka but has reached 60m (197ft).

It is the traditional species for Christmas
trees and is widely planted for that purpose.
The yellowish white timber, called white
deal or whitewood, is used for almost every
indoor purpose—joinery, boxes, pulp, plywood, etc—but is not durable outdoors.
It is heavier but not so elastic as sitka.
Specially selected slow grown samples are
used for making violins and other musical
instruments. The needles are far less
prickly than those of sitka, shorter and
shining green on both sides; the young
shoots orange-brown and the female
flowers bright red; the cones are much
larger, 11–17cm (4⅓–6⅔in) with flatter,
stiffer scales. The bark is coppery brown
and flakes off in much smaller, thinner
scales. There is a strange type, called
'snake spruce', which has hardly any side

branches and is formed of straggling thin
shoots with the needles all round the twigs.
White spruce
(Picea glauca syn. *P. alba)*
Native from Alaska to Newfoundland, this
is one of the most widespread conifers in
Canada; the timber, usually called Canadian or Quebec spruce, has been exported
all over the world and is now one of the
main sources of woodpulp. The creamy
white wood is used for the same purposes
as Norway spruce and is always in demand.
Growing to 56m (183½ft) along the Peace
River, but more usually to about 36m
(118ft), white spruce is of narrow form with
almost white young shoots. The short,
stiff, slender needles, 1–1.5cm (⅖–⅗in) long,
have a pungent smell when crushed and are
almost round in section, with a bluish
tinge due to fine white lines on all surfaces.
The cones are small, tapering cylinders,
5–6cm (2–2⅓in) long and brown when ripe.
Black spruce
(Picea mariana syn. *P. nigra)*
With the same amazingly wide native
distribution as white spruce this species is

smaller, maximum about 30m (98ft), and of
less commercial value, its timber at its
best is rather stronger, but is less used
except for pulp. It differs from white spruce
in having white lines only on the underside
of the needles, the upper surface being dark
green. The twigs are pinkish-brown and
slightly hairy; the cones, usually crowded
in large numbers on the branches, are
shorter, 3–4cm (1⅙–1½in) in length.
Red spruce
(Picea rubens syn. *P. rubra)*
Native to northeastern USA and Nova
Scotia, this is an important woodpulp tree
with timber similar to black spruce, but
larger, growing up to 50m (164ft). Its special
features are dense, hairy, orange-brown
shoots, buds surrounded by long, thin
pointed scales; grass green, glossy, incurved, short pointed needles and long
ovoid cones 3–5cm (1⅙–2in) with crinkled
slightly toothed scales.
Engelmann spruce
(Picea engelmannii)
This is a mountain tree of northwestern
America and Canada, about the same size

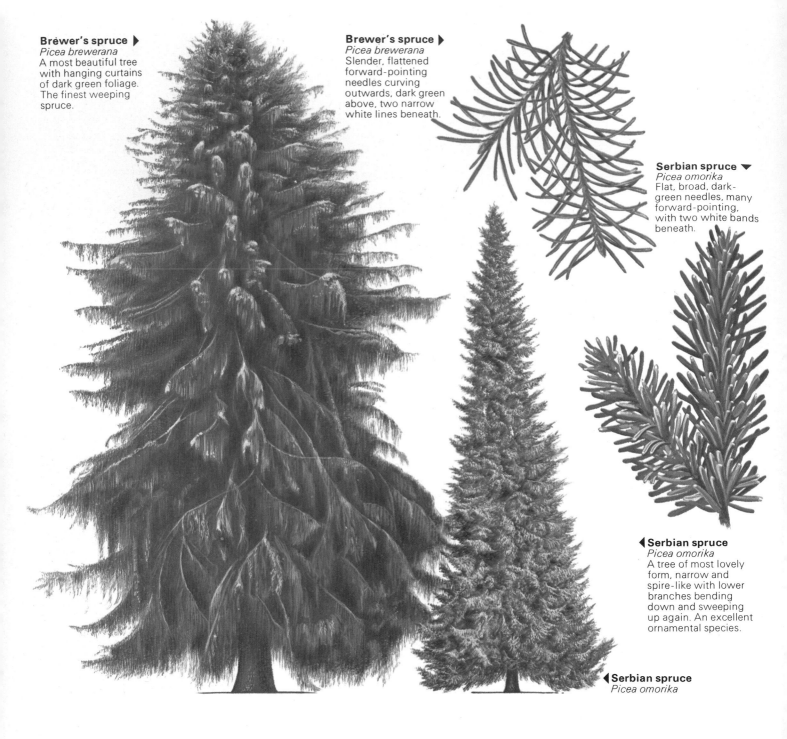

Brewer's spruce ▶
Picea brewerana
A most beautiful tree
with hanging curtains
of dark green foliage.
The finest weeping
spruce.

Brewer's spruce ▶
Picea brewerana
Slender, flattened
forward-pointing
needles curving
outwards, dark green
above, two narrow
white lines beneath.

Serbian spruce ▼
Picea omorika
Flat, broad, dark-
green needles, many
forward-pointing,
with two white bands
beneath.

◀ **Serbian spruce**
Picea omorika
A tree of most lovely
form, narrow and
spire-like with lower
branches bending
down and sweeping
up again. An excellent
ornamental species.

◀ **Serbian spruce**
Picea omorika

as white spruce. Because the light, straw-coloured timber is not strong, it is much used for pulp and general construction work where strength is not essential.

The blue-green needles are 2–3cm ($\frac{4}{5}$–1$\frac{1}{6}$in) long, soft and flexible, but with sharp points and foetid smell when bruised; the cones, 4–9cm (1$\frac{1}{2}$–3$\frac{1}{2}$in) long with thin scales and toothed margins, are shining brown when ripe, the bark reddish-brown, resinous and scaly. There is an attractive bluer cultivar 'Glauca', for ornamental planting.

Colorado or blue spruce
(Picea pungens)
Native to Colorado, eastern Utah and New Mexico, this high elevation tree ranges from 1,800–3,000m (5,904–9,840ft). It is of no great value for timber but has attractive bluish, stiff needles and has given rise to many beautiful cultivars selected from the bluest wild forms. These go under the general name *P. pungens*, 'Glauca', but are further identified by cultivar names such as: 'Koster', 'Moerkeimii', 'Thomsen', 'Spekii', etc, and include many very

striking trees with colours ranging from very blue to almost silver, much in demand for parks and gardens.

Morinda or West Himalayan spruce
(Picea smithiana syn. *Picea morinda)*
For many years the acknowledged king of weeping spruces, this splendid tree grows up to 60m (197ft) in its native mountains with long hanging shoots clad in well-spaced, forward curved, dark green needles, 3–4cm (1$\frac{1}{6}$–1$\frac{1}{2}$in) long, shiny, slender and nearly round in section. The cones are large, 10–15cm (4–6in) long, tapering at each end, shining brown when ripe, with smooth rounded scales. A fine, stately, pleasing tree.

Brewer's spruce
(Picea brewerana)
From the mountains of northwest California and southwest Oregon, this is the great rival to the morinda spruce. It is a smaller tree, seldom above 36m (118ft), but with wonderful curtains of dark drooping side shoots hanging from each downward-sweeping branch, with hardly any lateral growth between the branches, giving a

unique and very beautiful form. The flat, dark green, shining needles, 2–3.5cm ($\frac{4}{5}$–1$\frac{3}{8}$in) long, point forwards and curve outwards with two thin silver lines on the underside. The cones are smaller, 8–12cm (3$\frac{1}{8}$–4$\frac{2}{3}$in), the female flowers dark red.

This is one of the most beautiful of all conifers and has virtually replaced morinda for ornamental planting. It is rather frost tender.

Serbian spruce
(Picea omorika)
A tree of quite different shape, the Serbian spruce has a very slender spirelike form with short upper branches ascending or horizontal, while the lower ones droop but turn up at the ends, resulting in a very beautiful tree that is rightly finding its way into more parks and gardens. Its flat, dark green needles have two broad silver bands beneath, the female flowers, 1.5–2.5cm ($\frac{3}{5}$–1in) high, are crimson and the cones, 4–6cm (1$\frac{1}{2}$–2$\frac{2}{3}$in) long, are pointed, very resinous, a remarkable blackish-blue for a while, turning dark brown when ripe and very numerous near the top of the tree.

Sargent spruce ▶
Picea brachytyla
Beautiful flat green
needles pure silver
beneath, very striking.
Purple-brown cones
with slightly reflexed
scale-tips.

◀ Oriental spruce
Picea orientalis
Broadly conic with
densely foliaged,
rather crooked
branches. A rather
dark tree.

▲ Tiger tail spruce
Picea polita
Remarkable for its
very sharp, rigid,
pointed, curved
radiating needles;
the stoutest of any
spruce.

▲ Oriental spruce
Picea orientalis
Very short, shiny,
dark-green, square-
section needles.
Small cones.

◀ Oriental spruce
Picea orientalis

Above: Serbian spruce (*Picea omorika*). The
small, pointed, resinous cones are a remarkable
blue colour before turning dark brown later.

Below: Likiang spruce (*Picea likiangensis*).
A lovely, erect, red female flower, with small,
red male flower buds and green new shoots.

Oriental spruce
(Picea orientalis)

This large tree, up to 55m (180ft) tall with
girth up to 3m (10ft) in its native Asia Minor
and Caucasus, is recognized by its very
short needles, 0.5–1cm ($\frac{1}{5}$–$\frac{2}{5}$in), the shortest
of any spruce, shiny dark green, round
ended and set on hairy pale brown shoots.
The cones, 5–8cm (2–3$\frac{1}{8}$in) long, are curved,
pointed, resinous and grey-brown when
ripe. The timber is basically similar to that
of Norway spruce.

We now come to a large group of spruces
from the Far East of which we can only
mention a few of the most interesting.

Likiang spruce
(Picea likiangensis)

This fine tree, up to 35m (115ft) tall and 3m
(10ft) girth from southwest China, is
valued locally for its timber but elsewhere
mainly as an ornamental species noted
for its masses of flowers. The males are
red at first, opening to golden cylinders,
while the females are erect, scarlet and
about 2cm ($\frac{4}{5}$in) high. The leaf buds hang
like green jewels in the dark tree.

Sargent spruce
(Picea brachytyla)

Unfortunately this beautiful Chinese tree
has been ruthlessly cut for timber and is
now much less common, but it is a fine
ornamental species with marvellous silver-
backed needles and purple-brown cones.

Tiger tail spruce
(Picea polita)

This Japanese tree is grown purely for
ornament and the fascination of its amazingly aggressive, sickle-shaped needles,
1.5–2cm ($\frac{3}{5}$–$\frac{4}{5}$in) long, stout, rigid, set all
round its shoots and with very sharp hard
points—a truly fearsome prospect! It is of
narrow conic form, slow growing and with
large cones, 6–10 × 3.5–4.5cm (up to
4 × 1$\frac{3}{4}$) when open.

Koyama's spruce
(Picea koyamai)

Another Japanese species valued for good
form, of conic shape, this has ascending branches and beautiful cones, 5–10cm
(2–4in) long, usually very plentiful and
colourful, at first green-edged purple,
then lilac-brown and finally pinkish-
brown with silvery edges to the scales.

Dragon spruce
(Picea asperata)

This mountain tree is from northern China
where its timber is used locally, but it is
mainly planted as an ornamental species
and will grow near the coast better than
many species. It is broadly conic with
upturned branches and stiff bluish-green
needles, 1.5–2cm ($\frac{3}{5}$–$\frac{4}{5}$in) long, radiating
round the twigs and tipped with sharp
yellow spines. The cones are 2–14cm
($\frac{4}{5}$–5$\frac{1}{2}$in) long, green at first with purple-
edged scales and later pale brown.

Before leaving the spruces it should be
mentioned that many dwarf forms are
cultivated to adorn our rockeries. Some of
the best-known of these are:

P. albertiana conica   *P. mariana nana*
P. abies procumbens   *P. abies pumila*
P. abies nidiformis   *P. abies pygmea*
P. abies clanbrassiliana

A few species are also used for Bonsai
indoor decoration.

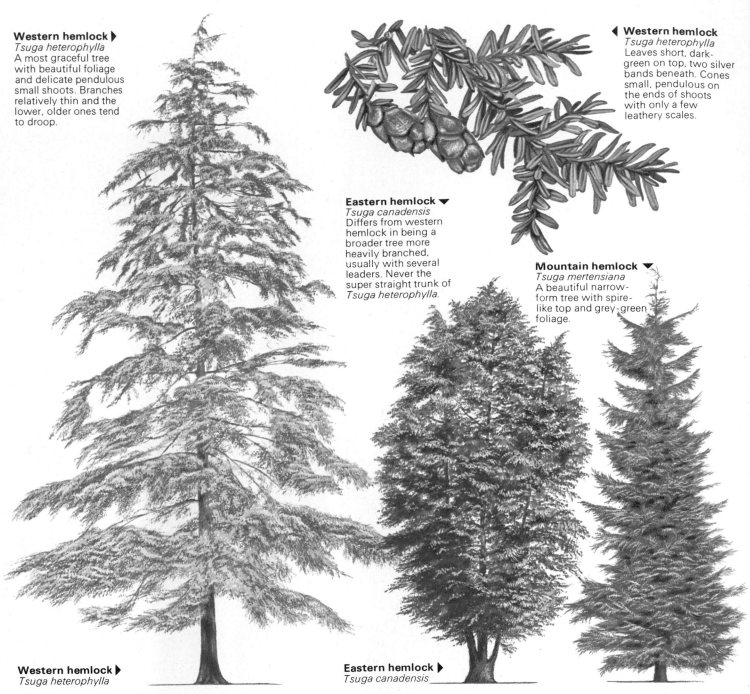

Western hemlock ▶
Tsuga heterophylla
A most graceful tree with beautiful foliage and delicate pendulous small shoots. Branches relatively thin and the lower, older ones tend to droop.

◀ **Western hemlock**
Tsuga heterophylla
Leaves short, dark-green on top, two silver bands beneath. Cones small, pendulous on the ends of shoots with only a few leathery scales.

Eastern hemlock ▼
Tsuga canadensis
Differs from western hemlock in being a broader tree more heavily branched, usually with several leaders. Never the super straight trunk of *Tsuga heterophylla*.

Mountain hemlock ▼
Tsuga mertensiana
A beautiful narrow-form tree with spire-like top and grey-green foliage.

Western hemlock ▶
Tsuga heterophylla

Eastern hemlock ▶
Tsuga canadensis

Hemlocks

Originating from North America, east Asia and the Himalayas, there are nine species in this small coniferous genus, closely related to the spruces; they include one important timber tree and several good ornamentals. The common name 'hemlock' is unfortunate because they are not at all poisonous and their only likeness to the well-known umbelliferous herb is that the crushed foliage of some of them has a similar scent.

Western hemlock
(*Tsuga heterophylla*)
The largest, best known and most valuable timber species, this is a giant North American tree often over 60m (197ft) tall with one record of almost 83m (272ft). It is one of the most beautiful of all the conifers, of superb narrowly conical form with slender rather pendulous shoots and flat needles, parted on each side of the shoot, green above but with two bright silver bands beneath and of variable length, those in the upper rows being only 5–7mm ($\frac{1}{5}$–$\frac{1}{4}$in) long but in the lower ranks 1.5–2cm ($\frac{3}{5}$–$\frac{4}{5}$in). It is a species that makes excellent hedges.

Above: Western hemlock (*Tsuga heterophylla*). Young trees, branches weighed down with snow. One of the most graceful of all conifers.

The small, globular male flowers are red at first but yellow when the pollen is shed, and the females are purple ovoids about 6mm ($\frac{1}{4}$in) long. Cones, often very numerous, are pendulous on the ends of small shoots, bluntly ovoid, 2–3cm ($\frac{4}{5}$–$1\frac{1}{6}$in) long with a few leathery scales, green at first but pale brown when ripe. The seeds are extremely small with short wings and run at 400,000 to the kg (over 180,000 per lb).

Western hemlock bark is very rich in tannin and has been extensively used in the American leather industry; it is smooth at first but on older trees becomes shallowly fissured into irregular small plates.

The yellowish timber is light in weight, straight grained, durable and has a wide range of uses. The species is fast growing and increasingly used in the forestry of many countries.

Eastern hemlock
(*Tsuga canadensis*)
This is a smaller and more bushy species from Canada and eastern USA. Its needles taper more than those of western hemlock and some of those on the top side of

Eastern hemlock ▲
Tsuga canadensis
Cones narrower than in
western hemlock and
the needles taper more
with some turned over
so as to show the
silvery underside.

▼ **Mountain hemlock**
Tsuga mertensiana
Needles point forwards
and are set radially
round the shoots, grey
or silvery green on
both surfaces.

▼ **Northern Japanese
hemlock**
Tsuga diversifolia
Has shorter, stouter
leaves than the others
with very bright silver
lines beneath.

▲
Chinese hemlock
Tsuga chinensis
Differs from western
hemlock as follows:
Sparser leaves with
bands on lower side
greenish instead of
white. Small shoots
more nodding.

Right: Eastern hemlock (*Tsuga canadensis*).
The finely fissured bark of an old tree. The trunk
nearly always divides near the ground.

Below: Western hemlock (*Tsuga heterophylla*).
The reddish-yellow, resin-free timber.

the shoots often twist so that the silver
bands are uppermost. The cones are
similar but rather smaller than those of
T. heterophylla.

It is an important softwood of the northeastern states, as well as Pennsylvania,
Michigan and Wisconsin. It is much used
for house framing and shiplap cladding;
the poorer logs are used as pulpwood.

Carolina hemlock
(Tsuga caroliniana)
Another American species, from the Al-
legheny mountains, this has a broad
pyramidal form and dense branches with
upswept tips. The glossy green needles are
slender, 1–2cm ($\frac{2}{5}$–$\frac{4}{5}$in) long and set at
irregular angles to the stems.

Mountain hemlock
*(Tsuga mertensiana syns. T. pattoniana
and T. hookeriana)*
A beautiful high-elevation tree from
western North America, this grows up to
45m (147$\frac{1}{2}$ft) tall, of narrow form with a
spire-like top and dense uneven-length
branches with drooping small twigs.

The needles, 1.5–2.5cm ($\frac{3}{5}$–1in) long,

set radially on the shoots, are usually
grey-green all over, but on some trees,
often called 'Glauca', they are of a beautiful blue-grey hue. The cones, spruce-like,
much larger than those of any other
hemlock, often up to 7cm (2$\frac{3}{4}$in) long.

Because the wood is light, soft and
brittle this species is not much used in
forestry, but is planted as an ornamental.

Southern Japanese hemlock
(Tsuga sieboldii)
This medium-sized tree from southern
Japan has broad shining dark-green
notched needles, 7–20mm ($\frac{1}{4}$–$\frac{4}{5}$in) long and
of broadly conic form sometimes with
multiple stems. The reddish-brown timber
is nicely grained and valued for furniture
and building purposes. The bark is used for
tanning.

Northern Japanese hemlock
(Tsuga diversifolia)
This comes from northern Japan, has
shorter, less shiny needles with better
silver bands on the lower surface, and is a
smaller, less valuable tree. Both the
Japanese species have ovoid-conic cones

measuring about 2–2.5cm ($\frac{4}{5}$–1in) long.

Chinese hemlock
(Tsuga chinensis)
From central and west China where it
grows up to 30m (98ft) tall, this is rather
similar to *T. heterophylla* in form and
foliage but with rather larger and rounder
cones. The timber is used for building
purposes and for roofing shingles.

Himalayan hemlock
(Tsuga dumosa syn. T. brunoniana)
This tall graceful, pendulous-branched
tree from the eastern Himalayas grows up
to 36m (118ft) tall. It has slender needles
up to 3cm (1$\frac{1}{6}$in) long with broad silver
bands on the underside. It is a tender
species only succeeding in mild areas and
its rather inferior timber is not exported.

Jeffrey's hybrid hemlock
(Tsuga × jeffreyi)
This is a hybrid between *T. heterophylla*
and *T. mertensiana* but is disappointing
and of no special value. It has olive-green
rather sparse needles and tends to be of
broad bushy form—very surprising considering its parents!

◄ Douglas fir
Pseudotsuga menziesii
One of the finest of
conifers, combining
the qualities of
grandeur, great size,
fast growth and
valuable timber.
Slenderly conic when
young, more columnar
with age, but with an
irregular outline.
Beautiful dense foliage.

Douglas fir ▲
Pseudotsuga menziesii
Soft needles, aromatic
when bruised, green
above with two silver
lines beneath.
Purplish-green upright
female flowers, male
flowers pendulous and
yellow when ripe.

Douglas fir ▶
Pseudotsuga menziesii
Beautiful and unique
pendulous cones,
rich brown when
mature, with a three-
pronged tongue-like
bract projecting
forwards beyond
each scale.

Blue or ▶
Colorado Douglas fir
Pseudotsuga menziesii
var. *glauca*
Has blue-grey foliage
and smaller cones
with the trident bracts
bent outwards away
from the cones.

◄ Douglas fir
Pseudotsuga menziesii

Douglas Firs

The natural range of Douglas fir
(*Pseudotsuga menziesii*) runs from the
Alaskan border right through the western
seaboard to Mexico. It was first discovered
by the Scottish botanist Archibald Men-
zies on Captain Vancouver's expedition
in 1792. David Douglas introduced it into
Britain in 1827.

Douglas fir is one of the world's tallest
tree species; there are still living specimens in British Columbia of over 94m
(308ft). It is not now possible to verify some
of the early claims of felled trees measuring
over 127m (416½ft). The famous flagpole at
the Royal Botanic Gardens, Kew, erected
in 1919, is a single spar of Douglas fir 65m
(213ft) high, 30cm (12in) in diameter at the
top and weighed 18 tons when felled.

One of the most important timber trees,
Douglas fir is known as Oregon pine or
British Columbian pine in the trade and in
addition to the very large natural forests
in North America it is now used for forestry
in most of western Europe, New Zealand,
Australia and South Africa. Its very wide
range of uses includes constructional

work, doors, plywood, panelling, flooring,
masts, spars, sleepers (cross-ties) and
pulping. The timber is light pinkish in
colour with orange-brown markings, and
the springwood of the annual rings is pale,
in marked contrast to the red-brown of the
summerwood. It is strong, machines well
and when flat-sawn gives very attractive
grain markings.

Unfortunately, Douglas fir is rather
liable to be uprooted by severe gales,
particularly where it is growing on shallower soils, and sites subject to smoke,
fumes, salt winds, severe spring frosts or
very alkaline conditions should be
avoided; but on good, reasonably sheltered
sites it grows splendidly, often making
annual shoots 1–2m (3¼–6½ft) in length.

Compared with many other conifers it
is a relatively easy species to identify,
having several good key-characters. The
needles are arranged in two loose ranks,
dark green above with two silvery white
bands on the lower surface, and when
crushed they emit a strong, fragrant, fruity
resinous odour, hence the Italian name

'abeto odoroso'—fragrant fir. If the needles
are pulled off the twig they leave a small
round smooth scar, as is the case with
silver firs. Often little specks of white
fluff will be found on the needles, especially
on the under surface; these are caused by
attacks of an aphid—*Adelyes cooleyi*.

The buds are reddish-brown, spindle-
shaped and rather like short beech buds.
Male flowers are in blunt-conic clusters on
the underside of the twigs, pink at first
then golden as pollen is shed; female
flowers are at the side of the shoots and
turn upwards to form erect, crimson, cone-
like tufts turning green later. The cones
are pendulous, 5–8cm (2–3⅛in) long, 2–2½cm
(⅘–1in) broad, light brown and with very
characteristic trident bracts protruding
between the cone scales. The small winged
seeds are a much lighter brown on one
side than the other and number 100,000
to a kilogram (45,000/lb). The seeds
germinate easily and natural regeneration
on the forest floor is common where enough
light is available.

On old trees the bark is very rugged and

Above: Douglas fir (*Pseudotsuga menziesii*). The bark of a young tree, showing the blisters that contain pungent clear resin.

Below: Douglas fir (*Pseudotsuga menziesii*). The contrasting orange and yellow grain of the valuable timber, often known as Oregon pine.

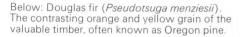

deeply fissured but on young trees, and near the top of older ones, it is smooth except for numerous blisters which exude pungent-smelling clear resin if burst.

Young trees grown in the open are narrowly conical with long slender leading shoots, but mature trees, though still fairly slender for their height, become rather flatter at the top and the heavy lower branches droop markedly.

Other species and varieties of Douglas fir include the following:

Above: Douglas fir (*Pseudotsuga menziesii*). The bole of a mature tree, showing the deeply fissured bark broken up into irregular plates.

Left: Douglas fir (*Pseudotsuga menziesii*). One-year seedlings on the forest floor. Douglas fir grows well on all but very alkaline soils.

Blue or Colorado Douglas fir
(*Pseudotsuga menziesii* var. *glauca*)
A smaller tree from the drier side of the Rocky Mountains, this is identified by blue-grey foliage and the upturned bracts of the rather smaller cones. The bark is much darker too. It will grow in colder areas than *P. menziesii*.

Fraser River Douglas fir
(*Pseudotsuga menziesii* var. *caesia*)
This comes from the inland Fraser River area, and has grey-green, stouter needles, mottled buds and stouter twigs.

Large-coned Douglas fir
(*Pseudotsuga macrocarpa*)
From southwest California and San Bernardino mountains, this is not common and has stiffer needles and large cones, 8–18cm (3⅛–7in).

Japanese Douglas fir
(*Pseudotsuga japonica*)
This is a much smaller tree—rare and of little importance. It has notched needles spread all round the shoot and without the fragrance of the other Douglas needles. Branches tend to grow level.

The Pine Family

The natural range of pines is amazing—in fact, from the Arctic Circle to the equator; and there is scarcely a country where a member of this great conifer group cannot survive; some possess extraordinary rugged hardness and tenacity while others need really warm conditions to grow well. Their value to man is immense for not only are they one of the world's greatest sources of timber but they also provide pioneer species for fixing areas of blown sand, shelter on rocky and exposed sites, nurse species and shelter belts in forestry and agriculture, suppliers of resin, turpentine and various chemicals and edible pine kernels. In addition they give us many very beautiful and interesting ornamental trees.

The outstanding general characteristic of pines is that their evergreen leaves are in the form of long narrow 'needles' varying in length from 3–45cm ($1\frac{1}{6}$–18in) and in bundles of twos, three or fives, each group enclosed at the base by a little sheath. The number of needles in a bunch is almost constant for each species, thus enabling the pines to be grouped according to this factor, which helps enormously with their identification.

Most of the buds are brownish or reddish-brown, many are pointed though some are more cylindrical with rounded tips; they are often very resinous. The male flowers are usually in dense clusters of small ovoid units at the base of new shoots, often orange or pinkish before opening to shed their clouds of golden pollen; whilst the female flowers are very small red globes, one to five in number for most species, right at the tips of the newly expanding shoots.

Pine cones are mainly hard and woody though a few are more leathery; they vary greatly in size and shape from small and almost round to very long and thin, and are formed of overlapping scales each concealing a pair of seeds, usually winged. The cones vary in weight from a few grams to 2kg ($4\frac{1}{2}$lb).

Squirrels and birds, such as crossbills, break up cones to get at the seeds and the skeletal remains are often seen scattered around the base of many pine trees.

The majority of mature pines have rough, often deeply fissured bark scaling off in irregular plates; the colour is usually fairly dark, but orange and reddish shades are not rare. Scots pine and lace-bark pine have unusual barks which are described in the individual species notes.

In form most young pines are conic with narrowly pointed tops and regular whorls of branches, but in later life the majority, if free of competition, become broader and more rounded at the top, while some, like stone pine, finally develop crowns shaped like broad umbrellas. As regards age, there is great variation between the different species; nearly all reach 100 years, many between 200 and 500 years, but one — the bristlecone pine (*Pinus longaeva*)—is regarded as the oldest living thing on earth. It is older than the sequoia trees, having reached 4,900 years and still alive in desert conditions at 3,000m (9,840ft) elevation in the White Mountains of California. These ancient trees have given us facts and figures enabling some

Above left: Maritime pine (*Pinus pinaster*). Coastal trees deformed by gales; blown over when young, they have recovered and grown into these twisted shapes.

Above: A stand of Scots pine (*Pinus sylvestris*). This is one of the most widely spread pines, growing throughout Europe and into Siberia. As well as adding grace and beauty to the landscape, it also yields a valuable, sturdy timber.

Right: Stone pine (*Pinus pinea*). The broad crown will characteristically flatten with age.

errors in the Carbon 14 dating methods to be corrected.

A large specialized book would be needed to do justice to the pine family and all we can do in the very limited available space is to try and give a glimpse of just a few of the most interesting species, offering apologies if anyone's favourites are omitted! An interesting way of grouping the selected species to be dealt with will be according to their particular uses and capabilities, starting with the hardiest, then dealing with the timber producers and finally those of special interest.

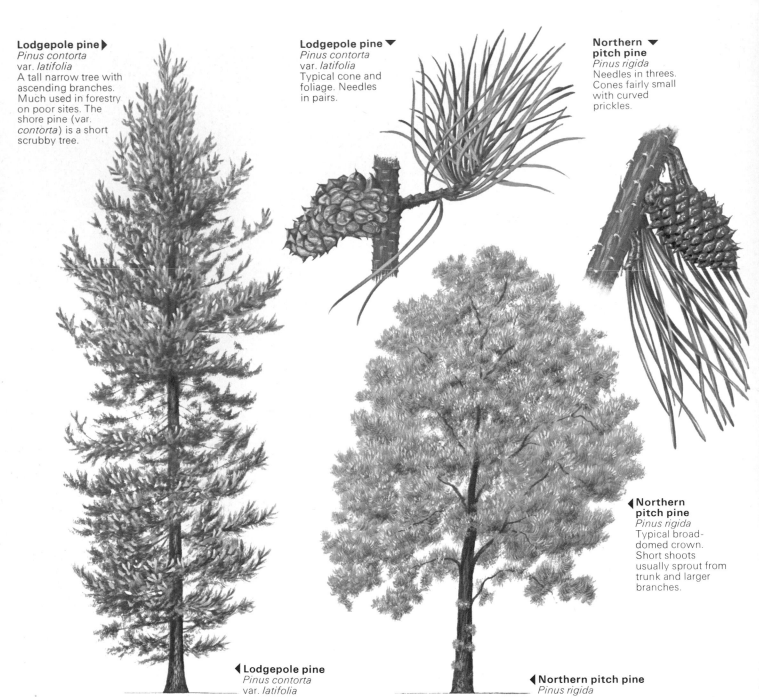

Lodgepole pine ▶
Pinus contorta
var. *latifolia*
A tall narrow tree with ascending branches. Much used in forestry on poor sites. The shore pine (var. *contorta*) is a short scrubby tree.

Lodgepole pine ▼
Pinus contorta
var. *latifolia*
Typical cone and foliage. Needles in pairs.

Northern ▼
pitch pine
Pinus rigida
Needles in threes. Cones fairly small with curved prickles.

◀ **Northern**
pitch pine
Pinus rigida
Typical broad-domed crown. Short shoots usually sprout from trunk and larger branches.

◀ **Lodgepole pine**
Pinus contorta
var. *latifolia*

◀ **Northern pitch pine**
Pinus rigida

Pioneer Pines

Jack pine
(Pinus banksiana)
Native to Canada from near the Arctic Circle to the Great Lakes, this small, two-needled pine is one of the hardiest of all trees, tolerating severe conditions of exposure, low temperature, poor soils and low rainfall. It is an important timber and pulpwood species.

Its special characteristic is its cones, which are 3–6cm ($1\frac{1}{6}$–$2\frac{1}{3}$in) long, ovoid, pointed and bent so that they face forward along the shoot.

Lodgepole pine
(Pinus contorta)
This species is usually divided into two varieties—beach or shore pine (*P. contorta* var. *contorta*) and true lodgepole pine (*P. contorta* var. *latifolia*).

The shore pine ranges from southeastern Alaska to California, a short scrubby tree but an excellent pioneer, vegetation suppressor and shelter-belt species, tolerant of sea-winds and bad soils and much used in forestry. The paired needles are short (4–5cm; $1\frac{1}{2}$–2in) and

twisted (hence the name 'contorta') and the cones about 5cm (2in) long, pointing down the stem, with prickles on the scales.

The lodgepole pine, so called because it was used for the support poles for the huts of North American Indians, grows further inland, from the Yukon to Colorado, with a great range of elevation, 450–3,200m (1,476–10,496ft). It is taller and straighter than the shore pine; it is useful in forestry, being a very hardy species.

The timber, though often knotty, is quite strong and works well. The needles are slightly longer than those of shore pine and not so densely set.

Below: Lodgepole pine (*Pinus contorta*). Yellowish, quite strong, easily worked timber.

Scrub pine
(Pinus virginiana)
This is a pioneer species in the eastern United States, growing on poor eroded soils and often coming in after 'slash' burning. Its timber is poor and often used for pulp and firewood. The special feature of scrub pine is that its young shoots are purplish and covered with a glaucous film. The needles are in pairs, 3–6cm ($1\frac{1}{6}$–$2\frac{1}{3}$in) and the cones small (3–7cm; $1\frac{1}{6}$–$2\frac{3}{4}$in), with sharp prickles.

Northern pitch pine
(Pinus rigida)
Similar in range and pioneer capabilities to scrub pine, this species has better timber, though inferior to that of longleaf pine (*P. palustris*); it is much used for low-grade work and for firewood. Northern pine has a special feature that enables it to resist forest fires remarkably well—it can put out sprouts of new growth even through the thick bark of an old trunk, so that if the crown is burnt the tree may well recover. The needles are in threes, 8–12cm ($3\frac{1}{8}$–$4\frac{3}{4}$in) long, and the cones small, 3–6cm ($1\frac{1}{6}$–$2\frac{1}{3}$in).

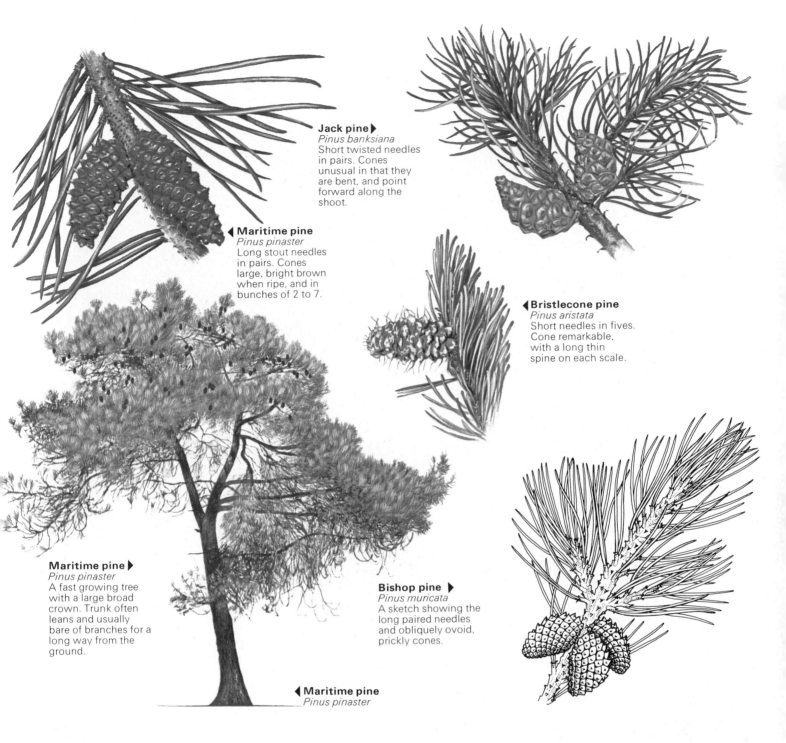

Jack pine ▶
Pinus banksiana
Short twisted needles in pairs. Cones unusual in that they are bent, and point forward along the shoot.

◀ Maritime pine
Pinus pinaster
Long stout needles in pairs. Cones large, bright brown when ripe, and in bunches of 2 to 7.

◀ Bristlecone pine
Pinus aristata
Short needles in fives. Cone remarkable, with a long thin spine on each scale.

Maritime pine ▶
Pinus pinaster
A fast growing tree with a large broad crown. Trunk often leans and usually bare of branches for a long way from the ground.

Bishop pine ▶
Pinus muricata
A sketch showing the long paired needles and obliquely ovoid, prickly cones.

◀ Maritime pine
Pinus pinaster

Mountain pine
(Pinus uncinata)

This tree and its bushy variety (*P. mugo*) are native to the Alps and the Pyrenees and are only used in forestry as pioneer crops on poor high-altitude ground, as nurse-crops or as snowbreak belts.

They have short needles (4–6cm; $1\frac{1}{2}$–$2\frac{1}{3}$in) in pairs and small cones (4–5cm; $1\frac{1}{2}$–2in) with the basal scales turned backwards.

Bishop pine
(Pinus muricata)

Native along the California coast, the strong point about this tree is its remarkable resistance to salty winds, and in many countries it is an obvious choice for coastal shelter belts.

This is often called prickly pine because of its special botanical feature—obliquely ovoid, prickly cones about 8×6cm ($3\frac{1}{8} \times 2\frac{1}{3}$in) in regular whorls of from three to seven that still remain on the branches for anything up to 40 years and are often found still on trunks up to 50cm (20in) in diameter. The paired needles are 7–15cm ($2\frac{3}{4}$–6in) long, the cylindrical buds often

coated with white resin. The timber is of moderate quality, but in short supply.

Austrian pine
(Pinus nigra var. austriaca)

Native to Austria, Central Italy and the Balkans, this is another species eminently suitable for shelter belts, even close to the coast, but it has the unusual advantage of tolerating alkaline and clay soils. It is widely used in many countries for windbreaks, both in forestry and agriculture, but is too coarsely branched for good timber. The dense, paired, stiff needles, 8–14cm ($3\frac{1}{8}$–$5\frac{1}{2}$in) long, are very dark green and unusually resistant to smoke and fumes. The cones are pointed, narrow ovoid, 5–8cm (2–$3\frac{1}{8}$in) long, set at a wide angle to the stems.

Maritime pine
(Pinus pinaster)

This rather coarse, rapidly growing, two-needled pine, native to the central and west Mediterranean region, does not succeed in cold climates or on heavy soils but is used on a large scale in the light sandy areas of southwest France, where it was the

centre of the resin tapping industry and very successful in fixing sand dunes. It was this pine that made Bournemouth, England famous for its lovely pine-woods but, sadly, foolish development has now ruined nearly all of them. One of its special features is its large cones, 12–18cm ($4\frac{3}{4}$–7in) long, in whorls of three to six, green at first, then a wonderful chocolate colour and finally a rich shining brown, eventually shedding seeds with large shining wings.

Bristlecone pine
(Pinus aristata, also Pinus longaeva)

With a very limited distribution in the arid mountain regions of California, Nevada, Utah and Colorado, this species is of unique interest because certain specimens (recently dubbed *Pinus longaeva*) are the oldest living things on earth. Its special feature, apart from longevity, is its small spine-covered cones, 4–7cm ($1\frac{1}{2}$–$2\frac{3}{4}$in) long and often very resinous. The dense short needles, 4–7cm ($1\frac{1}{2}$–$2\frac{3}{4}$in) long, are in fives, its new shoots carry orange-coloured pubescence and the trunks of old specimens are twisted and very large.

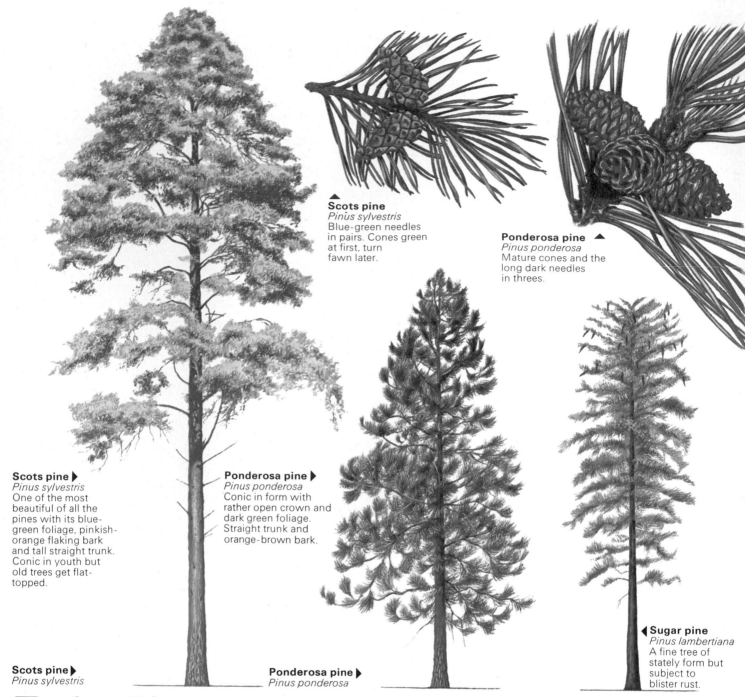

Scots pine
Pinus sylvestris
Blue-green needles in pairs. Cones green at first, turn fawn later.

Ponderosa pine ▲
Pinus ponderosa
Mature cones and the long dark needles in threes.

Scots pine ▶
Pinus sylvestris
One of the most beautiful of all the pines with its blue-green foliage, pinkish-orange flaking bark and tall straight trunk. Conic in youth but old trees get flat-topped.

Ponderosa pine ▶
Pinus ponderosa
Conic in form with rather open crown and dark green foliage. Straight trunk and orange-brown bark.

Scots pine ▶
Pinus sylvestris

Ponderosa pine ▶
Pinus ponderosa

◀ **Sugar pine**
Pinus lambertiana
A fine tree of stately form but subject to blister rust.

Timber Pines

Scots pine
(Pinus sylvestris)
This was the sole European pine to survive the Ice Ages and has a wide natural distribution from Scotland to Siberia and Lapland to Spain. It is one of the major timber trees with large forests in Russia and many parts of northern Europe. The cream and orange-brown timber is one of the most widely used softwoods, sold under many names such as Baltic fir, red deal, Archangel fir, etc, employed for countless purposes especially in the building trade. Scots pine seems to fit perfectly into wild mountain scenery and its special features are its beautiful blue-green paired needles, 5–10cm (2–4in) long, and the unique pinkish-orange flaking bark in the upper parts of the tree. Its pointed ovoid cones, known as 'deal apples' by some country people, are 5–8cm (2–3⅛in) long, green at first, becoming light brown as they mature and round when fully open.

Ponderosa pine
(Pinus ponderosa)
The most widely distributed of all the

Above: Scots pine (*Pinus sylvestris*). Clusters of male flowers on the point of shedding pollen.

native North American pines, with huge areas in the northwest and found at elevations from sea level to 3,000m (9,840ft), this is one of the largest and most important timber trees in the USA, growing up to 70m (229ft) high and 2.5m (8ft) in diameter and living to a great age—sometimes to over 700 years.

With its very deep tap-root it can grow where many species fail. The timber, strong and resinous with reddish-brown heartwood, is available in large sizes and is used for many purposes including heavy construction work, indoor woodwork, doors, floors, etc. Botanical features include needles in threes, 16–22cm (6⅓–8⅔in) long and crowded on the shoots, cones 7–10cm (2¾–4in) long, leaving the base on the branches when they are shed, and attractive orange and brown bark with scaly irregular plates. *Pinus jeffreyi* is very close to ponderosa but has larger cones, 15–18cm (6–7in) long.

Slash pine
(Pinus elliottii)
One of the most important timber trees in

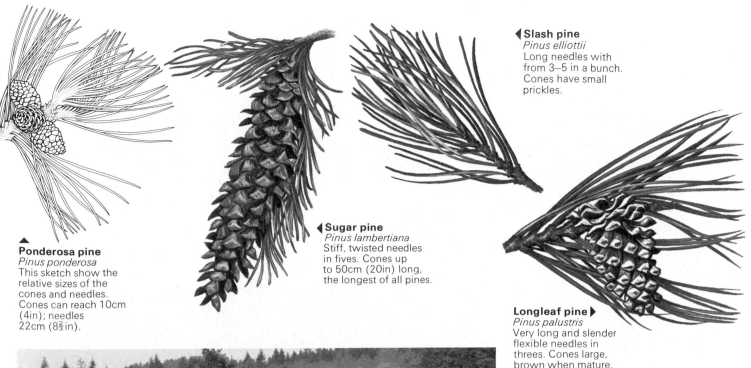

Ponderosa pine
Pinus ponderosa
This sketch show the
relative sizes of the
cones and needles.
Cones can reach 10cm
(4in); needles
22cm (8⅔in).

◀**Sugar pine**
Pinus lambertiana
Stiff, twisted needles
in fives. Cones up
to 50cm (20in) long,
the longest of all pines.

◀**Slash pine**
Pinus elliottii
Long needles with
from 3–5 in a bunch.
Cones have small
prickles.

Longleaf pine▶
Pinus palustris
Very long and slender
flexible needles in
threes. Cones large,
brown when mature.

Above: Scots pine (*Pinus sylvestris*). A sample
of the widely used, cream-coloured timber. It is
marketed under several names, including
European redwood and Baltic fir.

Left: Scots pine (*Pinus sylvestris*). The tall,
orange-brown trunks of these trees are a common
sight across Europe. Old trees are flat-topped.

Below: Slash pine (*Pinus elliottii*). The bark of
this pine is broken into a network of broad plates
that scale off in thin layers.

the southeastern United States with a
native range from the coastal plain of
South Carolina to central Florida and
Louisiana. A rapid grower, making 1½m
(5ft) annual shoots on good sites and
usually reaching about 30m (98ft) in
height. The timber is strong, orange-red,
resinous and used for a wide range of
building and joinery work. The needles,
20–30cm (8–12in) long, vary in numbers in
a bunch from two to five. The young shoots
are glaucous and the cones, 9–13cm
(3½–5in) long, are on short stalks.

Below: Longleaf pine (*Pinus palustris*). Straight-
grained, resinous, orange-tinted timber.

Sugar pine
(Pinus lambertiana)
This tree gets its name from a sugary
exudation obtained from the heartwood;
which has sometimes been used as a
sugar substitute. A native of Oregon and
California and the most valuable of all the
pines, growing up to 76m (249ft) in height
and to a diameter of 3m (10ft), it is a tree of
magnificent form with a long clean trunk
and a fine crown clothed in stiff, twisted
needles 8–11cm (3⅛–4⅓in) long and in
bundles of five. It has the longest of all
pine cones, 30–50cm (12–20in) on stalks
7–10cm (2¾–4in). The timber is soft, straight
grained and of very good quality, used
over a wide range of construction work,
building and joinery.

Longleaf pine
(Pinus palustris)
Though not a large tree, the tallest being
34m (111½ft) with a diameter of just over
1m (39in), longleaf is very valuable for its
first class orange-red timber, much in
demand wherever strength and durability
are essential and used the world over for
roof timbers, bridge building, interior
woodwork, flooring, decking, masts, etc.
It prefers a warm humid climate and is
native to the southeastern corner of the
USA. It has the longest needles of any
pine—up to 45cm (18in), in threes, slender
and flexible. The cones are large, 15–25cm
(6–10in) long by 5–8cm (2–3⅛in) broad, nut
brown when ripe.

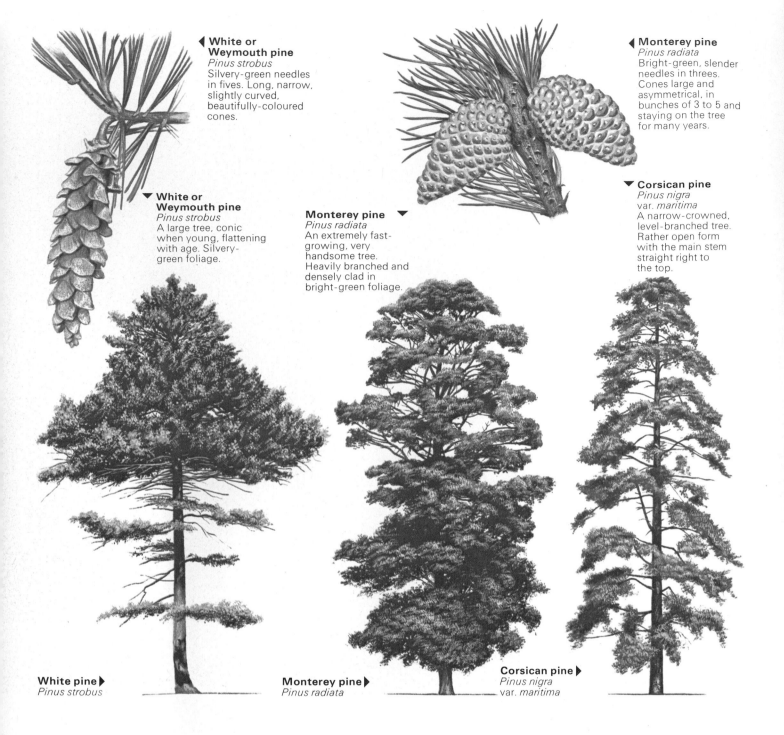

White or Weymouth pine
Pinus strobus
Silvery-green needles in fives. Long, narrow, slightly curved, beautifully-coloured cones.

Monterey pine
Pinus radiata
Bright-green, slender needles in threes. Cones large and asymmetrical, in bunches of 3 to 5 and staying on the tree for many years.

White or Weymouth pine
Pinus strobus
A large tree, conic when young, flattening with age. Silvery-green foliage.

Monterey pine
Pinus radiata
An extremely fast-growing, very handsome tree. Heavily branched and densely clad in bright-green foliage.

Corsican pine
Pinus nigra var. *maritima*
A narrow-crowned, level-branched tree. Rather open form with the main stem straight right to the top.

White pine
Pinus strobus

Monterey pine
Pinus radiata

Corsican pine
Pinus nigra var. *maritima*

Loblolly pine
(Pinus taeda)

Another tree of the southeastern United States that covers very large areas, this is the principal pine of North America and grows up to 39m (128ft) high with a useful tendency to prune itself, so that long clean stems are common, giving nice, soft, light-brown and cream timber, rather resinous and with much the same use as pitch pine though a rather lower quality. The rather stiff, slightly twisted needles are in threes and 14–23cm (5½–9in) long, while the smallish cones, 8–13cm (3⅛–5in) long, are almost sessile, with scales armed with reflexed prickles. It will not grow well in northern Europe.

White or Weymouth pine
(Pinus strobus)

This tree of eastern North America yields beautiful soft knot-free white timber that once supplied over half of Europe's needs as well as being in great demand in America and elsewhere. It was named after Viscount Weymouth who introduced it to Longleat, England, in 1705 but it quickly fell victim to blister rust disease and is not used in British forestry now, though it is still planted in parts of France and Germany. It is a large tree, reaching 65m (213ft) tall with a diameter of 3m (10ft). The silvery-green needles are in fives, 8–12cm (3⅛–4¾in) and the slightly curved, narrow cones, 10–20cm (4–8in) long, with rather broad thin scales, are often resinous and hang down on slender stalks.

Corsican pine
(Pinus nigra var. *maritima)*

Not so hardy as its close relation, Austrian pine, this is a larger, faster growing, more finely branched tree much used in forestry in many parts of Europe and native to Corsica, southern Italy and Sicily. Growing best on light soils, with fairly low rainfall, it gives higher volume more rapidly than Scots pine. The timber is inferior to that of Scots pine but is used for many purposes and is good for pulping. It grows to about 45m (147½ft) high and 1½m (5ft) in diameter and its paired needles, 12–18cm (4¾–7in) long, are not so stiff as those of Austrian pine. The buds are pointed and often coated with white resin, and the cones are the same as for Austrian pine, 5–8cm (2–3⅛in) long.

Bosnian pine
(Pinus leucodermis)

This tree from the Balkans is very close to Corsican pine and is worthy of mention because of its cones, similar in size and shape to those of Corsican pine, but of an extraordinary blue-black colour that makes them very attractive and conspicuous.

Monterey pine
(Pinus radiata)

Only native to one or two very small areas on the Monterey peninsula and in Cambria, California, this remarkable pine has quickly become of importance owing to its extraordinarily rapid growth and large size; it is now used in the forests of America, Europe, South Africa, Australia and New Zealand, becoming a major species in the last two countries. It grows to over 60m (197ft) with diameters up to 2m (6½ft) and in mild winters continues to grow throughout the year. Annual shoots of 2m (6½ft) are

Corsican pine
Pinus nigra
var. *maritima*
Needles in pairs.
Cones usually set
at 90° to the twig.

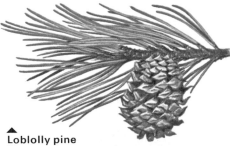

Loblolly pine
Pinus taeda
Stiff, twisted needles
in threes. Small
cones with reflexed
prickles.

Above: White or Weymouth pine (*Pinus strobus*). Pale, straw-coloured, excellent softwood timber.

Right: Corsican pine (*Pinus nigra* var. *maritima*). The edge of a fine plantation of mature trees in the New Forest, southern England.

Above: Monterey pine (*Pinus radiata*). The exceptionally rugged bark is deeply fissured into large, hard, irregular plates.

Right: Corsican pine (*Pinus nigra* var. *maritima*). Bark heavily fissured into long, irregular plates.

common and one Australian tree grew 6m (20ft) in its fifth year, while a New Zealand specimen *averaged* 1.2m (4ft) for 50 years! Needles are in threes, bright green, slender and dense, 10–15cm (4–6in). The cones are $10–15 \times 6–9$cm (up to $6 \times 3\frac{1}{2}$in) and very asymmetrical at the base, in whorls of three to six and retained on both branches and trunks for many, many years like those of bishop pine. The bark is very rugged, with deep fissures.

Shortleaf pine
(Pinus echinata)
This species has the widest natural distribution of any southeastern pine in the USA, growing in 22 states and covering 1,139,600 square km (440,000 sq miles), but is not much used in forestry elsewhere. The light-brown and cream timber is very variable but mostly of fairly good quality, and is used for a wide range of purposes. The needles, 7–13cm ($2\frac{3}{4}$–5in) long, are normally in pairs but sometimes in threes or fours; the cones are fairly small, measuring 4–6cm ($1\frac{1}{2}$–$2\frac{1}{3}$in) long, and often growing together in small clusters.

123

◄Stone pine
Pinus pinea
A large and beautiful cone with thick, hard scales much larger on one side than on the other. Stout needles in pairs.

▲
Coulter pine
Pinus coulteri
Noted for its very large, heavy cones with scales ending in strong, hooked spikes. Stout needles in threes.

Stone pine ►
Pinus pinea
This unique umbrella-shaped, wide crown is a well-known feature of the Mediterranean region. The heavy, low branches are often almost level.

Other Pines

Swiss stone pine or Arolla
(Pinus cembra)
This beautiful pine, native to the Alps, the Carpathians and Siberia, is such a perfect part of the wild mountain scenery that it is easy to forget that it is also a source of timber and that its seeds yield one of the edible 'pine kernels' collected in quantity, especially in Russia. The soft, yellowish timber is used locally for joinery, turnery and carving. Both the foliage and the cones are very attractive; the needles are in fives, 7–9cm ($2\frac{3}{4}$–$3\frac{1}{2}$in) long and marked with blue-white lines, while the barrel-shaped cones, about 8×6cm ($3\frac{1}{8} \times 2\frac{1}{3}$in), are at first blue-green but later brown and have two large edible seeds behind each scale.

Stone pine
(Pinus pinea)
With its large umbrella-shaped crown, stone pine is the most distinctive tree, other than the Italian cypress, all along the Mediterranean from Portugal to Asia Minor, forming a well loved and conspicuous part of the scenery. Apart from its shape its special features are its large,

Mexican white pine ▶
Pinus ayacahuite
Fine, long, pendulous cones, often with reflexed scales near the base. Slender, bluish-green needles in fives.

Mexican white pine ▼
Pinus ayacahuite
Young trees have rather open form, becoming denser with age. The lower branches grow long and level.

Bhutan pine ▶
Pinus wallichiana
Long, blue-green, pendulous needles in fives. Long, narrow, resinous cones.

Swiss stone pine ▼
or Arolla
Pinus cembra
Beautifully columnar when young, broadens with age. Branches turn up at the ends and the foliage is blue-green.

▲ **Swiss stone pine**
Pinus cembra
Needles, marked with silver lines, are in fives. Barrel-shaped, short cones have flat scales with projecting tips, blue-green at first, brown later. The large seeds are edible.

◀ **Swiss stone pine**
or Arolla
Pinus cembra

hard, ovoid or nearly round brown cones 10–13cm (4–5in) long by 8–10cm ($3\frac{1}{8}$–4in) broad with thick rounded scales which hide the very best and largest edible 'pine kernels', much in demand and sold under the other names—'pignons' or 'Pinocchi'. The stout needles, 12–15cm ($4\frac{3}{4}$–6in) long, are in pairs and the dark bark is fissured with reddish markings.

Bhutan pine
(Pinus wallichiana)
Native from Afghanistan to Nepal and growing at elevations from 1,800–3,700m (5,904–12,136ft), this very ornamental tree is much planted in many countries for its amenity value but in the Himalayas it is an important timber tree also used for resin tapping. The brownish wood is resinous with fine medullary rays and has a wide range of uses from building purposes to torches and firewood. Special features include long (16–22cm; $6\frac{1}{3}$–$8\frac{2}{3}$in), lax, blue-

Left: Bhutan pine (*Pinus wallichiana*). The graceful, sweeping branches and long, pendulous needles make this a fine ornamental tree. Note the pale yellow, male flowers.

green needles in fives and beautiful narrow resinous cones 20–30cm (8–12in) long.

An interesting hybrid between this tree and *Pinus ayacahuite* occurred at Weston-birt Arboretum, Gloucestershire, in 1904—*P. × holfordiana*, a fine vigorous tree with cones almost twice as wide but the same length as those of bhutan pine.

Mexican white pine
(Pinus ayacahuite)
Providing the best timber of any of the Mexican pines, but not used much in forestry elsewhere, this tree has a natural range from Mexico to Guatemala and is planted for its beauty in many countries. Its special features are fine pendulous cones, 20–40cm (8–16in) long by 6–12cm ($2\frac{1}{3}$–$4\frac{3}{4}$in) broad when open, having stout 2cm ($\frac{4}{5}$in) stalks and usually markedly reflexed scales, especially near the base; the long level branches are clothed in slender needles, 12–15cm ($4\frac{3}{4}$–6in) long, in bundles of five.

The timber is used in Mexico for general joinery and also for resin collection. The tree grows up to a height of 50m (164ft).

Coulter pine or big cone pine
(Pinus coulteri)
Not of any great commercial value, this southwest Californian tree is famous for its huge oblong ovoid cones up to 35cm (14in) long by 20cm (8in) broad and weighing anything up to 2kg ($4\frac{1}{2}$lb), with thick scales each mounted with a strong hooked spike like an eagle's claw. The tree grows to about 30m (98ft) tall, has a fairly broad crown and very rugged bark. Its needles are in threes, rather glaucous, stiff, stout and 20–28cm (8–11in) long.

Digger pine
(Pinus sabiniana)
Another Californian tree of no commercial value with large cones—reaching up to 24cm ($9\frac{1}{2}$in) long and 16cm ($6\frac{1}{3}$in) wide when open, and with short hooks on its scales. It has distinctive grey-green foliage.

Macedonian pine
(Pinus peuce)
This is a very attractive pine for ornamental planting and is not fussy about soil conditions. Native to the southwest Balkans, it grows to 30m (98ft) tall in a fairly

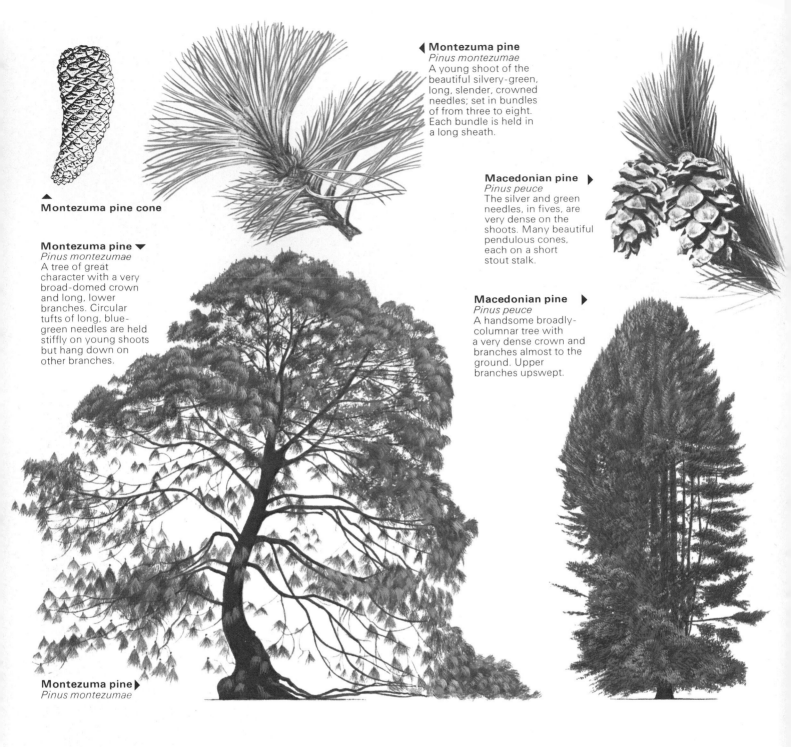

Montezuma pine cone

◀ Montezuma pine
Pinus montezumae
A young shoot of the
beautiful silvery-green,
long, slender, crowned
needles; set in bundles
of from three to eight.
Each bundle is held in
a long sheath.

Macedonian pine ▶
Pinus peuce
The silver and green
needles, in fives, are
very dense on the
shoots. Many beautiful
pendulous cones,
each on a short
stout stalk.

Montezuma pine ▼
Pinus montezumae
A tree of great
character with a very
broad-domed crown
and long, lower
branches. Circular
tufts of long, blue-
green needles are held
stiffly on young shoots
but hang down on
other branches.

Macedonian pine ▶
Pinus peuce
A handsome broadly-
columnar tree with
a very dense crown and
branches almost to the
ground. Upper
branches upswept.

Montezuma pine ▶
Pinus montezumae

broad columnar form and has beautiful
silver stomata lines on its densely set
needles 8–12cm ($3\frac{1}{8}$–$4\frac{3}{4}$in) long, curved at
the base, resinous, green at first then
ripening to a rich brown. The timber is
similar to that of Swiss stone pine and the
tree is not used in forestry, outside its
native land, as much as it deserves to be.

Montezuma pine
(Pinus montezumae)
A decidedly tender Mexican pine that will
not stand hard winters, this is one of the
most unusual and beautiful trees with its
wide spreading rounded crown, marvellous
blue-grey needles 25–40cm (10–16in) long,
slender and spreading stiffly round the
shoots. The small cones, 6–10cm ($2\frac{1}{3}$–4in)
long, are barrel shaped and with small
prickles on the scales.

In Mexico the timber is used for joinery
and resin is collected from the tree.

Japanese white pine
(Pinus parviflora)
Specially pruned specimens and dwarf
forms of this tree are a common feature in
the design of many Japanese parks and

gardens and it is also one of the main trees
used in Bonsai dwarfing for indoor use.
The larger forms grow up to 17m (56ft) tall
and the light soft timber is used in Japan
for general carpentry but is not exported
in any quantity. The form of this pine is
unusual with wide level or drooping
branches and short needles, 4–8cm ($1\frac{1}{2}$–
$3\frac{1}{8}$in), somewhat twisted and of a beautiful
blue-green. The cones are barrel shaped
when open, 5–6 × 3–4cm (up to $2\frac{1}{3}$ × $1\frac{1}{2}$in)
and when ripe are rich shades of brown.

Japanese black pine
(Pinus thunbergii)
Another Japanese pine much used for
Bonsai dwarfing, but in natural forests
this grows much larger than the Japanese
white pine, up to 40m (131ft) with diameters
up to 2m ($6\frac{1}{2}$ft), and is quite a valuable
timber tree as well as being used for resin
tapping. In other countries, especially
Australia, it is planted for coastal windbreaks and for stabilizing blown sand
areas.

Its special botanical features are the
small cones, 3–6cm ($1\frac{1}{6}$–$2\frac{1}{3}$in) long and

usually in large bunches, sometimes as
many as 40 or 50 in one group. The needles
are in pairs, 7–10cm ($2\frac{3}{4}$–4in) long, pointing
forwards and dense on the shoots.

Lace bark pine
(Pinus bungeana)
This tree is native to China, and is remarkable for its beautiful bark which flakes
away, as in a plane tree, resulting in
chalky white irregular patches scattered
in a grey-green matrix. The cones are very
attractive, barrel-shaped, 3–5 × 3–4cm (up
to 2 × $1\frac{1}{2}$in) with a small number of large
scales with sharp spines. Needles in
threes, 6–8cm ($2\frac{1}{3}$–$3\frac{1}{8}$in) long. Lace bark
pine is of no economic importance outside
China though it should be used more
than it is for ornamental planting.

Armand's pine
(Pinus armandii)
Native to the mountains of west China
this also is of no great importance except as
an ornamental tree. It is planted mainly
for its beautiful cones, 10–18cm long, 6–9cm
wide (up to 7 × $3\frac{1}{2}$in), erect in the first year,
pendulous the next year, bright, blue-

◀ Armand's pine
Pinus armandii
Noted for its numerous, beautiful, large cones, erect and blue-green at first, brown and pendent later. The long bright green needles, set in fives, are rather sparsely grouped, mainly at the ends of the somewhat bare twigs.

Japanese umbrella pine ▼
Sciadopitys verticillata
Each of the glossy green leaves, arranged like the spokes of an umbrella, consists of two needles fused together. The small ovoid cones have only a few large scales.

▼ Japanese white pine
Pinus parviflora
Short very twisted blue-green needles in fives. Small barrel-shaped cones blue-green at first, later orange-brown.

◀ Japanese white pine
Pinus parviflora
A striking tree with beautiful, silvery, blue-green foliage mainly on the upper side of the wide level branches with their upturned ends. Seldom very tall and often of broad irregular shape.

◀ Japanese white pine
Pinus parviflora

green at first then changing to light brown with red-brown inside the scales, which are thick, large and often resinous. The needles are in fives, 12–14cm (4¾–5½in) long with a drooping habit.

Knobcone pine
(Pinus attenuata)
Native to southwestern USA, this tree is of special interest because of its amazing asymmetrical cones, 10–14cm (4–5½in) long, with stout spines on the scales and remaining on the branches in bunches for very many years.

Japanese umbrella pine
(Sciadopitys verticillata)
Not a true pine, but included in the great Pinaceae family, this unique tree has its needle-like leaves grouped in whorls of from 15 to 30, arranged like the spokes of an umbrella frame, with each whorl spaced out from the next one along the twig. Each of the dark green glossy leaves, 9–12cm (3½–4¾in) long, actually consists of two needles fused together. The ovoid cones are small, 4–7cm (1½–2¾in) with a few large scales.

Right: Lace bark pine (*Pinus bungeana*). The bole of this tree, showing the remarkable bark that flakes off to reveal patches of many colours, including grey, pink and white.

Below: Japanese umbrella pine (*Sciadopitys verticillata*). The bark flakes off in strips.

A guide to the BROADLEAVES

The dense canopy of a sugar maple
enables it to trap every possible ray of light available,
and thus ensures that, in the fierce
competition among broadleaves
for adequate light, space and nutrients,
this particular tree will survive.

*T*housands of species of broadleaved trees thrive in temperate regions. (Tropical rain forest has even more.) The vast range in size and shape represents more than 60 plant families. All belong to the true flowering plants or Angiosperms—that huge group with seeds protectively borne in the seed case or ovary. Biologically, broadleaved trees thus have an advantage over the conifers. They also tend to have larger, more variable leaves, fruits and flowers. Apart from a few groups, such as the palms, almost all broadleaved trees are dicotyledons, producing a pair of cotyledons or seed leaves from each seed. Broadleaved trees in general are often called 'hardwoods' because many yield hard and durable timber. But on poor soils or very exposed sites, few have the conifers' pioneering abilities.

In temperate regions, most species of broadleaved tree shed leaves at the onset of winter—a device that reduces the risk of damage from frost, wind and desiccation. For man, seasonal leaf fall and new growth bring accidental delights in the form of spring buds, a lush summer canopy, rich autumn colours and the delicate tracery of bare twigs and branches in winter.

Ecologically, a broadleaved deciduous forest is far richer than an evergreen coniferous forest. Because its dead leaves and branches yield relatively more nourishment, they support more kinds of plant and animal, and in larger numbers. But the spacing of trees is important: few plants thrive under a dense beech canopy, for example. Then, too, spacing affects the trees themselves. The best specimens grow widely spaced in hedgerow, parkland or garden.

The following guide features the principal broadleaved trees of temperate and Mediterranean regions. The drawings are not to scale; tree and leaf sizes are given in the text. For most groups one major species has been presented as a dominant illustration.

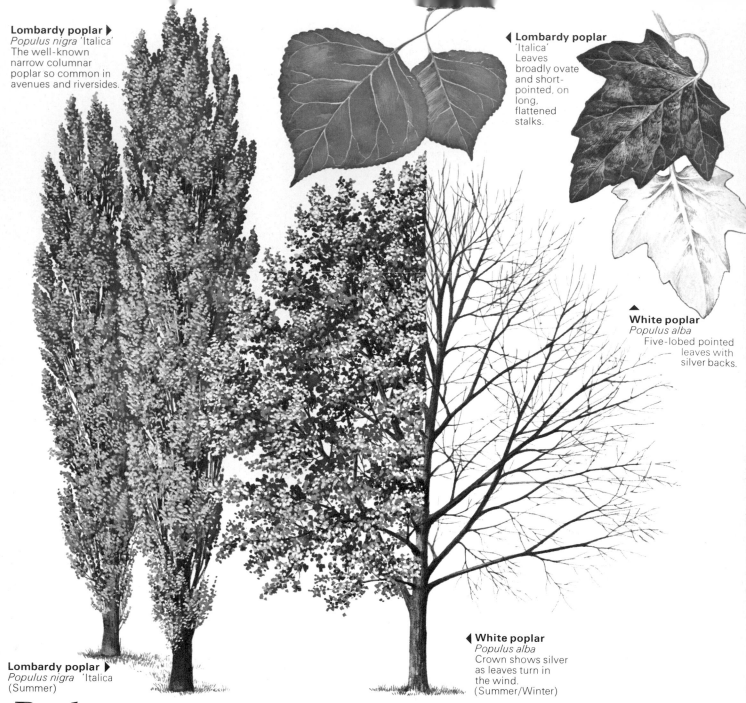

Lombardy poplar ▶
Populus nigra 'Italica'
The well-known
narrow columnar
poplar so common in
avenues and riversides.

◀ Lombardy poplar
'Italica'
Leaves
broadly ovate
and short-
pointed, on
long,
flattened
stalks.

▲ White poplar
Populus alba
Five-lobed pointed
leaves with
silver backs.

Lombardy poplar ▶
Populus nigra 'Italica'
(Summer)

◀ White poplar
Populus alba
Crown shows silver
as leaves turn in
the wind.
(Summer/Winter)

Poplars

Poplars are famous for their rapid growth, long-stalked trembling leaves and large colourful catkins. Over 30 species of this genus grow in northern temperate regions. These are grouped here under four headings: balsams, white poplars, aspens and black poplars.

Balsam poplars

This group has aromatic winter buds and young leaves, sticky bud scales, large leaves and long attractive catkins. It includes the following species:

Black cottonwood or western balsam
(Populus trichocarpa)
Native from Alaska to California, this is the largest American poplar, growing up to 60m (197ft) tall. It yields good timber and is used for many hybrids. Its scent fills the spring air. The large pointed leaves (10–30cm; 4–12in) are whitish beneath; the bark tends to peel off.

Balsam poplar or 'Tacamahaca'
(Populus balsamifera)
Another American tree, this is smaller, has poorer timber than *trichocarpa*, and sends up many suckers. The vigorous 'TT20' is a cross between this and *P. trichocarpa*.

Balm of Gilead or Ontario poplar
(Populus × candicans)
This is another highly scented species but should not be used for timber growth as it is particularly susceptible to canker and suckers prolifically. A cultivar with cream and pink patches on the leaves, 'Aurora', is suitable for amenity planting.

White poplars

The leaves are white beneath, and on top when just opened; new shoots also are white. The catkins are crimson and grey and the bark is pitted with small diamond shaped boles.

White poplar
(Populus alba)
This is a European tree, rarely taller than 25m (82ft); the trunk is seldom upright and the branches twist; the twigs are very white when young. It is canker-resistant, and the timber, reddish in colour, is harder than that of most poplars. The three- to five-lobed leaves are 4–6cm (1½–2in) across with brilliant silver undersides, making a beautiful picture when blown by the wind and seen against a blue sky.

Grey poplar
(Populus canescens)
From Europe and western Asia, this species also has good canker-resistance. It is larger than *P. alba*, with better, whiter timber. Neither the twigs nor the rounded leaves are quite as white.

Aspens

Trees in this group have roundish leaves with long lateral stalks which are in constant movement. They yield excellent, very pale-grained timber. They sucker freely and are not easy to raise from cuttings.

Aspen
(Populus tremula)
This native tree of Europe and Asia Minor seldom grows above 20m (65½ft) tall. The bark is fairly smooth with horizontal markings. The male catkins are grey and rather stout. The roundish leaves, 4–6 × 5–7cm (1½–2⅓ × 2–2¾in), with a few large

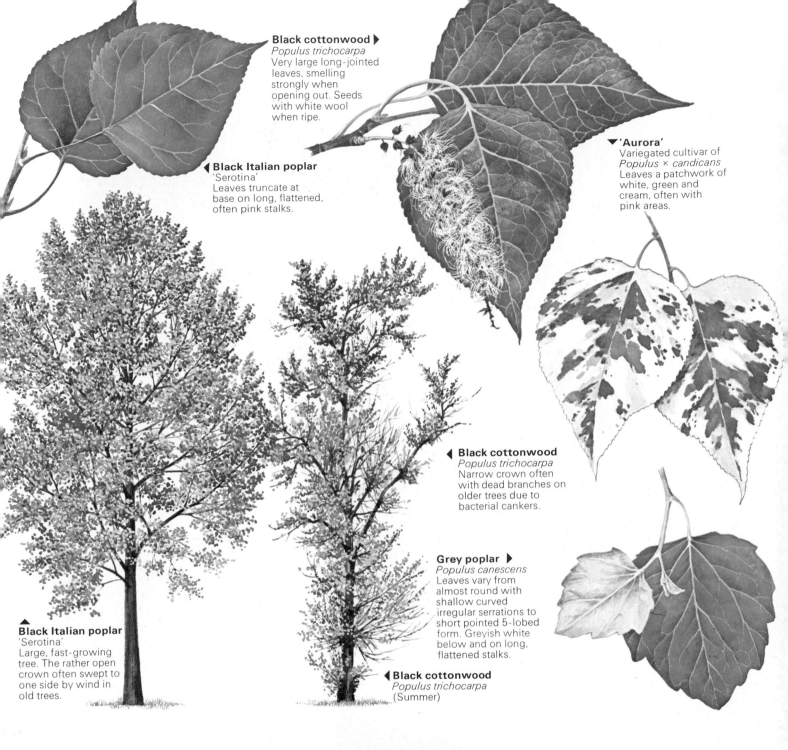

Black cottonwood ▶
Populus trichocarpa
Very large long-jointed leaves, smelling strongly when opening out. Seeds with white wool when ripe.

◀ Black Italian poplar
'Serotina'
Leaves truncate at base on long, flattened, often pink stalks.

▼ 'Aurora'
Variegated cultivar of *Populus × candicans*
Leaves a patchwork of white, green and cream, often with pink areas.

◀ Black cottonwood
Populus trichocarpa
Narrow crown often with dead branches on older trees due to bacterial cankers.

Grey poplar ▶
Populus canescens
Leaves vary from almost round with shallow curved irregular serrations to short pointed 5-lobed form. Greyish white below and on long, flattened stalks.

◀ Black cottonwood
Populus trichocarpa
(Summer)

▲ Black Italian poplar
'Serotina'
Large, fast-growing tree. The rather open crown often swept to one side by wind in old trees.

blunt teeth, are coppery at first, soon becoming grey-green.

Quaking aspen
(Populus tremuloides)
One of the most widely distributed trees in North America, from Alaska to Newfoundland, and the only Californian native to reach the Arctic Circle. Larger than *P. tremula* (up to 30m; 98ft) it has finely toothed leaves, slender catkins and timber of poor quality.

Black poplars and their hybrids
Black poplars form a very large group, including many hybrids and special clones; only a few characteristics apply to them all. Their leaves, none of which have white undersides, appear comparatively late in the season and have compressed slender stalks. Most of the old trees have rugged bark.

True black poplar
(Populus nigra)
This is one of the original European species but is seldom planted now and is becoming rare in many countries. It grows up to 35m (115ft) tall, with many large

Above: True black poplar (*Populus nigra*). The short stout bole of an old tree showing the typically rugged bark and presence of burrs.

branches, mostly ascending, and is domed at the top when old; large burrs are usual on the short stout trunk. It has fine crimson catkins. *Populus nigra* is one of the parents of many good hybrid species of poplar.

Lombardy poplar
(Populus nigra 'Italica'*)*
The well-known and much used fastigiate poplar, this variety originated in Italy but is now common in many countries. It grows to a height of 35m (115ft), with a beautiful narrow upright form.

Black Italian poplar
('Serotina')
Widespread throughout Europe, this very large tree, up to 42m (138ft), originally a French hybrid, has large branches, fairly level at first, then sweeping upwards to form an open wide crown, often one-sided. It has long red catkins, up to 12cm (4¾in). The timber is soft but useful for packing cases and a variety of small articles. There is a cultivar with golden leaves, 'Serotina Aurea'.

'Robusta'
A black poplar hybrid of great vigour, with annual shoots up to 4m (13ft), this is a valuable tree. Its spring leaves are a marvellous orange-red colour.

We should consider the following single

Above: Black cottonwood (*Populus trichocarpa*). A mature tree showing bark fissured into ridges.

Above: Black Italian poplar ('Serotina'). The long red catkins of this male only cultivar.

Below: A fine avenue of hybrid black poplars lining a road in northern France.

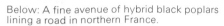

Above: Goat or pussy willow (*Salix caprea*). The beautiful, golden male catkins in spring.

Below: Crack willow (*Salix fragilis*). Old pollarded trees with very rugged, furrowed bark.

Willows

poplar outside the above groups:

Chinese necklace poplar

(Populus lasiocarpa)

A particularly attractive Chinese tree, *P. lasiocarpa* grows to 20m (65½ft) and has enormous heart-shaped leaves, up to 35cm (14in) long with red stalks and midribs. The common name is derived from the little round green fruits strung along the ripe catkin.

Poplars have been the subject of much experimental breeding work, particularly by the Dutch, resulting in about 400 hybrids and special clones; those obtained by crossing American and European trees are known as 'Euramerican' hybrids.

Despite all this work there are still only a few species and clones that are reasonably resistant to the very serious disease known as bacterial canker, which ruins the trees for either timber or amenity. Some of the most resistant are: 'Serotina', 'Gelrica', 'Eugenei', 'Robusta', 'Fritzi-Pauley', 'Scott-Pauley', 'TT32', *P. nigra* 'Italica', *P. nigra* var. *betulifolia*, *P. can-*

escens, P. alba and *P. tremula*—though this last one is rather less immune.

In America poplars are called 'cottonwoods' because of their white, downy seeds. Because of their fast growth, often over 2m (6½ft) a year, and fair resistance to smoke they are often planted in and around towns, particularly for screens and avenues, but caution is needed because their thirsty roots can cause subsoil shrinkage and upset the foundations of buildings. They have characteristically broad leaves and their drooping catkins develop male and female on separate trees.

For forestry poplars have the advantage of giving a high volume in a short time and the white to pale yellow wide-ringed, soft timber has wide markets. It is preferred to all others for matches, and for fruit boxes; it is used also for a wide variety of purposes, including plywood, wood-wool, packing cases, flooring, kitchen utensils, wagon bottoms and rough boarding. The American fire service has a slogan 'One tree can make a million matches: one match can burn a million trees!'

This genus with over 300 species has the widest geographical distribution of any tree—right across the northern hemisphere and down into South America and South Africa. Their identification has been greatly complicated by frequent hybrids and only a few of the main examples can be considered here. They vary from creeping pioneer species to tall trees, some of which yield valuable timber, but many of them are shrubby with no marked central trunk. The buds of all willows are enclosed in a single rounded scale and, with rare exceptions, every tree is either wholly male or wholly female. The open female catkins with their whitish stigmas are usually silvery green while the males have golden anthers. The seeds are minute, each bearing a mass of fluffy white hairs, and will only germinate on damp soil; this explains why willows only spread along watersides or on marshes. They are usually propagated by cuttings which root easily; in fact willow pegs or stakes driven into the ground very often take root and many a fence post starts sprouting. In most species

Left: Crack willow (*Salix fragilis*). Young leaves and the slender, pale green female catkins, which grow to maximum length of about 10cm (4in).

Right: White willow (*Salix alba*). A riverside view of two mature white willow trees showing the characteristic dense crowns of blue-green foliage. Willows are often seen beside streams because their wind-brown seeds are viable for only a few weeks and need damp soil for germination.

Below: Cricket bat willow (*Salix alba* 'Coerulea'). A row of well-spaced trees growing along the bank of a stream. This cultivar of white willow is raised from cuttings and planted in the fertile soil found near water. The timber is harvested when the trees are about 50cm (20in) in diameter.

the leaves are long, narrow and alternate, but there are exceptions.

The well-known 'mophead' willows have been pollarded—that is, cut back every few years just above cattle-grazing level, to provide a continuous supply of straight young stems easily harvested for such purposes as hurdles, fruit baskets, wooden shoes (sabots), fencing material, fish-traps, and firewood. The timber is pale brown, often tinged with pink, with white sapwood, soft, light, and easy to work or to split; it has sometimes been used for matches instead of poplar, and for cricket bats but for the latter only special varieties give the best quality.

Some of the main species are described here.

Crack willow
(Salix fragilis)

Common and with a wide range across Europe, western Siberia, and extending into Persia, this species grows to 30m (98ft) tall, with long upswept branches, heavy and twisted on old trees, which are broadly domed and often become slanted. The

Left: A sketch showing the twig and bud of white willow (*Salix alba*). The twigs, buds and leaves are covered with silvery hairs.

Right: A sample of timber from the cricket bat willow (*Salix alba* 'Coerulea'). Although exceptionally light in weight it can withstand sudden impact.

twigs snap off very easily at the base: hence the name 'crack' willow. The male catkins are yellow, 2–5cm ($\frac{4}{5}$–2in), the females pale green 6–10cm ($2\frac{1}{3}$–4in). The narrow lanceolate leaves, 10–18cm (4–7in) long, are usually finely tapered, glossy green above and grey-green beneath, and hang evenly on the twigs. The bark on old trees is very rugged, deeply furrowed, and tends to flake off. The pale red timber is light and tough. One of its most interesting characteristics is that it withstands friction extremely well.

White willow
(Salix alba)

This tree is similar in size and distribution to the crack willow but has a denser crown, more pendulous long, slender twigs, male catkins 4–6cm ($1\frac{1}{2}$–$2\frac{1}{3}$in) and females 4–7cm ($1\frac{1}{2}$–$2\frac{3}{4}$in). The leaves are shorter, closer together and set more irregularly on the twigs, bluer green above and much whiter beneath. The timber is of better quality and rather whiter.

The many crosses and special clones from this species include the following:

White willow ▶
Salix alba
A most graceful tree with ascending branches but long pendulous twigs. Leaves silvery as they turn in the wind.

White willow ▶
Salix alba
Beautiful, long, narrow serrated leaves grey-green above, silver beneath. Twigs not brittle.

Crack willow ▼
Salix fragilis
Often pollarded. Leaves bright-green on top, grey-green below. Twigs brittle at joints.

◀ **White willow**
Salix alba
(Summer)

◀ **Crack willow**
Salix fragilis
(Summer/Winter)

Cricket bat or blue willow
(Salix alba 'Coerulea')
This cultivar, together with special hybrids and clones from it, is specially grown to provide top class cricket bats, a unique industry requiring good soil by streamsides to give exceptionally rapid and upright growth, ready for cutting from 12 to 15 years.

There is a bacterial disease, 'water mark', that seriously affects the timber, causing dark staining. This is a serious plague to growers and research work is still in progress.

'Coerulea' is of conic upright form, has slender purple shoots, bluish grey-green leaves and a narrow crown.

Weeping willow
('Tristis')
There is great confusion about weeping willows and as usual hybrids have made the problem worse. The original weeping willow is *Salix babylonica*, a native of China and probably not the tree referred to in the Bible; it is used much less often than the larger, more vigorous hybrid, with much yellower twigs, called *Salix vitellina* var. *pendula* (syns. 'Tristis' and 'Chrysocoma'), a cross between *S. vitellina* and *S. babylonica*.

All the weeping willows are distinguished by cascades of beautiful pendulous slender shoots, often hanging to touch the water beneath.

Scarlet willow or coral-bark willow
('Chermesina')
This is a special cultivar of *Salix alba* with orange-scarlet twigs, and is very conspicuous and beautiful in winter. As usual the names are confusing: it may be called 'Chermesina' or 'Chrysostella', or even 'Britzensis'.

Contorted willow
(Salix matsudana 'Tortuosa')
A cultivar of the Japanese tree *S. matsudana*, this tree has amazingly contorted branches, twigs and leaves.

Bay willow
(Salix pentandra)
Native to Europe and northern Asia and growing to 20m (65½ft), this broad-crowned tree has grey-brown fissured bark, shiny green twigs, large, glossy, dark green leaves, 6–12cm (2⅓–4¾in) long, finely serrated, glaucous beneath and looking like bay leaves. The yellow catkins are 3–6cm (1⅙–2⅓in) long. It is a good amenity species.

Black willow
(Salix nigra)
This North American species is the largest of all the willows, reaching a height of over 40m (131ft) in the Mississippi valleys. Narrow bright green leaves up to 13cm (5in) long and catkins flowering after the leaves are fully out. The bark is dark brown, rough and scaly. The timber is of poor quality and is mainly used for boxes.

Violet willow
(Salix daphnoides)
The special characteristic of this small tree, native to Europe, Central Asia and the Himalayas, is its highly coloured shoots, dark purple with a bright white bloom. To give the best effect it should be cut back every two or three years.

The following species are smaller and more bushy in growth:

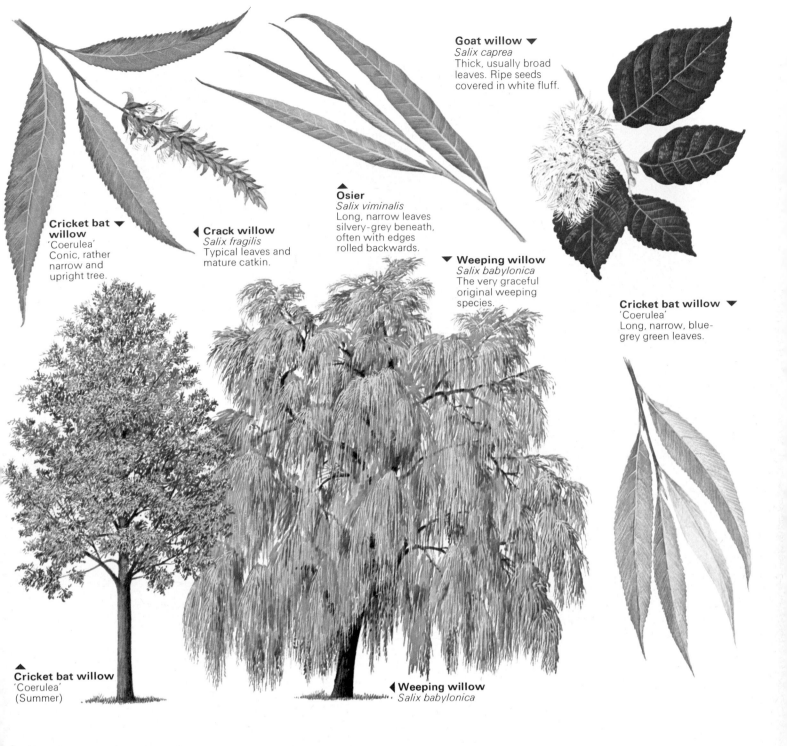

Cricket bat willow ▼
'Coerulea' Conic, rather narrow and upright tree.

◄ **Crack willow**
Salix fragilis
Typical leaves and mature catkin.

▲ **Osier**
Salix viminalis
Long, narrow leaves silvery-grey beneath, often with edges rolled backwards.

Goat willow ▼
Salix caprea
Thick, usually broad leaves. Ripe seeds covered in white fluff.

▼ **Weeping willow**
Salix babylonica
The very graceful original weeping species.

Cricket bat willow ▼
'Coerulea'
Long, narrow, blue-grey green leaves.

▲ **Cricket bat willow**
'Coerulea'
(Summer)

◄ **Weeping willow**
Salix babylonica

Goat willow, sallow or pussy willow
(Salix caprea)
Well-known and much loved for its heavy crop of beautiful short fat catkins in early spring, all silky-silver at first then the males turning golden-yellow and the females silvery-green, this bushy small tree is native to Europe and northern Asia. If not cut back it will grow up to 12m (39ft) tall on favourable wet sites, but will survive on very poor rough ground where goats roam and feed on its early foliage—hence 'goat' willow.

Flowering branches of *S. caprea* used to be gathered on the Sunday before Easter known as Palm Sunday. When the seeds are ripe the catkins are like balls of white fluff. The leaves vary in size and shape—anything from small lanceolate 3–4cm (1⅙–1½in) long to large broadly rounded 6cm (2⅓in) across, or oblong up to 9cm (3½in) long. In general the leaves are grey-green, serrate or entire, often wrinkled and on short red stalks. The shoots on old trees are short and knobbly.

Some botanists have distinguished several species, but in view of all the intermediate forms, such distinction is very doubtful.

Osier willows
A most important group of special clones and hybrids nearly all derived from the common osier *(Salix viminalis)*, is specifically grown and specially harvested for the basket and willow-weaving trade, with local names such as 'long skein', 'red root', 'brown merrin', 'mottled Spaniard', 'glib skins', 'Lincolnshire Dutch', 'Brittany green' and so on.

Osier stool beds are raised from cuttings and harvested annually as 'rods', most of these are peeled but some are used with the bark on. The conversion of these rods into baskets, furniture and fish traps is a highly skilled trade many hundreds of years old, and happily by no means dead yet.

In general osier leaves are narrower than those of most willows, silvery-grey and often hairy beneath, varying in length from 7–25cm (2¾–10in). The shoots vary over a whole range of colours—red, yellow, purple, brown, green, cream, to almost black.

Lastly there are three interesting pioneer dwarf willows often surviving naturally under extremely adverse conditions. They are often used in large rock gardens.

Creeping willow
(Salix repens)
This low sprawling shrub, usually less than 1m (3¼ft) high, is native to Europe and northern Asia and grows both on wet sites and on sandy wastes. The leaves are about 2cm (⅘in) long, oblong and silvery beneath.

Lapland willow
(Salix lapponum)
Reticulated willow
(Salix reticulata)
These two are pioneer low-growing shrubs usually at high elevations in northern Europe, Lapland, Siberia and Alaska, and persisting right into the Arctic Circle. The leaves are longer than those of *S. repens*, 2.5–6cm (1–2⅓in), with a marked network of veins in the case of *S. reticulata*.

Common walnut ▼
Juglans regia
A splendid wide-crowned tree with sinuous branches.

Common walnut ▲
Juglans regia
Large pinnate entire leaves with usually 7 leaflets and yellow-green veins.

◄ **Common walnut**
Juglans regia
(Summer)

◄ **Common walnut**
Juglans regia
(Autumn/Winter)

Walnuts

There is something aristocratic about a walnut tree; it offers only the very best both in timber and delicious nuts. The Latin name *Juglans* means the nut of Jove or Jupiter and the name walnut is derived from the old English words meaning 'foreign nut'.

The fifteen or so different species of walnut together show a wide distribution from North and South America, China and Japan to North Asia and all over Europe.

Common or English walnut
(Juglans regia)

This is the best-known species, a broad-crowned tree up to 23m (75½ft) in height, with light-grey, rugged bark, fissured between fairly broad plates. In common with all the walnuts it has the interesting special characteristic of air-pockets in the pith, so-called chambered pith, which can be seen clearly if a twig is split open.

New growth is easily damaged by frost but fortunately spring flushing is very late, the flowers and leaves not breaking out until late May or early June; when the foliage is young it is of a beautiful reddish-brown colour which does not give way to green until the large alternate pinnate leaves, 20 to 40cm (8–16in) long with 3 to 9 (usually 7) smooth-edged leaflets are well expanded. The mature leaves smell acrid when crushed and the sap from them stains the hands.

The male catkins are fat, 5–8cm (2–3⅛in) long, reddish at first but turning yellowish green before they fall, but the female flowers are very small, yellow-green and found in small clusters of from 2–5 at the end of some of the younger twigs.

The delicious nuts are large, 3–5cm (1⅙–2in) diameter and only about 90 per kg (40 per lb) and are always much in demand, for pickling, before the shells harden, and for dessert, cake decorations and flavouring. Surprisingly the largest orchards of English walnut are found in California.

Walnut timber, in varying shades of brown colour, and patterned with streaks and curves of both lighter and darker shades, is strong, tough, elastic and highly valued for furniture and gun-butts. The beautifully grained 'burr-walnut' fetches

Above: A bole of common walnut (*Juglans regia*) showing the grey bark deeply fissured into a typical pattern of hard, irregular ridges.

Right: A flowering twig of the common walnut (*Juglans regia*) with small female flowers developing amidst the coppery young leaves (at the top of the picture) and an immature male catkin forming lower down on the twig.

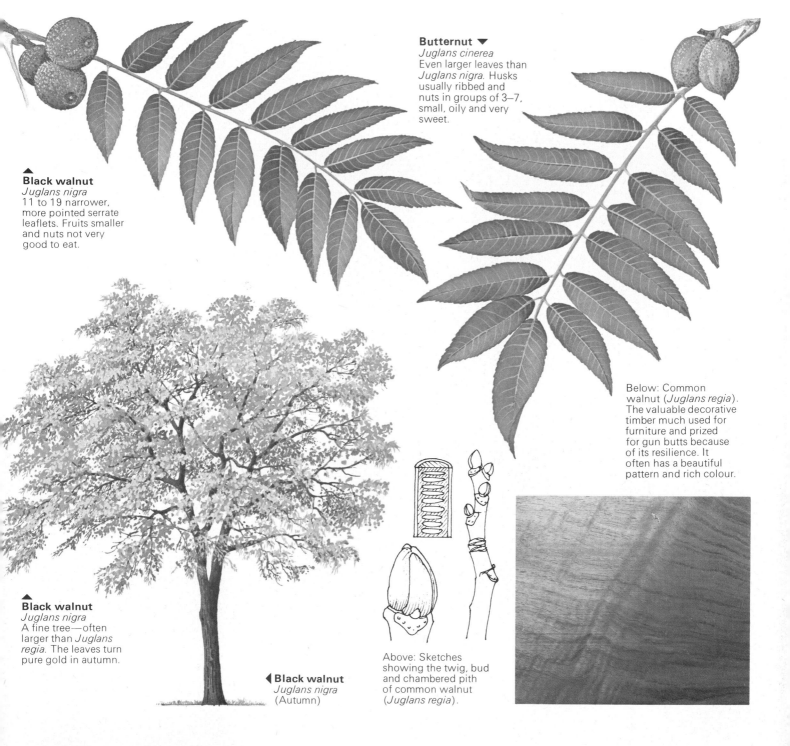

Butternut ▼
Juglans cinerea
Even larger leaves than
Juglans nigra. Husks
usually ribbed and
nuts in groups of 3–7,
small, oily and very
sweet.

▲
Black walnut
Juglans nigra
11 to 19 narrower,
more pointed serrate
leaflets. Fruits smaller
and nuts not very
good to eat.

▲
Black walnut
Juglans nigra
A fine tree—often
larger than *Juglans
regia*. The leaves turn
pure gold in autumn.

◄ **Black walnut**
Juglans nigra
(Autumn)

Above: Sketches
showing the twig, bud
and chambered pith
of common walnut
(*Juglans regia*).

Below: Common
walnut (*Juglans regia*).
The valuable decorative
timber much used for
furniture and prized
for gun butts because
of its resilience. It
often has a beautiful
pattern and rich colour.

very high prices as veneer; these burrs are large swellings on the trunk caused by abnormal cambium growth owing to infection by fungi, bacteria or other agents. This is an interesting example of diseased wood being more valuable than healthy timber. The best burr veneers come from *Juglans regia* trees in the Caucasus.

The finest nuts come from the French special clones such as the 'Franquette' cultivar, and there is a cut-leaved cultivar of common walnut called 'Laciniata'.

Black walnut
(Juglans nigra)
An American tree, now introduced into many other countries, the black walnut is hardier, taller (up to 33m; 108ft) and less spreading than the common walnut and has larger leaves (30–50cm; 12–20in) with many more leaflets: 11–23, averaging 15. The nuts are much inferior to those of the common walnut and the timber, though very good and strong, has less beautiful markings and grain.

There is a fine cut-leaved cultivar called 'Laciniata'. Hybrids have been made between common walnut and black walnut under the general name of *Juglans × intermedia*, but most of them have inferior nuts.

Butternut
(Juglans cinerea)
Another American species, this has sweet and oily nuts and leaves even larger than those of black walnut—up to 80cm (32in) or more in length. The wood is lighter in colour and softer than that of black walnut.

Japanese walnut
(Juglans ailantifolia)
This Japanese species is scattered through Europe and the USA. It is a smaller tree than all the others—up to 15m (49ft) but has huge leaves up to 1m (39in) long with 11–12 leaflets, and the male catkins are up to 30cm (12in) long. A close relation, (*J. hindsii*), is a favourite tree in California.

Other species
Californian walnut (*Juglans californica*) is native to southern Carolina; Arizona walnut (*J. major*) is found in the canyons of the southwestern United States and northwestern Mexico; little walnut (*J. microcarpa*) has a wide range to the east.

Bitternut ▼
Carya cordiformis
An irregular, rather
narrow not very dense
crown. Mid-green
foliage. Trunk seldom
very stout.

Bitternut ▶
Carya cordiformis
Large leaves with
seven to nine leaflets.
Rounded ridged fruit
with thin-shelled nuts.

Bitternut ▼
Carya cordiformis
Beautiful golden
autumn colour.
Branches mainly long
and ascending, except
the lowest ones.

◀Bitternut
Carya cordiformis
(Summer)

◀Bitternut
Carya cordiformis
(Autumn/Winter)

Hickories and Wingnuts

The hickories are closely related to the walnuts—in fact the name *Carya* is from the Greek for a walnut tree—but they are more graceful, usually of narrower form and with less dense crowns.

There are about twenty-two species, nearly all from North America, where they are well represented in the large forest areas of the eastern States, but only a few of the hardiest species can withstand more vigorous climatic conditions.

An interesting distinction between the walnuts and the hickories is that if a twig of the former species is slit open with a knife it will be found to have chambered pith while in the hickories the pith is solid.

Hickory timber in America corresponds to ash in Europe and is used for the same purposes where elasticity and strength are the essential requirements, such as handles, sports gear, spokes and oars. The heartwood is reddish-brown and the sapwood almost white; the timber is rather heavier than ash. Where maximum elasticity is needed only the sapwood is used.

In general the hickories have alternate buds, compound serrate leaves with from 3–17 leaflets, the foliage giving rich golden autumn colours. Male flowers are in the form of three-pronged catkins and female flowers are clustered at the top of new shoots. The nuts are usually smaller than walnuts, often more pointed, and with four grooves or narrow wings on the husks.

Five main species are described here.

Bitternut

(Carya cordiformis)

This tree is one of the hardiest of all the hickories. It is the commonest in America, ranging all over the central and eastern states and as far north as Quebec and northern Wisconsin. Its special feature is its curving yellow winter buds. The leaves have 7–9 sub-sessile leaflets, the middle pair the longest, turning golden in autumn; the bark is finely ridged.

Pecan

(Carya illinoensis)

A large and splendid tree but the least hardy of all the hickories, this is a native of the Mississippi basin and difficult to grow at all in Europe further north than central France. The oblong nuts are delicious and always in great demand.

The leaves are very large—up to 80cm (32in) long with 13–17 graceful curving leaflets; the bark is rough and fissured.

Mockernut or bigbud hickory

(Carya tomentosa)

As the common names indicate, the bud is large, $2 \times 1\frac{1}{2}$cm ($\frac{4}{5} \times \frac{3}{5}$in), or even larger, and densely hairy and the nuts, 3–4cm ($1\frac{1}{6} \times 1\frac{1}{2}$in) in diameter, are very often empty. The large leaves, up to 50cm (20in), are fragrant, turn deep gold in autumn and have 7 leaflets. Its timber is of high quality and the bark is only slightly fissured. Mockernut is widely distributed in southeastern USA, particularly in the Mississippi, Missouri and Ohio basins.

Shagbark hickory

(Carya ovata)

This tree is native to eastern USA and the mountains of northeast Mexico. As its name implies, it is the bark that makes this species easy to identify; at about 25 years it starts becoming shaggy and flaking; on old trees it is quite amazing,

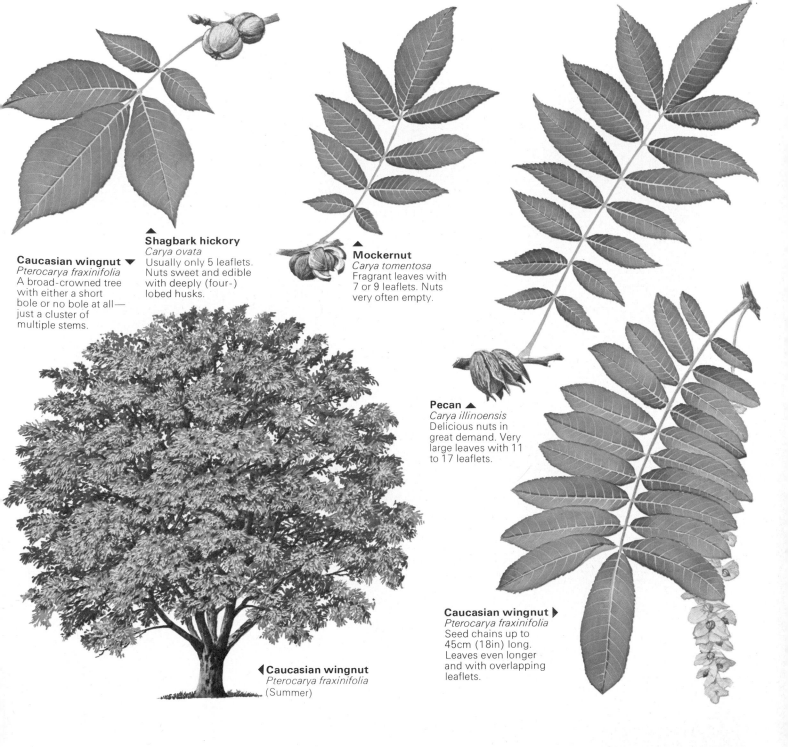

Caucasian wingnut ▼
Pterocarya fraxinifolia
A broad-crowned tree
with either a short
bole or no bole at all—
just a cluster of
multiple stems.

Shagbark hickory
Carya ovata
Usually only 5 leaflets.
Nuts sweet and edible
with deeply (four-)
lobed husks.

Mockernut
Carya tomentosa
Fragrant leaves with
7 or 9 leaflets. Nuts
very often empty.

Pecan ▲
Carya illinoensis
Delicious nuts in
great demand. Very
large leaves with 11
to 17 leaflets.

◀ **Caucasian wingnut**
Pterocarya fraxinifolia
(Summer)

Caucasian wingnut ▶
Pterocarya fraxinifolia
Seed chains up to
45cm (18in) long.
Leaves even longer
and with overlapping
leaflets.

with tattered strips curling away in all directions—a feature that may help to prevent squirrels getting the nuts too easily. The leaves are large, 45–65cm (18–26in), the leaflets rather hard and thick and usually 3 to 5 in number. The nuts are very good to eat and about 4cm (1½in) in diameter.

Big shell bark hickory
(Carya laciniosa)
The bark of this species flakes away in curiously overlaid curving scales, narrower than in *C. ovata*. Its leaves are particularly large, up to 80cm (32in), turn yellow in autumn, and usually have 7 leaflets. The nuts are similar to those of *C. ovata* but not so good to eat. It is native in the USA, from western New York to Iowa and from Michigan to Tennessee.

The wingnuts belong to the walnut family (Juglandaceae) and the twigs have the same type of chambered pith. They have large pinnate leaves, sometimes up to 60cm (24in) long, the toothed leaflets varying from 5 to 27 in number; the small

male and female flowers are on separate catkins, the female ones much longer than the males, forming a conspicuous and very characteristic feature of the species. The trees are a very striking sight when festooned with their long greenish-yellow catkins and have been rather neglected for ornamental planting, but their trunks tend to be rough and divided and of little value for timber.

There are eight species, six from China, one Japanese and one from the Caucasus.

Caucasian wingnut
(Pterocarya fraxinifolia)
This is the most widely used species and the largest growing (up to 31m; 101½ft). Its female catkins lengthen up to as much as 50cm (20in) before the autumn. The leaves, up to 60cm (24in) long, have from 9–27 crowded overlapping leaflets, shiny green above and paler beneath.

Other species
In Japan, *P. rhoifolia* is one of the finest trees in the Mt Hakkoda area where it reaches 30m (98ft) in height and grows to

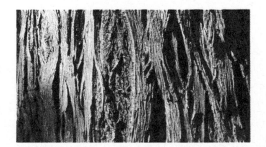

Above: Shagbark hickory (*Carya ovata*). This remarkable bark curls away from the trunk in a pattern of thin strips and plates.

an elevation of 1,220m (4,000ft). The two main species in China are *P. hupehensis* of the western mountains and *P. paliuris* of the central areas. The latter has remarkable circular winged seeds up to 7cm (2¾in) in diameter, looking like little cymbals.

The hybrid wingnut, *Pterocarya × rehderana* (a cross between *P. caucasica* and *P. stenoptera*) from the Arnold Arboretum, USA, is an excellent ornamental species with particularly prolific catkins.

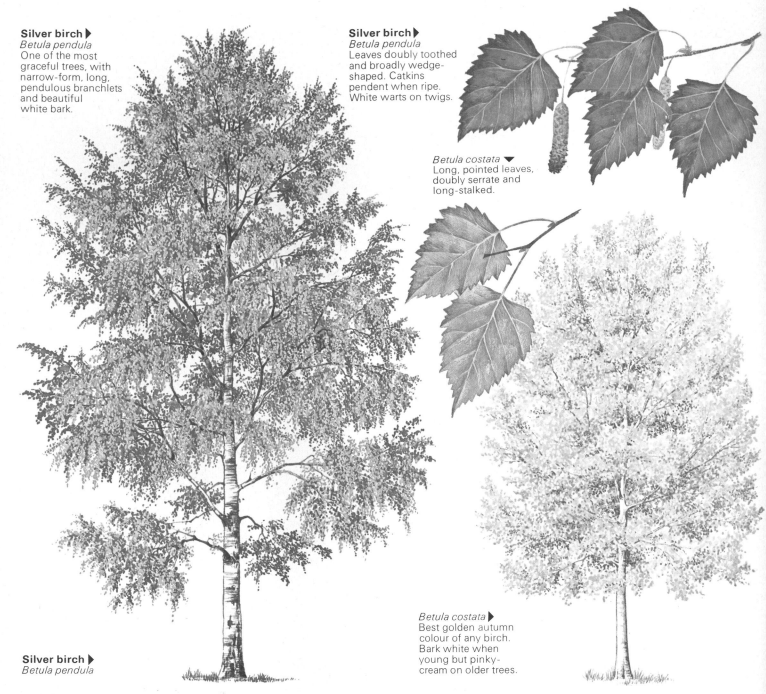

Silver birch ▶
Betula pendula
One of the most
graceful trees, with
narrow-form, long,
pendulous branchlets
and beautiful
white bark.

Silver birch ▶
Betula pendula
Leaves doubly toothed
and broadly wedge-
shaped. Catkins
pendent when ripe.
White warts on twigs.

Betula costata ▼
Long, pointed leaves,
doubly serrate and
long-stalked.

Silver birch ▶
Betula pendula

Betula costata ▶
Best golden autumn
colour of any birch.
Bark white when
young but pinky-
cream on older trees.

Birches

There are over 40 species of this genus in Europe, Asia, the Himalayas and North America; some grow even within the Arctic Circle in Iceland, Greenland and Alaska. All have their flowers in catkins, the males drooping, the females upright; the seeds are small, often 3 million per kg (1,400,000/lb); the leaves are alternate. The strikingly white bark, unusually tough and waterproof, is the dominant feature of many birches and has been used by mankind for thousands of years for a remarkable range of purposes, such as portable canoes by American Indians, roofing tiles by the Lapps and Norwegians, leggings by the Lapps, tanning Russian leather, Swiss Alpenhorns, and writing paper, baskets and boxes.

Most birch timber is strong, fairly hard but easily worked, variable in colour from white to brown and used for such purposes as plywood, veneers, turnery, furniture, carvings and boxes, and for firewood in Canada, Scandinavia and the Alpine regions of Europe. Two particularly popular and valuable types are the black

Above: Paper birch (*Betula papyrifera*). The bole has very white, horizontally peeling bark, usually with pinkish markings.

and brown flecked 'masur' birch of Sweden and the wavy grained 'flamy' birch.

Silver birch

(*Betula pendula* syn. *B. verrucosa*)

Common in Europe and Asia, this species grows to 30m (98ft), having a narrow form, branches ascending when young but pendulous later, twigs with whitish warts, and doubly serrate pointed leaves. The white or pinkish-white bark is often marked with black diamond-shaped ridges low on older trunks. In winter the twigs make a lovely purple haze against the sky.

'Dalecarlica', a Swedish cultivar of silver birch, has a narrow form, ascending branches, long pendulous twigs and deeply cut long-pointed leaves. 'Youngii' (syn. *Betula pendula* 'Pendula') is a grafted round-headed pendulous form.

Downy or white birch

(*Betula pubescens*)

Similar to the silver birch in size and distribution, the downy birch differs as follows: the branches are less pendulous and the twigs are hairy, not warty; the bark is whiter at middle age and without the

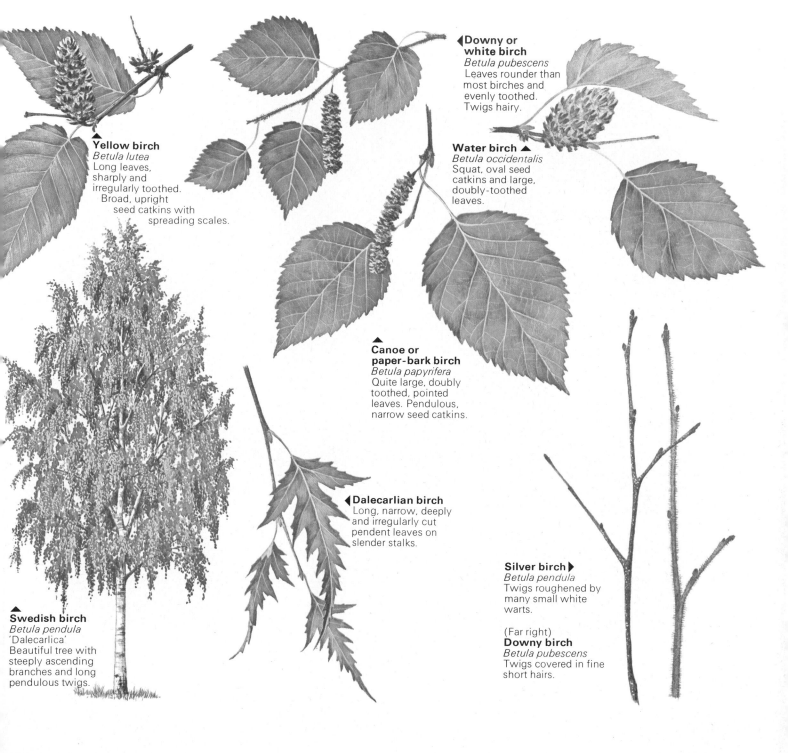

▲ Yellow birch
Betula lutea
Long leaves, sharply and irregularly toothed. Broad, upright seed catkins with spreading scales.

◀ Downy or white birch
Betula pubescens
Leaves rounder than most birches and evenly toothed. Twigs hairy.

Water birch ▲
Betula occidentalis
Squat, oval seed catkins and large, doubly-toothed leaves.

▲ Canoe or paper-bark birch
Betula papyrifera
Quite large, doubly toothed, pointed leaves. Pendulous, narrow seed catkins.

◀ Dalecarlian birch
Long, narrow, deeply and irregularly cut pendent leaves on slender stalks.

Silver birch ▶
Betula pendula
Twigs roughened by many small white warts.

(Far right)
Downy birch
Betula pubescens
Twigs covered in fine short hairs.

▲ Swedish birch
Betula pendula 'Dalecarlica'
Beautiful tree with steeply ascending branches and long pendulous twigs.

black diamonds; the leaves are rounder, more evenly serrated, and on downy stalks.

Canoe or paper-bark birch
(Betula papyrifera)
This is the canoe birch of the American Indians. It grows to 40m (131ft) tall and has smooth, peeling bark varying from cream to orange-pink, often strongly marked by horizontal bands; the leaves, 4–10cm (1½–4in), have stout hairy stalks. The timber is good and has a wide range of uses.

Japanese red birch or Maximowicz's birch
(Betula maximowicziana)
A fine vigorous tree, up to 30m (98ft) tall, this has the largest leaves of any birch (8–14cm × 6–11cm; 3⅛–5½ × 2⅓–4⅓in), shaped like lime leaves. The male catkins grow to 9–14cm (3½–5½in), the females 3–7cm (1⅙–2¾in), in racemes of two to four. The reddish bark becomes greyer with age.

Erman's birch
(Betula ermanii)
This native of Japan, Manchuria and northeast Asia grows to 30m (98ft) tall. It has broad cylindrical catkins and leaves

6–9cm (2⅓–3½in) long. The bark is white in young trees, turning pinkish with horizontal stripes and shredding off later.

Yellow birch
(Betula lutea syn. B. alleghaniensis)
This species from eastern North America, grows to 30m (98ft) tall. The shoots have a characteristic scent of oil of wintergreen when crushed. The leaves, 8–11cm × 4–6cm (3⅛–4⅓in × 1½–2⅓in), pointed and doubly serrated, turn bright yellow in autumn. The bark is silvery-yellow, peeling to show golden-brown. The timber is good, light to reddish-brown in colour, strong, tough often with nice grain, and much used for doors, interior trim and furniture.

Water birch
(Betula occidentalis syn. B. fontinalis)
A native of the west coast of North America from Canada to California, liking wet sites, this small, often bushy, tree (5–10m; 16½–33ft) has broad, ovate, doubly serrate leaves 2–5cm (⅘–2in), and squat catkins.

River birch
(Betula nigra)
An eastern USA species growing to 30m

(98ft) tall, river birch is distinguished by its bark—silvery brown at first then dark blackish-red-brown, flaking off in rolls and tatters from both trunk and branches. Its glossy green leaves have markedly double-serrate margins.

Betula costata
The special features of this handsome Asian birch are its very white bark and the wonderful deep gold colour of its leaves in autumn.

Cherry or sweet birch
(Betula lenta)
This tree from the northeastern USA gets its name from its reddish-brown bark, rather like that of a cherry; it is aromatic when young. The finely serrate leaves are edged with whisker-like points and turn orange and gold in autumn. In common with yellow birch, the shoots of *B. lenta*, are a source of oil of wintergreen.

Dwarf birch
(Betula nana)
This round-leaved bush extends from northern Asia and Europe right up to the Arctic Circle in Greenland and Alaska.

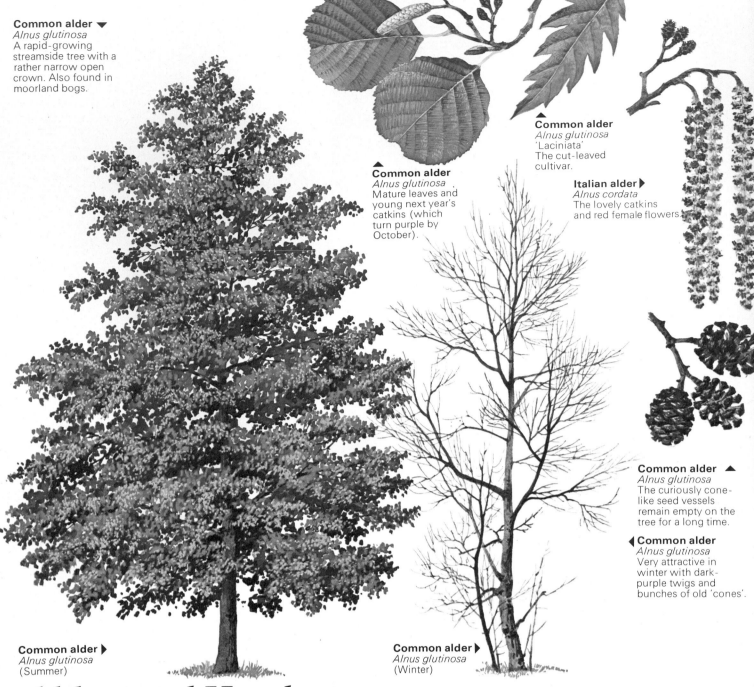

Common alder ▼
Alnus glutinosa
A rapid-growing
streamside tree with a
rather narrow open
crown. Also found in
moorland bogs.

Common alder ▲
Alnus glutinosa
Mature leaves and
young next year's
catkins (which
turn purple by
October).

Common alder
Alnus glutinosa
'Laciniata'
The cut-leaved
cultivar.

Italian alder ▶
Alnus cordata
The lovely catkins
and red female flowers.

Common alder ▲
Alnus glutinosa
The curiously cone-
like seed vessels
remain empty on the
tree for a long time.

◀ **Common alder**
Alnus glutinosa
Very attractive in
winter with dark-
purple twigs and
bunches of old 'cones'.

Common alder ▶
Alnus glutinosa
(Summer)

Common alder ▶
Alnus glutinosa
(Winter)

Alders and Hornbeams

A genus of about 30 species growing mainly in the northern hemisphere, alders are associated with streamsides and other wet sites. The buds form on short stalks and the rounded leaves are alternate; the fruit is a small, woody ovoid, cone-like in structure and very persistent on the twigs. Nodules caused by nitrogen-fixing bacteria, *Schinzia alni*, form on the roots. When a tree is felled the cut end turns bright orange-red. Several species tend to throw up suckers from the roots. The timber is soft but lasts well in water.

Common or black alder

(Alnus glutinosa)

Native throughout Europe, and North Africa, this streamside tree grows to about 28m (92ft) tall with ascending branches and usually narrow form. It has purplish buds on short stalks, broad leaves up to 7×10cm ($2\frac{3}{4}$–4in) with rounded apex and wavy, shallow-toothed margin. The male catkins 6–12cm ($2\frac{1}{3}$–$4\frac{3}{4}$in), several together, are purple in winter, turning yellow tinged crimson when ripe; the female flowers are dark red 5–6mm ($\frac{1}{5}$–$\frac{1}{4}$in) long,

in short, erect small clusters; seeds form in a hard woody cone 10–18mm ($\frac{2}{5}$–$\frac{2}{3}$in) long. The grey-brown bark is shallowly fissured on older trees. The timber, creamy when fresh but quickly turning light reddish-brown, is used for waterside structures, clogs, turnery and carving, and for making charcoal to be used in gunpowder.

Himalayan alder

(Alnus nitida)

This fine alder, up to 35m (115ft) tall, is used as a timber tree in the Himalayas. It has ovate leaves 8–16cm ($3\frac{1}{8}$–$6\frac{1}{4}$in) long, and flowers in the autumn, with male catkins up to 16cm ($6\frac{1}{3}$in); the fruits are erect, 2–4cm ($\frac{4}{5}$–$1\frac{1}{2}$in) long.

Green alder

(Alnus viridis)

A small bushy species growing in central European mountains, with clumps of erect hazel-like stems.

Italian alder

(Alnus cordata)

Native to Corsica and southern Italy, this is the most handsome of all the alders, growing to 27m ($88\frac{1}{2}$ft) tall, with beautiful

shining green leaves, fine pink and gold male catkins and bright crimson little female flowers.

It will grow on drier sites than the common alder and is well worth planting, both for forestry and as an amenity tree.

Red or Oregon alder

(Alnus rubra syn. A. oregona)

Common right down the west coast of North America from Alaska to California, this is a smaller tree than *A. cordata*. The buds are red usually, though on some trees they may be mostly green, and the ovate, bluntly pointed leaves have finely toothed edges. It is a useful soil improver and nursery species but is less reliable than the grey alder, *Alnus incana*.

Grey alder

(Alnus incana)

Native to Europe, the Caucasus and eastern North America, this is a hardy species, tolerating colder sites than most alders. Its leaves are distinct: ovate, coarsely toothed, dull green above, greyish beneath, often with pubescent surfaces, sometimes pointed, sometimes rounded.

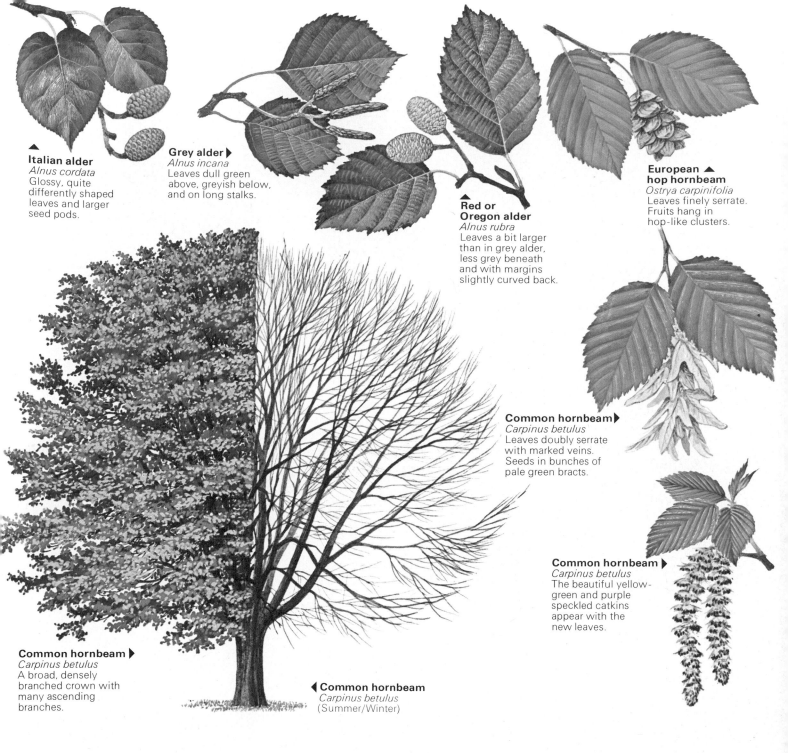

Italian alder
Alnus cordata
Glossy, quite differently shaped leaves and larger seed pods.

Grey alder ▶
Alnus incana
Leaves dull green above, greyish below, and on long stalks.

▲ **Red or Oregon alder**
Alnus rubra
Leaves a bit larger than in grey alder, less grey beneath and with margins slightly curved back.

European ▲
hop hornbeam
Ostrya carpinifolia
Leaves finely serrate. Fruits hang in hop-like clusters.

Common hornbeam ▶
Carpinus betulus
Leaves doubly serrate with marked veins. Seeds in bunches of pale green bracts.

Common hornbeam ▶
Carpinus betulus
A broad, densely branched crown with many ascending branches.

◀ **Common hornbeam**
Carpinus betulus
(Summer/Winter)

Common hornbeam ▶
Carpinus betulus
The beautiful yellow-green and purple speckled catkins appear with the new leaves.

A genus of about 20 species, hornbeams grow in the northern temperate zone and are at their best in rich soil on low ground. Superficially they are similar in appearance to birches, but they have readily distinguished characteristics. The alternate leaves are sharp-pointed and finely serrated; the catkins are enclosed in buds during the winter; the small nut-like fruits are enclosed in three-pointed bracts that hang in bunches. The boles, which are elliptical rather than circular, tend to become fluted. The timber is very hard, horny and cross-grained.

Common hornbeam
(Carpinus betulus)
Native to Europe and Asia Minor, this species grows to about 25m (82ft) tall, with sinuous ascending branches and an irregular crown. The bark is silver-grey striped with fawn, and develops rather large flat ridges; the boles of old trees are deeply fluted, eccentric and twisted. The slender buds are closely appressed and sharp pointed; the leaves are oblong-obovate, pointed, 7–10cm ($2\frac{3}{4}$–4in) long,

sharply double-toothed, with about 15 pairs of conspicuous parallel veins, becoming golden in the autumn; abundant yellow-green catkins 3–10cm ($1\frac{1}{6}$–4in) long, appear in spring. The fruit forms in hanging clusters of green bracts, 3–3.5cm ($1\frac{1}{6}$–$1\frac{3}{8}$in) long, enclosing ribbed nutlets (6–8mm; $\frac{1}{4}$–$\frac{5}{16}$in).

The greyish-cream timber, very hard and tough, was once used for such things as ox-yokes, cogs for watermills, and butchers' blocks, or dyed black as an ebony substitute. Common hornbeam was often grown as coppice for firewood.

There are many cultivars of this species, including two good street trees: 'Fastigiata' syn. 'Pyramidalis' of pyramidal form with many ascending branches, and 'Columnaris' of very narrow form.

American hornbeam
(Carpinus caroliniana)
An eastern North American tree seldom above 13m ($42\frac{1}{2}$ft) tall, this species has characteristics similar to common hornbeam but is broader in form and has oval buds and very attractive autumn colours.

Hop hornbeams
Trees in this group are very like hornbeams but the catkins are naked in winter and the nutlets are enclosed in bladder-like sheaths.

Eastern hop hornbeam
(Ostrya virginiana)
This is a round-topped tree up to 9m (30ft) found mainly in dry soils of eastern North America. The bark is reddish-brown and shaggy in appearance; the timber, often called ironwood, is hard and heavy.

European hop hornbeam
(Ostrya carpinifolia)
From southern Europe and Asia Minor, up to 20m ($65\frac{1}{2}$ft) tall, this has leaves like common hornbeam, but in this case the nutlets hang in hop-like bunches about 3–6cm ($1\frac{1}{6}$×$2\frac{1}{3}$in) long.

Japanese hop hornbeam
(Ostrya japonica)
Though very like the European species, this is a much larger tree, up to 32m (105ft) tall, whose timber is valued in Japan for furniture and flooring. It has densely pubescent twigs.

143

Common hazel ▲
Corylus avellana
Twigs hairy, leaves orbicular with
short points and irregular teeth.

Filbert ▲
Corylus maxima
Larger in both leaf
and nut than common
hazel. Nuts enclosed
by bracts.

Beaked hazel ▲
Corylus cornuta
Leaves slightly smaller
than in filbert but
bracts extend in a long
point beyond the nut.

Purple-leafed filbert ▲
Corylus maxima
'Purpurea'
Has very dark purple
leaves and contrasts
well with other shrubs.

◀ **Common hazel**
Corylus avellana
Many stemmed when
grown as coppice.
Good yellow and
brown autumn colours.

Common hazel ▶
Corylus avellana
(Autumn/Winter)

Hazels

Fifteen species of this genus of deciduous trees and shrubs occur in the northern temperate regions. They all have alternate, toothed leaves, male and female flowers on the same tree, with all male flowers in pendent catkins.

Turkish hazel
(Corylus colurna)
A fine tree, native to southeastern Europe and Asia Minor, the largest of the group and of stately pyramidal form, Turkish hazel grows up to 25m (82ft) tall. It has brown scaly bark, large leaves up to 14cm (5½in) long and clusters of edible nuts covered by whiskery husks. It should be more widely planted.

Chinese hazel
(Corylus chinensis)
Another large tree, this is similar to Turkish hazel but native to central and western China.

American hazel
(Corylus americana)
This shrub, up to 4m (13ft), from eastern North America, is very like common European hazel described below but has poorer, slightly flattened nuts enclosed in very long involucres.

Common European hazel or cobnut
(Corylus avellana)
Native to Europe, Western Asia and North Africa, this small tree has been the friend of man since prehistoric times because it has yielded various woody products he has needed for his survival: weapons (such as spears), firewood, roofing material, fish traps, wattle for the 'wattle and daub' panels used in cottages and farm buildings, interwoven hurdles, fencing poles and flower stakes. It has also been valuable for its nut crop and as cover for game birds. For hundreds of years it has been treated as a coppice crop, cut on a rotation at about seven year intervals, thus supplying a continuous harvest of small pole material, and incidentally the ideal conditions for the growth of bluebells, primroses, wood anemonies, red campions, and many other plants; it is sad that such forestry methods are now seldom practised and hurdle-making is a vanishing craft.

The small brown ovoid buds of common hazel are set on distinctly hairy twigs opening to give irregularly toothed, rounded leaves 5–9cm (2–3½in) long, downy on both surfaces. In their short, unopened form the male catkins can be seen all the winter and in January, growing up to 7cm (2¾in) long, pale yellow with golden pollen blowing in the wind. The female flowers are plump little upright greenish buds 3–5mm (⅛–⅕in) long, tipped with vivid crimson styles; the nuts, one to four together, each in a leafy cup, are pale green at first, ripening to golden brown.

Filbert
(Corylus maxima)
Native to southern Europe, this tree closely resembles common hazel, except that it grows taller and has larger superior nuts enclosed in very long husks. There are various special strains planted for nut crops in southern Europe and in California, and a purple-leaved cultivar ('Purpurea') known as purple hazel.

Beaked hazel
(Corylus cornuta syn. *Corylus rostrata)*
This shrub from eastern and central USA

Left: A coppiced growth of common hazel (*Corylus avellana*). Though never a true timber tree, common hazel has great importance in the forest and folk history of Europe because it was encouraged, and indeed planted, over wide areas of woodland. The owner of a hazel coppice cut one seventh of it every year and used the harvest for firewood, stakes for fences and plants, and poles for odd jobs. The fresh green stems were woven in the fields to make hurdle fences. Now no longer grown commercially, hazel coppices persist to provide havens for wild flowers and ground cover for birds escaping from their predators.

Below: The bark of older hazel stems is marked by a network of fissures and ridges.

Right: Common hazel (*Corylus avellana*). The beautiful male catkins that open in early spring on bare branches. Throughout the winter these catkins can be seen in their compact, unopened form, but once open they become much more conspicuous as the familiar yellow 'lamb's tails', releasing clouds of pollen in the wind. The female flowers, by contrast, are tiny, green, bud-shaped structures with crimson stigmas at their tips. During the summer they expand rapidly to become groups of nuts, each white-fleshed with a brown shell.

Far right: A close view of hazel male catkins showing the clusters of yellow-tipped stamens.

seldom grows above 3m (10ft) high, with the special characteristic of long, bristly, beaked husks protruding 2–4cm ($\frac{4}{5}$–1$\frac{1}{2}$in) beyond the nuts.

Corkscrew hazel
(Corylus avellana 'Contorta')
A slow-growing shrub with strangely twisted twigs and branches, this is used for ornamental planting.

Common beech ▶
Fagus sylvatica
A truly magnificent
tree with a dense
rounded crown, wide-
spreading branches
and excellent autumn
colours.

▲ Common beech
Fagus sylvatica
The oval bright green
leaves have wavy
margins and prominent
veins. Nuts in prickly
husks.

Common beech ▶
Fagus sylvatica
(Summer)

Common beech ▶
Fagus sylvatica
(Autumn/Winter)

Beeches

There are only ten species in this genus, all growing in northern temperate regions, but they include some very important trees both from the commercial aspect and for amenity purposes. All are deciduous, the leaves, developing from long, slender buds are alternate and parallel-veined, and in most species turn an attractive bronze colour in autumn. The male flowers open in bunches on slender stalks, and the nuts form in four-lobed woody husks. The bark is smooth and the dense, even-grained timber is very valuable.

Common beech

(Fagus sylvatica)

This splendid tree, a native of Europe, has long and with good reason been called the 'Queen of the Forest'. Growing to over 40m (131ft) tall, with stately form and huge domed crown, it is indeed a magnificent sight with great silver-grey branches spreading from its sturdy buttressed bole up into the dense upper greenery and, on old open-grown trees, outwards to form a great circle of deep shade as much as 35m

(115ft) in diameter. In the past many trees were pollarded, resulting in a very short bole and many heavy branches, but when grown under expert forest management beech will provide long clean trunks of perfect timber, straight-grained and free from knots. Characteristically the wood is pinkish-buff, speckled with small darker brown flecks, even-grained, with no very marked difference between the spring and summer wood. It is fairly hard, strong, easily worked and much in demand for furniture, especially chairs, flooring, handles and turnery, veneers, plywood, and modern densified boards; and of course for making excellent firewood.

The slender, long-pointed, red-brown buds are 1.5–2cm ($\frac{3}{5}$–$\frac{4}{5}$in) long and the leaves emerge a lovely fresh green edged with delicate silver hairs; when mature they are obovate, 4–8cm × 3–6cm (up to $3\frac{1}{8}$ × $2\frac{1}{3}$in) with well-marked parallel veins and slightly wavy edges.

Flowering occurs in May, just as the leaves expand, the males being in the form of little golden tassels on long stalks while

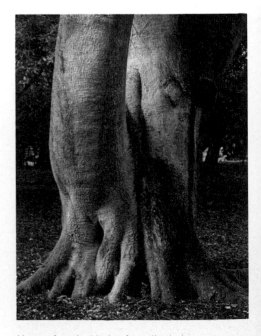

Above: A typical bole of a pollarded common beech. Algae give the bark a green tinge.

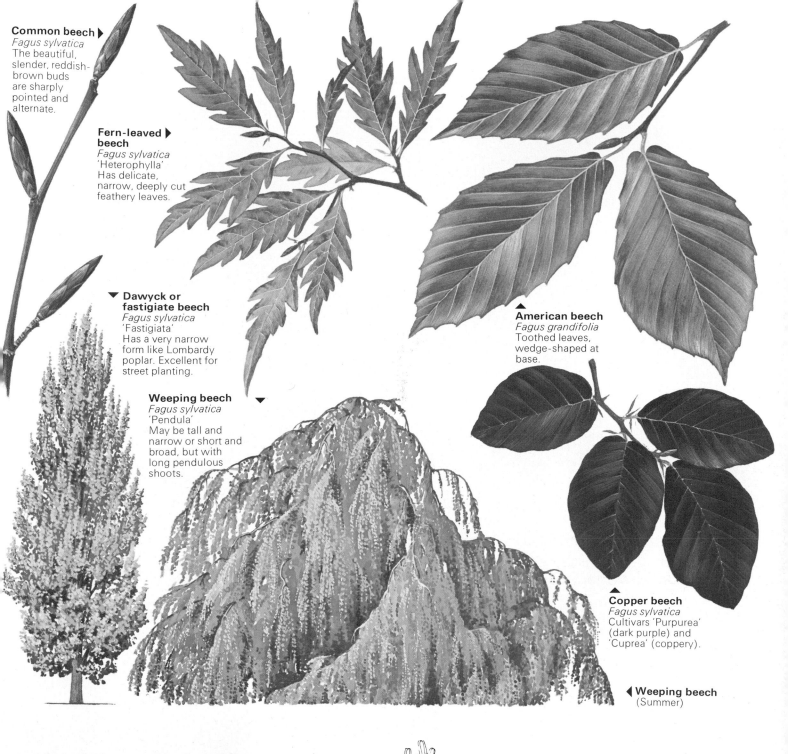

Common beech ▶
Fagus sylvatica
The beautiful,
slender, reddish-
brown buds
are sharply
pointed and
alternate.

Fern-leaved ▶
beech
Fagus sylvatica
'Heterophylla'
Has delicate,
narrow, deeply cut
feathery leaves.

▼ **Dawyck or**
fastigiate beech
Fagus sylvatica
'Fastigiata'
Has a very narrow
form like Lombardy
poplar. Excellent for
street planting.

Weeping beech ▼
Fagus sylvatica
'Pendula'
May be tall and
narrow or short and
broad, but with
long pendulous
shoots.

▲ **American beech**
Fagus grandifolia
Toothed leaves,
wedge-shaped at
base.

▲ **Copper beech**
Fagus sylvatica
Cultivars 'Purpurea'
(dark purple) and
'Cuprea' (coppery).

◀ **Weeping beech**
(Summer)

Left: Flowers of common
beech, females upright
and inconspicuous,
males pendent and
plentiful.
Note the new leaves
edged with silver hairs.

Right: Details of common
beech flowers; male
(top) with numerous
stamens, female
(bottom) with three-
lobed styles.

the females are more upright, on shorter
stouter stalks, with fine silver filaments
tinged with pink and green.

Beech nuts, collectively known as
'mast', are triangular, short-pointed 1.5–
2cm ($\frac{3}{5}$–$\frac{4}{5}$in) long, shining brown and
usually develop two to each husk; the
husks are four-lobed and covered with
short prickles.

Common beech does well on chalk and
limestone soils where it is often the climax
species. Its foliage is dense, casting a deep
shade so that the ground beneath is usually
bare of vegetation. It is a favourite species
for avenues, large gardens and parks.

There are several cultivars, only some of
which are described here.

Copper beech 'Cuprea', and **purple**
beech 'Purpurea'. These two common
and conspicuous forms have, respectively,
coppery-red and dark purple leaves; both
have weeping varieties.

Fern-leaved beech 'Heterophylla': A

Left: A sample of prepared beech timber showing
its warm colour and attractively flecked even
grain. Beech is an important wood for furniture.

Left: New Zealand black beech (*Nothofagus solandri*), one of several species of southern beeches native to the southern hemisphere. This evergreen species forms a broad-crowned tree with a short thick bole when open grown, but develops a long clean trunk when grown in a close-spaced plantation. (Southern beeches are featured on page 244).

Below: Spring in a beechwood (*Fagus sylvatica*). This is one of the most beautiful of all sylvan scenes, with delicate green foliage contrasting with sunlit patches on the rich brown forest floor. In a beech tree's crown the slender twigs run side by side, so close that their foliage forms a dense canopy that intercepts almost every ray of sunlight. Even diffuse light is cut down to about a fifth of that outside the wood, and this dense shade does not allow any green plants to thrive on the forest floor. Forest folk-lore asserts that the drip of rain from beech leaves poisons plant growth below, but what really happens is that the ground is starved of life-giving light.

Above: Nuts of the sweet chestnut (*Castanea sativa*). An opened burr showing silky silver lining and the poorly developed nuts typical of colder climates. The old styles can be seen still bunched on the tips of the nuts.

Below: Bark of the sweet chestnut (*Castanea sativa*). Showing the beautiful network of hard heavy ridges, usually spirally arranged.

handsome and graceful tree with long leaves deeply cut into narrow pointed lobes giving a fern-like appearance.

Weeping beech 'Pendula': An eye-catching tree with long weeping shoots.

Dawyck or fastigiate beech 'Fastigiata': A remarkable variety with narrowly ascending branches giving a form like Lombardy poplar; very suitable for street planting.

Contorted beech 'Tortuosa': A rare form with contorted stem and branches.

American beech

(Fagus grandifolia syn. *F. ferruginea)*

The only beech native to America, where it is found mainly in the eastern area, this is a fine tree, almost as large as common beech, with larger, more pointed leaves up to 13cm (5in) long with coarsely serrate edges and silver-grey bark, often blotched with dark patches. Sucker growth is common in this species. The timber is similar to common beech.

Oriental beech

(Fagus orientalis)

Native to Asia Minor, Persia and Bulgaria, this species is of similar size to common beech but has a more upright form, a fluted bole, darker grey bark and more pointed leaves. The timber is good but the fluting results in more waste.

Chinese beech

(Fagus englerana)

This beautiful tree, seldom above 20m (65½ft) tall, is from central China. It has very slender long buds, sea-green leaves with deckled wavy edges, turning to fine orange, brown and gold autumn colours.

Japanese beech

(Fagus japonica)

This grows up to 25m (82ft) tall, but with a short bole quickly dividing into large branches. The nuts protrude beyond the husks for about two-thirds of their length.

Siebold's beech

(Fagus crenata syn. *sieboldii)*

Another Japanese species larger than *F. japonica*, this has a longer, straighter trunk and yields good timber. It is closely allied to common beech but is distinguished by long strap-like bristles at the base of the nut husks.

Sweet Chestnuts

Ten species of this genus grow in the temperate regions but the devastating chestnut blight bark disease (*Endothea parasitica*) has already virtually wiped out the American *Castanea dentata* and is a serious threat to the others; it is already in Italy and Spain and may spread through France to Britain. All species prefer warm sites and grow best on light soils and southern aspects.

Sweet chestnuts are stately trees that live to five hundred years or sometimes longer. The timber of young trees is tough and durable but in older trees it deteriorates and becomes of little use except as firewood. The bark starts smooth and brown, but soon splits into longer spiralling fissures. The nuts, growing in sharp-prickled husks, two or three together, are large and in warm climates provide a popular and highly nutritious food.

Sweet or Spanish chestnut

(Castanea sativa)

A native of southern Europe, western Asia and North Africa, this large handsome tree grows to 35m (115ft) tall with

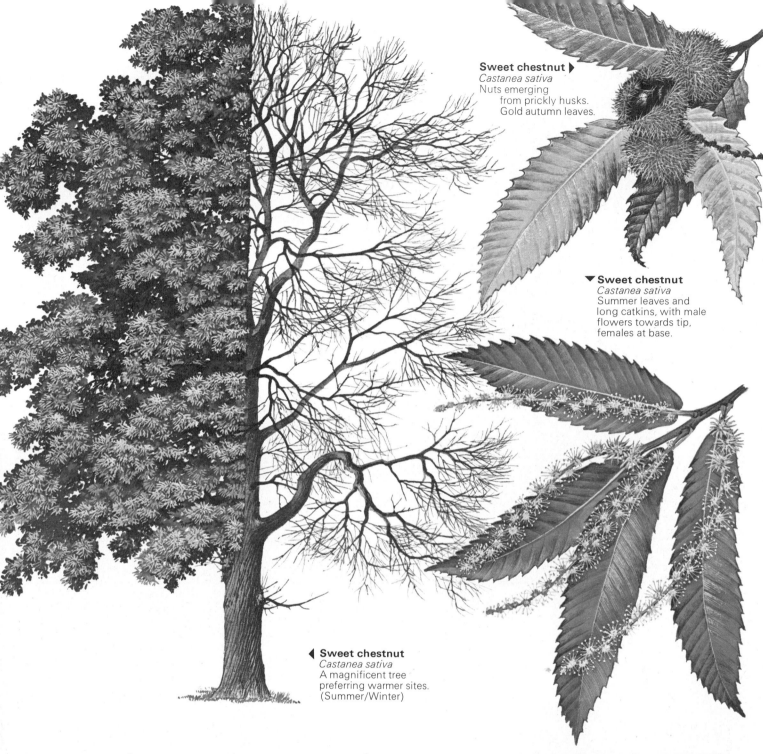

Sweet chestnut ▶
Castanea sativa
Nuts emerging
from prickly husks.
Gold autumn leaves.

▼ **Sweet chestnut**
Castanea sativa
Summer leaves and
long catkins, with male
flowers towards tip,
females at base.

◀ **Sweet chestnut**
Castanea sativa
A magnificent tree
preferring warmer sites.
(Summer/Winter)

girths up to 13m (42½ft). It was introduced to Britain by the Romans because polenta (chestnut meal) was a staple ration for their soldiers. The bark is deeply fissured into long ridges, often spirally arranged. It has large, glossy green, hard texture leaves, 14–20cm × 5–9cm (up to 8 × 3½in), sharply serrate and with prominent parallel veins. The heavily scented, cord-like, pale yellow catkins, 16–25cm (6⅓–10in) long, appear in summer; the glossy brown nuts, held in tough prickly green husks are eaten raw, roasted, boiled or crystallized into 'marrons glacés'.

The light brown timber may be offered as 'oak' but is not so strong and lacks the medullary rays that give oak its beautiful grain. Large trees are very liable to 'ring-shakes', which ruin the timber when sawn up, but this tree is usually grown as coppice on a 10 to 15 year rotation and converted into cleft fencing material, hop-poles, and similar products.

Chinese chestnut
(Castanea mollissima)
This species from China and Korea grows to about 20m (65½ft) and is the most resistant to chestnut blight. Both leaves and nuts of the Chinese chestnut are smaller than those of *Castanea sativa*.

Japanese chestnut
(Castanea crenata)
A small Japanese tree, also fairly resistant to blight, with leaves nearly as large as in *C. sativa* but having grey down on the underside. The original stock has poor nuts but special strains have been developed, giving excellent crops widely used in Japan.

Golden chestnut
(Castanopsis chrysophylla syn. Chrysolepis chrysophylla)
Native to Oregon and California, this evergreen tree grows to 40m (131ft) with very large girths and is not as severely affected by the blight as *C. dentata* or *C. sativa*. It takes two years to ripen and the leaves, 5–14cm (2–5½in) long, are coated with minute golden scales beneath. The native name is 'Chinquapin' meaning chestnut, which it is indeed, although botanists have called it *Castanopsis*.

Above: Sweet chestnut stakes, to be used for 'chespaling' fencing. Repeated coppicing of sweet chestnut trees results in the growth of a bundle of pole-like branches. These are cut off at regular intervals, cleft into triangular stakes and finally bound with wire.

Common oak ▼
Quercus robur
A broad-crowned,
heavy-branched tree
with a stout trunk.

▲ **Common oak**
Quercus robur
Acorns borne on
long stalks, leaves
are stalkless.

Common oak ▶
Quercus robur
(Summer)

Red oak ▶
Quercus rubra
(Autumn/Winter)

Oaks

There are over 300 species of oak in the northern temperate regions, as well as many hybrids and special clones. Most oak species share the following characteristics. They all have seeds in the form of acorns but these vary greatly in size, shape and form of the cups. The buds are usually in clusters, often with several about the same size, resulting in the numbers of large irregular branches that give most oaks their characteristic rugged crowns. The male flowers develop in the form of drooping catkins, with fewer females, on short stalks, erect above the males.

The tough, exceptionally strong timber is brownish, with a small amount of whitish less durable sapwood, and usually has the distinctive feature of conspicuous 'medullary rays', which show clearly on the cross section of a log as paler lines radiating from the central core, and give the timber the beautiful grain pattern so often seen on good furniture.

The few oaks selected for description here start with some major timber trees.

Common or pedunculate oak
(Quercus robur syn. *Quercus pedunculata)*
A large tree, up to 37m (121ft) tall, native to Europe, the Caucasus, Asia Minor and North Africa, this familiar species often lives for 500 years and even, rarely, to 1,000 years; it has a large, spreading crown, often wider than tall, with massive twisting branches which made it the best species for the 'crucks' and curves needed for wooden-frame houses and ships. The leaves have a somewhat wavy surface, often bunched together, auricled at the base, oblong-obovate 8–12cm ($3\frac{1}{8}$–$4\frac{3}{4}$in) long, with four to six pairs of rounded lobes and a very short stalk—(3–7mm; $\frac{1}{8}$–$\frac{1}{4}$in). The flowers appear in April or May, the males in green clusters on a hanging stalk 5–7.5cm (2–3in) long, the females on short erect stalks above the male catkins, and the acorns, 2–4cm ($\frac{4}{5}$–$1\frac{1}{2}$in) long, often develop in pairs, with 3–7cm ($1\frac{1}{6}$–$2\frac{3}{4}$in) stalks and shallow cups.

The demand for this excellent timber tree far exceeds the supply and many of our forest economists are too shortsighted to see that in a hundred years time it will have extreme rarity value.

Sessile or durmast oak
(Quercus petraea syn. *Quercus sessiliflora)*
This has much the same native distribution as *Q. robur* but tends to prefer higher ground. Its leaves are flatter, more leathery, less bunched, and have five to nine pairs of rounded, less deeply cut

Below: A cross-section of common oak (*Quercus robur*), showing the conspicuous medullary rays.

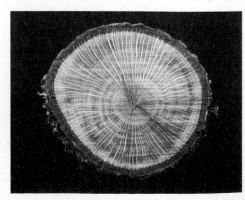

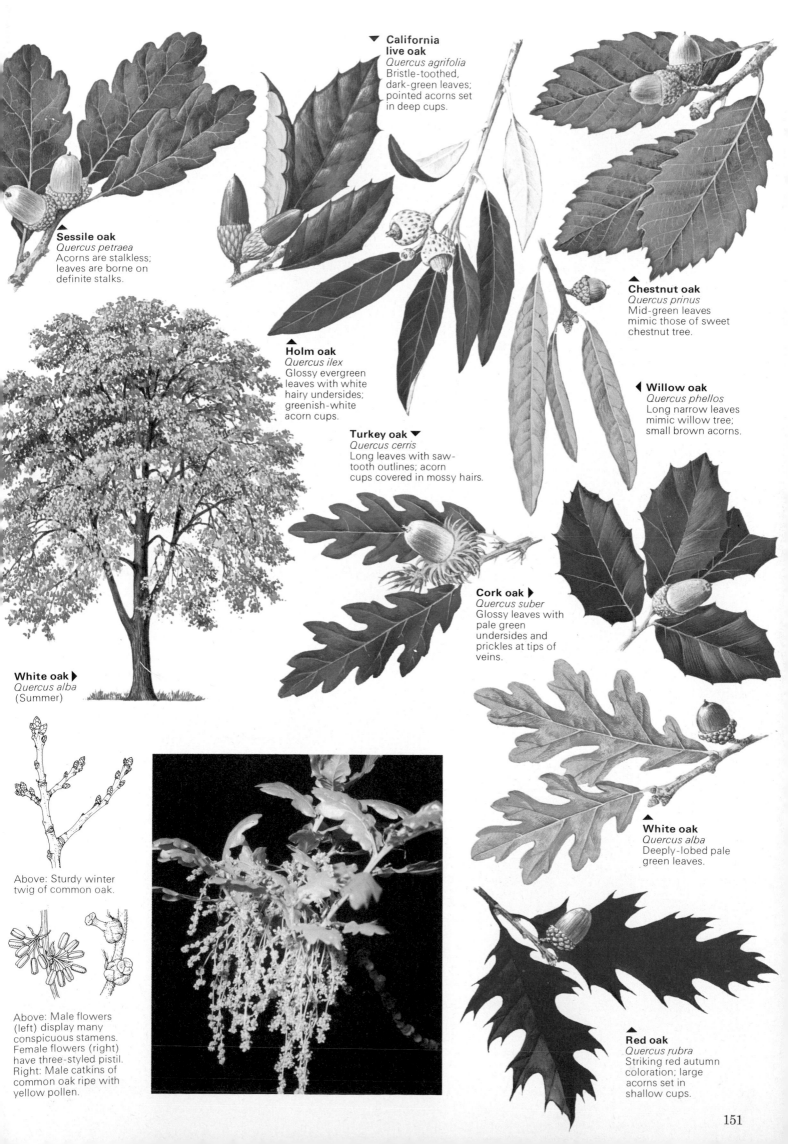

California live oak
Quercus agrifolia
Bristle-toothed,
dark-green leaves;
pointed acorns set
in deep cups.

Sessile oak
Quercus petraea
Acorns are stalkless;
leaves are borne on
definite stalks.

Chestnut oak
Quercus prinus
Mid-green leaves
mimic those of sweet
chestnut tree.

Holm oak
Quercus ilex
Glossy evergreen
leaves with white
hairy undersides;
greenish-white
acorn cups.

Willow oak
Quercus phellos
Long narrow leaves
mimic willow tree;
small brown acorns.

Turkey oak ▼
Quercus cerris
Long leaves with saw-
tooth outlines; acorn
cups covered in mossy hairs.

Cork oak ▶
Quercus suber
Glossy leaves with
pale green
undersides and
prickles at tips of
veins.

White oak ▶
Quercus alba
(Summer)

White oak
Quercus alba
Deeply-lobed pale
green leaves.

Above: Sturdy winter
twig of common oak.

Above: Male flowers
(left) display many
conspicuous stamens.
Female flowers (right)
have three-styled pistil.
Right: Male catkins of
common oak ripe with
yellow pollen.

Red oak
Quercus rubra
Striking red autumn
coloration; large
acorns set in
shallow cups.

lobes, on leaf stalks 1–2cm ($\frac{2}{5}$–$\frac{4}{5}$in) long; the acorns have no stalks. It is less frequently found in old forests because its smaller, straighter branches made it less suitable for the curved timber required in the past, and its smaller crop of acorns provided less mast for foraging pigs. Now, however, when rapid straight growth is required by the timber trade, durmast oak is planted. Its timber is almost identical to that of common oak and it is the main species in several European forests.

White oak
(Quercus alba)
This magnificent tree, up to 45m (147$\frac{1}{2}$ft) tall, from eastern and central USA produces splendid timber, very similar to that of *Quercus robur*, and is a major species over large areas of American forests. The large leaves, 8–12cm (3$\frac{1}{8}$–4$\frac{3}{4}$in) broad by 16–20cm (6$\frac{1}{3}$–8in) long, narrow sharply towards the stalk, and have four to six pairs of round-ended lobes glossy green above, whitish underneath, turning to a purple colour in the autumn. The acorns are about 2cm ($\frac{4}{5}$in) long in shallow cups.

Red oak
(Quercus borealis syn. Quercus rubra)
Native and widespread in Canada and northeastern USA, red oak grows up to 40m (131ft) tall. The large oblong leaves 12–24cm (4$\frac{3}{4}$–9$\frac{1}{2}$in) long, with acute points on the variable-sized lobes, start bright-yellow in the spring, usually becoming a fine deep red in the autumn but this is variable; some trees remain dark brown. It is a fast-growing tree, with annual shoots up to 2m (6$\frac{1}{2}$ft). It yields good pale reddish-brown timber, straight-grained and easy to cleave but not quite so strong as *Quercus robur* or *Quercus alba*.

Burr oak
(Quercus macrocarpa)
This is another large and widely distributed North American species that provides timber very similar to *Q. alba*. On good sites it may reach 52m (170$\frac{1}{2}$ft) with straight trunk and diameter up to 2m (6$\frac{1}{2}$ft). Its special feature is its broadly ovate chestnut-brown acorns, 2.5–5cm (1–2in) long,

finely pubescent at the apex and set in cups with a fringe of hairs round the top and pointed, raised scales. The leaves are very large 15–26cm (6–10$\frac{1}{4}$in), and irregularly lobed.

Japanese oak
(Quercus mongolica)
Native to Japan, Korea, northern China and eastern Siberia, this tree grows to a height of about 30m (98ft) and provides the Japanese oak timber so widely imported and now easier to obtain than common oak, *Quercus robur*. It has coarsely toothed oblong-obovate leaves 10–20cm (4–8in) long, on short stalks and crowded at the ends of the twigs; the acorns have a fringed cup. The timber is excellent, a little softer and straighter grained than common oak without such a beautiful figure when quarter-sawn, but widely used for furniture and flooring. The top-grade timber comes from a variety, *Quercus mongolica* var. *grosseserrata*, a rather taller, straighter tree, up to 40m (131ft), with smaller leaves and fringed acorn cups.

Chestnut or tanbark oak
(Quercus prinus)
A handsome round-headed tree, up to 30m (98ft) tall, chestnut oak is native to central and southern USA. The leaves 10–18cm (4–7in) long by 4–8cm (1$\frac{1}{2}$–3$\frac{1}{8}$in) wide, resemble those of sweet chestnut but the lobes are more rounded and less sharp pointed, with 10 to 14 parallel veins, and maturing to rich crimson colours in autumn; the ovoid acorns are 2.5–3.5cm (1–1$\frac{3}{8}$in) long. The brown timber is hard and heavy, and the bark is rich in tannin.

Post oak
(Quercus stellata)
Common in south-central and south-eastern USA, this tree seldom reaches 30m (98ft). The large, broad leaves (10–20cm × 5–10cm; up to 8×4in), have two or three pairs of broad lobes of which the centre pair is much the largest. It is slower-growing than *Q. alba* but has equally good timber with a wide range of uses.

The following group includes interesting

or ornamental species which are not notably good for timber.

Holm oak
(Quercus ilex)
This southern European tree is one of the most widely used evergreen oaks and grows up to 30m (98ft) with a broad-domed very dense crown and usually large low branches. Its bark is blackish brown, shallowly fissured into small rectangular plates. The terminal buds have some curled whiskers and the leaves are dense on the twigs, very variable in size and shape, lanceolate or oval, entire or toothed, wavy-edged or flat and anything from 3–12cm (1$\frac{1}{6}$–4$\frac{3}{4}$in) long. In late June, when the new leaves have just emerged, the tree is a dull gold colour but for the rest of the year dark green. It survives well near the sea. The small acorns 1.5–2cm ($\frac{3}{5}$–$\frac{4}{5}$in) long are often half-enclosed in the cup of felted scales.

Cork oak
(Quercus suber)
The thick soft outer bark of this medium-sized tree from southern Europe and North Africa is still the world's main source of cork. The outer bark is carefully harvested from the standing trees and grows again and again at intervals of eight to ten years for further supplies. Soon after stripping, the trunks turn a rich red colour and look most remarkable. The hard, oblong-ovate evergreen leaves are lustrous dark green above with whitish pubescence below, the margins wavy with shallow spine-tipped lobes.

Natural and variable hybrids occur between *Quercus suber* and *Quercus cerris* —these are called 'Spanish oak' (*Quercus* × *hispanica*) and are usually semi-evergreen and have harder bark than *Quercus suber*. One such hybrid quite often seen is the ornamental Lucombe oak (*Quercus* × *hispanica* 'Lucombeana').

Willow oak
(Quercus phellos)
A deciduous tree up to 30m (98ft) tall from eastern USA, with ascending branches and a domed crown. Its special feature is its

Left: Golden oak (*Quercus robur* 'Concordia') an attractive small tree with yellow leaves throughout summer.

Below: Common oak (*Quercus robur*). A splendid light-brown timber with great strength.

Right: Common oak (*Quercus robur*). Late summer in an oak woodland composed principally of mature pollarded trees about 150 years old.

Below: Sessile or durmast oak (*Quercus petraea*). Winter twigs and buds, which are large and ovoid, orange-brown with dark tips.

narrow, entire, willow-like leaves, 5–12cm (2–4¾in) long and about 1.5–2cm (⅗–⅘in) wide, pointed at both ends which turn pale-yellow in autumn. Its small acorns, about 1cm (⅖in) long with shallow cups, take two years to ripen. The timber is coarse-grained, pale reddish-brown, strong and used locally for general rough work.

Scarlet oak
(Quercus coccinea)

Another American species, sometimes confused with red oak, this is a smaller tree. The leaves also are smaller than in red oak, on longer stalks with about three widely spaced, pointed lobes cut in nearly to the midrib, and have more regular deep-red autumn colouring which starts irregularly over the tree. The small acorns develop in shallow, large-scaled cups.

Turkey oak
(Quercus cerris)

Native to southern Europe and southwest Asia this vigorous tree, up to 40m (131ft) tall, is slender when young but broadly domed in maturity. The pale brown buds are pubescent and surrounded by long, twisted whiskers, and the thin narrow-oblong, rough-surfaced leaves are 7–15cm (2¾–6in) long, with a variable number of quite deeply-cut lobes. Yellowish male catkins 5–7cm (2–2¾in) long, grow in bunches; sessile acorns develop in mossy cups with long, pale-green pointed scales.

Mirbecks oak
(Quercus canariensis syn. *Quercus mirbeckii)*

A handsome tree native to North Africa and Spain, up to 30m (98ft) tall, partly evergreen, often with some green and some brown leaves in winter. Oblong-obovate leaves vary from 8–20cm × 5–11cm (up to 8 × 4⅓in), with 6–12 pairs of small pointed lobes and red stalks.

Pin oak
(Quercus palustris)

A native of northeastern USA, up to 40m (131ft) tall, with a main stem growing well into the crown, pin oak is so-called because if often has many small, stiff, pin-like branches on its trunk and larger limbs. These produce small knots in the timber.

Live oak
(Quercus virginiana)

A massive evergreen tree typical of the lower coastal plain of southeastern USA. This species seldom grows over 20m (65½ft) tall but is often as much as 40m (131ft) wide, with a short thick bole and enormous branches which are often moss-covered. The oblong leaves are usually entire, 4–12cm (1½–4¾in) long, dark green above, and whitish below, with revolute margins. California live oak *(Quercus agrifolia)* is another evergreen species very like *Q. ilex.*

Black oak
(Quercus velutina)

Widely spread in eastern and central USA, up to 45m (147½ft) tall, this has leaves like *Q. borealis* but their autumn colour is brown. The bark is blackish-brown but the inner layer is orange and yields a yellow dye called 'quercitron'.

Chestnut oaks

Besides *Quercus prinus* described above, there are three other species whose leaves resemble those of sweet chestnut:

Japanese chestnut oak *(Quercus acutissima)* with really spiny edged leaves.

Chestnut-leaved oak *(Quercus castaneifolia)* from Persia and the Caucasus with fat acorns 2cm (⅘in) across and less spiny-edged leaves.

Chinkapin or yellow chestnut oak *(Quercus muhlenbergii)* from central-eastern USA. The leaves are without the very sharp points along the edges, and the acorns are sweeter than with other oaks.

Lastly **Maingay's oak** *(Quercus maingayi)*, native in the Malay Peninsula, should be mentioned because of its immense acorns—up to 7cm (2¾in) long.

Oaks have played a leading part in the great broadleaved forests in Europe, North America and the temperate regions of Asia and their tough timbers have been exceptionally valuable to man throughout history. Early man used the wood for roofing supports, palisades, trackways over swampy ground, bridges, and for coffins. Acorns were fed to pigs, cattle, deer, and other grazing animals.

The bark was harvested for tanning leather, and in some species cut up for cork; oak-galls were used for making writing ink. Small branch-wood and coppice poles were burnt under controlled conditions in earth-covered mounds in the forests to produce charcoal for the iron, steel, glass and gunpowder industries, as well as for special fuel, filters, rubber products and medical uses.

Cleft-oak is particularly valuable as it provided 'clapboards' (literally 'cleft-boards') for cladding buildings, and material for strong baskets (called 'spelks', 'skips' or 'whiskets').

Larger branches and trunks provided the beams, often curved, for countless timber-framed houses and farm buildings, as well as for the magnificent roof trusses in nearly all the early great buildings.

Lastly we come to that very special use for oak that was to affect the destinies of man so much—the construction of the strong sea-going ships that opened up exploration of so many lands—the 'Hearts of Oak' ships whose immensely strong timbers, again often curved, came from the great forests of England. There is no other timber comparable to oak for these great ships.

Oaks are also of great ecological significance—woods and forests of the deciduous species of oak are unusually rich in variety of species, not only of plants, but of mammals, birds, insects and fungi; it is therefore of great importance that we do not allow purely economic pressures to ruin these exceptional nature reserves.

Several factors, all favouring a rich ecology, contribute to the special value of oakwoods in this respect. The crowns are fairly open so that the trees do not cast a heavy shade; in the past many oakwoods were run on a coppicing rotation, thus providing very different shade conditions in different years.

◀ English elm
Ulmus procera
A truly magnificent
tree.

▲ English elm
Ulmus procera
Harshly rough leaves.
The small seeds are
seldom fertile and
often not central in
the membranes.

◀ English elm
Ulmus procera
(Summer)

◀ Wych elm
Ulmus glabra
Autumn/Winter

Elms

There are about 20 species of this genus in the northern temperate regions but as there are many hybrids and special clones exact identification is difficult. Only a few of the best known examples can be dealt with here. They all have alternate leaves, usually rough to the touch, lop-sided at the base, and almost all are deciduous. In some species the twigs tend to develop corky winged ridges.

A point of special interest is that several species only rarely produce fertile seeds and are propagated instead by sucker growth with the result that their characteristics do not vary by cross-fertilization and their offspring are remarkably uniform. The development of prolific suckers from the roots makes elms particularly suitable for hedgerows because they can be constantly increased without replanting; also, having large crowns, they are good shade and shelter trees for cattle.

Nearly all elms yield valuable timber, usually in large sizes. Tragically the so-called "Dutch" elm disease has devastated the elms in many countries.

English elm

(Ulmus procera syn. *Ulmus campestris)*
A magnificent, tall, stately tree up to 40m (131ft) high with girths to 7m (23ft) or more; it develops a large-domed crown with lesser domes on the ends of large ascending branches. Unfortunately it is not very deep-rooted and is therefore liable to be thrown by gales, especially on wet sites. It was probably brought to England at the time of the Anglo-Saxon settlements about AD 500 and became for centuries one of the main features of hedgerows and parklands. The English elm, once very popular, has been widely planted throughout Europe and America.

The small, ovoid, dark brown winter buds are only 2–3mm (up to $\frac{1}{8}$in) long; the darkish green leaves are doubly toothed, with a very rough upper surface, strongly marked parallel veins, lop-sided at base, variable shape and size, 4–8cm (1½–3⅛in) long, usually fairly orbicular but shortly pointed. The red stamens of the small flowers massed on the bare twigs give a crimson haze against the sky in late

Above: English elm (*Ulmus procera*). The mature bark is hard, grey-brown and deeply fissured into a pattern of irregular plates.

February to mid-March, developing later into bunches of small infertile seeds, each near the tip of a round green membrane.

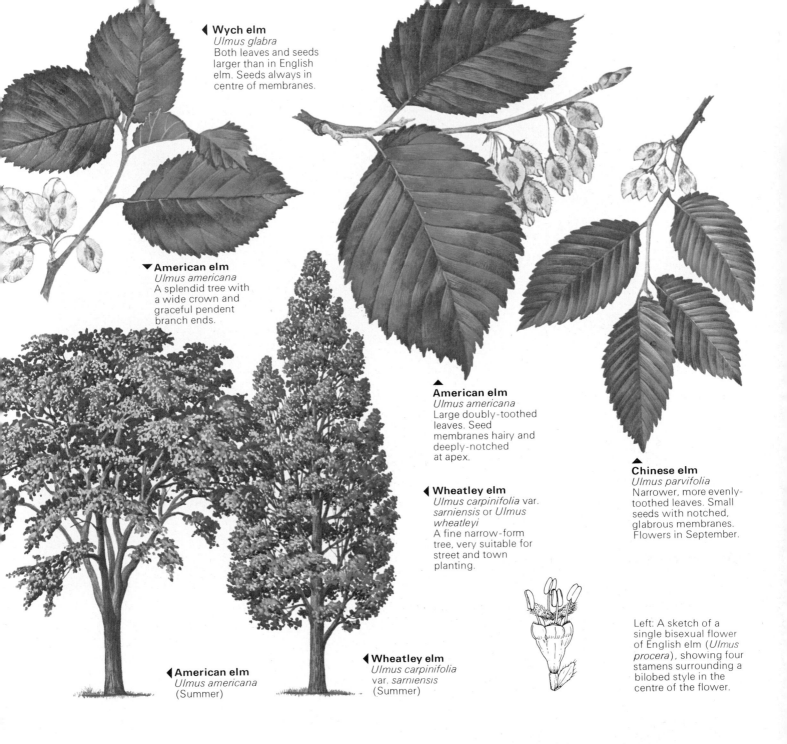

◄ Wych elm
Ulmus glabra
Both leaves and seeds larger than in English elm. Seeds always in centre of membranes.

▼ American elm
Ulmus americana
A splendid tree with a wide crown and graceful pendent branch ends.

▲ American elm
Ulmus americana
Large doubly-toothed leaves. Seed membranes hairy and deeply-notched at apex.

◄ Wheatley elm
Ulmus carpinifolia var. *sarniensis* or *Ulmus wheatleyi*
A fine narrow-form tree, very suitable for street and town planting.

▲ Chinese elm
Ulmus parvifolia
Narrower, more evenly-toothed leaves. Small seeds with notched, glabrous membranes. Flowers in September.

◄ American elm
Ulmus americana
(Summer)

◄ Wheatley elm
Ulmus carpinifolia var. *sarniensis*
(Summer)

Left: A sketch of a single bisexual flower of English elm (*Ulmus procera*), showing four stamens surrounding a bilobed style in the centre of the flower.

The dark, grey-brown bark is deeply fissured into short irregular plates and the valuable brown timber, with creamy sapwood, is well-known for its toughness, durability when wet, and coarse irregular grain, which gives strong resistance to splitting. It is available in large sizes and always in great demand for a wide range of uses, including water pipes (in former days), coffins, wheel hubs, sea groynes, lock construction, chair seats and other furniture. Many an 'oak' beam in old houses was in fact elm! Elm burrs fetch high prices for veneer work.

Wych elm
(Ulmus glabra)
This native of Britain and western Asia has a wider, more rounded outline than English elm, with a less definite main stem and more arching branches; the bark is smoother, with longer, shallower fissures. The buds are darker and a little larger; the leaves much larger (up to 15cm; 6in). The timber is similar but has straighter grain.

Wych elm seldom produces sucker growth but its rather larger seeds are very fertile. Camperdown elm is a common, grafted, weeping cultivar with large leaves up to 20×12cm ($8 \times 4\frac{3}{4}$in) and a broad head of spreading tortuous branches.

American white elm
(Ulmus americana)
A splendid tree widely used in America, this is equal in size to *U. glabra* but the branches are gracefully pendulous; the leaves are longer and more pointed and have long stalks. The timber is good and much straighter-grained than English elm.

There are several cultivars; 'Pendula' is a favourite avenue tree.

Smooth-leafed elm
(Ulmus carpinifolia syn. *Ulmus nitens)*
Native to Europe, western Asia and North Africa this is the common elm of the European continent. Seldom as large as *U. americana* it has a much narrower, more upright form, smaller leaves and particularly long bark fissures. As its name implies, it has smoother, shinier leaves than most elms; twigs often have corky ridges, as in 'Suberosa'. Its timber is similar to that of English elm.

Above: English elm (*Ulmus procera*). Clusters of the beautiful, feathery red flowers.

At least two of its other many varieties should be noted.

Wheatley or Jersey elm
(Ulmus carpinifolia var. *sarniensis* syn. *Ulmus wheatleyi)*
This tree has a narrow-pointed pyramidal form, with many steeply ascending

Above: Smooth-leafed elm (*Ulmus procera*). Flowers just bursting from the buds; they are not quite as red as those of English elm and the white styles are distinctive.

Right: Wheatley or Jersey elm (*Ulmus carpinifolia* var. *sarniensis*). A fine row of this narrow-form tree, characterized by its steeply ascending branches and pointed crown. Widely planted as a roadside tree.

Below: A golden-leafed cultivar of English elm (*Ulmus procera* 'Louis van Houtte'). This handsome tree retains golden-yellow foliage throughout the summer and is an ideal subject for ornamental planting in parks and gardens.

branches and is very suitable for street and motorway planting. There is a golden-leaved Wheatley elm, 'Aurea', sometimes called 'Dicksonii'.

Cornish elm

(*Ulmus carpinifolia* var. *cornubiensis* syn. *Ulmus stricta*)

When young this variety is very like Wheatley elm though not so dense; in later life its rather sparse ascending branches become rounded at the top, giving the tree a narrow fan-like form with little foliage except near the branch ends: another good street tree. 'Wredei' is a golden-leaved cultivar of *U. carpinifolia* with small shiny leaves.

Dutch elm hybrids

(*Ulmus* × *hollandica*)

This large group of hybrids between *Ulmus glabra* and *Ulmus carpinifolia* is widely used in Europe. Two of the best known are described here.

Dutch elm

('Hollandica' syn. *Ulmus major*)

A large tree up to 40m (131ft) high with wide open crown and somewhat pendulous branch ends, this shoots suckers both from roots and from the upper surface of old branches. The leaves are large, up to 15 × 8cm (6 × 3⅛in), and rough. The timber is like that of English elm.

Huntingdon elm

(*Ulmus* × *hollandica* 'Vegeta')

Similar to Dutch elm in size this has straighter and more steeply ascending branches and leaves with long stalks. The flowers are larger and later than those of most elms. The timber is similar to that of other Dutch elms.

Chinese elm

(*Ulmus parvifolia*)

A native of China, Japan and Korea, this evergreen or semi-evergreen tree has very small, fairly narrow leaves, only 3–4cm (1⅙–1½in) long; it flowers in autumn.

Slippery elm

(*Ulmus rubra* syn. *Ulmus fulva*)

A native of central and eastern North America this medium-sized tree has a mucilaginous inner bark and rough leaves like those of *Ulmus glabra*. A demulcent milk-food can be made from the bark.

'Dutch' elm disease

This disease did not come from Holland and was only called 'Dutch' because most of the early research work on it was carried out in the Netherlands. It probably originated from Asia and has occurred widely in Europe, Canada and the USA. The most recent outbreak started in 1968 and is still spreading.

The die-back and death is caused by the fungus *Ceratocystis ulmi*, which is carried from tree to tree by bark beetles of the genus *Scolytus*. Spores of the fungi enter the twigs where the beetles have eaten away the bark and quickly spread through the springwood vessels, killing the affected branches, partly by a toxic substance produced by the fungi and partly by gumming up the water conduction vessels. First signs are yellowing of the foliage, often as early as June, followed by die-back of the branch starting at the twig ends which turn down forming little 'shepherds' crooks'. In severe cases the tree may die in one season, but often it takes a couple of years. If affected twigs are

cut through, the blocked vessels are shown up by dark dots and lines in the annual rings. In rare cases, a tree will become diseased and then recover.

Much work has been done on control measures but no sure cure has yet been found, although injection of control chemicals into the tree trunk has worked in some cases. Severely affected trees should be felled, branch wood and all bark from the trunk and larger branches burnt before the emergence of the adult beetles in April so as to minimize the spread of the disease. In practice, however, it has seldom been possible to do this before the epidemic has become widespread.

Much tree breeding has been done in the attempt to obtain a really resistant strain. The best so far is the 'Commelin' elm, a Dutch hybrid, but even this has not been resistant to the present strain of the disease in Britain. Until such time as better progress can be made it is wisest to replace the elms by other species such as oak, beech, ash, sycamore, chestnut, lime, grey poplar or plane.

Above: The effect of Dutch elm disease on a specimen of English elm (*Ulmus procera*). The fungus *Ceratocystis ulmi* has killed part of the tree and one year after the photograph was taken the whole tree became affected.

Right: English elm bark pecked by birds in search of the *Scolytus* beetles that form part of their diet. Although these beetles can spread Dutch elm disease, such torn bark does not necessarily mean that the tree is infected.

Below: An adult *Scolytus* beetle and several larvae in the bark of an English elm tree.

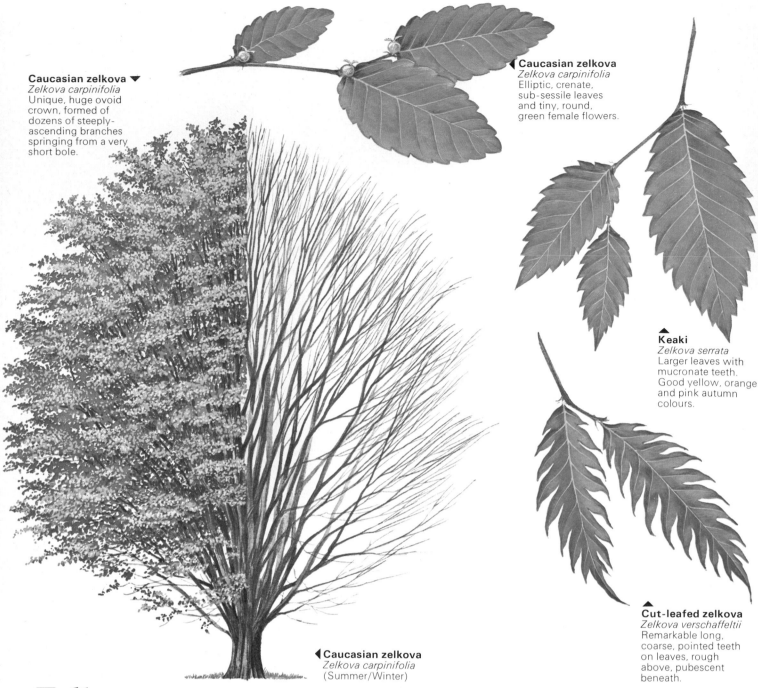

Caucasian zelkova ▼
Zelkova carpinifolia
Unique, huge ovoid
crown, formed of
dozens of steeply-
ascending branches
springing from a very
short bole.

◀ **Caucasian zelkova**
Zelkova carpinifolia
Elliptic, crenate,
sub-sessile leaves
and tiny, round,
green female flowers.

▲ **Keaki**
Zelkova serrata
Larger leaves with
mucronate teeth.
Good yellow, orange
and pink autumn
colours.

▲ **Cut-leafed zelkova**
Zelkova verschaffeltii
Remarkable long,
coarse, pointed teeth
on leaves, rough
above, pubescent
beneath.

◀ **Caucasian zelkova**
Zelkova carpinifolia
(Summer/Winter)

Zelkovas

A small group of broadleaved deciduous trees from East Asia, Crete and the Caucasus, the zelkovas are in many ways closely related to the elms but fortunately less liable to Dutch elm disease—though not completely immune.

Caucasian zelkova
(Zelkova carpinifolia syn. *Z. crenata)*

This tree from the Caucasus mountains is perhaps the best known, growing up to 35m (115ft) with a short beech-like trunk that usually divides into a mass of long, steeply ascending branches, creating a high oblong-oval bush shape. The bark is rather like beech but peels off in flakes revealing small orange-pink patches. The timber is tough, durable and of good quality but is rarely if ever exported; the form of the tree would prevent any long large balks. The alternate, acute elliptical leaves, $5–12 \times 3–6$cm (up to $4\frac{3}{4} \times 2\frac{1}{3}$in), are crenate and toothed, almost sessile, dark green above with scattered hairs, pale green beneath and more downy especially near the veins, turning to orange-brown in the autumn. The flowers are small,

greenish and inconspicuous, the fruit the size of a small pea with narrow ribs.

Keaki or Japanese zelkova
(Zelkova serrata syn. *Z. acuminata)*

A much valued timber tree in Japan and Korea, growing to 35m (115ft), this has low arching branches forming a broad, round-topped crown. The wood is often beautifully grained and used for quality furniture and cabinet work, while the normal grained trunks, being very durable, are employed for arches, gateways and pillars.

The leaves are sharply toothed, instead of crenate, more acutely pointed and tend to be pendulous. Autumn shades are very fine—mixed yellow, pink and orange.

Cut-leafed zelkova
(Zelkova verschaffeltii)

Probably of Caucasian origin, the special feature of this species is its sharply acute toothed edges of the leaves, cut much more deeply than other zelkovas.

Chinese zelkova
(Zelkova sinica)

This species is remarkable for its orange-pink bark, zigzag twigs and uncut leaves.

Above: Caucasian zelkova (*Zelkova carpinifolia*). The bole of a mature tree, showing the smooth bark with orange patches where flaking occurs.

Lastly there is *Z. cretica* from Crete, a delicate, slender small tree with drooping tips to its ascending branches and narrow leaves with small rounded notches.

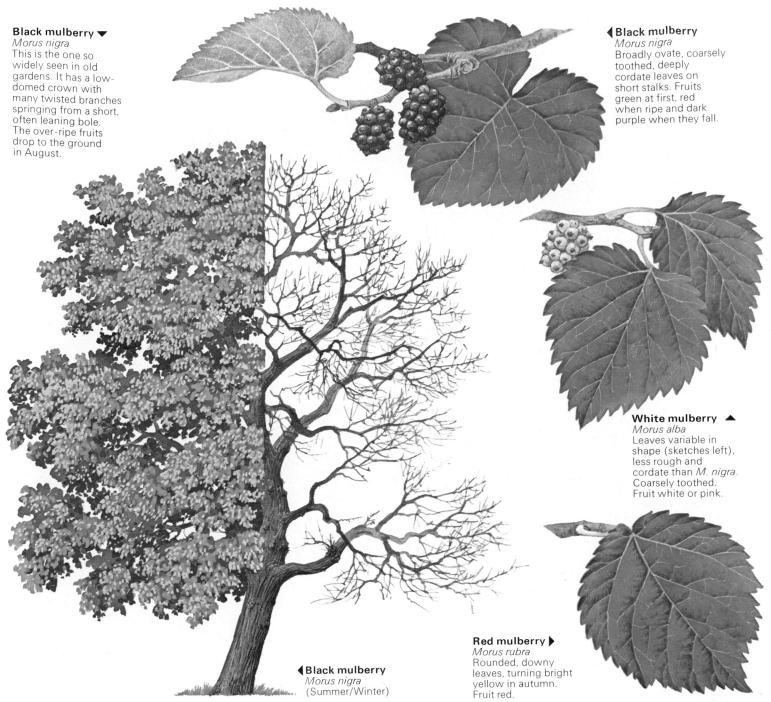

Black mulberry ▼
Morus nigra
This is the one so widely seen in old gardens. It has a low-domed crown with many twisted branches springing from a short, often leaning bole. The over-ripe fruits drop to the ground in August.

◀**Black mulberry**
Morus nigra
Broadly ovate, coarsely toothed, deeply cordate leaves on short stalks. Fruits green at first, red when ripe and dark purple when they fall.

White mulberry ▲
Morus alba
Leaves variable in shape (sketches left), less rough and cordate than *M. nigra*. Coarsely toothed. Fruit white or pink.

◀**Black mulberry**
Morus nigra
(Summer/Winter)

Red mulberry ▶
Morus rubra
Rounded, downy leaves, turning bright yellow in autumn. Fruit red.

Mulberries

The mulberries belong to the Moraceae, a huge family with over a thousand species, growing mainly in the tropics, and having the special characteristic of milky sap; figs are one of the best known members of this group.

There are about a dozen true mulberries (*Morus*) coming from China, the USA, Mexico, Iran and Russia and they are usually associated in our minds with the silk-worm industry because the caterpillars feed on their leaves.

Black mulberry
(*Morus nigra*)
Originally from Persia (Iran), this is the most widely planted mulberry. It has been cultivated for thousands of years and is a fashionable feature of large old gardens. Its cordate, hairy, crenate leaves, 8–14cm ($3\frac{1}{8}$–$5\frac{1}{2}$in) long, with stout stalks, are roughly heart-shaped but have a distinct point; deep green above, much paler beneath, they turn pale gold in autumn. The small clusters of pale greenish flowers are only about 1cm ($\frac{2}{5}$in) long and the well-known fruits, rather like rough rasp-

berries, are rather acid when red but become sweeter as they turn through dark crimson to almost black; they make a terrible mess on the ground beneath the trees. The tree has a broad rounded crown, seldom more than 12m (39ft) high and quickly develops an old, gnarled appearance, often with burrs and bosses on the trunk and larger branches; the bark is pinkish-brown and finely fissured. The timber with its deep brown heartwood and yellowish sapwood is very attractive but only available in small sizes suitable for turnery and carving.

Chinese white mulberry
(*Morus alba*)
This is a narrower, taller, faster growing tree up to 18m (59ft) high, with unusually variable leaves, sometimes like black mulberry but often with large, rounded, irregular lobes. Its pinkish-white fruits are not so good to eat as those of the black mulberry, *M. nigra*, but the leaves are the best for feeding silkworms, although in France black mulberries were often used for that purpose.

Red mulberry
(*Morus rubra*)
This species from the USA is the largest of the mulberry trees, growing up to 25m (82ft) with a diameter up to 1.5m (5ft), with a dense rounded crown, spreading branches and brown scaly bark. The fruits are mainly fed to animals and poultry.

Mexican mulberry
(*Morus microphylla*)
A much smaller tree, also from the USA and Mexico, this has small leaves only 5–7cm (2–$2\frac{3}{4}$in) long.

Russian mulberry
(*Morus antarctica*)
The hardiest of the mulberries, this has even smaller leaves than the Mexican variety.

For ornamental use some cut-leaved and weeping cultivars of several of the mulberries have been developed. Among those most widely available are cultivars of white mulberry known as 'Laciniata', 'Nana', 'Pendula' and 'Pyramidalis'.

◄ Tulip tree
Liriodendron tulipifera
Leaves seem
'cut off' at the ends.
Fruit body a
narrow erect core
of papery scales. ▶

▼ Southern magnolia or bull bay
Magnolia grandiflora
One of the finest
evergreen trees.

Cucumber tree ▶
Magnolia acuminata
Large, upright-form
tree. Foliage hides
the greenish-yellow
flowers.

Tulip tree ▲
Liriodendron tulipifera
A fine, tall tree with
bright gold autumn
colour.
(Autumn/Winter)

Magnolias and Tulip Trees

This large group of about forty species, mostly from America, East Asia and the Himalayas, includes some of the finest flowering trees; they may be evergreen or deciduous, and have large solitary terminal flowers, cone-like fruits and buds, each with a single scale.

Southern, laurel or bull bay magnolia
(Magnolia grandiflora)
This species from southeastern USA is one of the finest of all flowering evergreen trees, growing up to 24m (79ft) tall with large, rich, green, glossy leather leaves up to 24×12cm ($9\frac{1}{2} \times 4\frac{3}{4}$in), but normally about 15×7cm ($6 \times 2\frac{3}{4}$in). The fragrant creamy-white flowers, 18–25cm (7–10in) across, have six thick petals and flower from July to October. The fruits are narrowly ovoid, about 6×3cm ($2\frac{1}{3} \times 1\frac{1}{8}$in) with purple-green pubescent scales; the bark is dark greyish-green with only shallow fissures. In colder localities it is best grown against a south-facing wall.

Chinese evergreen magnolia
(Magnolia delavayi)
Another evergreen, this species is from southwest China and only grows up to about 15m (49ft) tall; it has dull, grey-green, very wide leaves about 22×16cm ($8\frac{2}{3} \times 6\frac{1}{3}$in) and much larger fruits, up to 14cm ($5\frac{1}{2}$in) long. The flowers are similar to those of *M. grandiflora* but not quite so large and the bark is lighter coloured and of a more corky consistency.

Cucumber tree
(Magnolia acuminata)
The special feature of this deciduous American tree, which reaches 30m (98ft) tall, is its curious fruit—like, small, short, upright cucumbers, about 8×4cm ($3\frac{1}{8} \times 1\frac{1}{2}$in), green at first but turning through pink to red. The greenish-yellow flowers, about 10cm (4in) across, are not very noticeable amongst the large, pointed, broadly elliptic glossy-green leaves about 20×12cm ($8 \times 4\frac{3}{4}$in).

Large-leafed cucumber tree
(Magnolia macrophylla)
Another American species, this is similar to, though smaller than *M. acuminata*, with enormous blunt-pointed, bright green auricled leaves, 20–70cm (8–27$\frac{1}{2}$in) long by 15–38cm (6–15in) wide, and larger creamy-white flowers which usually grow up to 20cm (8in) across.

Japanese magnolia
(Magnolia stellata)
With its masses of pure white fragrant flowers on the bare branches in early spring this small rounded tree, up to 2m (6$\frac{1}{2}$ft) tall, is one of the best loved of all the magnolias. Each flower has from 12 to 18 narrow petals about 4–5cm (1$\frac{1}{2}$–2in) long. It is very suitable for small gardens but is liable to frost damage owing to its early flowering.

There is a cultivar 'Rosea' which has beautiful pinkish-purple tinged petals, deeper in colour when in bud.

Lily tree or 'Yulan'
(Magnolia denudata syn. *M. conspicua)*
This beautiful Chinese species up to 15m (49ft) tall is often seen in temple gardens. Its pure white flowers open even earlier than those of *M. stellata* and are often spoilt by frost. A special feature is its winter buds which are covered with shaggy hairs.

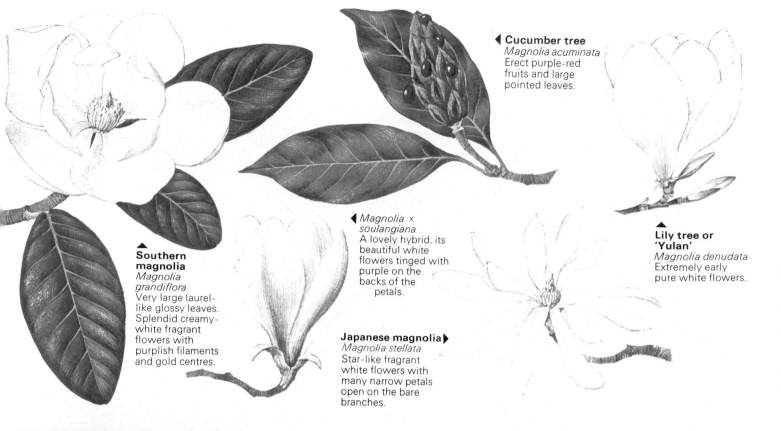

Cucumber tree
Magnolia acuminata
Erect purple-red
fruits and large
pointed leaves.

◀ *Magnolia ×
soulangiana*
A lovely hybrid, its
beautiful white
flowers tinged with
purple on the
backs of the
petals.

**Lily tree or
'Yulan'**
Magnolia denudata
Extremely early
pure white flowers.

▲ **Southern
magnolia**
*Magnolia
grandiflora*
Very large laurel-
like glossy leaves.
Splendid creamy-
white fragrant
flowers with
purplish filaments
and gold centres.

Japanese magnolia ▶
Magnolia stellata
Star-like fragrant
white flowers with
many narrow petals
open on the bare
branches.

Above: Southern magnolia (*Magnolia grandiflora*). A mature tree with dark, fairly smooth bark.

Above: *Magnolia × soulangiana*. A magnificent
specimen in full flower in a parkland setting.

Japanese big-leafed magnolia
(Magnolia obovata)
Noted for its whorls of large pale green
leaves up to 30 × 15cm (12 × 6in) and fine
fragrant white flowers up to 18cm (7in)
across, tinged with purple on the back,
this does not compete with *M. macrophylla*
for size of leaf.

Magnolia × soulangiana
This hybrid between *M. denudata* and *M.
obovata* is one of the most popular of all the
magnolias with its vigorous growth, up to
8m (26ft) high and very broad, tulip-shaped
white, rose-backed flowers starting on
bare branches but persisting until after
the leaves are out. It flowers a little later
and is therefore less often frost damaged
than some other species.

There are many special clones of this
excellent species such as 'Rustica rubra'
with rich red flowers and 'Lennei' with
larger leaves and purple-backed flowers.

**Campbell's magnolia or
'Pink lily tree'**
(Magnolia campbellii)
A magnificent Himalayan species, reaching 20m (65½ft) tall, this grows up to 3,000m
(9,840ft) elevation, with large rose-pink
flowers up to 30m (12in) across and shiny
green-grey leaves 15 × 10cm (6 × 4in).

Unfortunately it does not flower until
about 20 years old and is too early flushing
for cold districts.

Only two species of tulip tree exist, the
best known is from North America.
Tulip tree
(Liriodendron tulipifera)
This fine ornamental tree grows to a
height of 57m (187ft), with a tall, many-
domed crown and very heavy lower
branches. The bark is much-fissured when
mature, light orange-brown in colour and
often with burrs. It is an important timber
tree in America, known under various
trade names such as whitewood, canary
whitewood and yellow poplar, a yellowish
or yellow-brown wood, soft, even-grained
and a favourite for very many uses including plywood, joinery, turnery, piano parts
and when of curly grain for veneers.
Everything about the tree seems out of the
ordinary—the buds, about 1cm ($\frac{2}{5}$in) long,
are brown in colour, bloomed with lilac,
flattened with curved tips; the unique
leaves are saddle-shaped, four-lobed and
truncated at the ends, 10–15 × 15–20cm
(up to 6 × 8in) on long stalks; autumn
colour pure bright gold turning sometimes to rich brown. The flowers appear in
early summer, tulip-shaped at first, then
widening out; they have six petals 4–5cm
(1½–2in) long, pale greenish-yellow with
orange markings near the base and many
fleshy yellow stamens. The fruit is a papery,
erect, narrow-pointed cone 4–5cm (1½–2in)
long, seeds with long narrow wings. Unfortunately the trees seldom flower in the
first 15 to 20 years.

Chinese tulip tree
(Liriodendron chinensis)
This smaller species only grows to about
20m (65½ft), with more deeply waisted
leaves and rather smaller but very similar
flowers. The fruit is rather longer.

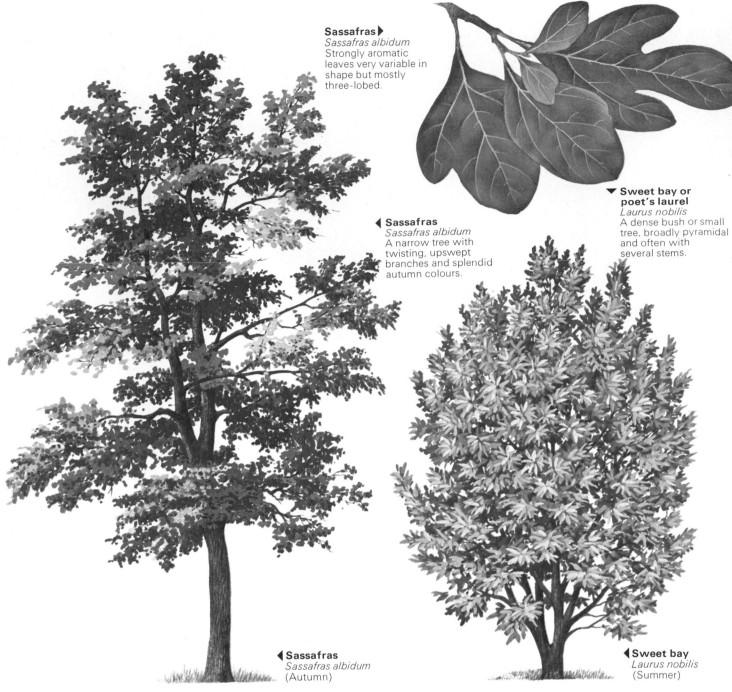

Sassafras ▶
Sassafras albidum
Strongly aromatic leaves very variable in shape but mostly three-lobed.

◀ Sassafras
Sassafras albidum
A narrow tree with twisting, upswept branches and splendid autumn colours.

▼ Sweet bay or poet's laurel
Laurus nobilis
A dense bush or small tree, broadly pyramidal and often with several stems.

◀ Sassafras
Sassafras albidum
(Autumn)

◀ Sweet bay
Laurus nobilis
(Summer)

Laurels, Sassafras and Sweet Gums

There is only one true laurel, *Laurus nobilis*, and both the common so-called laurels (cherry and Portugal) are in fact members of the great *Prunus* genus and are dealt with under that heading.

Sweet bay, bay tree or poet's laurel
(Laurus nobilis)

Native to the Mediterranean, and growing to about 18m (59ft), this is the famous species whose leaves were used to crown the heroes of olden times and are still gathered for flavouring savoury dishes and for scenting linen in drawers and cupboards with the characteristic aroma.

The dark, evergreen, leathery lanceolate leaves are finely toothed and 6–10 × 2–3cm (up to 4 × 1⅛in), often with red basal veins; the pale yellow flowers, about 1cm (⅖in) across, are produced in small umbels at the base of the leaves, the sexes being on separate trees. The fruit is a green, shiny, slightly oval berry, about 1cm (⅖in) across, turning black when ripe. On young trees the blackish-grey bark is fairly smooth but as the tree ages it gradually becomes wrinkled and cracked.

Californian laurel or Oregon myrtle
(Umbellularia californica)

The tree is called *Umbellularia* because the little yellowish-green flowers, only 5mm (⅕in) across, are borne in small umbels about 2cm (⅘in) wide. It is very similar to *Laurus nobilis* except that its leaves are narrower, of a duller greyish-green, and it is a larger species growing up to as much as 30m (98ft) tall.

The leaves are extremely pungent when crushed and if the very strong scent is inhaled it may cause quite severe head pains—in fact it is locally known as the headache tree. The timber is particularly tough and hard.

A very small group of only three species closely related to the true laurels. Only *Sassafras albidum* is at all well known.

Common sassafras
(Sassafras albidum syn. *S. officinale)*

An interesting eastern American species growing to 30m (98ft) tall with upswept twisting branches and grey bark with irregular dark fissures. Its thin, mid-green

Above: Sweet bay or poet's laurel (*Laurus nobilis*). The bole typically divides into several stems, with smooth grey bark on young trees.

Sweet bay ▲
Laurus nobilis
Berries green,
turning to shining
black.

◄ **Sweet bay**
Laurus nobilis
The leathery, crinkly-
edged leaves are
very aromatic.

◄ **Sweet gum**
Liquidambar styraciflua
The long-stalked
leaves are maple-like
but alternate. Seeds in
prickly globes.

◄ **Californian laurel**
*Umbellularia
californica*
Very pungent pointed
leaves. Flowers pale
yellowish-green in
small rounded umbels.

◄ **Sweet gum**
*Liquidambar
Styraciflua*
A fine tree with truly
remarkable autumn
colours, sometimes
wholly bright-red but
more often a wonderful
mixture of purples,
reds, orange, yellow
and green.

◄ **Sweet gum**
Liquidambar styraciflua
(Autumn)

leaves are remarkable for varying greatly in size and shape, even on the same branch, from entire simple ovals to regular three-lobed form or even lop-sided two-lobed shapes, 10–18 × 5–8cm (up to 7 × 3⅛in) on short, often red stalks; they display brilliant yellow and red autumn colours. The small yellowish-green flowers, about 8mm (5/16in) across, are in racemes 3–6cm (1⅙–2⅓in) long, male and female usually on separate trees; they are not very beautiful or conspicuous and the fruit is only a small bluish-black ovoid about 1cm (⅖in) long. The brown timber is brittle, soft and coarse-grained but resists damp well and is used for fence-posts and cooperage.

The whole tree is very aromatic; the bark and roots are sometimes used to brew a kind of tea, and oil of sassafras is used for soaps and liniments.

Sweet gums are so called because they exude a fragrant yellow resinous gum. Of the six species in this little group only three are commonly met with, the best known and by far the most widely planted

being the following American species.
Sweet gum
(Liquidambar styraciflua)
This tree grows up to 40m (131ft) tall and 2m (6½ft) in diameter in its native areas and yields the beautiful, reddish-brown timber exported under the trade name of satin walnut, to be used for furniture, joinery, veneers and barrels. The balsam resin-gum known as 'styrex' or 'storax', used for perfumes and medicines, originated from this tree, and was obtained by bruising the bark, but in more recent years most of it has come from the oriental species mentioned below. The leaves, 10–15cm (4–6in) long, with from 3 to 7 lobes, are like maple leaves but are alternate on the twigs; the yellowish-green flowers are small, in little round clusters, not at all conspicuous, and the fruits are burr-like, roundish clusters, 2–3cm (⅘–1⅙in) across when fully developed, hanging on stalks about 4–5cm (1½–2in) long, either singly or several together. The rough grey bark is much fissured between heavy ridges. This is one of the finest of all trees for autumn colours,

Above: Sweet gum (*Liquidambar styraciflua*). A striking display of autumn colours, the large leaves turning a mixture of reds, golds and greens. A wonderful tree for gardens.

showing great variation between different specimens. Some turn to a blaze of pure crimson, others give an amazing mixture of green, gold and red, or a striking blend of just red and gold. Because of this wonderful display, liquidambars are widely planted in parks and gardens of many countries.
Oriental sweet gum
(Liquidambar orientalis)
Native to Asia Minor, this tree is the main source of balsam resin and grows to 30m (98ft) with orange-brown flaking bark and five-lobed, hairless leaves on long slender stalks. It has attractive autumn colours.
Chinese sweet gum
(Liquidambar formosana)
This tree grows to about the same size as the American species and its timber has been much used for making tea chests and general local joinery. It is distinguished by its hairy young shoots and leaves, and by the heavily buttressed trunk.

London plane ▼
Platanus × hispanica
Very large trees that
succeed well in towns.
Bark flakes off leaving
creamy patches.
Seed balls remain over
the winter.

London plane ▶
Platanus × hispanica
Typical leaves and
seed balls.

Oriental plane ▼
Platanus orientalis
Typical deeply cut
leaves and seed
balls.

London plane ▶
Platanus × hispanica
(Summer/Winter)

Buttonwood ▶
*Platanus
occidentalis*
Shallow-lobed
leaves. Seed balls
less spiny.

Planes

The trees described here belong to the
Platanaceae family and are known in
England as planes. Confusion occurs
because Americans call them sycamores.

London plane

(Platanus × hispanica syn. *P. × acerifolia)*
One of the most vigorous and certainly the
most widely planted member of the family,
this is a cross between the American plane
(buttonwood), *P. occidentalis* and the
oriental plane, *P. orientalis*. This magnificent tree, often exceeding 36m (118ft)
in height, is ideal for town planting in
parks, squares and boulevards and is a
famous feature of London. It is wind-firm,
resistant to smoke and fumes and, if space
is restricted, it will stand repeated and
severe cutting back with no ill effects;
thus it is widely planted in Europe, New
Zealand and both North and South
America. It is a fast grower, often putting
on 1–2m ($3\frac{1}{4}$–$6\frac{1}{2}$ft) a year when young, and
in open ground develops a majestic crown
of large, spreading, twisting branches,
beautiful against the sky in winter and, in
summer, clothed with striking, large (up

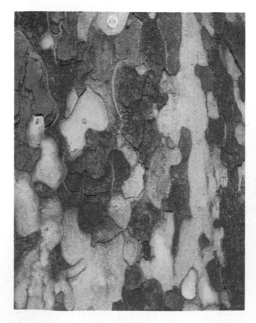

Above: London plane bark (*Platanus ×
hispanica*), showing irregular patches revealed
by the shedding of bark flakes.

Above: Oriental plane (*Platanus orientalis*).
The huge bole with scaling bark and deeply
cut, pointed-lobed leaves.

Above: London planes (*Platanus x hispanica*). Spring foliage on an avenue of pollarded trees.

to 20 × 23cm; 8 × 9in) five-lobed maple-like leaves arranged alternately.

Other special characteristics are: bark that flakes off in irregular patches to give a lovely mottled pattern; seeds in hanging balls up to 4cm (1½in) across in strings of from 2 to 6; leaf stalks whose bases encircle and enclose the next year's buds, which when mature are red-brown, ovoid and with slightly curved tips. The timber, sometimes called lacewood, is pinkish-brown, strong yet easily worked, often beautifully grained and much prized for furniture, turnery and veneers.

Oriental plane or chinar
(Platanus orientalis)
Native to southeast Europe, Asia Minor and Kashmir, this is another splendid tree, even larger and more vigorous than London plane, many specimens exceeding 45m (147½ft) in height with girth over 15m (49ft), but much less hardy and not nearly so common. It is referred to in the Old Testament in connection with events about 480 BC and is one of the longest living broadleaved trees, often exceeding 500 years, with a few trees perhaps approaching as much as 1,000 years.

The characteristics of oriental plane are: deeply cut five-lobed leaves up to 18 × 20cm (7 × 8in) in size; very broad crown with crooked trunk and large limbs often touching the ground; fruit balls rather smaller than those of London plane. The timber is good but the short, usually crooked, trunk spoils it for commercial use.

Buttonwood or American sycamore
(Platanus occidentalis)
This is the largest broadleaved tree in America, with heights up to 53m (174ft) and girth up to 16m (52½ft); it ranges across all the states east of the Great Plains except for Minnesota.

Of very rapid early growth, with records of reaching 13m (42½ft) in ten years, it has a narrower crown and straighter trunk than oriental plane. The timber is excellent, with an interlocked grain. The tree is used in the forestry of the southwestern states.

Buttonwood leaves normally have only three distinct lobes, which are shallowly divided; the seed balls are smoother

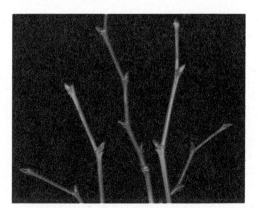

Above: Twigs of London plane (*Platanus x hispanica*). Note the pointed buds.

than those of the other planes and usually only have one ball to each stalk.

Other species
The Californian sycamore (*P. racemosa*) and the Arizona sycamore (*P. wrightii*) are smaller trees, usually of poor form, occurring along streams in canyons of the southwestern United States.

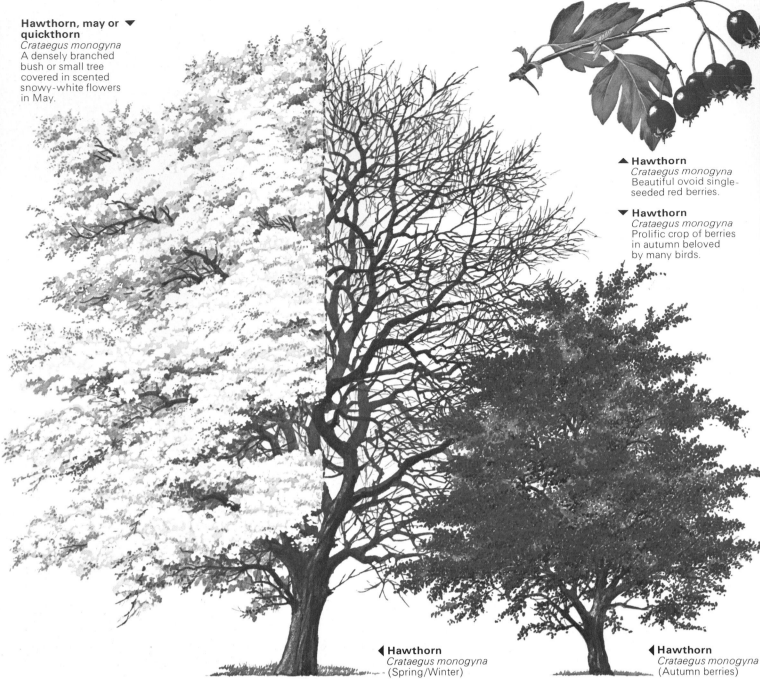

Hawthorn, may or quickthorn ▼
Crataegus monogyna
A densely branched bush or small tree covered in scented snowy-white flowers in May.

▲ **Hawthorn**
Crataegus monogyna
Beautiful ovoid single-seeded red berries.

▼ **Hawthorn**
Crataegus monogyna
Prolific crop of berries in autumn beloved by many birds.

◄ **Hawthorn**
Crataegus monogyna
(Spring/Winter)

◄ **Hawthorn**
Crataegus monogyna
(Autumn berries)

Hawthorns

The hawthorns are a small section within the very large *Crataegus* or thorns group which contains several hundred species, mostly American, many of them only shrubs and outside the range of this book. The following notes will introduce some of those that become trees.

Cockspur thorn
(Crataegus crus-galli)

A North American species much used in many countries for street and garden planting, with nice red berries and unusual rich orange autumn colours. A flat-topped, wide-spreading small tree seldom more than 6m (20ft) high with glabrous, obovate, serrate leaves about 6 × 3cm (2⅓ × 1⅛in), purple-brown twigs with frequent thorns, white flowers 1.5cm (⅗in) in diameter in erect bunches. There are hybrids between this thorn and others; some have larger flowers, others bigger leaves, others redder autumn shades.

Downy or red haw
(Crataegus mollis)

A fine small tree from central USA, this has white hairs on young twigs, large rather

downy leaves, truncate or heart-shaped at the base, 5–12cm (2–4¾in) long, with glandular-toothed edges; white flowers, 2.5cm (1in) across, on stalks thickly coated with white hairs and red, rather downy berries up to 2.5cm (1in) in diameter.

Scarlet haw
(Crataegus coccinea syn. *C. pedicellata)*

Also from the USA, this is very like red haw but has glabrous young shoots, leaves wedge-shaped at the base, and smaller berries, about 1–1.5cm (⅖–⅗in) in diameter, that tend to be pendulous.

Washington thorn
(Crataegus phaenopyrum syn. *C. cordata)*

This is famous for its red autumn colours and its bright red berries persisting through the winter.

Crataegus macracanthia

A small eastern North American tree with

Left: Hawthorn (*Crataegus monogyna*). When allowed to grow to tree size, hawthorn has attractive gnarled and fluted bark with a finely fissured surface. In ideal growing conditions it will reach a height of about 15m (49ft).

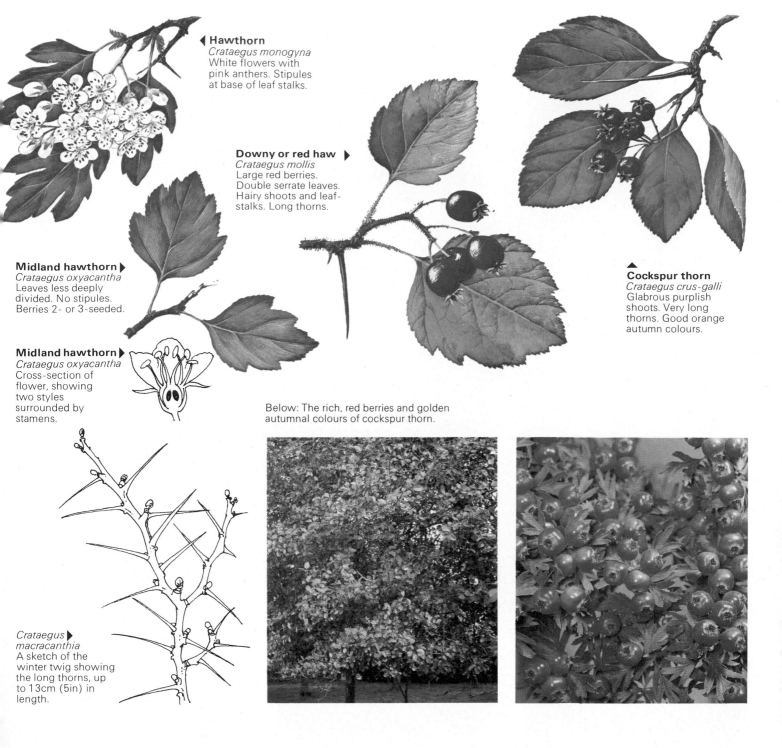

◄ Hawthorn
Crataegus monogyna
White flowers with
pink anthers. Stipules
at base of leaf stalks.

Downy or red haw ►
Crataegus mollis
Large red berries.
Double serrate leaves.
Hairy shoots and leaf-
stalks. Long thorns.

Midland hawthorn ►
Crataegus oxyacantha
Leaves less deeply
divided. No stipules.
Berries 2- or 3-seeded.

Midland hawthorn ►
Crataegus oxyacantha
Cross-section of
flower, showing
two styles
surrounded by
stamens.

▲ Cockspur thorn
Crataegus crus-galli
Glabrous purplish
shoots. Very long
thorns. Good orange
autumn colours.

Below: The rich, red berries and golden
autumnal colours of cockspur thorn.

*Crataegus ►
macracanthia*
A sketch of the
winter twig showing
the long thorns, up
to 13cm (5in) in
length.

abundant huge thorns up to 13cm (5in)
long—a most formidable obstacle! It has
white flowers 2cm (⅘in) across with yellow
anthers and bright crimson berries 1–1.5cm
(⅖–⅗in) in diameter.

Hawthorn, may or quickthorn
(Crataegus monogyna)
Native from Europe right across to Afghanistan, this is the most common of all
hedging species, its thorny nature, dense
branch growth and ability to withstand
constant cutting back making it ideal for
that purpose. But left alone it will develop
into a small rugged tree up to 15m (49ft)
high with a very strong trunk, often fluted,
with bark flaking off in irregular scales.
The rate at which it invaded chalk downland and other spare ground in England
after the rabbits had been almost all killed
by myxomatosis was quite amazing. The
common local name 'May' is easily under-
stood for in that month hawthorn is covered
in snowy white blossom and the country-
side seems filled with its strongly scented
whiteness. Country people often call the
young leaves 'bread and cheese' because

they have a nutty flavour and are eaten by
children. When mature the dark shining
green leaves are about 5–7×4–5cm (up to
2¾×2in), coarsely toothed, irregularly
lobed with two leafy bracts at the base of
the short stalks. The twigs are reddish-
brown with straight sharp thorns; the very
small brown buds open into white flowers
1.5cm (⅗in) across, in dense bunches;
the red berries are abundant, ovoid, about
1cm (⅖in) long and single seeded.

Midland hawthorn
(Crataegus oxyacantha)
Mainly confined to heavy soils and more
shady sites in southern England and
Europe, this is almost the same as 'May'
but has shallower lobed leaves without
bracts at the base of the stalks and the
berries are two- or three-seeded.

Glastonbury thorn
(Crataegus praecox syn. C. biflora)
This variety of hawthorn produces some
flowers in winter as well as in May—
which has led to a whole crop of legends,
and mythological tales, relating to Glas-
tonbury, southwest England.

Above: Oriental thorn (*Crataegus orientalis*).
Coral or orange-red berries, deeply cut leaves
pale on the underside.

Crataegus pinnatifida
China has given us several thorns, this
being the best known species. It has long
irregularly lobed leaves with red and gold
autumn colours and large red berries
1.5cm (⅗in) in diameter with small dots on
the skin. It has a variety, *major*, cultivated
for its large red edible berries.

Oriental thorn
(Crataegus orientalis syn. C. laciniata)
This has deeply cut triangular or lozenge-
shaped dark green leaves covered with
grey down underneath, white flowers and
roundish, hairy, coral or orange-red berries
1.5–2cm (⅗–⅘in) in diameter.

There are many cultivated varieties of
hawthorn including 'Paul's scarlet' (*Coccinea Plena*) with double red flowers,
much used in parks, streets and gardens;
'Rosea', with pink flowers; 'Pendula',
with weeping habit, and 'Plena', with
double white flowers.

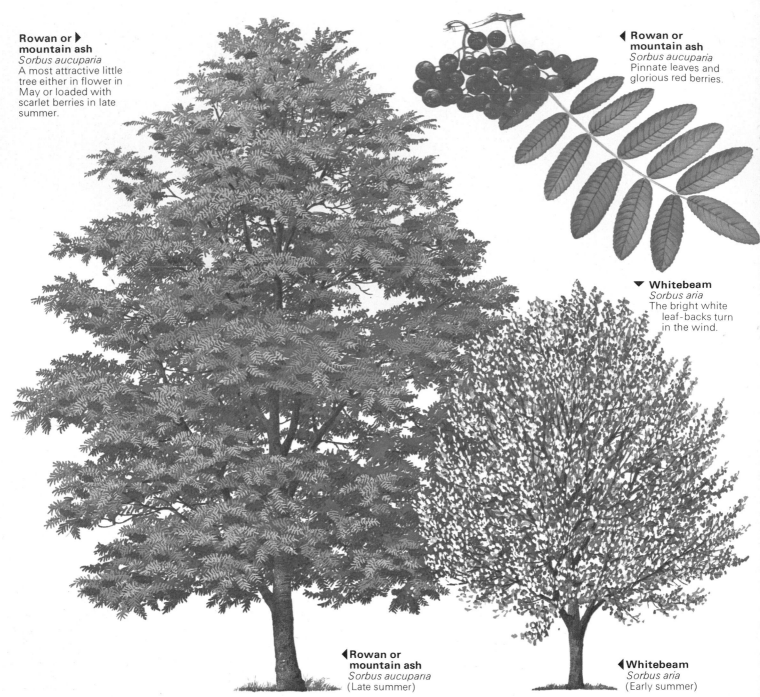

Rowan or mountain ash ▶
Sorbus aucuparia
A most attractive little tree either in flower in May or loaded with scarlet berries in late summer.

◀ Rowan or mountain ash
Sorbus aucuparia
Pinnate leaves and glorious red berries.

▼ Whitebeam
Sorbus aria
The bright white leaf-backs turn in the wind.

◀Rowan or mountain ash
Sorbus aucuparia
(Late summer)

◀Whitebeam
Sorbus aria
(Early summer)

Mountain Ash, Whitebeams and Service Trees

This branch of the great Rosaceae family used to come under the name of 'Sorbus', then it was changed to 'Pyrus' and now it is back again to 'Sorbus'. It contains about 80 northern temperate species ranging from Scotland to the Himalayas and down to Mexico, mostly with attractive berries and pinnate leaves.

Rowan or mountain ash
(Sorbus aucuparia)
Spread widely over Europe and also in parts of Asia and North Africa, this very hardy, beautiful little tree occasionally reaches 20m (65½ft) but usually only about 10m (33ft); it survives in Scotland up to 1,000m (3,280ft); higher than any other tree in that country, and is famous for its masses of striking orange-red berries, up to 1cm (⅖in) across, in dense bunches, which are used to make an unusual smoky flavoured jelly. It has an irregular shaped crown, strongly ascending branches and steely-grey bark, smooth at first, a bit scaly when old. The buds are ovoid with curved tips, dark purplish, often with grey hairs; leaves pinnate, up

to 20cm (8in) long with from 9 to 17 tooth-edged leaflets, dark green above, paler below with very variable autumn colours; they can be quite dull or lovely reds and gold. The white flowers are in dense corymbs, 8–15cm (3⅛–6in) across, with woolly stems. The tough timber has reddish-brown heartwood and, in areas where wood is scarce, is used for tool handles, carving and turnery.

There are several cultivated varieties with different coloured berries and various leaf forms. Rowan belongs to rocky mountain country but is also much used as an ornamental in parks and gardens.

American mountain ash
(Sorbus americana)
This is similar to rowan but has sticky buds, rather larger leaves, smaller flowers and berries slightly longer than broad. A close relation, *S. decora*, has large red berries 1.5cm (⅗in) across.

Vilmorin's rowan
(Sorbus vilmorinii)
From China, this tree is distinguished by its smaller leaves, deep red autumn colours

and beautiful pink berries. There are other Chinese species such as *S. sargentiana*, small and bushy with deep red buds, large pinnate leaves up to 35cm (14in) long, small red berries and excellent gold and red autumn colours; and *S. hupehensis* with rather pendulous grey-green leaves, glaucous beneath, white and pink berries and more rounded flower corymbs.

Kashmir rowan
(Sorbus cashmiriana)
This lovely Indian species has pink flowers and white berries on pink stalks.

Whitebeam
(Sorbus aria)
This very beautiful tree thrives in chalk and limestone soils and is native to Europe; its unique feature is its wonderful oval, doubly toothed leaves, 6–9 × 4–5cm (up to 3½ × 2in), with marked veins, bright green above but covered with silver down beneath—marvellous when turning in the wind and in spring when the buds open into pure white spikes, like magnolia flower buds. The heavily scented flowers are creamy white, about 1.5cm (⅗in) across

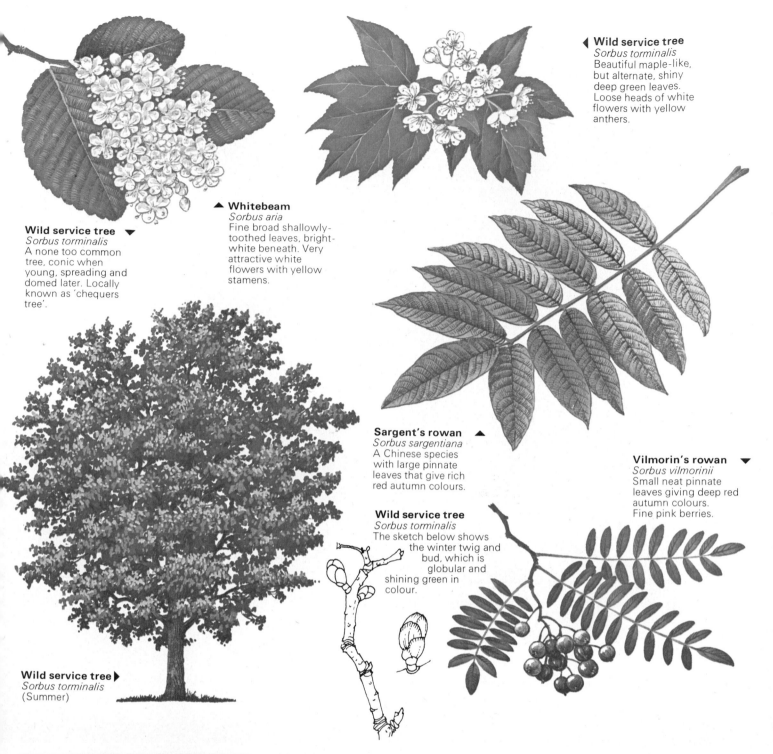

Wild service tree ▼
Sorbus torminalis
A none too common tree, conic when young, spreading and domed later. Locally known as 'chequers tree'.

▲ Whitebeam
Sorbus aria
Fine broad shallowly-toothed leaves, bright-white beneath. Very attractive white flowers with yellow stamens.

◄ Wild service tree
Sorbus torminalis
Beautiful maple-like, but alternate, shiny deep green leaves. Loose heads of white flowers with yellow anthers.

Sargent's rowan ▲
Sorbus sargentiana
A Chinese species with large pinnate leaves that give rich red autumn colours.

Vilmorin's rowan ▼
Sorbus vilmorinii
Small neat pinnate leaves giving deep red autumn colours. Fine pink berries.

Wild service tree
Sorbus torminalis
The sketch below shows the winter twig and bud, which is globular and shining green in colour.

Wild service tree ▶
Sorbus torminalis
(Summer)

Above: Whitebeam (*Sorbus aria*), with its silver-grey bark which, on older trees, is broken up by long, irregular fissures.

and in corymbs about 6–9cm (2⅓–3½in) in diameter; the bright red berries are 1–1.5cm (⅖–⅗in) long, roundish-oval, contrasting with the white-backed leaves. In autumn the leaves are a pinkish shade on the back when they fall. The bark is smooth and light grey between long irregular fissures. There are several cultivars available.

Swedish whitebeam
(Sorbus intermedia)
This is very similar to *S. aria* but has pinnately lobed leaves and the berries are a little larger. It is a smaller, narrower form tree from Sweden, the Baltic States and Germany, very tolerant of smoke and poor soil and often used as a street tree.

Other whitebeams
There are two very large leaved white-beams—*S. cuspidata* from the Himalayas, with leaves up to 22 × 14cm (8⅔ × 5½in) and 'Mitchellii' from Westonbirt Arboretum, with large round leaves up to 15cm (6in) in diameter.

Sorbus alnifolia from Japan and Korea has small white-backed leaves, fine red berries and good autumn colours.

Wild service tree
(Sorbus torminalis)
Native to Europe, but not common any-

where, this is a small dome-crowned tree with ovate alternate leaves about 7 × 9cm (2¾ × 3½in), lobed like a maple leaf and doubly toothed, turning dark purple in autumn. White flowers, 1–1.5cm (⅖–⅗in) across, are grouped in rather loose corymbs 6–9cm (2⅓–3½in) in diameter. The berries, reddish-brown when ripe, obovoid, 1cm (⅖in) long, quite sweet and of gritty texture, have been used for flavouring beer. The bark is fissured into many scales.

True service tree
(Sorbus domestica)
From South and East Europe, western Asia and North Africa, this is very like rowan but with larger flowers—about 1.5cm (⅗in) across—and much larger berries, 2–3cm (⅘–1⅙in) long, varying in shape from round to pear-shaped and brown tinged with red when ripe.

Service tree of Fontainebleau
(Sorbus × latifolia)
A hybrid between whitebeam and wild service tree, varying greatly in shape and size of leaf and shape and colour of berries; basically intermediate between parents.

European crab ▼
Malus sylvestris
A small, very dense crown with twisting branches.

European crab ▶
Malus sylvestris
Flowers white and pink. Leaves deep-green above, whitish-green beneath.

Japanese crab ▼
Malus floribunda
A broad-crowned tree with masses of red buds opening to pink flowers.

◀**European crab**
Malus sylvestris
(Summer/Winter)

◀**Japanese crab**
Malus floribunda
(Spring)

Apples

There are about 30 species of wild apple trees in the north temperate regions and it would be hard to estimate how many hybrids and cultivars have been raised from them either for fruit or ornament—undoubtedly many hundreds. Here we shall not consider the huge fruit production aspect but confine ourselves to a few of the original crab apples and some of their most important progeny, which together are second only to cherries in popularity for ornamental planting the world over.

European crab apple
(Malus sylvestris syn. M. pumila)
Native to Europe and southwestern Asia, this is the progenitor of the domestic apple orchard, but it took generations of skilled work to transform its small sour fruit, really only suitable for making a special jelly, into sweeter and much larger apples. The special features of this original crab apple are: bushy form with dense twisting branches, seldom more than 8m (26ft) high, often quite thorny leaves 4–6 × 3–4cm (up to $2\frac{1}{3} \times 1\frac{1}{2}$in) of variable shape,

ovate or elliptic, may be pointed or fiarly round-ended, deep green and rather shiny above, whitish green and pubescent beneath; rather small mainly white flowers, sometimes with a pink tinge especially on the buds; fruit nearly round, about 2.5 × 3cm ($1 \times 1\frac{1}{6}$in), yellow with some red markings. The bark of the European crab is grey-brown in colour and fissured into irregular small plates.

The main ornamental varieties have differences in the colour of the fruits rather than of the flowers. 'John Downie' is well known for its white flowers and quite large orange and red fruits.

Siberian crab apple
(Malus baccata)
A common very hardy native tree in Siberia, Manchuria and northern China, this grows up to 10m (33ft) tall with a tendency to pendulous branches and rather narrow leaves, 3–6 × 2–2.5cm (up to $2\frac{1}{3} \times$ 1in), flowers white on slender stalks; fruit bright red.

Siberian crab has yielded large numbers of hybrids and cultivars providing a

wonderful range of ornamental trees much used in the gardens of the world. Examples are 'Lemoinei' with crimson-purple flowers, 'Eleyi' with bright red-purple flowers, 'Robusta' with bright scarlet cherry-like fruits and 'Golden Hornet' with bright yellow fruits—the last two cultivars both retain their fruits for months, well past leaf-fall.
(Malus niedzwetzkyana)
From southwest Siberia and Turkestan, this tree is very closely related to *M. baccata* but has purple-red flowers and young leaves flushed with red.

Japanese crab apple
(Malus floribunda)
One of the most beautiful Japanese trees, not very tall with arching branches, prolific rosy red flowers and either yellow or red small fruits.

Chinese crab apple
(Malus spectabilis)
A fine tree from north China this has large, slightly double, bright rosy-pink flowers up to 5.5cm ($2\frac{1}{6}$in) across, turning pale pink later; and small yellow fruits.

'John Downie'
A cultivar of
Malus sylvestris
with masses of white
flowers and beautiful
orange and red fruits.

'Lemoinei' Cultivar of ▼
Malus × purpurea
The beautiful crimson
flowers. Note that
some of the new
leaves are red.

'Lemoinei' A cultivar ▼
of *Malus × purpurea*
with Siberian crab
blood in its veins. Has
masses of crimson-
purple flowers in
spring.

Hupeh or ▶
tea crab apple
Malus hupehensis
Small orange and red
fruits on long stalks.

◀ **American or**
sweet crab
Malus coronaria
Fine, large, beautifully-
scented pink-white
flowers.

◀ **'Lemoinei'** Cultivar of
Malus × purpurea
(Spring)

Hupeh or tea crab apple
(Malus hupehensis)
This is another Chinese species with stiff
ascending branches, small abundant
bunches of pink and white flowers and
small orange and red fruits. Sometimes
used in China as a substitute for tea.

American or sweet crab apple
(Malus coronaria)
Native to eastern North America, this tree
has large beautifully scented pink and
white flowers on long stalks, yellowish-
green orange-shaped fruits; the leaves,
5–14cm (2–5½in), colour well in autumn.

Prairie crab apple
(Malus ioensis)
This is very close to garland crab but often
has spines on the tips of its twigs and
more downy twigs and leaves.

Sikkim crab apple
(Malus sikkimensis)
This low, bushy Himalayan tree has
remarkable rigid branching spurs on the
trunk at the base of the branches, flowers
pink in bud, white when out, and abundant
very small, pear-shaped dark red fruits.

Above: Japanese crab apple (*Malus floribunda*).
The flowers, which are very abundant, are rosy-
red in bud and white when fully open.

Right: Common crab apple (*Malus sylvestris*).
The bole of an old tree with finely fissured bark
flaking away in irregular thin plates.

Wild peach ▼
Prunus persica
A broad, bushy, small tree bearing beautiful round fruits, yellow at first, later suffused with red.

Blackthorn or sloe ▶
Prunus spinosa
Sharply-toothed ovate leaves. Small fruits with wonderful blue bloom.

▼ **Blackthorn or sloe**
Prunus spinosa
Densely packed twisting thorny branches. Its snowy-white flowers are one of the joys of early spring.

◀ **Wild peach**
Prunus persica
(Summer)

◀ **Blackthorn or sloe**
Prunus spinosa
(Spring/Winter)

Plums, Apricots, Peaches and Almonds

This is another very large group from the Rosaceae family. It includes the cherries and cherry laurels, and over 200 species from temperate regions, as well as countless hybrids and cultivars, all with alternate leaves and five petals. A small representative selection will be considered here, again concentrating on the wild species and the cultivated forms of special ornamental value.

Blackthorn or sloe
(Prunus spinosa)
A very aggressive bush or small tree that quickly spreads by sucker growth to form an impenetrable thicket armed with sharp black thorns and held together by its crooked interlacing branches. Native to Europe and northern Asia, it will grow to a maximum of about 7m (23ft) but more usually around 4m (13ft), and is a wonderful sight in spring when its bare black twigs are covered with masses of pure white flowers each 1.5cm ($\frac{3}{5}$in) across. The ovate, sharply toothed leaves, 2–4cm ($\frac{4}{5}$–1$\frac{1}{2}$in) long, turn a fawny gold in autumn. It is the

commonest wild plum and the fruit, known as a 'sloe', is about 1.5cm ($\frac{3}{5}$in) in diameter, blue-black and covered with a very beautiful bloom when ripe, harshly sour but used for making sloe-gin, sloe-wine and a tart jelly.

Bark on old stems is blackish-grey, breaking away in small flakes, with a tendency to horizontal markings; the tough, strong timber was much used for hay-rack teeth, flail swingles, walking sticks and Irish shillelagh clubs.

Bullace
(Prunus insititia)
Bullace has much the same native range as blackthorn but is much less common. It differs as follows: larger leaves, 4–8cm (1$\frac{1}{2}$–3$\frac{1}{8}$in) long, and more coarsely toothed; twigs not so thorny and lighter coloured bark; larger flowers, 1.5–2.5cm ($\frac{3}{5}$–1in) across, rounder fruits up to 2.5cm (1in) in diameter, yellow or black when ripe.

Wild plum
(Prunus communis syn. P. domestica)
Probably of Asian origin, this has been naturalized in Europe for hundreds of

years; it is very like bullace but the fruits are always black, and oblong, not round. Crosses and varieties of both bullace and wild plum have given rise to numerous cultivated plums including the damson.

Myrobalan or cherry plum
(Prunus cerasifera)
Native from the Balkans to central Asia, this is the earliest flowering wild plum—often a month before the blackthorn or the bullace. It is much used for hedges. Its fruits are round and red. 'Pissardii' is a cultivated variety of myrobalan with purplish-red leaves and white or slightly pink flowers; much used for both gardening and street planting.

American red plum
(Prunus americana)
This, the best known of the American wild plums, is native to the eastern and central states and as far south as Georgia and New Mexico. It is the ancestor of many orchard plums; a strong grower up to 10m (33ft) tall with sharply toothed leaves, 7–11cm (2$\frac{3}{4}$–4$\frac{1}{3}$in) long and pure white flowers, 2.5cm (1in) across in stalkless umbels. The almost

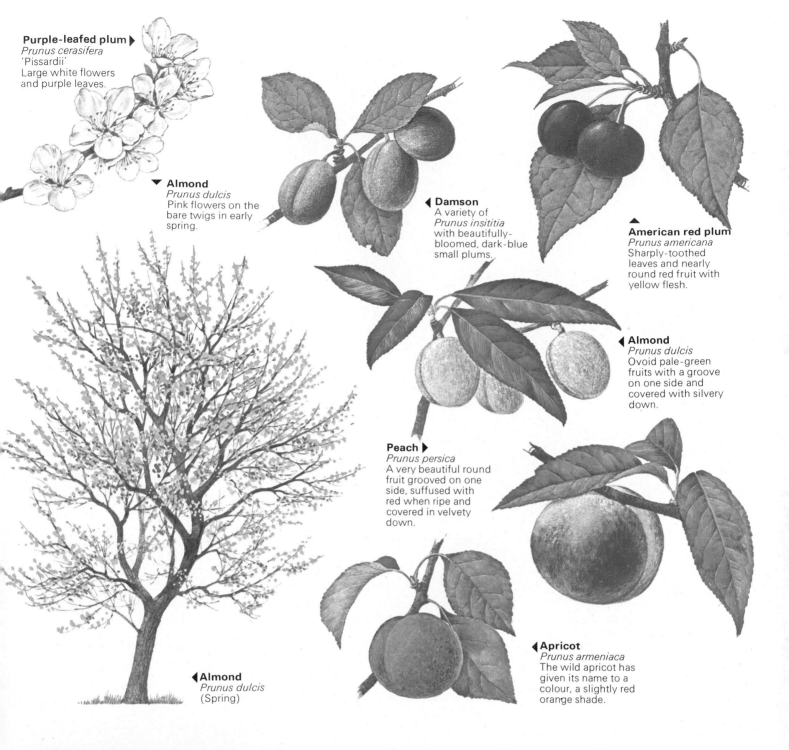

Purple-leafed plum ▶
Prunus cerasifera
'Pissardii'
Large white flowers
and purple leaves.

▼ Almond
Prunus dulcis
Pink flowers on the
bare twigs in early
spring.

◀ Damson
A variety of
Prunus insititia
with beautifully-
bloomed, dark-blue
small plums.

▲ American red plum
Prunus americana
Sharply-toothed
leaves and nearly
round red fruit with
yellow flesh.

◀ Almond
Prunus dulcis
Ovoid pale-green
fruits with a groove
on one side and
covered with silvery
down.

Peach ▶
Prunus persica
A very beautiful round
fruit grooved on one
side, suffused with
red when ripe and
covered in velvety
down.

◀ Apricot
Prunus armeniaca
The wild apricot has
given its name to a
colour, a slightly red
orange shade.

◀ Almond
Prunus dulcis
(Spring)

round fruits, about 2.5cm (1in) in diameter, are red with yellow flesh. Closely related is *P. mexicana*, a larger tree which has purplish red fruits.

Apricots are closely related to the plums but have flowers singly or in pairs, not so bunched as in plums and the skin of the fruits is velvety in the early stages.

Common apricot
(Prunus armeniaca)
Growing up to 10m (33ft) tall, this native of north China is a rounded form tree with broadly ovate leaves, 6–9cm ($2\frac{1}{3}$–$3\frac{1}{2}$in) long, set with rounded teeth; the white or pale pink flowers, 2.5cm (1in) across, are set singly and the round fruits, 3–4cm ($1\frac{1}{6}$–$1\frac{1}{2}$in) in diameter, are yellow, tinged with red. Some of its cultivars have larger fruits.

Left: Myrobalan plum (*Prunus cerasifera*). The trunk is seldom straight and usually divides into heavy branches quite low down on the tree. The bark of old trees shows a pattern of shallow, irregular fissures and thin peeling scales. This tree is often used to make dense hedges.

Japanese apricot
(Prunus mume)
This is much the same in size and form as *P. armeniaca* but has scented, pale rose flowers, larger, more pointed leaves and its yellow fruits are not very palatable. It is grown for its lovely flowers and has many cultivated varieties such as: 'Alboplena', with semi-double white flowers in winter months; 'Pendula', a weeping tree with pale pink flowers very early in the year, and 'Alphandii', which has sets of semi-double pink flowers.

Wild peach
(Prunus persica)
Although native to China, this tree has been cultivated in many countries for hundreds of years and now has dozens of varieties—some grown for their luscious fruits, others for the beauty of their flowers.

It is a small bushy tree up to 8m (26ft) tall and the original wild stock has long lanceolate pointed leaves, 7–15cm ($2\frac{3}{4}$–6in) long, finely toothed, with a glandular stalk about 1.5cm ($\frac{3}{5}$in) long. Unfortunately the

Above: Almond (*Prunus dulcis*). The familiar nuts of this small tree are contained within ovoid, light green fruits covered with silvery down.

Right: Almond (*Prunus dulcis*). The bole of a young tree showing the shiny grey bark. On old trees it is much darker and cracked into squares.

Below: Peach (*Prunus persica*). A close-up of the beautiful rose-pink flowers with golden anthers that cover this bushy tree every spring.

Above: Willow-leafed pear (*Pyrus salicifolia*). A fine specimen in a park setting that shows the rounded crown, pendulous branches and masses of white flowers typical of this species.

Below: Pear (*Pyrus communis*). A sample of the even-grained timber harvested from this tree. It is used for precision and decorative articles.

Pears

leaves are often reddened and deformed by a fungal disease called Peach Leaf Curl.

The rose-pink flowers, 2.5–4cm (1–1½in) across, make a wonderful show in spring and the fruit is globose, 5–8cm (2–3⅛in) in diameter, covered with velvety down, with a shallow groove on one side. When ripe they are golden suffused with red and exceedingly sweet and juicy. The stone is grooved and very hard.

Some of the cultivated varieties are very beautiful: 'Alba' and 'Alboplena', with single and double white flowers respectively; 'Russell's Red', with double crimson flowers; 'Klara Mayer', with double pink flowers; 'Aurora', with dense clusters of double rose-pink flowers with fringed petals; 'Pendula', a weeping form with masses of white flowers.

David's peach
(Prunus davidiana)
Another Chinese species, this flowers exceptionally early and therefore needs shelter in areas liable to frosts. The twigs are grey in winter and the leaves like those of almond. The flowers are pure white,

2.5cm (1in) across and produced singly; fruits very downy, 3–4cm (1⅙–1½in) in diameter, yellow, with thin flesh and a large pitted stone.

Almond
(Prunus dulcis syn. *P. amygdalus)*
This is the only common wild species, well loved for its beautiful early spring large pink flowers, 2.5–4cm (1–1½in) across and very widely planted in gardens, streets and parks. A small tree, native to North Africa and western Asia and very close to a peach—in fact the large flowered 'Almond', so often used for ornamental planting, is a hybrid between almond and peach, sometimes called 'Pollardii'.

Almond has finely toothed lanceolate leaves, 7–12cm (2¾–4¾in) long, often turning red and becoming deformed by the Peach Leaf Curl disease.

The light green fruits are ovoid, rather flattened, 4–5cm (1½–2in) long, grooved on one side and covered with silvery down. Inside is a pale brown pitted nut containing the well known kernel.

A group of about 20 species in the north temperate region characterized by flowers in umbel-like corymbs and fruits with a certain 'gritty' texture, especially when unripe. A small selection of the wild and ornamental species will be considered here, omitting the large number of hybrids and cultivars produced for marketing the fruits. Unlike apples, pears have only a minimal depression at the point where the stalk joins the fruit.

Common pear
(Pyrus communis)
Native to Europe and western Asia, a tall, fairly narrow tree with a rounded top when mature and branches that tend to ascend first and then bend over towards the end; this grows up to 18m (59ft), with dark bark cracking into squarish plates.

The reddish-fawn timber, sometimes called 'fruit wood', is of excellent quality, hard and even-grained and used for furniture, drawing instruments, woodcut blocks, carving, turnery and veneers. Leaves ovate to elliptic, 5–8cm (2–3⅛in) long, on stalks 2–4cm (⅘–1½in) long, finely

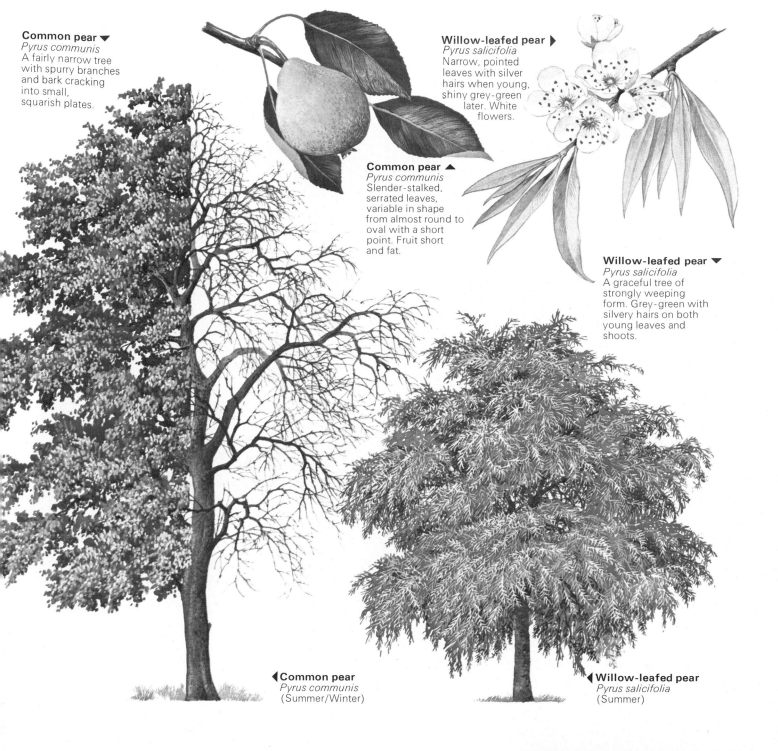

Common pear ▼
Pyrus communis
A fairly narrow tree with spurry branches and bark cracking into small, squarish plates.

Common pear ▲
Pyrus communis
Slender-stalked, serrated leaves, variable in shape from almost round to oval with a short point. Fruit short and fat.

Willow-leafed pear ▶
Pyrus salicifolia
Narrow, pointed leaves with silver hairs when young, shiny grey-green later. White flowers.

Willow-leafed pear ▼
Pyrus salicifolia
A graceful tree of strongly weeping form. Grey-green with silvery hairs on both young leaves and shoots.

◀**Common pear**
Pyrus communis
(Summer/Winter)

◀**Willow-leafed pear**
Pyrus salicifolia
(Summer)

crenate, dark shiny green above, paler beneath. The branches have many short stiff spurs, sometimes spiny; masses of white flower, emerge before the leaves are fully out, 2–3.5cm ($\frac{4}{5}$–$1\frac{3}{8}$in) across in little bunches. The fruit is small, 2.5–5cm (1–2in) long, sometimes rather round.

Willow-leafed pear
(Pyrus salicifolia)
This very ornamental small tree, again from Europe and western Asia, grows to about 9m (29$\frac{1}{2}$ft), with ascending branches markedly pendulous at the end, and a rounded crown. The more weeping types are often named as 'Pendula'. It has beautiful silver-green, willow-like leaves, tapered at both ends and with lots of white hairy down, especially when young. The small pure white flowers are closely packed in small clusters, the calyx and flower stems covered in white wool. Fruits are small, typically pear-shaped and 2.5–3.5cm (1–1$\frac{3}{8}$in) long.

Callery pear
(Pyrus calleryana)
This Chinese species is noted for fine red

autumn colours and masses of foamy white flowers in spring. Its branches are thorny and the very small brown fruit rather round. Two special clones from this species are 'Bradford', particularly resistant to polluted atmosphere and to fire blight disease, and 'Chanticleer', a tree noted for its narrow pyramidal shape.

Ussarian pear
(Pyrus ussuriensis)
This very hardy pear from northeast Asia has pink buds and pinkish-white flowers. The fruit is small and not good to eat. Some cultivars have extra pink flowers.

Mediterranean pear
(Pyrus nivalis)
Another European species, this is grown in France for its fruit (which is very sweet when rather over-ripe) and in many countries for its abundant pure white flowers in spring and narrow oval leaves that when young are coated with pure white down and look most striking.

Sand pear
(Pyrus sinensis)
Native to northern Asia and planted in

Above: Mediterranean pear (*Pyrus nivalis*). The fissured grey bark of this attractive small tree.

China and Japan for its quite large fruits—up to 12cm (4$\frac{3}{4}$in) long and very variable in both colour and form, usually speckled yellow and brown but sometimes marked with red or almost pure yellow; they tend to be sour but are good for stewing and keep much longer than most pears.

Gean or wild cherry ▼
Prunus avium
A fine mature tree. Young ones have very straight branches. Leaves red and yellow in the autumn.

Gean or ▶ wild cherry
Prunus avium
The white flowers and bronze young leaves open together. A perfect spring picture.

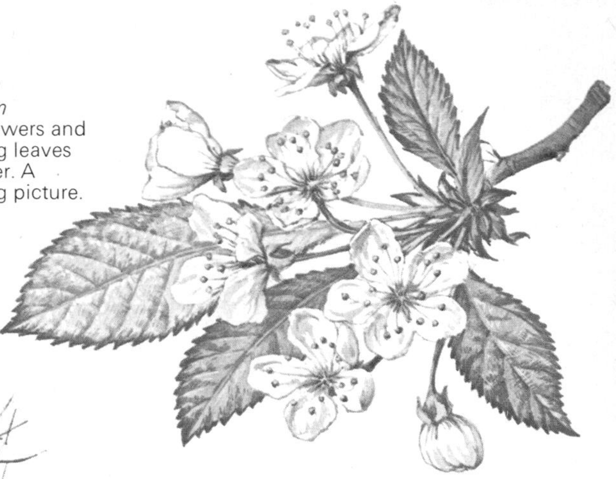

▼ Cherry laurel
Prunus laurocerasus
Often grown as a hedge or shrubbery but will form a small tree if given space.

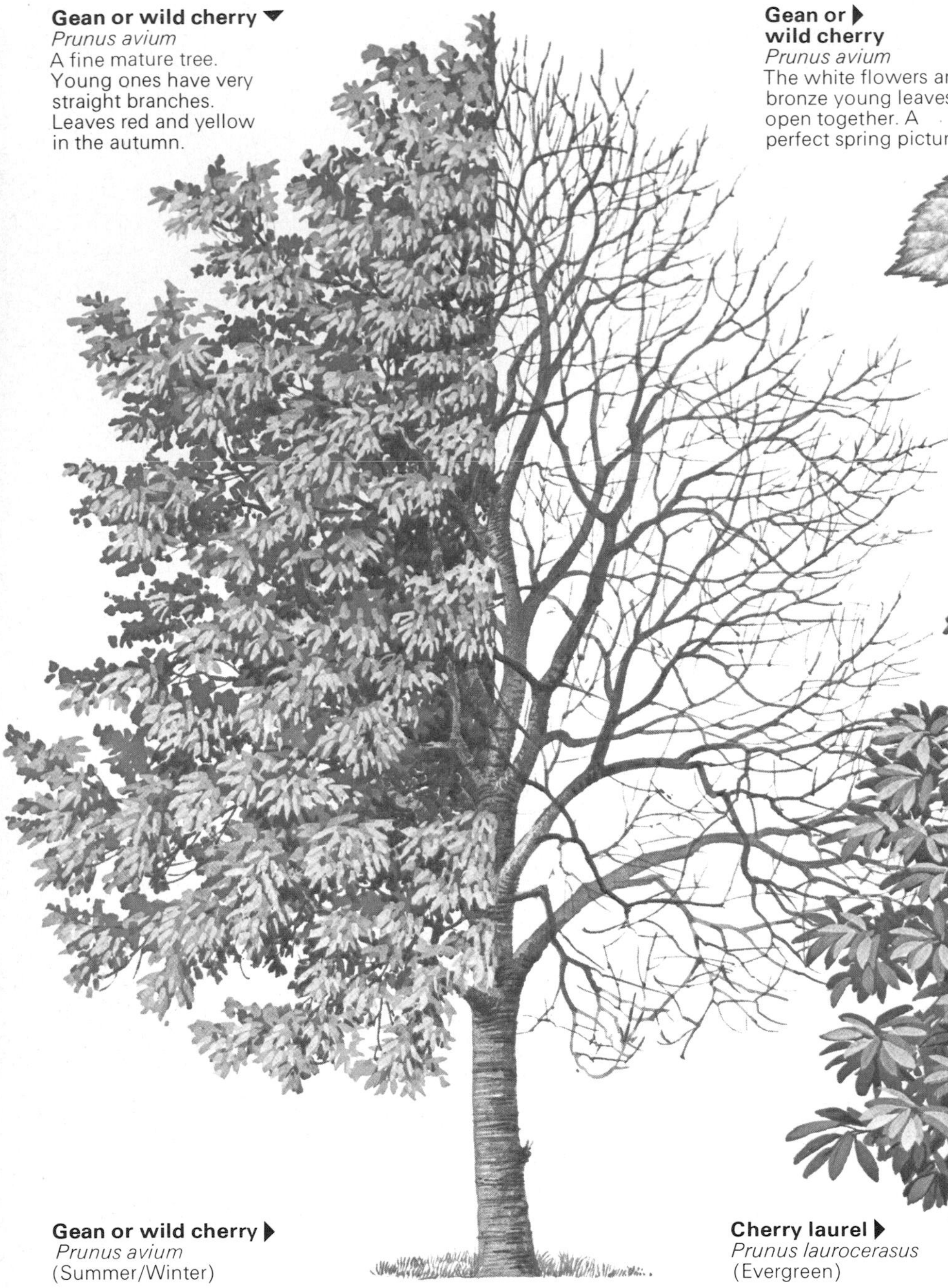

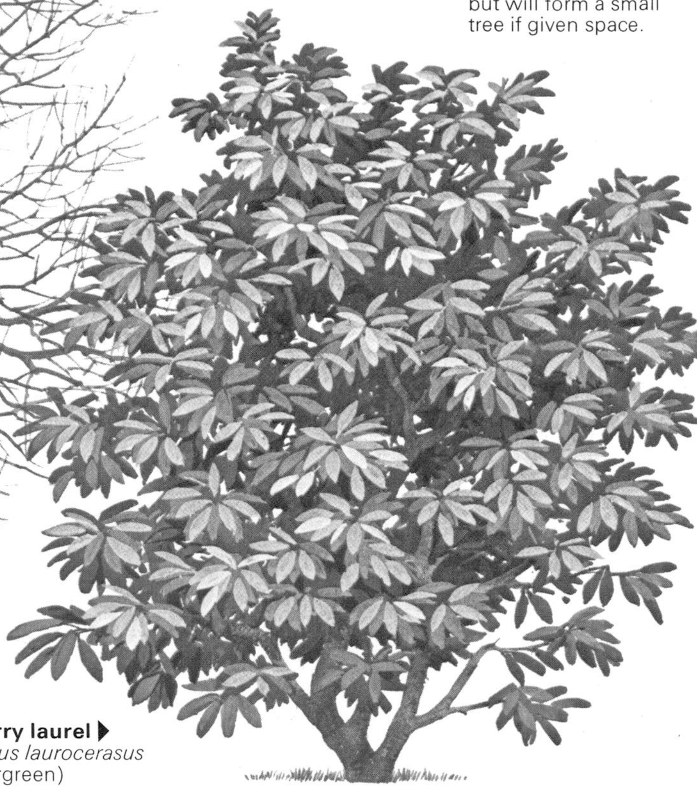

Gean or wild cherry ▶
Prunus avium
(Summer/Winter)

Cherry laurel ▶
Prunus laurocerasus
(Evergreen)

Cherries and Cherry Laurels

This is the largest and most successful of all groups of spring flowering trees. The wild species will be described here, together with a few of the best hybrids and cultivars selected from the huge number available. All the cherries have small one-stoned fruits and the leaves, though really alternate, often tend to be rather bunched together.

Gean or wild cherry
(Prunus avium)
Gean is one parent of many cultivated cherries, particularly the black-fruited ones, and is native to Europe, western Asia and North Africa. It is a tree of great vigour, up to 30m (98ft) tall, conic, with open, whorled branches when young, becoming dome-crowned with age. The bark is beautiful, greyish or reddish, with prominent horizontal bands of brown lenticel scars, and peels away across the stem like birch bark. If grown as a forest tree it develops long clean trunks and the slightly scented golden brown timber is much valued for high class furniture, turnery, veneers, shop-fittings and ornamental boxes. The pointed buds are shining red-brown and the oblong, sharply toothed pointed leaves, 7–10cm ($2\frac{3}{4}$–4in) long, set on short grooved stalks, turn yellow and red in autumn. There are masses of white flowers, 2.5–3cm (1–$1\frac{1}{6}$in) across, set in clusters on stalks 3–5cm ($1\frac{1}{6}$–2in) long and the fruit, red to blackish-red when ripe, is almost round, 2–2.5cm ($\frac{4}{5}$–1in) in diameter.

The cultivar 'Plena' is one of the finest double white cherries, growing to about 20m ($65\frac{1}{2}$ft) tall; it has flowers up to 4cm ($1\frac{1}{2}$in) across, which appear in great profusion. It seldom sets any fruits.

Bird cherry
(Prunus padus)
Another European and Asian species, this much smaller tree has completely different flowers; small, white, fragrant and densely crowded on spikes 8–13cm ($3\frac{1}{8}$–5in) long, some semi-upright but mostly leaning over sideways. The fruit is a small round berry, black when ripe and 6–9mm ($\frac{1}{4}$–$\frac{1}{3}$in) in diameter, but sour to the taste. The rather leathery, finely toothed leaves are 8–12cm ($3\frac{1}{8}$–$4\frac{3}{4}$in) long and turn yellow, with a little red, in autumn. The timber is good, very like that of *P. avium*, but only available in small sizes. There is a cultivar 'Plena'—again, with larger, double-white, long-lasting flowers, and one 'Watereri' with very long spikes, up to 20cm (8in) of single white flowers.

Sour cherry
(Prunus cerasus)
Native to southeast Europe and southwest Asia and one of the parents of the 'Morello' cherry, this is a small bushy species that produces sucker growth and can be a nuisance. It has small red to blackish fruits, very sour and is of little importance, but its cultivar 'Rhexii' with double white flowers, 3–4cm ($1\frac{1}{6}$–$1\frac{1}{2}$in) in diameter, on long stalks, and later flowering than most cherries, is well worth growing.

Black or rum cherry
(Prunus serotina)
This species is very like bird cherry but differs as follows: the flower spikes are more upright, the leaves are very glossy dark green and the fruits red, turning dark purple, not black; they are used in the

Portugal laurel ▶
Prunus lusitanica
Oval berries, turning
black later. Leathery
leaves on red stalks.

▲
Bird cherry
Prunus padus
Small flowers crowded
on long spikes, quite
unlike gean. Young
leaves yellowish-
green at first.

◀ **Black or
rum cherry**
Prunus serotina
Berries round and
dark purple, not really
black. Leaves often
wider than shown.
Teeth incurved.

▲
Cherry laurel
Prunus laurocerasus
Larger round berries.
Large leathery, glossy
leaves on yellow-
green stalks.

Left: Portugal laurel (*Prunus lusitanica*).
The shining green leaves and beautiful slender
spikes of fragrant white flowers.

Below: Gean or wild cherry (*Prunus avium*).
Cross-section of log, showing dark heartwood.

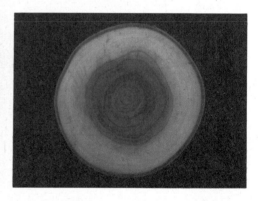

USA for flavouring rum and brandy. The timber is highly valued by cabinet makers. Unfortunately this tree is an alternate host of *Myzus persicae*, an aphid carrier of the sugar beet virus disease; consequently there are a great many areas where it should not be planted.

Manchurian cherry
(Prunus maackii)
This tree from Korea and Manchuria has small fragrant white flowers 1cm ($\frac{2}{5}$in) across in rather round racemes and is not much used in ornamental planting except for its beautiful multicoloured bark, which has mixed browns, reds, golds and greys and peels off in horizontal strips very similar to that of birch.

Cherry laurel
(Prunus laurocerasus)
This very well-known species is much used for hedges and screens; native to southeast Europe and Asia Minor, it is an evergreen with large, leathery, glossy, broadly lanceolate leaves, up to 18×6cm ($7 \times 2\frac{1}{3}$in), with slightly toothed margins and stout

Above: Manchurian cherry (*Prunus maackii*).
Beautiful peeling bark of mixed golds, browns
and greys. Smooth and shiny when young.

2cm ($\frac{4}{5}$in) stalks. It grows to a maximum of 14m (46ft) and has upright spikes of small fragrant white flowers, 8–14cm ($3\frac{1}{8}$–$5\frac{1}{2}$in) tall, followed by berries, 1–2cm ($\frac{2}{5}$–$\frac{4}{5}$in) long, green at first, then red, finally turning to black. The leaves smell of almonds if crushed and are very poisonous, containing prussic acid; they are sometimes used by entomologists for making insect-killing bottles. The bark is blackish brown in colour.

Portugal laurel
(Prunus lusitanica)
A strong growing, handsome, evergreen, bushy tree from Spain and Portugal, occasionally reaching 15m (49ft) high, with oblong, ovate, leathery, coarsely toothed leaves, glossy dark green above, yellow-green on the lower surface. The buds are narrow, acute and bright red-brown. Masses of creamy white fragrant flowers grow in dense spikes 12–23cm ($4\frac{3}{4}$–9in) long, followed by small red berries, about 1cm ($\frac{2}{5}$in) long, turning black when ripe. There are several attractive cultivars of this species of laurel.

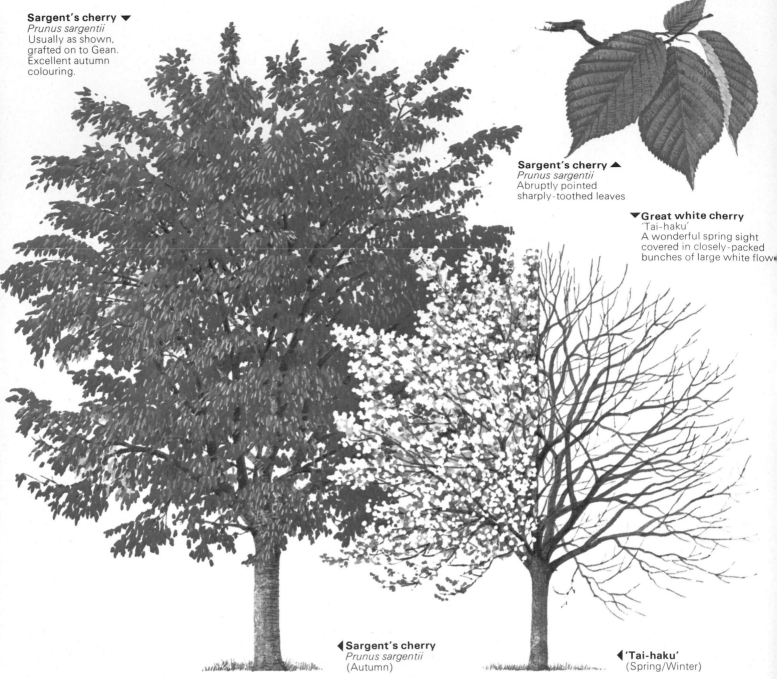

Sargent's cherry ▼
Prunus sargentii
Usually as shown,
grafted on to Gean.
Excellent autumn
colouring.

Sargent's cherry ▲
Prunus sargentii
Abruptly pointed
sharply-toothed leaves

▼Great white cherry
'Tai-haku'
A wonderful spring sight
covered in closely-packed
bunches of large white flow

◀Sargent's cherry
Prunus sargentii
(Autumn)

◀'Tai-haku'
(Spring/Winter)

Japanese Cherries

This group comprises around 100 named varieties—some native species, but mainly cultivars and hybrids. The exact origin of many of them would be very hard to trace and a large number are now simply known by their Japanese local names, even though some of the original parents probably came from China hundreds of years ago. One such example is *Prunus serrulata*, from which a great many beautiful trees have been developed.

White-flowering species

'Tai-haku', the great white cherry, probably the finest of all the whites with masses of large single flowers and rich copper-red young leaves, is a wide growing vigorous tree reaching 12m (39ft) high—a marvellous sight on a bright spring day. Other good white cultivars are 'Shirotae', sometimes called 'Mount Fuji'—a fine semi-double flowered tree with young leaves green and a low crown with long level branches. Then there is the winter-flowering 'Autumnalis', a cultivar of *P. subhirtella*, with semi-double white

Above: Japanese cherry (*Prunus serrulata*). The bark is typically marked by horizontal lenticels.

Right: The narrow spire and profuse pink flowers of 'Amanogawa', one of many different Japanese cherries that grace gardens all over the world.

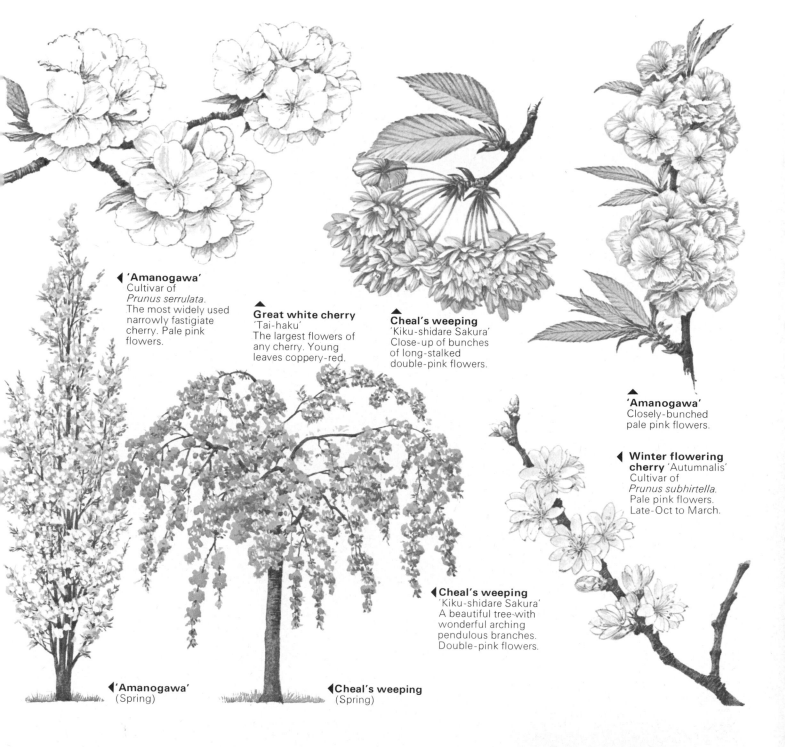

'Amanogawa'
Cultivar of *Prunus serrulata*. The most widely used narrowly fastigiate cherry. Pale pink flowers.

Great white cherry 'Tai-haku'
The largest flowers of any cherry. Young leaves coppery-red.

Cheal's weeping 'Kiku-shidare Sakura'
Close-up of bunches of long-stalked double-pink flowers.

'Amanogawa'
Closely-bunched pale pink flowers.

Winter flowering cherry 'Autumnalis'
Cultivar of *Prunus subhirtella*. Pale pink flowers. Late-Oct to March.

Cheal's weeping 'Kiku-shidare Sakura'
A beautiful tree with wonderful arching pendulous branches. Double-pink flowers.

'Amanogawa' (Spring)

Cheal's weeping (Spring)

flowers. 'Longipes' ('Shimidsu Sakura') is pink in the bud but opening pure white with wide spreading branches.

Pink-flowering species

Among the pink-flowering cherries, the most popular species in Tokyo is 'Yoshino' (*P.* × *yedoensis*), completely covered with scented pink flowers in spring. It grows to a good moderate height for street use. *P. sargentii*, the great mountain cherry, seen so wonderfully on the slopes of Fujiyama, is widely used in many countries. It is a large, fast-growing tree up to 25m (82ft) with reddish young leaves and bunches of large pink flowers on wide-angled branches. Its timber is much used in Japan, and gives fine red and gold autumn colours. A fringed petal, semi-double pink is 'Accolade', a cross between *P. sargentii* and *P. subhirtella*, with broad open crown and flowers in bunches all the way up the branches, opening before the leaves appear.

'Kanzan', very widely planted especially in gardens and streets, shows its bronze-purple young leaves first, followed by masses of deep pink flower buds bursting into semi-double pink flowers on strongly ascending branches. The leaves colour well in autumn. 'Fukubana', another cultivar of *P. subhirtella*, is a smaller tree with long, wand-like branches, giving deeper pink semi-double flowers sometimes described as rose-madder.

'Amanogawa' is an impressive narrow form tree, which forms a very narrow column with bronze young leaves and almost upright clusters of fragrant semi-double pale pink flowers. Another good narrow form tree is the hybrid *P.* × *schmittii* with pale pink flowers and the special feature of beautiful, dark, red-brown bark with horizontal stripes.

Hillier's 'Spire' is not quite so narrow but all the branches ascend sharply and it is an excellent street tree with masses of pink flowers and good autumn colouring.

Two pendulous types are Cheal's weeping cherry (Kiku-shidare Sakura), with double pink flowers and *P. subhirtella* 'Pendula' with single pink flowers.

Above: The bole of the hybrid Japanese cherry *Prunus × schmittii* showing the characteristic red-brown bark marked with horizontal stripes.

Judas tree ▼
Cercis siliquastrum
Round-headed dense crown. The purple seed-pods show up against the dark green foliage.

Judas tree ▶
Cercis siliquastrum
The beautiful rosy-pink, pea-type flowers.

▼ **Pagoda or scholar's tree**
Sophora japonica
Broad-crowned with large contorted branches and delicate foliage.

▲ **Judas tree**
Cercis siliquastrum
(Late summer)

▲ **Pagoda or scholar's tree**
Sophora japonica
(Early summer)

Judas Trees, Redbuds and Sophoras

This is a small genus of seven species from North America, southern Europe and East Asia. It has alternate, simple, entire leaves, rounded, heart-shaped at the base and with 5 or 7 prominent veins. An unusual feature is that the pink, pea-type flowers occur in clusters on quite thick branches, or on the trunk itself, as well as on younger shoots.

Judas tree

(Cercis siliquastrum)

The French name for this tree is 'L'arbre de Judée', meaning 'Tree of Judaea'—much more sensible than the widely used term Judas tree.

Native to southern Europe and western Asia, this is the species most often seen in European parks and gardens, growing to about 12m (39ft) but usually of rather bushy habit with rounded crown and, on older trees, drooping branches. The buds are dark red, the leaves round, 6–10cm (2⅓–4in) across, dark green above, glaucous beneath and with green and red stalks. Bright rosy-pink flowers in small bunches cover the tree in spring—a wonderful

sight. The flat seed-pods, about 8 × 12cm (3⅛ × 4¾in), usually in large numbers, are beautifully coloured, passing from green to purple and finally light brown; they are a special feature of the species. There is a white flowered cultivar 'Alba'.

Eastern American redbud

(Cercis canadensis)

Very similar to Judas tree, but the leaves are larger and more pointed, the flowers slightly smaller and the tree of narrower form. It is one of the most beautiful American trees and so common as to be a feature of the spring landscape in the eastern and central states. It also has a white cultivar 'Alba'. The other main American species is the western redbud (*C. occidentalis*), a much smaller tree, native to California, with both leaves and flowers very like the Judas tree.

Chinese redbud

(Cercis chinensis)

The largest of all the redbuds, sometimes reaching 20m (65½ft), it is very similar to eastern American redbud, but its leaves are less glaucous beneath, the flowers a

little larger, and the seed-pods rather larger and more pointed. It is a more tender species than most of the others.

Also from China there is *C. racemosa*, growing up to 10m (33ft) and with lovely rose-pink flowers hanging in racemes up to 10cm (4in) long with from 20 to 40 blossoms on each one. Its young twigs are distinct in that they are very downy.

Belonging to the great pea family, Leguminosae, there are about twenty sophora tree species but only two or three are commonly used.

Pagoda or scholar's tree

(Sophora japonica)

Native to China and Korea, this splendid deciduous tree deserves much wider use; it reaches 25m (82ft) high and about the same width, and its only drawback is that it does not flower until about 30 years old.

It is very like *Robinia* but of wider and more rounded form with massive contorted branches, pinnate alternate leaves, 15–25cm (6–10in) long with from 9 to 15 entire

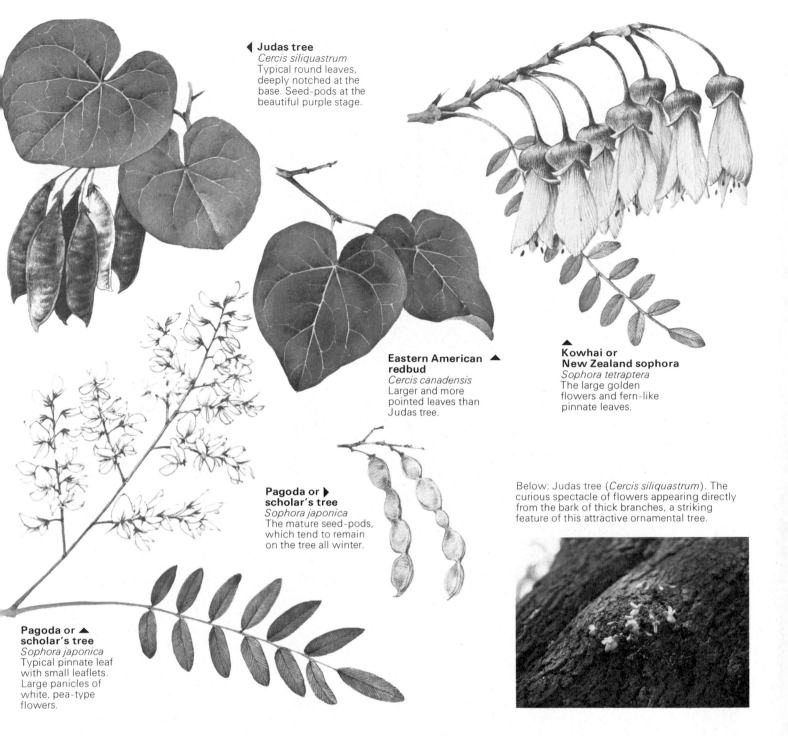

◀ Judas tree
Cercis siliquastrum
Typical round leaves,
deeply notched at the
base. Seed-pods at the
beautiful purple stage.

**Eastern American ▲
redbud**
Cercis canadensis
Larger and more
pointed leaves than
Judas tree.

**Kowhai or
New Zealand sophora**
Sophora tetraptera
The large golden
flowers and fern-like
pinnate leaves.

**Pagoda or ▶
scholar's tree**
Sophora japonica
The mature seed-pods,
which tend to remain
on the tree all winter.

**Pagoda or ▲
scholar's tree**
Sophora japonica
Typical pinnate leaf
with small leaflets.
Large panicles of
white, pea-type
flowers.

Below: Judas tree (*Cercis siliquastrum*). The
curious spectacle of flowers appearing directly
from the bark of thick branches, a striking
feature of this attractive ornamental tree.

Below: Judas tree (*Cercis siliquastrum*). A
mature tree in full bloom. The pink flowers
appear in May and later give way to seed-pods
that turn from purple to brown.

pointed, narrowly ovate leaflets, 3–5cm
(1⅙–2in) long. The flowers, not out until
late summer, are in terminal panicles,
15–25cm (6–10in) long with pubescent
stems and beautiful creamy white flowers,
sometimes almost yellow. The seed-pods
are small, 5–10cm (2–4in) long. Mature
bark is grey-brown and corrugated, rather
like ash. A very picturesque cultivar,
'Pendula', has even more contorted
branches and long pendulous shoots.

Kowhai
(Sophora tetraptera)
This is a very beautiful New Zealand tree,
up to 15m (49ft) tall, with slender zig-zag
branches. It has smaller, more fern-like
leaves than *S. japonica* with a very variable
number of leaflets—anything from 7 to 70.
The flowers are tubular 3–5cm (1⅙–2in)
long, come out in late spring and are
golden-yellow; seed-pods are 5–20cm (2–
8in) long with four wings.

(Sophora viciifolia)
This small bush-like species grows wild
in China, spreading freely. The pinnate
leaves, 3–7cm (1⅙–2¾in) long have 7 to 10
pairs of small oval leaflets; the flowers are
bluish-white, with a blue calyx. Young
twigs are downy, but as the tree ages the
twigs become spiny.

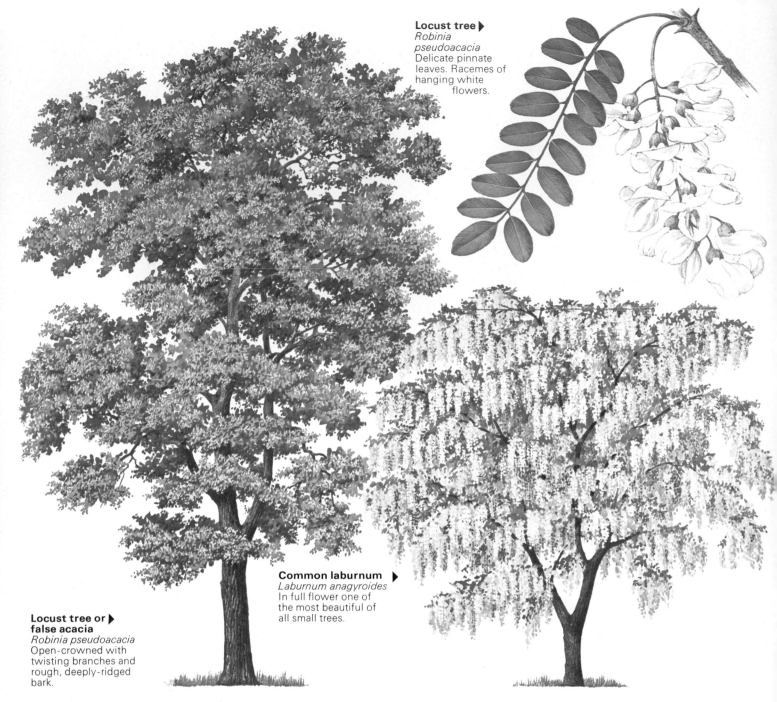

Locust tree ▶
Robinia pseudoacacia
Delicate pinnate leaves. Racemes of hanging white flowers.

Common laburnum ▶
Laburnum anagyroides
In full flower one of the most beautiful of all small trees.

Locust tree or ▶ false acacia
Robinia pseudoacacia
Open-crowned with twisting branches and rough, deeply-ridged bark.

Locusts and Laburnums

Locust is a loosely used name applied to a number of different trees and shrubs. The ones considered here belong to three genera: *Ceratonia, Gleditsia* and *Robinia*.

Carob or locust bean
(Ceratonia siliqua)

This, the true locust bean, is native to the eastern Mediterranean region, a small broad tree, seldom up to 15m (49ft), with dense racemes of small reddish flowers, large brown pods, up to 30cm (12in) long by 3–4cm (1⅙–1½in) wide, containing very hard dark seeds called 'carats' in early times, and probably the origin of the weight unit for gold and diamonds. The pods are formed of a mealy pulp, sweet and edible, and years ago they were commonly sold, in a dried state, in greengrocers' shops. The pinnate leaves have 4 to 6 glossy roundish leaflets.

Honey locusts
(Gleditsia)

A group of about a dozen species from North and South America, Africa and Asia, whose special features are the for- midable thorns on their trunks and branches, large pinnate or bi-pinnate leaves, small inconspicuous flowers, and hard seeds in pods. The best known species is *G. triacanthos*, the honey locust, from western USA, a large tree up to 45m (147½ft) tall, whose crown tends to be broadest at the top, with lovely fern-like pinnate or bi-pinnate leaves, 10–20cm (4–8in) long with 14–32 oblong lauceolate, glossy, bright green, shallowly toothed leaflets, 1.5–4cm (⅗–1½in) long and turning gold in autumn. The buds are protected by spines and large thorns, up to 25cm (10in) long, which also protect the branches and trunk; the greenish flowers are very small. The pods are large, 20–40cm (8–16in) by 2–3cm (⅘–1⅕in), twisted, and yellow-green ripening to brown. The timber is tough and strong and sometimes used for furniture.

There are two cultivars worth noting: 'Sunburst', with rich gold leaves and 'Inermis', without spines.

Japanese locust
(Gleditsia japonica)

This smaller tree has very small leaflets, 1.5–2.5cm (⅗–1in), giving a wonderful fern-like appearance; the scimitar shaped pods are slightly smaller than those of the honey locust.

Chinese honey locust
(Gleditsia sinensis)

Another small tree, this one from Peking, has larger leaflets than the Japanese tree; with pods which are not twisted and with more erect thorns.

Caspian locust
(Gleditsia caspica)

This tree from northern Iran, up to 12m (39ft) high, has leaflets 2.5–4.5cm (1–1¾in), larger than those of *G. triacanthos*. It is the most heavily thorned of all, with masses of huge spikes, some up to 30cm (12in) long.

There are two more species worth mention- ing—water locust (*G. aquatica*)—a very flat topped tree with very small, oblique diamond-shaped pods not more than 5cm (2in) long; and the coronilla (*G. amor- phoides*) from Brazil and Argentina, a larger tree up to 25m (82ft) with longer pods—up to 10cm (4in).

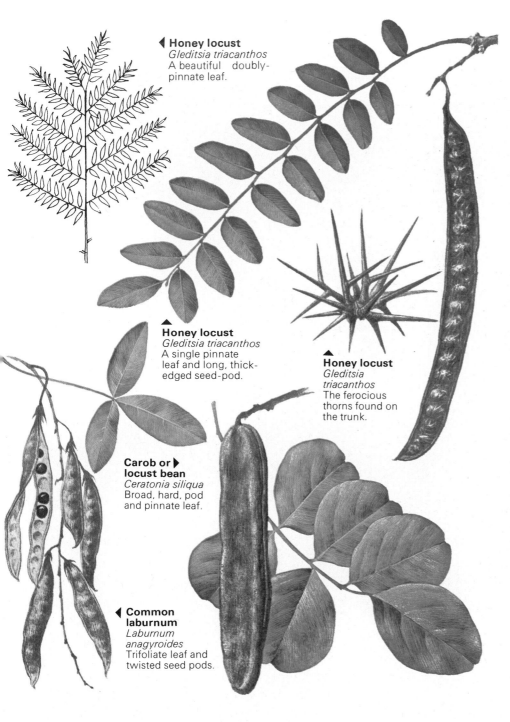

◄ Honey locust
Gleditsia triacanthos
A beautiful doubly-pinnate leaf.

▲ Honey locust
Gleditsia triacanthos
A single pinnate leaf and long, thick-edged seed-pod.

▲ Honey locust
Gleditsia triacanthos
The ferocious thorns found on the trunk.

Carob or ▶ locust bean
Ceratonia siliqua
Broad, hard, pod and pinnate leaf.

◄ Common laburnum
Laburnum anagyroides
Trifoliate leaf and twisted seed pods.

Locust trees
(Robinia)
About twenty species, all from North America and Mexico with only a few of any special value.

Black locust, locust tree or false acacia
(Robinia pseudoacacia)
This fine tree from eastern USA grows to about 30m (98ft), with a rough open crown broadest at the top, deeply ridged and fissured bark, alternate pinnate leaves 15–20cm (6–8in) long with 11 to 19 oval entire leaflets each with a minute spine on its rounded end, and short paired spines at each bud, making the twigs very prickly. The scented white flowers grow in racemes, 10–20cm (4–8in) long, and fairly narrow seed pods, 5–10cm (2–4in) long, ripen to dark brown with black seeds. Unfortunately the branches split away from the trunk rather easily in gales or snowstorms, often spoiling the shape of the tree.

The golden-brown timber has yellow sapwood, is very tough and strong and particularly durable in the soil and so

valued for gate posts and fencing. It was also used for 'tree-nails' in ship building.

There are many nurserymen's cultivars of this tree offering different coloured flowers, golden leaves, thornless twigs, and contorted or dwarf forms.

Rose acacia
(Robinis hispidas)
From southeast USA, this is a straggling bushy species with short racemes of rose coloured flowers and shoots covered in crimson bristles. *Robinia kelseyi* is almost the same as this species.

Clammy locust
(Robinia viscosa)
Native to Carolina, this is a small pink-flowered tree having young branches covered with sticky glandular hairs.

Also worthy of mention are *Robinia luxuriana*, noted for its bristly pods, and the cultivar 'Inermis', which has a small rounded crown of spineless branches.

Belonging to the Leguminosae family this very small genus consists of three

species, two native to central and southern Europe and the other to Greece and Asia Minor, all with deciduous, trifoliate, alternate leaves, yellow flowers in long racemes and seeds in clusters of small pods. Because of an alkaloid in the sap the leaves and seeds are poisonous.

Common laburnum or golden rain
(Laburnum anagyroides syn. L. vulgare)
This is the common laburnum, one of the most widely used ornamental trees, particularly in Europe, where it is a common feature of gardens great and small, and often planted as a street tree. There are few more striking sights than a well shaped laburnum covered with its golden rain of pendulous bright yellow flowers, each raceme 15–25cm (6–10in) long; but children in particular should be warned that its leaves and seeds are poisonous. The slender seed-pods, 5–8cm (2–3⅛in) long, are grey-green above, silky and silvery on the underside. After a few years the attractive bark on the trunk is shiny, pale brown with fine fissures and the beautiful timber has rich brown heartwood, marked with gold flecks, contrasting with pale yellow sapwood. Unfortunately, the wood is only obtainable in small sizes, but it is much valued for ornamental work and turnery. In gardens, the trees are often kept small by pruning but if allowed to grow naturally they will reach about 12m (39ft) with ascending arching branches.

Scotch laburnum
(Laburnum alpinum)
Another European species only differing from *L. vulgare* in having less hairy and larger leaves, 8–13cm (3⅛–5in) long, flowers more widely spaced on rather longer racemes, 20–35cm (8–14in) and seed-pods with a distinct wing along the upper edge.

Hybrids
There is an excellent hybrid between the common and the Scottish laburnums, called *L. vossii* or *L. × watereri*, which is now used more often than either of its parents because of its magnificent racemes, 25–50cm (10–20in) long with the flowers densely arranged, and also because many of the flowers are sterile, resulting in far fewer of the poisonous seed-pods, thus making it safer for children.

By grafting one of the brooms, *Cytisus purpureus*, on to the common laburnum a very interesting graft-hybrid or 'chimaera', called *Laburnocytisus adamii*, can be made, thus producing a small tree which bears three types of flowers—some like common yellow laburnum, some in short bunches of purple flowers and others long racemes of pinkish purple flowers—a quite remarkable sight.

Laburnum caramanicum
This species from Greece and Asia Minor forms a small, narrow crowned tree with most branches nearly erect. Its special feature is its erect yellow flower racemes, 7–18cm (2¾–7in) long, but it is subject to spring frost damage and is not much used.

Moroccan broom or pea-tree
(Cytisus battandieri)
This is not a laburnum, but so close in appearance that it seems appropriate to mention it here. A shrub or small tree growing rapidly to about 6 or 7m (up to 23ft), it has laburnum-like silky leaves and dense clusters of pineapple-scented, bright yellow flowers in mid-summer.

Tree of heaven ▲
Ailanthus altissima
The very large leaves
smell foul when
crushed. Central stems
often red. Leaflets
have glands behind
basal teeth.

◄**Tree of heaven**
Ailanthus altissima
A magnificent tree
with strongly ascending
branches and glorious
foliage.

◄**Tree of heaven**
Ailanthus altissima
(Summer)

Trees of Heaven and Sumacs

The tree of heaven's Latin name is a translation of *ailantes*, an Indonesian word signifying 'tree tall enough to smite the skies'. In German it has become Gotterbaum, meaning 'tree of the gods'. Although its Latin specific name, *altissima*, signifies 'very tallest tree', the records are disappointing; it has seldom reached 32m (105ft). In the eastern United States and parts of southern Europe the tree of heaven has become completely naturalized, and is regarded as part of the general flora.

Tree of heaven
(Ailanthus altissima)

This is a good example of an impressive tree cultivated mainly for its lovely foliage. Its timber, pale brown, soft and weak, is rarely used. The flower spikes are lax, with only tiny blossoms, but the autumn fruits can clothe the dark green foliage in a brilliant cloth of gold. Native to China, the tree of heaven was introduced to Europe, America and various subtropical countries about the middle of the eighteenth century. It soon became a popular tree for street, park and garden planting because it grows

vigorously, tolerates town smoke and presents a rich exotic appearance that suggests some warm 'tropic' land.

This is largely due to its huge compound leaves, which may reach a length of 60cm (24in) on normal trees, or a full metre (39in), on coppiced shoots. Each leaf resembles a branch; it has up to fifty small side leaflets, plus a solitary one at its tip. When the leaves open very late in spring, they are bronze in colour. They soon turn dark green, and break up in autumn without changing colour, leaving their midribs attached, for a while, to the tree's real branches. Each leaflet has a short stalk and a broad base which bears two swellings or glands that serve no known purpose.

The flowers open in midsummer, in large, loose panicles of tiny white blossoms, all of one sex, though both sexes can occur on one tree. They have a rather acrid, unpleasant odour. Each blossom may be male, with ten stamens bearing yellow anthers, or female, with a central pistil. They soon fade and the tree then attracts little attention until early autumn, when

the large seed-wings turn from green to gold; at the same time the central zone of each wing, holding one small round seed, becomes a rich orange-crimson shade. When the wind-borne seed sprouts next spring the wing remains attached to it, resting on the surface of the ground. A little shoot springs up, bearing two green, oval seed-leaves. These are succeeded by the first true leaves, which have only three leaflets each; larger and longer compound leaves follow.

This genus of some 150 species belongs to the great cashew family, Anacardiaceae. Its leaves may be large and pinnate or simple, some deciduous, some evergreen and several rather poisonous.

Stagshorn sumac
(Rhus typhina)

One of the most remarkable features of this small, rather flat-topped deciduous tree from North America is that its very thick twigs are covered with red-brown hairs, reminiscent of stags' antlers in their 'velvet' stage. The large pinnate leaves,

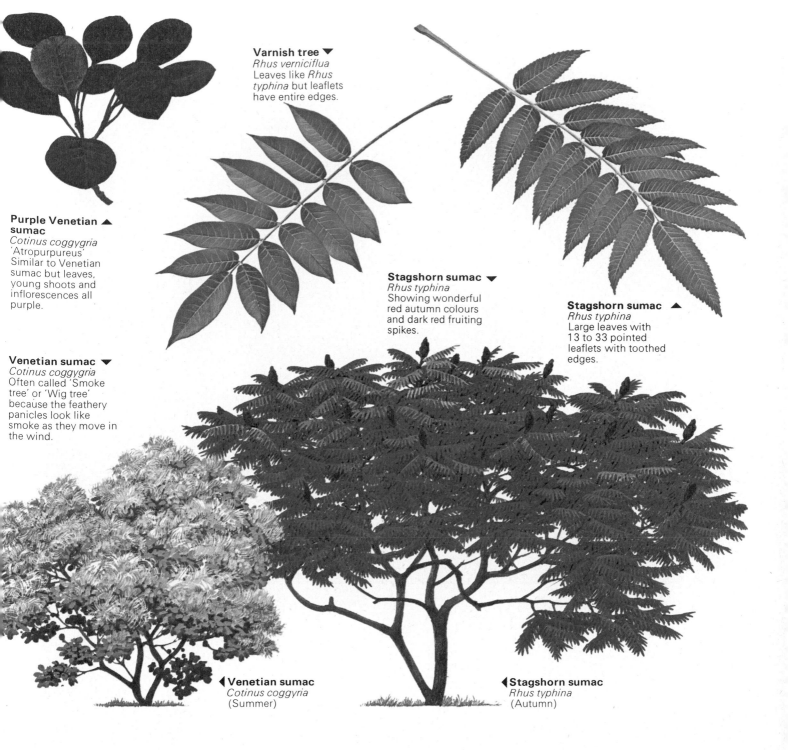

Purple Venetian ▲ sumac
Cotinus coggygria 'Atropurpureus' Similar to Venetian sumac but leaves, young shoots and inflorescences all purple.

Varnish tree ▼
Rhus verniciflua Leaves like *Rhus typhina* but leaflets have entire edges.

Venetian sumac ▼
Cotinus coggygria Often called 'Smoke tree' or 'Wig tree' because the feathery panicles look like smoke as they move in the wind.

Stagshorn sumac ▼
Rhus typhina Showing wonderful red autumn colours and dark red fruiting spikes.

Stagshorn sumac ▲
Rhus typhina Large leaves with 13 to 33 pointed leaflets with toothed edges.

◀ **Venetian sumac**
Cotinus coggyria (Summer)

◀ **Stagshorn sumac**
Rhus typhina (Autumn)

hairy when young, are 25–60cm (10–24in) long, with from 13 to 31 pointed, lanceolate, toothed leaflets from 5–10cm (2–4in) long; in the autumn they turn flaming orange, red and purple. Male and female flowers are on separate trees, taking the form of spikes or panicles made up of a large number of very small flowers; the male panicles are rather lax, reddish-green and up to 30cm (12in) tall, the female ones denser and smaller—up to 20cm (8in) tall, turning later to a red hairy 'candle-flame' of seeds which remain on the tree long after all the leaves have fallen. The stems are full of an acrid, milky sap. Because of its magnificent foliage and splendid autumn colours it is widely planted as an ornamental species though it has the drawback of sending up numerous sucker shoots. The timber is useless but the pithy stems were once hollowed out by North American Indians for tubes and pipes; the speckled bark is rich in tannin.

There is a very handsome cultivar 'Laciniata' with deeply cut leaflets which, give the whole leaf a doubly pinnate effect.

Smooth sumac
(Rhus glabra)
Another North American species very close to *R. typhina* but with smooth twigs and leaves, without pubescence. This one also has a splendid cut-leaved cultivar called 'Laciniata' that turns orange, yellow and red in autumn.

Venetian sumac
(Cotinus coggygria syn. *Rhus cotinus)*
This species is often called 'Smoke tree' or 'Wig tree' because of its remarkable hairy, feathery inflorescent panicles, which are pink at first then turn grey, giving a 'smoky' appearance to the whole bush. Native to central and southern Europe, it usually forms a rounded bush up to 4m (13ft) high with simple obovate or orbicular leaves about 4–8cm ($1\frac{1}{2}$–$3\frac{1}{8}$in) long with well-marked parallel veins and thin stalks. The loose panicles bear no flowers and are just a mass of silky hairs; the leaves turn yellow in late autumn. A strong yellow dye is obtained from the twigs.

There is a cultivar 'Atropurpureus' with purple leaves, twigs and panicles.

Varnish tree
(Rhus verniciflua)
This attractive small tree, up to 15m (49ft) tall, comes from China, Japan and the Himalayas, and supplies lacquer for furniture. Its leaves are very like those of *R. typhina* but have entire margins. The yellowish white flowers are very small and borne in large loose panicles.

Poison ivy
Rhus toxicodendron
This is the 'poison ivy' of the eastern USA, a deciduous climbing or spreading shrub, with leaves composed of three leaflets and small dull-white flowers. Its yellowish milk-like sap is very poisonous and with some people causes a painful rash on contact with the leaves.

Poison sumac
(Toxicodendron vernix)
Another North American species with large leaves similar to those of *R. typhina*; the sap is even more poisonous than that of poison ivy. It is often planted for its wonderful red and gold autumn colours but should always be labelled 'poisonous'.

Holly
Ilex aquifolium
A very dense crown of dark glossy green evergreen leaves. These are very spiny on the lower branches, but near the top of the tree the leaves are oval and pointed with hardly any spines.

Holly
Ilex aquifolium
Typical prickly leaves and red berries.

Box
Buxus sempervirens
An attractive bush or small tree usually with several stems. Old specimens often lean. Native on chalk and limestone soils.

Holly
Ilex aquifolium
(An evergreen tree)

Box
Buxus sempervirens
(An evergreen tree)

Box and Holly

Box and holly are among the few evergreen broadleaved trees that thrive in northern Europe. Both are limited to the western seaboard where winters are comparatively mild, and neither is hardy under the severer climates found further east; thus they flourish on the fringe of a Mediterranean climate flora adapted to mild wet winters, followed by hot dry summers. As a result, they have thick, leathery leaves with waxy surfaces that slow down water loss through transpiration.

Box

(Buxus sempervirens)

In box the leaves are set in pairs, and each has a neat oval shape, dark green above, paler below. The foliage is shade-tolerant and this enables close-ranked leaves to flourish beside one another. Hence the trees can be trained to form a dense hedge or be trained into shapes to resemble, for example, birds or castle battlements, by the art of tree sculpture known as topiary. Its dwarf form, called 'Suffruticosa', is widely cultivated for low hedges throughout Europe and North America.

In late spring box opens clusters of little yellow flowers set in leaf axils. Male flowers develop on the outer edges of each cluster, and female ones at its centre. All have four yellow sepals and four yellow petals. Male flowers bear four stamens with golden anthers, while female flowers have a single, flask-shaped, green pistil with three stigmas. After pollination by insects, the pistil ripens, by autumn, to a greyish-white, papery capsule bearing four reflexed points or horns. Within this lie several small, hard black seeds, which escape when the capsule splits. When they sprout in the following spring, each raises two oval seed-leaves, which wither and fall after one summer's growth; normal evergreen foliage follows.

Never a tall tree, box may develop a trunk about 15cm (6in) in diameter, clad in thin corky bark broken into pale brown squares, like the skin of a crocodile. Boxwood is bright orange-yellow, very hard, dark, heavy and stable. Before the advent of plastics, it was widely used for rulers, mathematical instruments, surgical aids and household utensils such as salt spoons. It was, and still is, a favourite medium for the finest wood sculpture, especially chessmen. Many fine illustrations were once printed with boxwood blocks, a process invented by the British artist, Thomas Bewick. He used boxwood end grain to gain fine texture and long wear.

Holly

(Ilex aquifolium)

Holly is familiar to everyone as a Christmas decoration. Its natural resistance to loss of moisture enables it to stay green for many days when it hangs waterless on a wall. Wild holly trees are common throughout western and southern Europe, but are not hardy in the east, where frost lasts longer. Holly's glossy, twisted leaves, dark green above and paler below, often bear characteristic prickles along their edges. In the typical wild form the upper leaves are oval and pointed, but spineless because there is no need for them to be protected against browsing animals at levels where they are out of reach. Garden strains do not always follow this simple

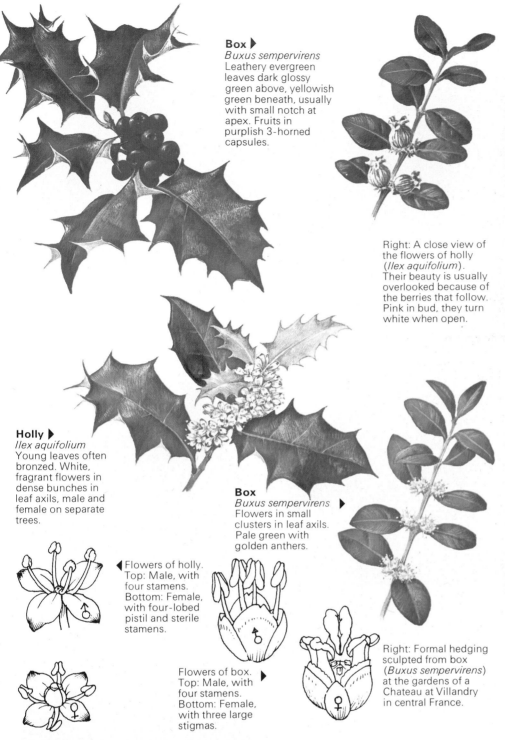

Box ▶
Buxus sempervirens
Leathery evergreen leaves dark glossy green above, yellowish green beneath, usually with small notch at apex. Fruits in purplish 3-horned capsules.

Right: A close view of the flowers of holly (*Ilex aquifolium*). Their beauty is usually overlooked because of the berries that follow. Pink in bud, they turn white when open.

Holly ▶
Ilex aquifolium
Young leaves often bronzed. White, fragrant flowers in dense bunches in leaf axils, male and female on separate trees.

Box
Buxus sempervirens ▶
Flowers in small clusters in leaf axils. Pale green with golden anthers.

◀ Flowers of holly. Top: Male, with four stamens. Bottom: Female, with four-lobed pistil and sterile stamens.

Flowers of box. ▶
Top: Male, with four stamens. Bottom: Female, with three large stigmas.

Right: Formal hedging sculpted from box (*Buxus sempervirens*) at the gardens of a Chateau at Villandry in central France.

Above: Holly (*Ilex aquifolium*). The bole of a mature tree showing the greenish-grey bark, smooth except for very fine irregular ridges.

rule. Some are spiny right to the top, others spineless right down to the bottom; 'hedgehog holly' even bears spines on the face of each leaf. There are some striking decorative cultivars, variegated with silver or gold on their leaves, or even red, white and green on the same leaf. The waxy surface of the foliage, which checks water loss, holds highly flammable substances; leaves flare like torches in a forest fire.

Every holly tree is either wholly male or wholly female. Nurserymen, who provide choice kinds grafted upon ordinary stocks, know the sex of each strain. Most people naturally prefer to plant females, which give promise of bright red, or possibly yellow, berries around midwinter. When hollies flower, in late spring, they open clusters of short-stalked blossoms along their outer twigs. The four petals of each flower have a waxy surface and are white, with purple tips. Male flowers have four prominent stamens with yellow anthers, while female flowers develop a squat, oval green pistil. The fruit, which ripens late in autumn, is a scarlet berry, holding four

hard brown seeds; birds scatter these when they attack the berry's soft, mealy yellow pulp, or swallow them and void them later. The first seed-leaves that appear when the seedling sprouts in the following spring, or sometimes a whole year later, are soft-textured, not hard.

Holly bark is smooth and grey, sometimes with an olive-green tinge. It holds a sticky substance and was once mashed and used to make birdlime. This substance held the feet of small birds firmly to twigs where they perched, making their capture easy; it is now illegal to use it. The wood, white or pale cream throughout, is exceptionally dense and heavy, yet soft and easily worked. It holds little water in relation to its dry weight, and so makes excellent firewood even if used fresh cut and 'green', without prior seasoning. Its main uses are for decorating, carving and cabinet work; for example, as a white inlay contrasting with darker woods or, when stained black, as a cheap substitute for ebony; smaller stems make sturdy walking sticks, or springy stocks for whips.

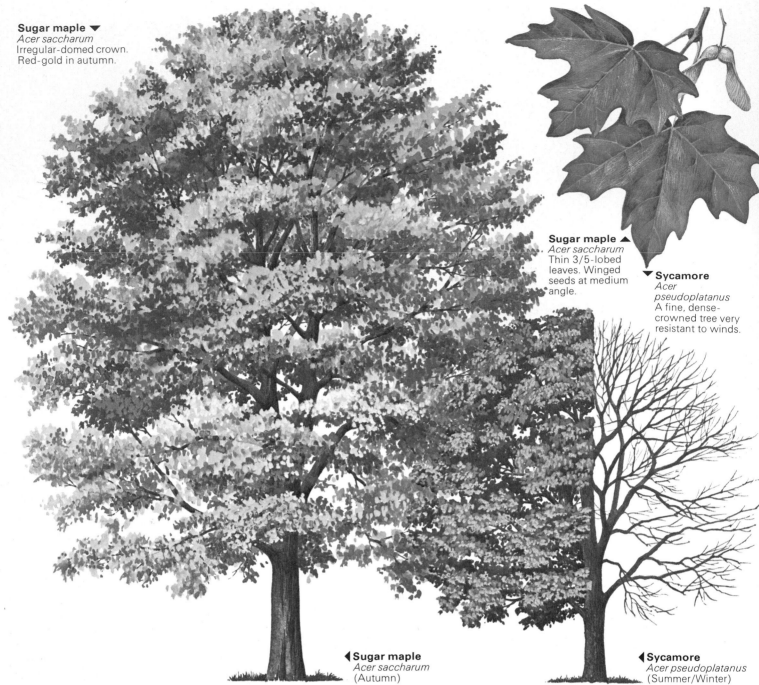

Sugar maple ▼
Acer saccharum
Irregular-domed crown.
Red-gold in autumn.

Sugar maple ▲
Acer saccharum
Thin 3/5-lobed
leaves. Winged
seeds at medium
angle.

▼ **Sycamore**
*Acer
pseudoplatanus*
A fine, dense-
crowned tree very
resistant to winds.

◀ **Sugar maple**
Acer saccharum
(Autumn)

◀ **Sycamore**
Acer pseudoplatanus
(Summer/Winter)

Maples

This large and important genus, of about 150 species in the north temperate regions, provides some of our finest ornamental trees, their special feature being marvellous autumn colours which are seen on the grandest scale in North America but, owing to the increasing use of the beautiful Japanese varieties, can now also be found in gardens, great and small, in many countries.

Canada displays the red leaf of a sugar maple (*Acer saccharum*) on its national flag and has no less than thirteen native species.

Several of the larger maples are important timber trees and their wood is used for furniture, cabinet work, the making of the bodywork of stringed instruments, flooring, turnery, and so on. A particular product in America is maple syrup made from the sap of the sugar maple.

The majority of maples have the following general characteristics: seeds in pairs, jointed at the base, each with a one-sided membranous wing; leaves opposite, usually lobed but a few are entire and nearly all are deciduous.

The following notes describe a representative selection starting with some of the larger species.

Sycamore
(Acer pseudoplatanus)

This splendid very hardy tree grows to 35m (115ft) tall with a large, broad, domed crown and girths up to 7m (23ft). Native and common over large areas in central and southern Europe, it was probably introduced by the Romans into Britain where it thrives even on exposed hill country. It has ovoid greenish buds, and the large leaves, up to 18×24cm ($7 \times 9\frac{1}{2}$in), usually wider than long, on 6–12cm ($2\frac{1}{3}$–$4\frac{3}{4}$in) stalks commonly have five coarsely and unevenly toothed lobes, often reddish in colour. The flowers hang in beautiful yellow-green tassels 6–12cm ($2\frac{1}{3}$–$4\frac{3}{4}$in) long, to be followed by bunches of winged seeds, green at first and later tinged with red, each pair being set and an angle of 70–120°. The bark on young trees is smooth, but in older trees it flakes off in squarish scales, often curled at the edge to expose pinkish fawn patches.

This is an important timber tree; the strong whitish wood has a fine natural lustre and a tendency to wavy grain. In some trees the timber has wonderful rippled markings, very valuable and much favoured for veneers and the bodywork of stringed instruments—in fact it is often called 'fiddle-back' maple. Normal sycamore timber is used for furniture, kitchen utensils, cabinet work, and turnery.

Mention should be made of 'Tar-spot' disease, which causes round black spots with yellow edges on sycamore leaves due to the attack of a fungus *Rhytisma acerinum*.

Two interesting cultivars of sycamore are 'Purpureum' with beautiful purple leaves, and 'Brilliantissimum', whose leaves emerge pink then turn light yellow and are very conspicuous till about August when they turn green.

Norway maple
(Acer platanoides)

A Scandinavian and North European

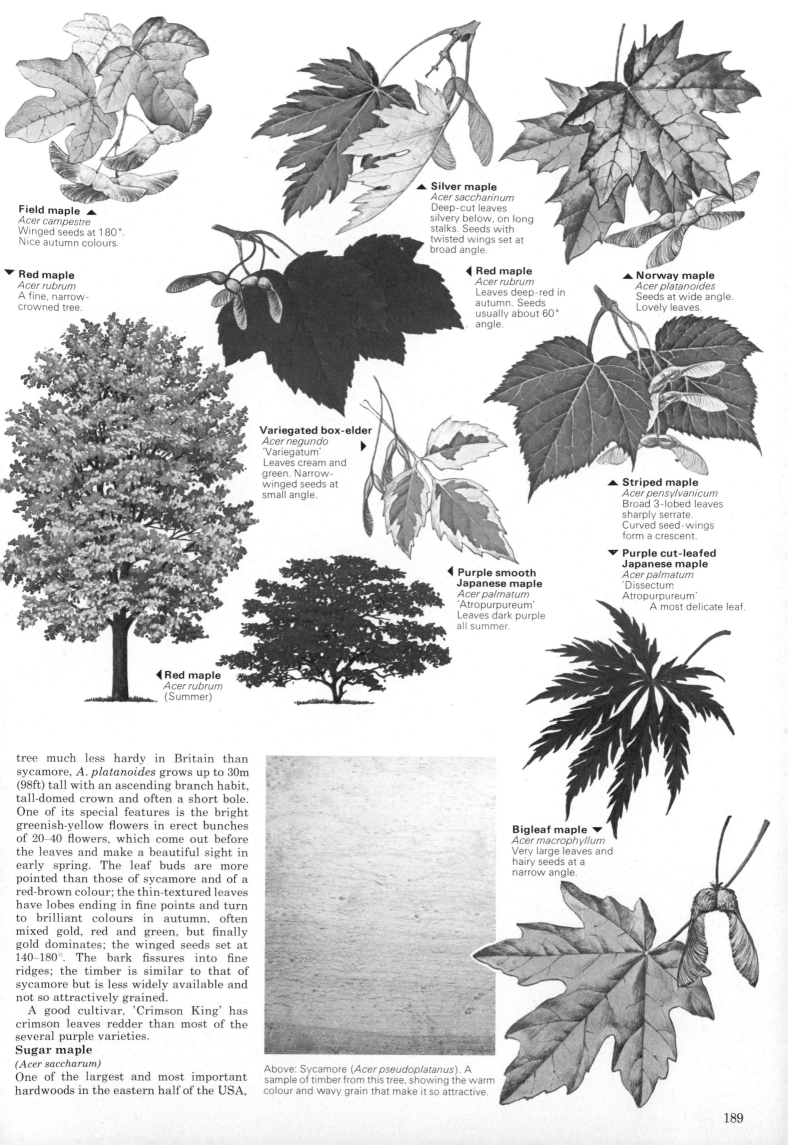

Field maple ▲
Acer campestre
Winged seeds at 180°.
Nice autumn colours.

▼ **Red maple**
Acer rubrum
A fine, narrow-
crowned tree.

▲ **Silver maple**
Acer saccharinum
Deep-cut leaves
silvery below, on long
stalks. Seeds with
twisted wings set at
broad angle.

◀ **Red maple**
Acer rubrum
Leaves deep-red in
autumn. Seeds
usually about 60°
angle.

▲ **Norway maple**
Acer platanoides
Seeds at wide angle.
Lovely leaves.

Variegated box-elder
Acer negundo
'Variegatum'
Leaves cream and
green. Narrow-
winged seeds at
small angle. ▶

▲ **Striped maple**
Acer pensylvanicum
Broad 3-lobed leaves
sharply serrate.
Curved seed-wings
form a crescent.

▼ **Purple cut-leafed
Japanese maple**
Acer palmatum
'Dissectum
Atropurpureum'
A most delicate leaf.

◀ **Purple smooth
Japanese maple**
Acer palmatum
'Atropurpureum'
Leaves dark purple
all summer.

◀ **Red maple**
Acer rubrum
(Summer)

Bigleaf maple ▼
Acer macrophyllum
Very large leaves and
hairy seeds at a
narrow angle.

tree much less hardy in Britain than
sycamore, *A. platanoides* grows up to 30m
(98ft) tall with an ascending branch habit,
tall-domed crown and often a short bole.
One of its special features is the bright
greenish-yellow flowers in erect bunches
of 20–40 flowers, which come out before
the leaves and make a beautiful sight in
early spring. The leaf buds are more
pointed than those of sycamore and of a
red-brown colour; the thin-textured leaves
have lobes ending in fine points and turn
to brilliant colours in autumn, often
mixed gold, red and green, but finally
gold dominates; the winged seeds set at
140–180°. The bark fissures into fine
ridges; the timber is similar to that of
sycamore but is less widely available and
not so attractively grained.

A good cultivar, 'Crimson King' has
crimson leaves redder than most of the
several purple varieties.

Sugar maple
(Acer saccharum)
One of the largest and most important
hardwoods in the eastern half of the USA,

Above: Sycamore (*Acer pseudoplatanus*). A
sample of timber from this tree, showing the warm
colour and wavy grain that make it so attractive.

sugar maple is not only a valuable timber tree and the source of maple sugar and maple syrup, obtained by tapping the sap in spring, but also one of the major species responsible for the magnificent autumn colours in North America. It grows to 35m (115ft) tall with an irregular-domed crown and its thin-textured leaf (8–12cm × 12–18cm; up to $4\frac{3}{4}$×7in), the emblem of Canada, has three to five pointed lobes and stalk 3–7cm ($1\frac{1}{6}$–$2\frac{3}{4}$in) long. The pale reddish-brown timber is hard, heavy and close-grained, and is used for a variety of purposes, including furniture, flooring and turnery.

Red maple
(Acer rubrum)
Red maple has much the same native distribution as sugar maple and the two often grow together. It is a smaller tree rarely above 30m (98ft). The smaller, narrower leaves have lobes more forward-pointing and more small teeth round the edges; autumn colours mainly marvellous bright reds. The timber is of poorer quality than that of sugar maple, but is used for similar purposes.

Silver maple
(Acer saccharinum syn. Acer dasycarpum)
Native to eastern and central North America, this is one of the largest and fastest growing of all the maples, up to 40m (131ft) tall, it is a graceful tree with a high-domed crown and many ascending branches, but rather apt to be damaged by gales. The beautiful finely cut leaves 8–9cm × 14–15cm (up to $3\frac{1}{2}$×6in) are green above and silvery beneath, with slender reddish stalks 8–12cm ($3\frac{1}{8}$–$4\frac{3}{4}$in) long; the flowers appear before the leaves in dense, greenish-yellow axillary clusters. The timber is not of the best quality and is not generally highly valued in the commercial world.

Bigleaf or Oregon maple
(Acer macrophyllum)
This is the only commercially important maple of the Pacific Coast region, with a native range from Alaska to California. It grows to 30m (98ft) and forms a tall-domed crown of ascending branches. It is notable for its very large three to five-lobed leaves, usually wider than long (18–30cm × 20–35 cm; up to 12 × 14in), glossy green above, paler beneath, on green or red stalks 15–25cm (6–10in) long. The sweetly-scented flowers hang in narrow racemes 12–20cm ($4\frac{3}{4}$–8in) long. This is one of the main timber maples; the wood is reddish-brown, often darker than most maple timbers, and much valued for a wide range of uses.

Cappadocian maple
(Acer cappadocicum)
This attractive maple from Turkey, the Caucasus, the Himalayas and China, with its wonderful pale gold autumn colour, deserves to be more widely planted, though it is of no importance as a timber tree. It grows to 25m (82ft) with a dense round crown and a short bole often surrounded by sucker growth. Its smooth-edged leaves 8×12cm–12×16cm (up to $4\frac{3}{4}$×$6\frac{1}{3}$in) on stalks 8–12cm ($3\frac{1}{8}$–$4\frac{3}{4}$in) long, have five to seven narrow-pointed lobes. There are two marked cultivars: 'Aureum' whose leaves are yellow in early spring, and 'Rubrum' with bright red young leaves; in both of these the leaves turn green by the summer.

Field maple
(Acer campestre)
This is the common hedgerow maple of Europe, and western Asia, often scrubby when cut back but when allowed to grow freely it makes a beautiful little tree up to 25m (82ft) tall and deserves to be more widely planted. The small leaves, 5–10cm (2–4in) across, have three main lobes and two small basal ones; they are usually broader than long and grow on slender stalks, 5–10cm (2–4in) long; in spring they are a pretty reddish colour, turning to gold in autumn. The yellow, red and green horizontally opposed winged seeds are also decorative. The older twigs often have narrow corky wings. It is of no importance as a timber tree, though the wood is hard and fine-grained.

Ash-leafed maple or box-elder
(Acer negundo)
An eastern North American species, this seldom grows above 20m ($65\frac{1}{2}$ft) tall. Each of the long-stalked pinnate leaves has five to seven leaflets much like those of ash or elder; their autumn colours are not remarkable. The pairs of narrow-winged seeds are bent inwards so that the wings are parallel.

The cultivar 'Variegatum' has leaves variegated with pure white and is more often planted than the original green type, but it tends to revert to green with sucker growths from the base.

Paperbark maple
(Acer griseum)
This small tree, seldom above 13m ($42\frac{1}{2}$ft) tall, has wonderful coppery-brown, shiny, peeling bark on both trunk and branches—making a beautiful contrast with the trifoliate leaves, which are dark grey-green above and bluish-white beneath. A native of western China it is one of the best of the ornamentals and gives good red autumn colours. The greenish-yellow flowers hang in little bunches of from three to five on long stalks, and the fat seeds have almost parallel broad wings.

Snake-bark maples
All the species in this little group, of which four examples are given below, share the characteristic of having the bark of the young trees vertically striped with silvery white lines—an attractive feature, especially in the winter when the leaves have fallen, leaving the branches bare.

Striped maple or moose-bark
(Acer pensylvanicum)
This tree from eastern Canada and northeastern USA grows up to 12m (39ft) tall with very erect branches and grey-green bark brilliantly striped with white lines. The large three-pointed leaves, 9–13cm × 20–22cm (up to 5 ×$8\frac{2}{3}$in), turn clear yellow in autumn.

Red snake-bark maple
(Acer capillipes)
This Japanese tree, up to 15m (49ft) tall, has green bark with white stripes and, again, very upright form. The leaves, about 9×12cm ($3\frac{1}{2}$×$4\frac{3}{4}$in), have large, pointed central lobes and two small side lobes, and turn to shades of red and yellow-orange in autumn.

Hers's maple
(Acer hersii)
Of Chinese origin, up to 15m (49ft) tall, with steeply ascending branches that arch out at the ends, A. hersii has smooth

olive-green bark with silver stripes tinged green. The thick, rather rubbery leaves, about 9×12cm ($3\frac{1}{2}$×$4\frac{3}{4}$in) are shallowly three-lobed with slightly crenate edges and turn a variety of oranges, yellows, and reds in autumn. The small green flowers are on arching racemes.

David's maple
(Acer davidii)
Another Chinese species, this is very variable and some botanists divide it into several separate species. It grows up to 18m (59ft) tall, the lower branches being level, upper ones ascending and arching over; the bark is olive-green with broad silver stripes. The leaves (not at all maple-like) are of a simple ovate shape with a pointed end, unevenly toothed, dark shiny green above and whitish green on the underside at the start of the season, turning to various autumn colours, some poor, others bright yellow, orange or red.

Japanese ornamental maples
Among the most attractive features of Japanese gardens for hundreds of years, these

Above: Norway maple (*Acer platanoides*). The beautiful panicles of yellow flowers that appear in late March, before the leaves come out.

Left: Sugar maple (*Acer saccharum*). The brilliant autumn colours of this important tree are a visual delight over wide areas of North America.

Below: Sycamore (*Acer pseudoplatanus*). The long buds burst as the large, three- to five-lobed leaves begin to unfold and expand in spring.

wonderful little trees have now become popular all over the temperate regions of the world, looking enchanting with their beautiful leaves, brilliant autumn colours and the delicate tracery of their sinuous branches. In Japan their small-sized, hard, fine-grained timbers are used for toy-making, turnery and musical instruments.

The two main species are *Acer japonicum* and *Acer palmatum* but there are many cultivars, particularly of the latter species, and the seedlings show great variation. Nearly all the Japanese maples now sold are cultivars and the original forms are seldom used. Some notes follow on a small selection of these species and cultivars.

Downy Japanese maple
(Acer japonicum)

A small broad-crowned tree, this grows to 10m (33ft) tall, with a short bole quickly dividing into many sinuous branches, with greyish bark. The light green almost circular leaves, about 7–12cm ($2\frac{3}{4}$–$4\frac{3}{4}$in) in diameter, with seven to eleven lobes cut not more than two-fifths towards the leaf base, have irregular small-toothed edges and silky hairs all over when just opened, both on leaves and stalks. Later they are only retained on the underside of the leaf veins. The small purple flowers, 1–1.5cm ($\frac{2}{5}$–$\frac{3}{5}$in) across, form in long-stalked nodding bunches; winged seed pairs, almost horizontally spread, are greenish on red stalks. Autumn colours are usually good, mainly reds with some golds, but less brilliant than with many of its cultivars.

'Vitifolium' is almost the same but can grow to a rather larger tree. The leaves also are rather larger and usually with nine to twelve lobes; the autumn colours are more brilliant. 'Filicifolium' syn. 'Aconitifolium' has leaves more deeply divided and serrated which turn a very rich ruby autumn colour.

Smooth Japanese maple
(Acer palmatum)

This grows up to 15m (49ft) tall and is often less broad than *Acer japonicum*, with the sinuous branches a little more ascending before they arch down; the bark tends to be browner. The green leaves have five to seven pointed lobes cut halfway or more toward the base, finely serrated edges and no pubescence. Purple flowers about 7mm ($\frac{1}{4}$in) across grow in rather erect small panicles; the pale-red winged seeds are in little bunches, with the pairs of wings set at 80 or 90°. Autumn colours are bronze or purple.

'Atropurpureum' has rich purple leaves throughout the summer, in some trees bronze, in others more red. There is a cultivar 'Dissectum Atropurpureum' with very deeply cut purple leaves.

'Osakazuki' is one of the best of all the cultivars. The leaves usually have seven long acuminate lobes and start as soft green in colour, often tinged with bronze or pink round the edges turning to brilliant scarlet in autumn; during the summer the bright-red winged seeds contrast well with the green foliage.

'Dissectum' has very deeply cut green leaves. 'Aureum' has light yellow leaves which turn deep gold in autumn. 'Senkaki', the coral bark maple, has coral red bark on the twigs and smaller branches, and small, deeply cut yellow-green leaves.

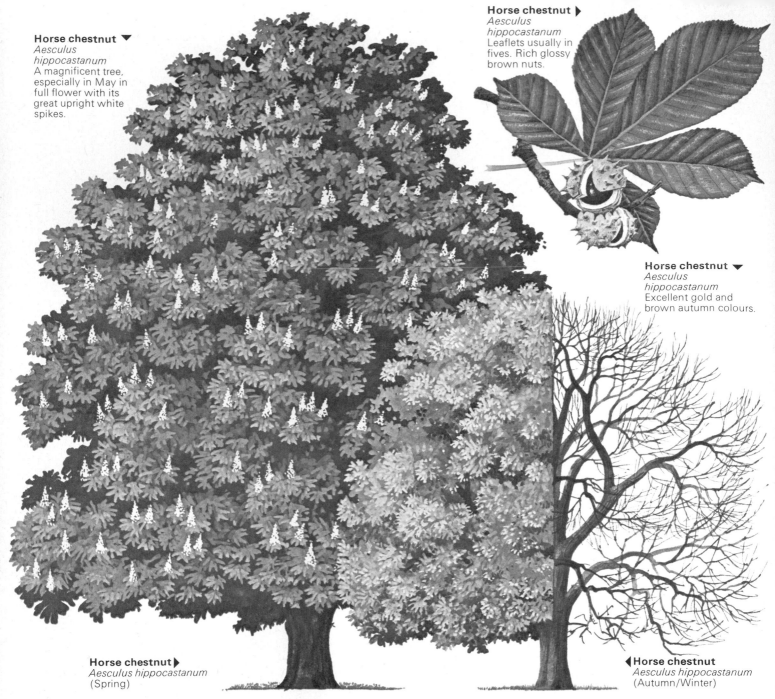

Horse chestnut ▼
Aesculus
hippocastanum
A magnificent tree,
especially in May in
full flower with its
great upright white
spikes.

Horse chestnut ▶
Aesculus
hippocastanum
Leaflets usually in
fives. Rich glossy
brown nuts.

Horse chestnut ▼
Aesculus
hippocastanum
Excellent gold and
brown autumn colours.

Horse chestnut ▶
Aesculus hippocastanum
(Spring)

◀ **Horse chestnut**
Aesculus hippocastanum
(Autumn/Winter)

Horse Chestnuts

Most of this group of over twenty species come from America, where they are called 'buckeyes' because the pale patch on the base of the dark nuts resembles the eye of a deer, but some are from southern Europe, China, Japan and the Himalayas. They all have large digitate leaves, erect panicles of flowers and big nuts. Their timber is soft and seldom used. Only the best known species are listed here:

Horse chestnut
(Aesculus hippocastanum)

This is one of the finest of all the broad-leaved trees, presenting a wonderful sight all through the year. It is of grand stature, up to 40m (131ft) tall, it has a huge domed crown and great spreading lower branches that bend downwards and then sweep up sharply towards the tips. Native to Albania and northern Greece but now spread widely through Europe, North America, and many other countries, horse chestnut is a favourite tree for parks and large gardens. It is loved for its large shining brown buds, sticky in spring and opening quickly; magnificent in late spring when

Above: Indian horse chestnut (*Aesculus indica*). The bole of this graceful tree showing the silvery bark with a fine network of shallow fissures.

Above right: Horse chestnut (*Aesculus hippocastanum*). Large, shiny, rich brown buds, sticky in spring. Leaf scars like horseshoes.

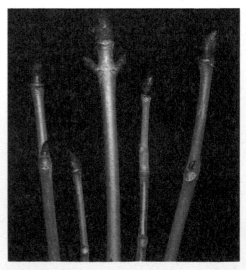

covered with its large upright spikes of white flowers, up to 26cm (10¼in) tall, each with its little patches of delicate yellow or pink; glorious in its rich autumn gold and abundant crop of large, rich brown, beautifully marked nuts or 'conkers' falling out of

◄ Sweet or yellow buckeye
Aesculus flava
Smaller, more shiny leaves than horse chestnut. Orange-red autumn colours. Nut husks without spines.

◄ Indian horse chestnut
Aesculus indica
Feathery flower spikes with long exserted curved stamens. Leaves, smaller, narrower and more shiny than in horse chestnut.

Red horse chestnut ▼
Aesculus × carnea
Much less vigorous than the white form, with both leaves and nuts smaller. Husks have few spines.

Red horse chestnut ▼
Aesculus × carnea
Short pinkish-red flower spikes, and darker, rougher leaves than white horse chestnut.

◄ Red horse chestnut
Aesculus × carnea
(Spring)

their prickly, globular, green husks.

Each large leaf has from 5 to 7 finely toothed leaflets, radiating from a fairly long stalk, the centre leaflet may be as large as 22×10cm ($8\frac{2}{3} \times 4$in) and broadest towards the tip. The leaf scars are large and marked like little horseshoes, even to the nail holes; but the name 'horse' chestnut probably comes from Turkey where the nuts were fed to horses and alleged to cure broken wind. Old trunks are often spirally fluted and the bark breaks away in irregular plates and scales. The timber is almost white, with no marked difference between heartwood and sapwood; soft and easily worked, it is sometimes used for turnery, brush backs, toys and fruit boxes.

Red horse chestnut
(Aesculus × carnea)
With its attractive dark pink flowers in spikes up to 20cm (8in) tall, this hybrid between *Ae. hippocastanum* and *Ae. pavia* is much smaller and slower growing than its white-flowered parent and very subject to stem cankers. Its nuts are also smaller and the husks have many fewer prickles.

Sweet or yellow buckeye
(Aesculus flava. syn. Ae. octandra)
Of the several American species this is the most vigorous, growing up to 32m (105ft), with twisting branches, yellow flowers in spikes up to 18cm (7in) high, smooth nuthusks and rather smooth, reddish-brown bark flaking in small scales.

Red buckeye
(Aesculus pavia)
This species seldom reaches above 12m (39ft); its flowers are darker red than those of *Ae. × carnea*. Another hybrid, *Ae. × planteriensis*, is a much more vigorous tree, reaching 25m (82ft), with larger pale pink flower spikes.

Ohio buckeye
(Aesculus glabra)
This is a fairly small river valley tree with creamy flowers. Its soft wood is used for various small utensils and was once much favoured for artificial limbs.

Dwarf buckeye or shrubby pavia
(Aesculus parviflora)
This species from southeastern USA is scarcely a tree, seldom more than 4m

(13ft) high and usually with a crowd of small stems from sucker growth, but it is hardy and has beautiful white flower spikes 20–32cm (8–12$\frac{3}{5}$in) high with lovely pinkish-white thread-like stamens.

Japanese horse chestnut
(Aesculus turbinata)
This is a very interesting tree growing up to 25m (82ft) high and remarkable for its enormously long stalked leaves with seven sessile leaflets, the largest of them up to 40×18cm (16×7in). The whole leaf may be 60cm (24in) across. The flowers are white with red or pink blotches, in spikes up to 26cm (10$\frac{1}{4}$in) high.

Indian horse chestnut
(Aesculus indica)
From the Himalayas, this tree reaches 30m (98ft) in India but seldom more than 20m (65$\frac{1}{2}$ft) elsewhere. It is a graceful tree with smaller, more shiny leaves than most chestnuts and very attractive feathery flower spikes up to 30cm (12in) tall. These are mainly white but have red and yellow blotches and projecting thin stamens that give a 'bottle brush' effect.

193

Common lime ▼
Tilia × *europaea*
Tall softly billowing
crown. Usually has
basal shoots on bole.

Common lime ▶
Tilia × *europaea*
Cordate leaves finely
toothed. Flowers
pale yellow.

▼ **Common lime**
Tilia × *europaea*
Branches ascend then
arch over and droop.

Common lime ▶
Tilia × *europaea*
(Summer)

Common lime ▶
Tilia × *europaea*
(Autumn/Winter)

Limes

The names *lime*, which was originally *line*, and *linden* both arise from the fibrous character of these trees' peculiar bark and derive from the old English *lin*, thread, and ultimately from the Latin *linum*, flax. Limes are called basswoods in America and this too arises from the fibrous bass or bast that lies just below the hard, smooth, grey outer bark. Though nowadays bast is only used by gardeners for tying bundles of plants, it once provided cordage for the Anglo-Saxons when they crossed the North Sea in simple open sailing boats around AD 500. American Indians also used lime cordage long ago.

There are about 30 species in the northern temperate zone; none of them are native in western North America though there are several in eastern USA. The particular characteristics of limes are their tough, fibrous inner bark, heart-shaped leaves oblique at the base, flowers in cymes from a stalk midway along a large membraneous bract, and buds with only two visible scales, one much larger than the other. Lime tree flowers are strongly scented and a great attraction for bees; lime honey is famous.

Unfortunately, many lime leaves are often attacked in the summer by swarms of aphids that cause sticky 'honeydew' to cover the foliage and drip off on to everything below the trees, finally developing black 'sooty-mould' fungi. Another, but far less troublesome, associate of lime leaves is the little red insect that causes nail-galls—little red spikes often seen projecting from the leaf surface.

Interbreeding has given rise to much confusion over the naming of varieties but the following notes cover a few of the better known trees.

Common lime

(Tilia × europaea syn. *Tilia vulgaris)*
A natural hybrid between *T. platyphyllos* and *T. cordata*, this is the commonest lime in Britain and also widespread in the rest of Europe. A fine tree, the tallest broadleaved species in Britain, reaching 46m (151ft) and living to a great age, anything from 500 to around 1,000 years. It is a graceful tree with a tall billowing crown formed of branches that first ascend and then arch over. It has long been a great favourite for garden training and many very old avenues can be found.

The ovoid red-brown buds open to unfurl heart-shaped leaves, 6–10cm ($2\frac{1}{3}$–4in) long, broad but with short-pointed tips, sharply serrate and smooth except for small whitish tufts in the main axils on the lower surface. The pendent, yellowish-white flowers, four to ten together, are very fragrant and ripen into hard broadly ovoid fruits 6–8mm ($\frac{1}{4}$–$\frac{5}{16}$in) in diameter, faintly ribbed and pubescent. The bark on old trees is fissured into a network of shallow ridges and the lower bole is commonly covered in burrs and dense thickets of small shoots.

The soft creamy-white to pale fawn timber is very evenly grained and particularly good for carving; it was much used by Grinling Gibbons around 1650. It is also useful for engineering patterns.

Large-leafed lime

(Tilia platyphyllos)
Native to Europe and Asia Minor, growing

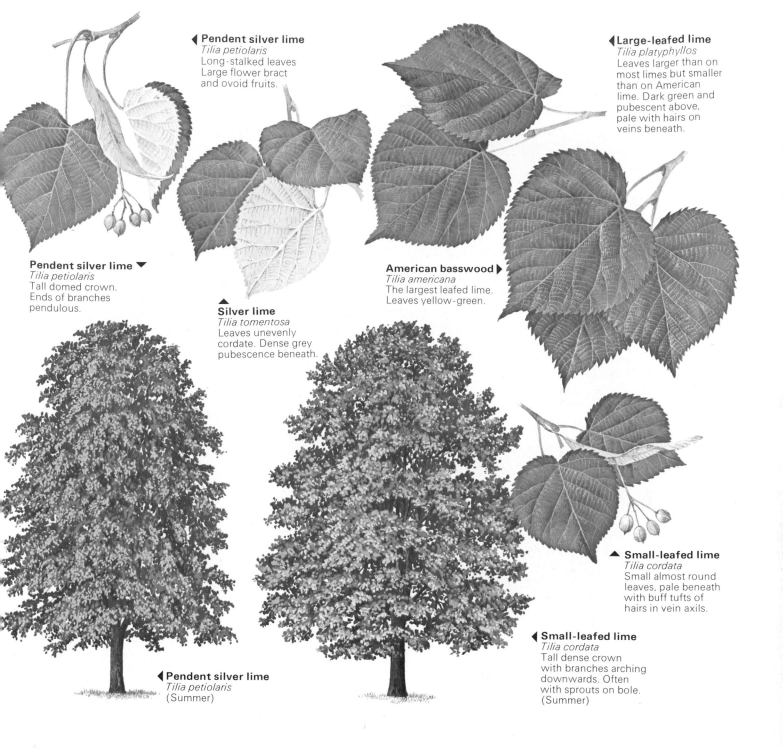

Pendent silver lime
Tilia petiolaris
Long-stalked leaves
Large flower bract
and ovoid fruits.

Large-leafed lime
Tilia platyphyllos
Leaves larger than on
most limes but smaller
than on American
lime. Dark green and
pubescent above,
pale with hairs on
veins beneath.

Pendent silver lime ▼
Tilia petiolaris
Tall domed crown.
Ends of branches
pendulous.

▲
Silver lime
Tilia tomentosa
Leaves unevenly
cordate. Dense grey
pubescence beneath.

American basswood ▶
Tilia americana
The largest leafed lime.
Leaves yellow-green.

◀ **Pendent silver lime**
Tilia petiolaris
(Summer)

▲ **Small-leafed lime**
Tilia cordata
Small almost round
leaves, pale beneath
with buff tufts of
hairs in vein axils.

◀ **Small-leafed lime**
Tilia cordata
Tall dense crown
with branches arching
downwards. Often
with sprouts on bole.
(Summer)

to 40m (131ft) tall with a narrow-domed
crown and branches more ascending than
in common lime, this is usually a clean
and shapely tree; its straight clean trunk
seldom has sprouts at the base. The leaves
are variable, from 8–16cm ($3\frac{1}{8}$–$6\frac{1}{3}$in) across,
deeply cordate, crenate and serrate, dark
green, sometimes but not always pubescent
on upper surfaces, pale green and densely
pubescent on the veins beneath. The
flowers grow in bunches of three to five,
and the flowering stalk bracts are large and
whitish-green; fruits are 8–10mm ($\frac{5}{16}$–$\frac{2}{5}$in)
in diameter, prominently five-ribbed and
densely pubescent.

There is a cut-leaved cultivar known as
'Laciniata' or 'Aspleniifolia'.
Small-leafed lime
(*Tilia cordata* syn. *Tilia parvifolia*)
Native to Europe, this rather smaller tree
is good where space is restricted. It is
slower-growing and reaches a maximum
height of 32m (105ft), with a tall, dense,
irregular crown. It flowers late in the
season; the fruits are thin-shelled and
smooth. Its leaves are slightly smaller

than those of the common lime, rounded,
more glaucous, and with orange or buff
tufts in the vein axils on the under-surface.
American basswood
(*Tilia americana* syn. *Tilia glabra*)
Up to 40m (131ft), this fine tree, native to
Canada and the USA, has very large
leaves, sometimes as much as 30cm × 20cm
(12 × 8in); unfortunately these are often
spoilt by the aphids common to so many
limes. The fruiting stem bracts are large,
up to 12cm by nearly 3cm ($4\frac{3}{4}$ × $1\frac{1}{6}$in); the
fruits are thick-shelled and without any
marked ribs. American basswood is valued
as a timber tree because of its large size;
it yields straight-grained, easily worked
soft wood. It is not abundant, however.
Silver or white lime
(*Tilia tomentosa*)
A fine broad-domed tree, up to 30m (98ft)
tall, with steeply ascending branches,
native to southeast Europe and southwest
Asia. Its rather special features are the
white woolly young shoots and the dense,
silvery-grey pubescence on the back of the
almost round leaves.

Oliver's lime
(*Tilia oliveri*)
Closely related to *Tilia tomentosa*, this
fine Chinese tree is one of the best limes
and deserves wider use. It grows to 25m
(82ft) tall with fairly straight ascending
branches and a high-domed crown. The
large leaves, up to 14 × 12cm ($5\frac{1}{2}$ × $4\frac{3}{4}$in),
are pointed at the tip, evenly cordate at
the base, with small, whitish, pointed
teeth and bright silvery undersides. Branch
scars are dark curved folds.
Pendent silver lime
(*Tilia petiolaris*)
Of doubtful origin, but probably from
eastern Europe, *T. petiolaris* is a beautiful
tree with rather sinuous ascending
branches and graceful pendent branchlets. It is usually grafted and forms a
narrow-domed crown reaching up to about
32m (105ft). The leaves are deeply cordate
on slender, white pubescent stalks, and
have white undersides. The flowers must
have a narcotic or intoxicating effect as
bees can often be found lying on the ground
beneath the tree, especially in the evening.

Tupelo or black gum ▶
Nyssa sylvatica
Mature leaves and
small egg-shaped
fruits in pairs on
long stalk.

Tupelo or black gum ▶
Nyssa sylvatica
One of the finest trees
for autumn colours,
mostly reds but some
gold in places.

Dove tree ▼
Davidia involucrata
Beautiful leaves and
small purplish flowers
with huge white bracts.

Dove tree ▼
Davidia involucrata
A remarkable sight
when festooned with
large white flower-
bracts.

Tupelo or black gum ▶
Nyssa sylvatica
(Autumn)

Dove tree ▶
Davidia involucrata
(Summer flowering)

Dove tree ▶
Davidia involucrata
Twig showing the
glossy very dark
red buds.

Tupelos and Dove Trees

There are only two tupelo species at all commonly seen, one from America and one from China. They are closely related to the dogwoods and dove trees.

Tupelo or black gum
(Nyssa sylvatica)

Native only to eastern North America but planted in many other temperate countries for its superb show of red and gold autumn colours. 'Nyssa' was a water nymph to the ancient Greeks, and this tree does prefer moist situations; when planted by the water's edge it gives marvellous autumn reflections. In America it reaches 30m (98ft) tall but elsewhere is seldom above 15–20m (49–65½ft) with a broadly conic crown, flattening out with age, and many level branches often turning up at the ends.

The red-brown buds are small and pointed, the glossy green leaves variable in both size and shape, from 5–12cm (2–4¾in) long, usually entire but sometimes with a few coarse teeth, normally oval and broadly pointed on a short stalk, occasionally longer and more elliptic, always very late flushing and turning to brilliant autumn colours. Both male and female flowers are inconspicuous, the former tiny yellow-green beads 3–4mm (up to $\frac{1}{6}$in) in diameter, the latter cylindric, about 4mm ($\frac{1}{4}$in) long, green with purple tips. The fruit, a blue-black egg-shaped berry, 1–1.5cm ($\frac{2}{5}$–$\frac{3}{5}$in) long, usually sets in pairs. Tupelo bark is grey, coarsely fissured into irregular rough narrow plates.

It is a tree deserving much wider use.

Chinese tupelo
Nyssa sinensis)

Not common except in its native haunts in central China, this is a small tree, usually less than 10m (33ft) in height but with the same wonderful autumn colours as *N. sylvatica*, from which it differs in having hairy red shoots, narrower leaves, which are not glossy above, and a broader crown.

Dove tree, ghost tree or handkerchief tree
(Davidia involucrata)

A single species from central and western China growing to a maximum of about 20m (65½ft), conical at first but later with a high domed crown and radiating branches, the upper ones ascending, the lower ones level. Its unique feature is the enormous white bracts around the flowers that may be as large as 22×11cm ($8\frac{2}{3} \times 4\frac{1}{3}$in) and hang from twigs like doves or handkerchiefs, looking ghostly at night. The cordate, beautifully veined leaves are broadly ovate with pointed ends, up to 16×13cm ($6\frac{1}{3} \times 5$in), coarsely toothed and white pubescence on the underside, often growing in small clusters. The dove tree has unusual shiny, deep red buds about 1–1.5cm ($\frac{2}{5}$–$\frac{3}{5}$in) long and ovoid. The sweet-smelling white flowers with purple stamens are dwarfed by the huge bracts; the ribbed fruits, about 3×2.5cm ($1\frac{1}{6} \times 1$in), on long stalks, are green at first, later turning purple. The bark is grey-brown, and tends to flake off in small pieces.

The variety *vilmoriniana*, sometimes treated as a separate species, really only differs in having glabrous leaves.

The dove tree deserves to be more widely planted as an ornamental species; it is very decorative when festooned with its hanging white flower-bracts.

Indian bean tree ▼
Catalpa bignonioides
A most impressive tree with a large wide-domed crown and heavy branches springing from a short, stout bole. The foliage is light-green and in winter the bunches of long seed-pods remain on the branches.

Indian bean tree ▶
Catalpa bignonioides
Very large, pale-green soft, wavy-edged leaves on long stalks. Striking flowers in broad panicles, white with frilled edges and spotted with purple and yellow.

Indian bean tree ▶
Catalpa bignonioides (Summer)

Indian bean tree ▶
Catalpa bignonioides
Very long, thin seedpods in small bunches, remaining on the twigs all winter.

Catalpas

This group consists of a few very attractive species from North America, eastern Asia and the West Indies, belonging to the large Bignonia family, and noted for their very large leaves and long slender seed-pods.

Indian bean tree
(Catalpa bignonioides)
A magnificent tree from southeastern USA, reaching 20m (65½ft) tall, often wider than it is high, with large spreading branches and a broad domed crown. The twigs are stout, pithy in the centre, with large leaf scars; the bright light-green leaves are conspicuous from a long way off, very large, 12–25cm × 9–20cm (up to 10 × 8in), often in whorls of three, entire, rounded with a short point, and soft with a slightly wavy edge. The beautiful flowers, very like those of horse chestnut but in broader panicles with larger individual bell-shaped flowers with frilled edges and yellow and purple spots, are produced in masses on older trees in midsummer. The slender dark brown seed-pods, 14–40cm (5½–16in) long, hang in bunches and tend to stay on the tree all the winter. The bark is pinkish-brown when young but on old trees becomes greyer, fissured into small irregular plates. The timber is very durable outdoors but of no commercial value.

There is a particularly striking golden leaved cultivar, 'Aurea', of great ornamental value as it contrasts wonderfully with the green of other trees.

Western catalpa
(Catalpa speciosa)
The largest of the catalpas, often over 30m (98ft) tall in its native southern central USA has an upright form and straighter stem than most others. Its leathery leaves are long pointed, up to 27cm × 22cm (10⅘ × 8⅔in) broad, with pale brown down on the lower surface. The flower panicles have fewer flowers than the Indian bean and the dark grey bark is deeply fissured into scaly ridges. The timber is valued for its remarkable resistance to wet soils.

Yellow catalpa
(Catalpa ovata)
A smaller tree from China, grows up to 12m (39ft) in height and has darker green, three-lobed leaves and yellowish flowers.

Farge's catalpa
(Catalpa fargesii)
This small tree from west China has a slender upright form, up to 20m (65½ft) high, its hard leather leaves are smaller than those of *C. speciosa* but with even longer points and soft white pubescence beneath; the pinkish flowers are speckled yellow and purple and on short panicles.

Below: Indian bean tree (*Catalpa bignonioides*). New leaves are dark bronzy purple at first.

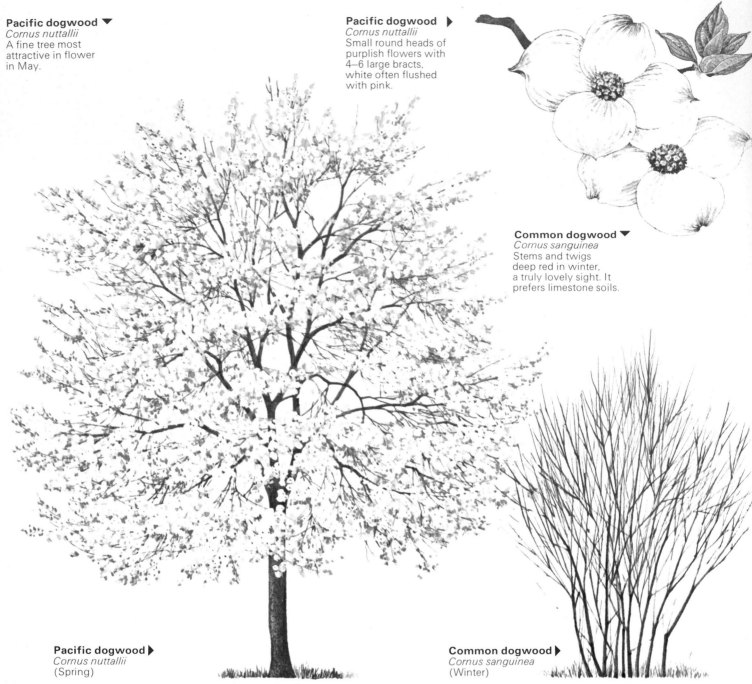

Pacific dogwood ▼
Cornus nuttallii
A fine tree most
attractive in flower
in May.

Pacific dogwood ▶
Cornus nuttallii
Small round heads of
purplish flowers with
4–6 large bracts,
white often flushed
with pink.

Common dogwood ▼
Cornus sanguinea
Stems and twigs
deep red in winter,
a truly lovely sight. It
prefers limestone soils.

Pacific dogwood ▶
Cornus nuttallii
(Spring)

Common dogwood ▶
Cornus sanguinea
(Winter)

Dogwoods and Elders

This outstandingly beautiful group of trees and shrubs, comprising about 40 species in all, is particularly well represented in America, but also grows in Europe, Siberia, China, Japan and the Himalayas. Most dogwood species have opposite leaves with veins arching towards the leaf-tip, small four-parted flowers, often backed by large showy pink or white bracts, ornamental berries and occasionally beautifully coloured stems. Only a small selection can be described here.

Pacific dogwood
(Cornus nuttallii)

The biggest of the American dogwoods, this species forms a magnificent tree, up to 30m (98ft) tall, with large white bracts to its flowers and wonderful gold and scarlet colours in autumn.

Flowering dogwood
(Cornus florida)

Native to eastern USA, this is a rather smaller tree that grows up to 15m (49ft), giving a mass of white or pink bracted flowers and autumn colours similar to those of *Cornus nuttallii*.

Nurserymen have made the most of the dogwoods in America and many lovely cultivars are to be seen in the parks and streets with different coloured bracts, usually pink or red.

Common dogwood or cornel
(Cornus sanguinea)

This dogwood, the main native species in Europe, is remarkable for its striking red stems, beautiful autumn colours and glossy black berries. It does well on alkaline soils and there is a variegated form commonly used in gardens. The hard, tough wood of the stems was used for making skewers and goads called 'dags' in old times and the original name was 'dagwood'.

Other red-stemmed dogwoods are *Cornus alba* from Siberia with fine red stems and bluish-white berries, with a specially good type 'Westonbirt Dogwood', developed at Westonbirt Arboretum in Gloucestershire, having extra brilliant red stems. Also *C. stolonifera* from North America is red-stemmed, with dark purplish-red twigs.

Cornelian cherry
(Cornus mas)

This striking European species is often bushy but sometimes up to 8m (26ft) high, and much loved for its little bunches of small yellow flowers in February and March on the leafless stems, and its bright red berries up to 2cm ($\frac{4}{5}$in) long.

Asiatic dogwood
(Cornus controversa)

This beautiful species comes from China, the Himalayas and Japan. It forms a large tree, up to 20m (65½ft), with remarkable, slender, horizontal branches and, unlike most dogwoods, alternate leaves; it has masses of small white flowers.

Japanese dogwood
(Cornus kousa)

This is a free flowering shrub or small tree up to 8m (26ft) tall with beautiful, slightly twisted, creamy white or pinkish, pointed bracts, four per flower, and excellent autumn colours. Its special features are its strange fruits, yellow at first then turning red like round hard raspberries on stalks up to 7cm (2¾in) long.

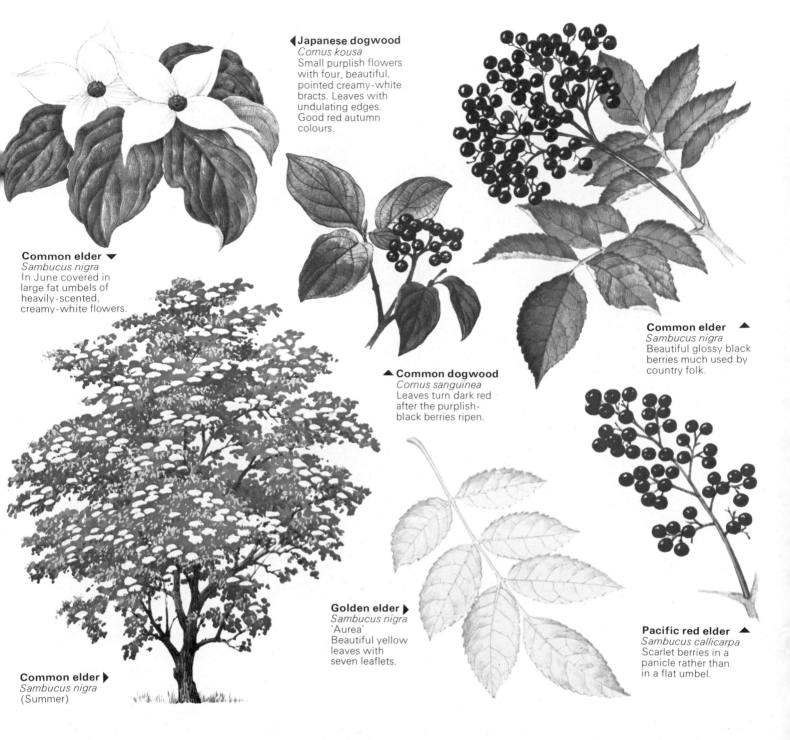

◄ Japanese dogwood
Cornus kousa
Small purplish flowers with four, beautiful, pointed creamy-white bracts. Leaves with undulating edges. Good red autumn colours.

Common elder ▼
Sambucus nigra
In June covered in large fat umbels of heavily-scented, creamy-white flowers.

▲ Common dogwood
Cornus sanguinea
Leaves turn dark red after the purplish-black berries ripen.

Common elder ▲
Sambucus nigra
Beautiful glossy black berries much used by country folk.

Golden elder ▶
Sambucus nigra 'Aurea'
Beautiful yellow leaves with seven leaflets.

Pacific red elder ▲
Sambucus callicarpa
Scarlet berries in a panicle rather than in a flat umbel.

Common elder ▶
Sambucus nigra
(Summer)

The elders, mainly from America and Europe, are an interesting and useful little group of deciduous shrubs and small trees characterized by opposite pinnate leaves always having an odd number, from 3–11, of toothed leaflets, young shoots lined with soft pith, clusters of small white, or yellowish-white flowers and berries varying from black to blue or red.

Common elder
(Sambucus nigra)
Native to Europe this is an amazingly hardy species, succeeding even on very poor or very alkaline soils, immune to rabbit damage, and tolerant of smoke and fumes, severe exposure and heavy shade. Country folk make much use of the elder: wines from the berries and the flowers; syrup for curing coughs and colds from the berries; elderflower water for various healing purposes. The pith is used in laboratories and by watch-makers as a cleaning material; hollowed out stems are used for pop-guns, blow pipes, whistles and flutes (the Greek word *sambuké* means a musical instrument).

In hedges elder is usually cut back and forms a bush, but left alone it will make a small tree up to 10m (33ft) high. The opposite leaves, 10–25cm (4–10in) long with from 3 to 7 toothed leaflets, emit a strong smell, especially when bruised; bunches used to be tied to horses' heads to help keep flies away. The white flowers also have a strong smell and occur in flat umbels, 10–20cm (4–8in) across. On young twigs the bark has conspicuous lenticels but on old trunks it has deep fissures.

There are many attractive cultivars such as golden elder with yellow leaves, cut-leaved elder, variegated elder and pink-flowered elder.

American elder
(Sambucus canadensis)
Closely allied to *S. nigra*, the eastern American elder is smaller, seldom more than 4m (13ft) high. Its leaves usually have more leaflets, the flower heads are not so flat and the berries are dark purple when ripe instead of black.

It has a cut-leaved cultivar 'Laciniata' and another with very large leaves and enormous flower heads called 'Maxima'.

Red-berried elder
(Sambucus racemosa)
Native to Europe, Asia Minor, northern China and Siberia, this species forms a growing shrub, only up to 4m (13ft) high. Its yellowish-white flowers are in pyramidal panicles and the bright red berries ripen in summer—much earlier than common elder. There are many cultivars, including cut-leaved, gold-leaved, white and pink-flowered ones.

The American species, *S. pubens*, is very close to *S. racemosa* but has downy leaves and shoots and brown pith.

Blue elderberry
(Sambucus coerulea)
Larger than most of the species, this elder grows up to 15m (49ft) with trunk diameter up to 50cm (20in). Native to western North America its berries, though black beneath, are covered with a pale blue bloom. The yellowish white flower umbels are large, 12–20cm (4¾–8in) across. It has a variety *S. velutina* with twigs and leaves clothed in grey velvety down.

Strawberry tree ▼
Arbutus unedo
A short evergreen tree with dense, rounded crown, broadly-spreading sinuous branches and dark green foliage.

Strawberry tree ▶
Arbutus unedo
The fruits take two years to mature so that the flowers and ripe fruits occur together. Very dark green serrated leaves.

▼ **Snowdrop tree**
Halesia monticola
A broad tree with widely spreading, almost level lower branches. Grey bark, pinkish in fissures.

Strawberry tree ▶
Arbutus unedo
(Evergreen)

◀ **Snowdrop tree**
Halesia monticola
(Spring flowering)

Strawberry, Snowbell and Snowdrop Tree

This is a small group of about a dozen evergreen species belonging to the great Ericaceae or heather family, with fruits rather like small round strawberries in appearance and native to the Mediterranean area, the North American continent and Ireland.

Strawberry tree
(Arbutus unedo)
This attractive Mediterranean species is also native to parts of Ireland. It is a small rounded tree from 4–14m (13–46ft) tall, usually with a short bole quickly dividing into several crooked stems; the bark is reddish and with age becomes grey-brown with scales. The leathery, serrated, shiny, dark-green leaves are 5–9×2–3cm (up to $3\frac{1}{2} \times 1\frac{1}{6}$in) in size with pinkish-green stalks, and the ivory-coloured flowers, like little waxen bells about 8mm ($\frac{5}{16}$in) across, hang in bunches, opening from October to December. The rough, pimply globose fruits, 1.5–2cm ($\frac{3}{5}-\frac{4}{5}$in) in diameter, take two years to mature and are green at first, then yellow and finally bright red, making a beautiful colour contrast with the

Above: Strawberry tree (*Arbutus unedo*). The divided bole with finely fissured, red-brown bark.

creamy white flowers; although edible they are insipid, and *unedo* (Latin) means 'I eat one—no more!'

Cyprus strawberry tree
(Arbutus andrachne)
This tree is very similar to *A. unedo* but its leaves are entire and smaller, its fruits smaller and smooth and it flowers in spring, not winter. Hybrids between these two species occur naturally in Greece and are known as × *andrachnoides*; many of them are rather spectacular ornamental trees with especially beautiful orange-red peeling bark.

Madrona
(Arbutus menziesii)
Commonly found wild from California to British Columbia, and conspicuous with its vivid orange-red bark, this magnificent tree reaches 30m (98ft) tall with oval, entire, leathery leaves, 5–12×5–7cm (up to $4\frac{3}{4} \times 2\frac{3}{4}$in) in size, dark shining green above but a wonderful ice-blue beneath. The small white flowers appear in spring in upright panicles and the fruits are only about 1cm ($\frac{2}{5}$in) in diameter.

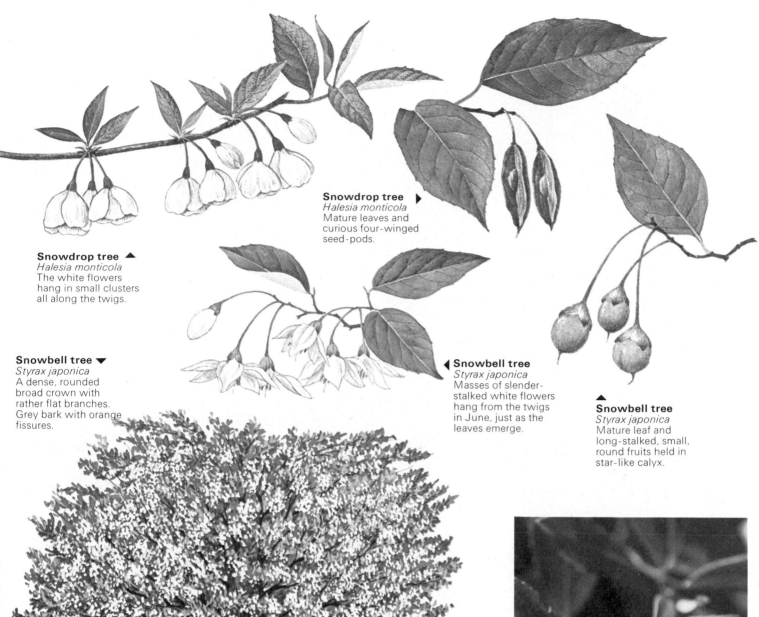

Snowdrop tree ▲
Halesia monticola
The white flowers hang in small clusters all along the twigs.

Snowdrop tree ▶
Halesia monticola
Mature leaves and curious four-winged seed-pods.

Snowbell tree ▼
Styrax japonica
A dense, rounded broad crown with rather flat branches. Grey bark with orange fissures.

◀ **Snowbell tree**
Styrax japonica
Masses of slender-stalked white flowers hang from the twigs in June, just as the leaves emerge.

▲
Snowbell tree
Styrax japonica
Mature leaf and long-stalked, small, round fruits held in star-like calyx.

◀**Snowbell tree**
Styrax japonica
(Summer flowering)

Snowbell and snowdrop trees are among the few members of the storax family (Styracaceae) that grow to tree size. They provide the gardener with a range of fine trees that thrive in a lime-free soil.

Snowbell tree
(Styrax japonica)
A small, rounded, deciduous tree from China and Japan, the snowbell tree grows to a height of about 12m (39ft) and has a tendency to be broader than tall, with arching upper branches and almost level lower ones. A special feature is the masses of bell-like white flowers on stalks up to 4cm ($1\frac{1}{2}$in) long, hanging in small bunches along the branches in June, later developing into smooth ovoid-globular fruits 1–1.5cm ($\frac{2}{5}$–$\frac{3}{5}$in) in diameter, silvery-green and topped by a star-like green calyx, often with purple tops to its five rounded lobes. The leaves are alternate, shiny green, broadly elliptic, 4–8cm ($1\frac{1}{2}$–$3\frac{1}{8}$in) long, pointed and with a few remote teeth along their wavy margins. On mature trees the bark is very attractive with pinkish-orange fissures between irregular grey ridges.

Snowdrop or silverbell tree
(Halesia monticola)
Quite a large, broadly conic tree up to 30m (98ft) tall, from the mountain areas of southeastern USA, bearing heavy crops of pendulous white flowers up to 3cm ($1\frac{1}{6}$in) long, on stalks 2cm ($\frac{4}{5}$in) long, just as the leaves are flushing in May. The bluntly jointed leaves are finely serrated, oblong-ovate, with conspicuous impressed veins. The fruits, almost pear-shaped, up to 5cm (2in) long with four narrow wings, are pale green at first but finally turn brown. The bark is dark-grey with pinkish fissures.

Halesia carolina is very similar to *H. monticola* but much smaller, only up to about 12m (39ft) tall, and with smaller leaves, flowers and fruits.

Right: Fruits of the strawberry tree (*Arbutus unedo*). These begin to ripen when the current year's flowers appear, having taken two years to reach maturity. In shades of yellow to red, the fruits make an attractive contrast to the dark green foliage but they are too acid to eat.

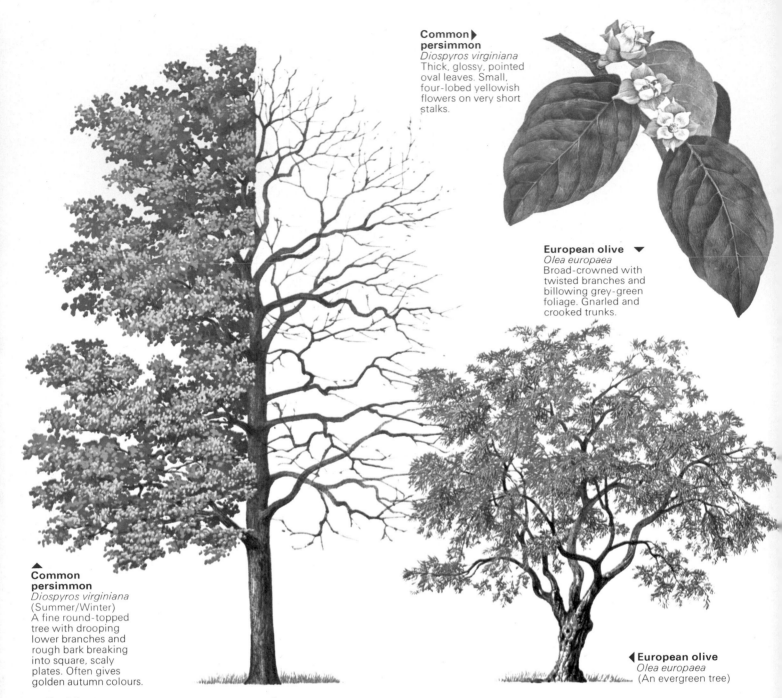

Common ▶ persimmon
Diospyros virginiana
Thick, glossy, pointed oval leaves. Small, four-lobed yellowish flowers on very short stalks.

European olive ▼
Olea europaea
Broad-crowned with twisted branches and billowing grey-green foliage. Gnarled and crooked trunks.

▲
Common persimmon
Diospyros virginiana
(Summer/Winter)
A fine round-topped tree with drooping lower branches and rough bark breaking into square, scaly plates. Often gives golden autumn colours.

◀ **European olive**
Olea europaea
(An evergreen tree)

Olives and Persimmons

The olives belong to the large family *Oleaceae*, a collection of some six hundred species of trees and shrubs including such well-known groups as ashes, privets, lilacs, forsythias, jasmines and osmanthus. Spread right across the world, there are about twenty trees represented in the true *Olea* group.

European olive

(Olea europaea)

By far the most important member of the group, this is native to Asia Minor and Syria. It has been cultivated since prehistoric times and is now grown all over the Mediterranean region with the best orchards in Spain, France, Italy and, more recently introduced, in California.

There is something timeless about the gnarled and twisted form of an old olive, and indeed they live to a very great age—a number of them are between 1,000 and 1,500 years old. The billowing silvery-green of an old olive grove, contrasting with the narrow spires of dark cypresses and the occasional umbrella-like crown of a mature stone pine, makes a beautiful peaceful scene typical of the Mediterranean region.

The lanceolate, or narrowly ovoid opposite evergreen leaves, 5–8cm (2–3$\frac{1}{8}$in) long, grey-green above, silvery beneath, are leathery and pitted; the white flowers, very small (0.5cm; $\frac{1}{5}$in), are in racemes, 3–6cm (1$\frac{1}{6}$–2$\frac{1}{3}$in) long; the familiar oval fruits, about 2–3cm ($\frac{4}{5}$–1$\frac{1}{6}$in) long, containing one hard stone, are green at first but ripen during the winter months, slowly turning through red to black. For eating they are harvested mainly in the green stage but for oil production they are allowed to ripen. For the finest grades of oil they are picked by hand, but more usually they are beaten off the branches and collected from the ground before the long and intricate process of crushing and clarifying.

Olive trees grow slowly, naturally reaching only a maximum height of about 15m (49ft), and are nearly always pruned to keep the branches low for harvesting. The form of old trees is extraordinary, with a rugged gnarled trunk, full of fissures and irregular cavities, and branches twisting and curving in all directions. The yellowish and brown timber, hard but smooth-grained and with attractive markings, is greatly valued for carving, turnery, inlay work, walking sticks and small joinery.

Other species

Olea laurifolia, from Africa, is one of the larger olives, reaching up to 25m (82ft) with diameters up to 1$\frac{1}{2}$m (4$\frac{1}{2}$ft), with shiny leaves (6–11cm; 2$\frac{1}{3}$–4$\frac{1}{3}$in) longer than those of most olives, sweet-smelling, creamy white flowers and fruits which, though good are much less valuable than those of the European tree. The hard brown timber weathers well outdoors and is used for sleepers, piles, stakes, and so on.

Olea africana, growing mainly in its native southern Africa, often in semi-desert conditions, has both flowers and fruits smaller than *O. europaea*. The timber is hard and durable but only used locally.

Olea hochstetteri correctly called East African olive, is often referred to as 'ironwood'; the timber is very like that of

Common persimmon
Diospyros virginiana
Medium-sized, round edible fruits, yellow to orange with red cheek.

Kaki-plum
Diospyros kaki
Beautiful, large, globose edible fruits, slightly grooved, yellow to orange colour. Leaves purple and orange in autumn.

European olive ▼
Olea europaea
The well-known oval fruits. Green at first, turning through red to black.

European olive ▲
Olea europaea
Grey-green lanceolate leathery leaves, silver beneath. Racemes of small white flowers.

Above: European olive (*Olea europaea*). The weirdly contorted and cavity-ridden boles so typical of old olive trees of the Mediterranean.

European olive but much harder and less easy to work.

Olea ferruginea is an Indian species, also called 'ironwood'. It yields a hard, heavy, tough, brown to purple timber which is very durable and takes an excellent polish; it is much valued for beautiful inlay work, and for small items such as tool handles and shafts.

Olea paniculata is an Australian species known as 'marblewood' (or sometimes yet again as ironwood), with tough durable timber, scented when freshly cut and used among other things for barrel staves and turnery. It is a large tree—up to 30m (98ft) with shiny stalked leaves up to 9cm (3½in) long and fruits only about 1.5cm (⅗in) long.

Olea fragrans, a Japanese tree, is noted for its wonderfully fragrant flowers and large leaves, up to 16cm (6⅓in) long.

Persimmons form a large group of mostly tropical and evergreen trees, though some are deciduous; all persimmons belong to the Ebony family (*Ebenaceae*).

Date plum
(Diospyros lotus)

This is a broad, dome-shaped evergreen tree, up to 14m (46ft) high, from China and Japan and across to western Asia, with luxuriant, glossy, dark green, oblong-ovate leaves, on short stalks, varying in size according to the age of the tree; on young trees they may be up to 18×5cm (7×2in) but are much smaller and broader on older specimens. The bark is dull grey and fissured into rectangular squarish plates. Male and female flowers are on separate trees, both types urn-shaped, cream and pink only about 7mm (¼in) long, the males two or three together, the females singly but closely placed in lines. The round fruits, 1–2cm (⅖–⅘in) in diameter are yellow and purple, and are unpalatable.

Common persimmon
(Diospyros virginiana)

This American species reaches up to 22m (72ft) tall with the lower branches often rather pendulous and the leaves similar to those of the date-plum though more pubescent beneath and with slightly tougher stalks. The flowers are longer, up to 1.5cm (⅗in) and the fruits much larger, 2–4cm (⅘–1½in) in diameter, pale orange, often with a red cheek, and edible though of rather poor flavour. Old trees have very attractive dark grey bark fissured into rectangular blocks. The timber is like ebony, almost black with paler sapwood, very hard and heavy and used for sporting goods, shoe-lasts and carving.

Kaki-plum or Chinese persimmon
(Diospyros kaki)

Growing to 15m (49ft) tall, this Chinese tree has the best fruits of any of the temperate region persimmons—up to 7cm (2¾in) in diameter, orange coloured and of much better flavour than the others. It is grown commercially for its fruit in California but its timber is inferior to that of *D. virginiana*. The leaves are much larger, 12–24cm (4¾–9½in) long, and rather markedly pubescent beneath.

Common ash ▼
Fraxinus excelsior
A tall open-crowned
tree with a domed top.
One of the largest
European hardwoods;
it prefers limestone
soils.

Common ash ▶
Fraxinus excelsior
Pinnate leaves and
winged seeds.

Manna or ▼
flowering ash
Fraxinus ornus
A smaller, rounder
form tree. A wonderful
sight in full flower.

◀**Common ash**
Fraxinus excelsior
(Summer/Winter)

◀**Manna ash**
Fraxinus ornus
(Spring)

Ashes

There are some 60 species in this genus, nearly all in the northern hemisphere and mainly moderate or large sized trees. All have opposite buds and in some these are completely black; all but one have pinnate leaves; most have wind pollinated flowers without petals; all have winged seeds. Several species yield excellent timber, of great value to men even in prehistoric times because the easily worked, yet very strong and exceptionally elastic wood has proved ideal for many of the tools that have contributed to civilization: handles for everything from stone age axes to modern tools, including spears, lances, pikes, plough-beams, cart shafts, coachwork, hoops, barrels, early aircraft, furniture, racquets, baseball bats, parallel bars, and turned woodware. For such uses the only real rival to ash is American hickory. To obtain the finest quality timber ash trees must be fast grown, straight-grained and free from knots. Ash timber is unusual in that each annual ring is made up of two exceptionally different layers—the springwood of large-

Above: Common ash (*Fraxinus excelsior*).
Silver-grey bark fissured into irregular plates.

pore structure is light and elastic, but the summerwood is much denser and stronger; this alternation of different qualities gives the timber its special strength and resilience.

A few main species are described here.

Common ash
(Fraxinus excelsior)
Native to Europe and Asia Minor, this is one of the largest and most important European broadleaved trees, growing up to 45m (147½ft) tall with girths up to 6m (20ft), with a tall-domed open crown. It has very distinct jet black, squat, conic buds. The pinnate leaves are 16–35cm (6⅓–14in) long with 9–13 leaflets, each broadly lanceolate, acuminate and serrate. The tree shows extraordinary sexual variation, not only do some trees have all female flowers, some all male and some mixed, but the flowers themselves are often mixed, even on the same twig; opening before the leaves, they occur in small feathery bunches, mixed purple, light yellow and green, small but very attractive. The winged, strap-shaped seeds (often

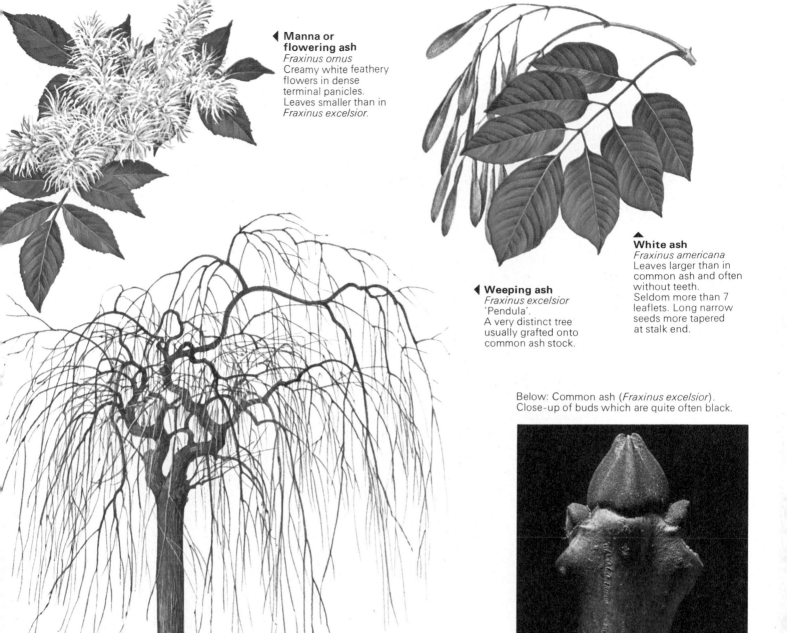

Manna or flowering ash
Fraxinus ornus
Creamy white feathery flowers in dense terminal panicles. Leaves smaller than in *Fraxinus excelsior*.

▲ **White ash**
Fraxinus americana
Leaves larger than in common ash and often without teeth. Seldom more than 7 leaflets. Long narrow seeds more tapered at stalk end.

◀ **Weeping ash**
Fraxinus excelsior
'Pendula'.
A very distinct tree usually grafted onto common ash stock.

◀ **Weeping ash**
Fraxinus excelsior
'Pendula'
(Winter)

Below: Common ash (*Fraxinus excelsior*). Close-up of buds which are quite often black.

called 'keys'), about 3–4cm ($1\frac{1}{6}$–$1\frac{1}{2}$in) long, on slender stalks 2–2.5cm ($\frac{4}{5}$–1in) long, hang in clusters; pale green at first, then yellowish and finally brown, they often remain on the tree all the winter.

The pale grey bark is smooth when young but later develops a beautiful

Below: Common ash (*Fraxinus excelsior*). A strong, elastic timber, always in great demand.

network of interwoven ridges and furrows. The valuable timber is very light brown, often tinged with pink and used for all the wide range of purposes listed in the introduction.

'Pendula' is a weeping type grafted on to common ash stock; 'Monophylla' syn. 'Diversifolia' is a remarkable freak with single simple leaves, ovate-oblong and variably toothed.

Manna or flowering ash
(*Fraxinus ornus*)
This beautiful tree up to 20m ($65\frac{1}{2}$ft) tall, from southern Europe and western Asia, is a remarkable sight when covered in masses of fragrant creamy-white flowers in late May. 'Manna' sugar is obtained from the sap.

Chinese flowering ash
(*Fraxinus mariesii*)
This is very similar to *F. ornus* but the leaves have only three to five leaflets.

White ash
(*Fraxinus americana*)
This splendid timber tree grows up to 40m (131ft) tall. The buds are dark brown, and

the leaves, up to 40cm (16in), have seven to nine large leaflets. The flowers, fruit and timber closely resemble those of common ash *Fraxinus excelsior*.

Oregon ash
(*Fraxinus latifolia* syn. *Fraxinus oregona*)
Another fine timber tree from western America, this is similar to white ash but not quite as large. It has unusually large side leaflets.

Red ash
(*Fraxinus pennsylvanica*)
A fast growing eastern North American tree, red ash is smaller than white ash, with poorer quality timber, red-brown buds, downy shoots and large leaves. It has a variety *lanceolata* (green ash), with much more slender leaves and leaflets and no down on the shoots.

Black ash
(*Fraxinus nigra*)
An important timber tree in western America, this grows almost as large as white ash. It has dark brown buds; the leaves have 7 to 11 slender, pointed leaflets and turn pale yellow in the autumn.

Tropical & Southern Hemisphere TREES

*The smooth, white, vellum-
like bark of the ghost gum (Eucalyptus papuana)
makes a striking contrast
with the red sands of Australia's
arid Northern Territory.*

*T*he tropical rain forest, that steamy, mysterious place, contains within its green boundaries a vast wealth of timber, fruits, gums and spices, all illuminated by vividly coloured flowers.

Among the first of the glittering prizes to be wrested from this seemingly inexhaustible treasury was that prince of timbers, mahogany. As early as 1588 the Spanish became aware of its special qualities of strength and durability, for they used this timber to build the hulls of their Armada fleet. And it was not long before the rain forest was made to surrender another of its hidden treasures, teak, an outstanding tropical hardwood.

Yet it was found that this precious vein was not inexhaustible. Soon the great battalions of teak and mahogany began to falter. Now a mighty trunk of teak is a rarer sight, and the search for substitutes goes on continuously. Cultivation in plantations has been less than successful, and the constant clearing of forest for agriculture has made conservation an urgent issue.

The tropical belt encompasses trees of wide contrast. At one extreme are the 'sea trees', the mangroves that survive by breathing through their stilt roots, while at the other are the desert trees, which search for water by sending out long roots beneath the sand.

The range of tropical fruits, spices and flowers is almost as great as that of timber. Figs have been familiar for centuries throughout the world since they can be transported dry, and our markets have long been flooded by other fruits.

There are the palms, too, which produce the largest seeds and leaves in the plant kingdom, and give us the date, the coconut and a host of beautiful trees. And in the southern subtropics we find the eucalypts of Australia—magnificent trees rivalling the giant redwoods in height and dazzling us with a unique display of vivid blooms and richly-textured bark.

Tropical Timber Trees

Only a small proportion of the hundreds of tree species in tropical rain forests are in general use by the local inhabitants, and a far lesser fraction finds its way into international trade. However, from the earliest days of European penetration into tropical regions, forest products have formed a substantial portion of return cargoes. Central and South America supplied woods from which coloured dyes were extracted. These dyes, ranging from yellow to purple, were more strongly coloured than those derived from temperate region plants, and they continued in use until synthetic aniline dyes almost completely superseded the vegetable product. Brazil, in South America, is so named because of the trade in *Caesalpinia echinata*, a leguminous tree which is a good source of a dye with the colour of glowing embers ('brasa' in Portuguese). The tree is now uncommon in the formerly extensive forests of the Atlantic seaboard of Brazil. It is no longer cut for dye production but is the preferred wood for bows of stringed musical instruments.

Tropical timbers familiar to consumers in temperate countries generally have one or both of two main functions. They may be substitutes for temperate timbers, or they may have desirable properties which are peculiar to themselves. Substitution depends only partly on equivalence of technical properties for a particular end use. Availability of the right quantities of the right sizes and qualities at a satisfactory price are also important factors. An example is the replacement of European oak in railway waggons and the bodies of heavy road vehicles by the Southeast Asian timber keruing (*Dipterocarpus* species). Keruing is 40 per cent stiffer than oak, and 20 per cent stronger in bending strength. It is weaker than oak in compression and shows more movement in service than is desirable (even after seasoning the timber shrinks and swells appreciably with changes in atmospheric humidity). But as keruing is available relatively cheaply in quantity with straight or shallowly interlocked grain and in long lengths, its substitution for oak in transport woodwork is largely a matter of economics.

Teak and teak substitutes

There are many examples of tropical timbers having desirable properties not possessed by those from the temperate zone. Perhaps the best known is teak (*Tectona grandis*), a tree of the monsoon forests of Southeast Asia. In its native region teak has been well known and used for hundreds, perhaps thousands, of years. Its strength properties are roughly equivalent to those of oak, and it works moderately well though the silica content has a marked blunting effect on ordinary steel tools. These properties are shared by many tropical timbers; teak is valued for its dimensional stability after seasoning, and its very high resistance to fungal decay and to attack by land-based insects or marine borers. For centuries it has been a preferred timber for boat building. Exposed to the open air, the golden brown surface of the fresh-cut wood bleaches rapidly to a silver grey but can be refreshed repeatedly by light sanding. The very characteristic smell of freshly cut wood is also regained by resurfacing. Teak is easily the highest priced tropical timber commonly entering international trade, and this has led to a number of effects which are repeated, to a lesser extent, in respect of other commonly used tropical woods.

In the long route from standing tree to dining-room table, the highest price per unit volume of wood is paid by the consumer. The import timber business is, at least in western Europe, old-established and complex. Although freight costs are a dominant element in the price of imported timber, the number of intermediary brokers and agents also keep prices up. The natural tendency is to use as little solid teak as is possible while still being able to describe the finished article as genuine teak. Legislation has recently been passed in Britain

to prohibit the term 'teak finish' in advertising furniture finished with imitation wood surfaces such as plastic and printed papers. Nearly all logs with irregular grain are converted to veneer, for overlying cheaper timbers or board, and so is an increasing proportion of straight-grained teak. Only in yachts built in Southeast Asia is a substantial amount of solid teak now used. Such is the reputation of the timber that the vast majority of fibreglass cruising yachts built in Europe still contain some teak trim, mostly in the interior finishing of the cabin where the special properties of teak are not required. This element of tradition plays an important part in maintaining a timber in demand. It is not peculiar to the use of tropical timbers but, in the face of diminishing supplies, it tends to make it harder to introduce technically satisfactory substitutes.

Such conservatism is not always evident in the countries of origin. Some forests in India, Burma and Thailand have magnificent working plans, documents which lay down how the forest authorities should manage the areas where teak is an important constituent in the mixture of species. The objective is to provide a continual supply of logs of the preferred large sizes. But the forests are remote, the forest services small and under-staffed, and all too often in some countries the quantity of illegally felled teak exceeds the amount which should be cut. The persistent regional, national and international demand for teak makes the small risks of illegal logging ever more worthwhile.

Harvesting teak Traditionally, teak is girdled and left to season on stump. That is, trees of market-able size have a wide strip of bark and cambium cut off all round the circumference with a hatchet or jungle knife, and the timber dries out slowly as the connections with the roots are severed and the huge roughly hairy leaves draw out the water from the sapwood. The trees are left standing for up to three years, long after the leaves have fallen, until the wood has lost enough water to float (green un-seasoned teak sinks). The trees are felled in the dry season and hauled by elephant, tractor or manpower to stream banks. In the wet season, the rivers flood and the logs are swept downstream in more or less organized rafts to the sawmills and veneer plants. With carefully sited control posts it is not difficult in theory to intercept rafts of logs not bearing the government ham-mer mark, and therefore not legally taken from the forests. In practice, the poorly paid field staff of the forest services have not had ap-preciable success in controlling illegal logging and the situation is, in general, not improving. Nearly all the governments in tropical countries are committed publicly to national integration through extensive road networks. As the roads push out into areas hitherto accessible only by boat in the wet season, so more forests are threat-ened by robbery. Thieves with caterpillar-tracked tractors and multiwheeled trucks can steal in a week the timber which should be marketed over decades. Yet this excessive cutting is inadequate to supply sufficient teak to all the markets to bring the price down. Moreover, behind the thieves come the landless peasants.

Teak plantations There is a very common belief in the tropics that the presence of forest indicates fertile land with a high potential for agriculture. Although this is far from universally true, experience with plantations of teak shows that the tree does best on deep well drained soils, and to this extent it is entirely understandable that the peasants clear and burn the forest whenever possible to satisfy their immediate needs for good farmland.

Faced with the reluctance of central governments to pass or to implement effective legislation to control destruction of existing forests (which is indeed a formidable task), many forest services have initiated plantation schemes for their more valuable timber trees. Fortunately, on suitable sites teak is a fast-growing tree. This and its well established reputation have led to its testing in many parts of the tropics. Further, although the sapwood is not naturally durable, it is easily impregnated with cheap preservatives by simple processes. Where there is a market for small dimension posts and poles for fencing, house poles, piling, tobacco-drying rails, etc., there is usually a good market for teak. This market is desirable because teak must be planted more densely than the spacing at which the final crop trees will stand. Height growth of teak more or less stops when the terminal shoot has flowered, so it is normal to force strong competition for light and hence growth in height in order to obtain logs of commercial length. To some extent it is now possible to delay flowering by careful selection of the geographical origin of the seeds used in the plantations, but fast initial height growth is still essential for commercial success. Three metres (10ft) a year is not unusual on a good soil for the first three years. By about ten years of age, height growth is slow even if flowering has not yet occurred, and forest management is concerned with maintaining rapid diameter growth as soon as height increment tails off.

Until recently it has been thought necessary to thin out the smaller trees and heavily branched specimens at intervals of a few years, but there is considerable evidence now that teak is self-thinning; mutual competition between trees in a plantation will cause the suppression and eventual death of smaller trees, leaving room for the larger ones to continue their more successful growth. Artificial thinning by foresters thus would not measur-

ably increase the growth of the naturally dominant trees, but could perhaps prevent two co-dominants from suppressing each other so that neither reached final crop size. Like most broadleaved trees, mature teak has a rather wide crown in relation to its trunk diameter, so the spacing between final crop trees is large and the timber volume yield per hectare is rather low (but usually much greater than in the natural forests where teak is only one among many constituent species). The most valuable part of a tree is usually the lowest trunk log, and unfortunately in plantations this is often fluted rather than cylindrical in teak. So the usable volume per tree for veneer peeling or saw timber is low. These inherent difficulties go some way towards explaining why the numerous trials of teak in plantations have not resulted in many more planting schemes on a commercial scale. Further, population increases in the countries where teak grows have boosted domestic sales. Even in Java, where the most extensive teak plantations lie, the volume available for export is small.

The search for substitutes The high price of teak with no likely prospect of a substantial increase in volume of wood on the international market has, over the years, led to a degree of substitution by other timbers with more or less similar properties. For a long time, importers have tended to consider a 'new' timber in terms of a potential substitute for one already well established. But increasing demand for wood and the availability of data from comprehensive trials by experienced timber-testing laboratories have helped to make more tropical timbers saleable under their own names. Industrialized high volume furniture making, for example, creates its own needs for timbers with certain properties which are not necessarily provided by woods more traditionally used. High speed sanders produce an irritant dust from many otherwise desirable tropical timbers, and require either a very good dust extraction system at the sander or the use of non-dusting woods.

There are advantages and disadvantages associated with modern woodworking machinery. As an advantage, it is necessary to have large volumes of wood with known and suitable properties.

After staining, painting or covering with veneers of other species (or plastic or paper finishes), the identities of the original timbers are effectively unimportant. This enables groups of species with similar properties to be marketed together, a partial compensation for the infrequent occurrence in mixed tropical rain forest of large marketable trees of any one species. Referring back to keruing, there are some seventy botanical species saleable under this timber name. Users who can tolerate a moderate degree of variation in properties can buy cheaper keruing from Malaysia, which will probably be a mixture of several similar species. Users demanding little variation will perhaps opt for the smaller range of species found at the geographical limits of the genus *Dipterocarpus* and often marketed under their local names (gurjun from India and Burma, yang from Thailand, apitong from the Philippines).

The ability to mix species for a particular end use is also helpful to forest managers in tropical

countries, who may otherwise be compelled to let their forests be heavily damaged by logging companies for the sake of one or two valuable trees per hectare. When more trees of more species can be extracted together at one time from a mixed tropical forest, the forest manager has greater opportunity for influencing the composition and stocking of the next generation of the forest. He has more space in which to raise an even-aged crop of his own choosing, with a lower likelihood that loggers will want to return to extract other trees from the remnant virgin forest before his new generation is ready for felling. Also, by concentrating the logging, the forest services have more opportunities for supervision of the logging companies, and to control careless damage to the remaining trees.

The natural virgin forest is frequently a mixture of many species, tree sizes and ages. Modern tractor and cable winch logging tends to severely damage the remaining forest in proportion to the amount of wood that it removes. It is easier to repair the damage from small areas of heavily logged forest than from large areas logged at a moderate intensity. In general, the high cost of modern logging equipment is such that the ecologically preferable light intensity logging is impracticable in mixed tropical forest. Further, concentrations of heavily logged forest are easier to protect against the depredations of the peasants who now almost invariably follow close behind the logging companies. It is a fortunate coincidence that the natural regeneration after heavy logging is, in all three of the great tropical rain forest areas (the Amazon basin, West Africa and the Congo basin, and Southeast Asia) rather rich in species with desirable timber properties from the point of view of industrial wood processing. These are: low to moderate specific gravity, colour white to pale red-brown, relatively easy to season and to work by machinery. However, natural regeneration of desirable species does not always occur after logging and it may be economically impossible to bring commercially understocked areas to a productive state. Therefore, in spite of the several apparent ecological and technical advantages of management by natural regeneration methods, most tropical forest services are putting the bulk of their efforts into man-made plantations. These are much more costly to establish and to maintain but the potential yields can be very high. Probably more important, though, are the social and political factors which so frequently override technical considerations.

High volume wood processing does have one especial disadvantage for tropical timbers. Countries anxious to promote one or a group

Below: Teak plantation in Southeast Asia. Although trials are being carried out, low yield remains one of several factors which make teak plantations inevitably uneconomical.

Below: Teak (*Tectona grandis*), a tropical tree which can reach 40m (131ft), produces a valuable, attractive wood for which world demand continues to exceed supply.

of species for a particular end use are frequently unable to assure continued regular supply. This is partly because of insufficient knowledge of the locations and compositions of their forest areas, and partly because of the traditionally anarchic state of production and marketing arrangements in those countries. There are numerous documented cases of sales contracts for particular species in specified grades of size and quality being fulfilled with a variety of species of variable properties in incorrect sizes and low quality. These cases are well remembered by the conservative importers and severely damage the prospects for the introduction into world trade of other species, or the same species when they become more readily available and quality control is better. For this reason several countries with an important tropical timber export trade are setting up or strengthening national and regional marketing organizations. These bodies promote contacts between importers and exporters, establish and enforce rules for quality grading of export timber, and arbitrate in disputes over fulfilment of contracts. If fairly and impartially run, and with a businesslike staff, such organizations can be very beneficial to all parties. The current good repute of West Malaysian timber is due in no small measure to the maintenance of standards of quality enforced in spite of poor prices and low demand during the world recession in 1974–76.

Most of the points made above apply especially to the high-priced and much-demanded teak. But as the supplies of large logs from virgin forest decline for other species, the same sets of factors have been seen to appear. Although overall the volume of tropical timbers harvested annually will almost certainly increase for many years, this is not at all the same as saying that there will be a continually increasing volume of good quality wood of any one species. Nor is there likely to be any diminution of price to the point at which it becomes detectable by the final consumer of the tropical timber.

Iroko Usually, a 'new' species enters world trade only after it has been well accepted in the country of origin, and even then there is a tendency for it to be named, misleadingly, as the timber it is thought to substitute or sup-

plement, qualified by a regional designation. For example, for many years, iroko *(Chlorophora excelsa* and *C. regia)* was sold in the international market as 'West African teak'. Strictly speaking, this term should mean *Tectona grandis* grown in West Africa. However, iroko has been proved by so much experience that it is now usually sold under its own name. Iroko is a tree of the moist semi-deciduous forests of West Africa, and is there associated with royalty — a 'king' tree — and so generally not felled by native farmers when they are clearing forests for village agriculture. It grows to a large size and, unlike true teak, the bole is usually nearly cylindrical. It is a truly majestic tree in the forest, with rough, dark brown bark and a heavy dark crown. The freshly cut stump oozes a rather opaque resin which can spread over the whole cut surface. The resin clears as it hardens to give an almost glassy surface, and this probably helps to make the stumps resistant to decay.

The pale yellow sapwood of iroko is clearly differentiated from the naturally durable medium brown heartwood, which will darken with age in the shade but bleaches like teak in the open. This is an im-

Below: Teak and its substitutes. Centre background (1): Teak (*Tectona grandis*), left (2): Cordia (*Cordia alliodora*), right (3): Iroko (*Chlorophora excelsa*) and, foreground (4): Afrormosia (*Pericopsis elata*).

portant factor in making it an acceptable substitute in boat building. The texture of the wood is more coarse and open than teak, and usually the grain is interlocked. The specific gravity of 0.64 is similar to the average value for teak (0.66) and is less variable with region of origin. Like teak, there is little movement after seasoning; iroko dries fairly rapidly with a tendency to slight splitting and distortion. It is a little inferior to teak in most strength properties but somewhat harder. This, together with the interlocked grain, requires more care in woodworking. Sometimes there are calcareous deposits in the heartwood known as stones. The stones can be the size of matchboxes and, being very hard, can cause damage to saws. There is no figuring in the wood, and iroko is invariably sawn. It does seem a pity, when one stands beside a huge, perfect and cylindrical log in a sawmill yard, that iroko does not peel well enough to produce veneers.

Whereas teak is easy to establish in plantations, iroko trials have not been successful. The two botanical species of iroko occupy overlapping geographical territories. *Chlorophora regia* is found in West Africa from the Gambia to eastern Ghana while *C. excelsa* occurs from Liberia across the continent to Zanzibar. The two species are found together in Liberia, the Ivory Coast and

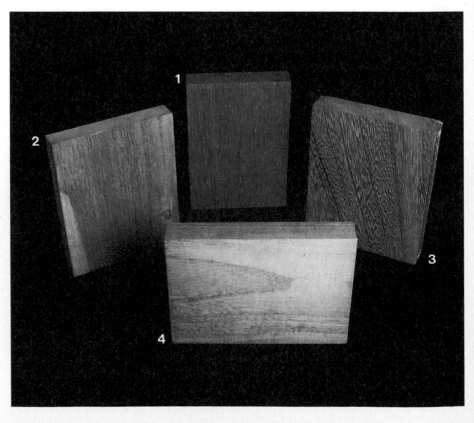

Ghana. *C. excelsa* is invariably attacked by the gall-forming psyllid insect *Phytolyma lata*. If *C. regia* is planted in an area where it does not occur naturally but *C. excelsa* does, the planted trees are not galled; but it may grow only slowly. Prospects for future crops of iroko thus depend on the natural regeneration in mixed forest. As there are no certain techniques for enhancing the growth rate of individual trees, and as the area of natural forest is diminishing continually because of clearance for farms, supplies of iroko to the world market are likely to be small.

Cordia Another timber sometimes used as a teak substitute is cordia. Usually this name refers to *Cordia millenii* from West Africa but smaller quantities reach world trade from *C. goeldiana* (now a rather uncommon tree in the Amazon basin) and from *C. alliodora* (mainly from Central America). Cordia is lighter in weight than teak, with specific gravity of about 0.43, a fairly coarse textured but lustrous wood with a pale gold to medium brown colour. Like iroko, the grain is interlocked. It seasons rapidly and shows little movement in use. The heartwood is durable, easy to work, finishes well and blunts tools less than iroko or teak. Unlike these two timbers, cordia has rather low strength but it is useful in furniture and it peels to make a good plywood somewhat like figured teak, but easily distinguishable by the absence of teak's characteristic smell.

Afrormosia A popular substitute for teak, especially for boats and high class cabinet work, is the Ghanaian timber afrormosia *(Pericopsis elata)*. This has the appearance of a fine-grained teak but lacks the slightly oily finish. It does not bleach on exposure but darkens with time. It shows little movement after seasoning, is stronger and harder than most teak and less blunting to steel tools. It is not a very common timber and it has not done well in plantation trials, so an indefinitely continued supply to world markets is unlikely.

Right: Asukesi forest reserve in Ghana, characteristic of the type of West African forest from which the bulk of tropical timber of that region is derived. Forest management throughout West Africa has now reached a highly organized stage in its development.

West African forests
It will be clear already that many of the most distinctive tropical timbers on the world market come from West Africa. It should not be imagined that tropical rain forest is a homogeneous vegetation type; far from it, the variations are immense and the range of botanically or physiognomically defined types far greater than that of the temperate zone. In West Africa the major types of forest occur in belts parallel to the east–west coastline of the Gulf of Guinea. The forests are tallest and most luxuriant, and have the greatest number of species close to the coast where they receive the full weight of the annual monsoon rains and the least effect of the desiccating sand-laden Harmattan wind sweeping south from the Sahara. As one progresses inland, north towards the desert, the forest types change. The average height of the trees lessens and there are marked alterations in the species present.

Above: Trimming the branches and foliage from an African hardwood log with a chainsaw. Many of the distinctive tropical timbers come from West Africa.

Above: Hardwood loading site in tropical Africa. Tropical timber is a diminishing resource and must be managed prudently if supplies are to be conserved and even replenished.

Near the coast only a few species lose their leaves regularly in the dry season but the further north one goes the higher the proportion of deciduous species. The average crown form of mature trees also changes. from the globular and hemispherical shape common in wet forests to an umbrella form and the flat-topped funnel shapes characteristic of the Sudan and Sahel zones fringing the Sahara.

There is no such clear trend in the wood properties of the changing species. A study of the wood density in the tropical zones of Central and South America has suggested that more than forty per cent of the wood volume has a specific gravity of more than 0.69 in tropical moist areas. These are, roughly, regions with 2,000 to 4,000mm (79 to 158in) of rain annually. In tropical wet forests, having 4,000 to 8,000mm (158 to 316in) of rain, the wood is mainly in the specific gravity range 0.40

to 0.59. As an extreme example, the lightest and most commercially desirable balsa *(Ochroma lagopus)* comes from the wettest of the forests on the Pacific slopes of the Andean foothills in Ecuador. In dry deciduous tropical forest, with 1,000 to 2,000mm (39 to 79in) of rain annually, the wood seems to be spread rather evenly across the specific gravity range from less than 0.30 (very light) to more than 0.69 (very heavy).

While this kind of information may be useful for broad-scale planning, within any one tract of tropical forest there is usually a wide range of timber densities and associated wood properties. Buyers of tropical timbers have, for some hundreds of years, also recognized regional variations within timbers which do not seem to be reflected in the characters of the flowers and fruits, the parts by which botanists classify the trees. It is reasonable to suppose

that a timber species occurring in West Africa from Sierra Leone to the Congo basin will show some variations from country to country, but whether these differences significantly affect the working properties of the timbers is not clear. The prices paid by importers do not entirely reflect differences between timbers, or between sources of supply for any one timber. Port facilities (or the lack of them), complexity of government bureaucracy and the expense of expediting its performance (that is, all too frequently, outright bribery), differential freight rates, frequency of shipping services, reliability of supply; these are a few of the factors affecting the importers' costs.

Increasingly influential, too, is the matter of long-term availability. In response to overseas demand, internal pressure for development capital, and other pressures, some tropical countries have permitted the logging of forests to take place at a much faster rate than they can be replaced by the natural growth of seedlings and saplings into market-

Below: Measuring a felled afzelia log in a forest clearing in tropical Africa. Average-sized trees can reach an impressive 30m (98ft) in height and 1m (39in) in diameter.

able trees. For some decades there has always seemed to be so much tropical forest available that a little local overcutting has not been perceived as a problem except by conservative foresters. Only relatively recently have politicians begun to realize that logging operations almost inevitably lead to forest destruction and the disappearance of a major source of wealth for countries which are almost invariably classed as 'developing'. We do not know how to domesticate and grow in plantations more than a very few of the favourite tropical timbers, and the area of plantations is negligible compared with the current demand. Only by careful logging at long intervals and by protecting the forest against encroachment can tropical countries hope to maintain supplies of most timbers. This is a hard truth to accept and most governments have neither the will nor the power to take effective and timely action on a sufficient scale.

Pale-coloured tropical woods

The increase in demand for wood, first for post-war reconstruction and later for development everywhere, has led to the marketing of almost all woods which exist in large quantities but especially those which can be processed by industrial machinery. We have discussed already what wood properties are favoured. Semi-skilled building labourers, and mass production workers in other trades, cannot select and treat to best advantage each piece of wood, as can a craftsman. The use of poorer qualities, containing more defects than were previously acceptable, has of course produced a demand for covering materials to improve visual acceptability. In some cases lower quality is technically quite adequate. For exampe, building research stations have shown that properly designed roof trusses can be made with far fewer and smaller timbers than are traditional.

When the finished product will be seen frequently, blemishes such as sound knots and irregular grain are in general disliked by customers in importing countries. At times, a manufacturer will wish to substitute a more expensive timber by a cheaper wood which is perhaps slightly different in colour. In both cases surface covering, especially by paints and varnishes,

improves marketability; under opaque paint the identity of a timber is very largely lost. So when post-war reconstruction demand for furniture began to push up the price of European beech the market was ready to accept timbers such as obeche or wawa (*Triplochiton scleroxylon*) from West Africa, virola (mainly *Virola* species and small quantities of *Dialyanthera*), hura (*Hura crepitans*) from South America, and ramin (*Gonystylus bancanus*) which comes from Sarawak.

Obeche Obeche has an open texture with a slightly interlocked grain. The creamy white to pale straw coloured timber is lightweight, specific gravity 0.38, and dries fairly rapidly although with some distortion unless the drying timber is constrained, for example by heavy concrete weights placed on the stack of lumber. Once seasoned the wood shows little movement. It is fairly elastic and resilient but has low strength. Its chief virtue, besides ready availability over the last three decades, is that it is very easy to work by both hand tools and machines. Obeche is a handsome, tall and fairly slim tree with a rather light crown. The palmately lobed leaves and winged fruit resemble those of maples and sycamores. Unfortunately obeche produces fruit infrequently and the seeds are liable to insect and smut fungus attack while still ripening on the tree. A considerable amount of research has been done in Ghana and Nigeria to develop methods of vegetative propagation but this has not yet progressed far enough for obeche to be considered as a major candidate for plantations.

Hura Unlike many tropical timbers, some of the paler lightweight woods have production areas reasonably secure from the threat of clearance for agriculture. These timbers grow in the fresh water and peat swamp forests, usually not far from coasts. An example of a fresh water swamp forest species is hura or sandbox (*Hura crepitans*) from South America. The young tree has a pale greenish photosynthetic bark and is fiercely armed with short, hard, very sharp conical prickles. The spines persist in the older trees. The milky sap is strongly caustic. Hura can grow to very large sizes. The timber varies in colour from white to yellowish brown, and the specific gravity is in the range 0.37 to 0.43. It is stronger than obeche and the texture is moderately fine and even. It seasons more easily and with less degrade, is similarly easy to work and very readily attacked by insects and fungi unless treated with a preservative. Nevertheless, until very recently, hura has been used in the Amazon river system principally as floating pontoons to support logs of denser timber on the long journey in rafts from riverine forest to sawmill.

Ramin For better quality joinery and mouldings (broom handles, picture frames and similar small-dimension products) a rather denser and finer textured wood is required than obeche or hura. Ramin from Sarawak and, latterly, Indonesian peat swamp forests, and idiobo *(Terminalia ivorensis)* from dryland forest in West Africa are in the specific gravity range 0.55 to 0.66. Ramin timber is uniform and creamy white in colour from Sarawak, somewhat yellowish from the western areas of Kalimantan (Indonesian Borneo). The texture is fine and even with a straight or slightly interlocked grain. Seasoning is easy and a tendency to end-splitting can be prevented by painting the ends of the boards with a tar-like sealing compound before building the drying stacks. Of course this makes the timber dry out more slowly. If a sawmill has insufficient lumber ready for shipment by an agreed date, it is a rather frequent practice for the sealing compound to be applied just before the boards are bundled for export, thus meeting the moisture content specifications in the contract, and blaming the splits on conditions during the voyage. Shrinkage and movement of timber in use are moderate. Strength properties are similar to those of European beech but ramin is stronger in compression and weaker in toughness and hardness. Ramin is very liable to fungal attack, especially the blue sapstain fungus, but this is easily prevented by a superficial dipping in a pentachlorphenate preservative; this is routine in the Sarawak mills. The silica content has a moderate blunting effect on steel tools.

Although ramin can reach large sizes, it is generally a small tree by tropical timber trade standards. A few countries prefer to import whole logs but for most end uses

this is inadvisable because of the inevitability of sapstaining during the voyage. This may not matter if the timber is to be painted; Italy continues to import large quantities of logs for the manufacture of window shutters and venetian blinds which are invariably painted. The swamp logging system in Borneo is based on sleds hauled by teams of four to eight men along skidways constructed of poles cut on site in the forest. Viewed from the air, the skidway system looks like a tree of ladders laid flat on the ground. The base of the 'tree' ends

Above: The dense undergrowth and close-growing nature of Southeast Asian tropical forests makes identification of tree species for felling and extraction purposes an extremely difficult operation.

beside a narrow-gauge railway which takes the logs to the sawmill. The Sarawak swamps may have depths of more than 25m (82ft) of peat, accumulated over the last five thousand years; the caterpillar tractor and truck logging systems used for most tropical forests cannot be supported by the very fragile superficial layer of interlaced roots overlying the soupy peat. Ramin seedlings are common in most areas where mature trees are also found, but they do not respond with extra growth to the great light intensity in logged forest. No silvicultural treatment has yet induced sufficient extra growth to establish a second crop of marketable trees. However, swamp logging does

Above: A timber extraction site in a forest in Papua New Guinea. Again, the nature of tropical forest growth precludes the use of sophisticated machinery such as that used in coniferous forests.

stimulate the growth of the well known red brown utility timbers, of which Southeast Asia is the chief supplier, timbers mainly of the family Dipterocarpaceae.

Light red tropical woods

By volume, the general purpose light red timbers make up by far the largest proportion of the world trade in tropical hardwoods. It is a rather one way trade: logs from Malaysia, Indonesia and the Philippines are shipped to Japan, Korea and Taiwan. Then veneers and plywood are exported from the latter countries to the United States. Increasingly the supplying countries are installing their own sawmills and plymills and taking

Below: Pale tropical hardwoods. (1) Hura (*Hura crepitans*), (2) Obeche (*Triplochiton scleroxylon*), (3) Virola (*Virola koschnyi*), (4) Ramin (*Gonystylus bancanus*), (5) Idigbo (*Terminalia ivorensis*).

hesitant steps towards curbing the export of unprocessed raw material. As usual, the transport system is a barrier. Japanese log ships have heavy cranes for picking up logs from rafts towed out to sea from estuaries in the producing countries. American ships carrying plywood need proper port facilities for loading their cargoes. Ports are few and far between in insular Southeast Asia where the coasts are often muddy and flat, the seas are shallow and nearly every river has a bar across the estuary. The construction of modern port facilities in such areas is technically difficult, and only very high volume trade in processed timber can justify the cost, so it is not likely that there will be a substantial reduction in log trade as long as the producing countries are in need of revenue.

All the tropical rain forest areas produce light, medium and dark red utility timbers with a considerable range in technical properties. Wherever possible retailers will call a tropical red wood 'mahogany'; most people have heard of this as an excellent timber and will pay accordingly. By United States' law, some dipterocarp timbers from the genera *Parashorea*, *Pentacme* and *Shorea* may be called Philippine mahoganies, but the name should be confined to the family Meliaceae and preferably to the three species of the genus *Swietenia*. The Dipterocarpaceae is a large family and produces nearly all the Southeast Asian timbers on the world market of general utility woods. The widespread use of local names, even though standardized within an

exporting country, is confusing for the importer and consumer. The same or closely allied timbers may be called meranti in West Malaysia and Sarawak, seraya in Sabah and Indonesia, and lauan or mahogany in the Philippines. West Malaysia was an early (pre-1939) proponent of exporting groups of botanically similar species under one established timber name, with a government-backed grading service so that a consignment of lumber would at least look the same from top to bottom plank in terms of colour and type and size of allowable defect. Although visual grading of lumber is now under some criticism because it is unrelated to end use requirements, it is relatively cheap to carry out and gives some security to both buyer and seller. Very few countries have progressed as far as West Malaysia in establishing a reliable sawn timber export service.

Because of historical links, most English reports and importers compare tropical timbers with the West African 'mahoganies' of the genera *Khaya* and *Entandrophragma*. These are not true mahoganies but belong to the family Meliaceae. Here I choose to avoid these comparisons and will describe briefly the properties of two light red timbers, kapur from Malaysia and *Calophyllum*-derived timber from the neotropics (Central and South America).

Kapur Kapur or Malayan camphor comes from the small dipterocarp genus *Dryobalanops*. The timber is a uniform colour in any one tree, but in a consignment may vary from light to deep reddish brown. The grain is straight or shallowly interlocked and the texture is coarse and even. Fine resin ducts occur in the timber and the odour of camphor fades with time. The specific gravity is in the range 0.72 to 0.80 and the strength properties are equivalent to those of teak and better than those of European beech. Kapur dries slowly, has a moderate blunting effect on steel tools and tends to give a fibrous finish. The heartwood is durable and resistant to treatment with preservative chemicals. Kapur is a tall and rather slender tree in the forest, and the timber is usually available in longer lengths than most tropical red woods. In some areas of Malayan lowland dipterocarp forest, kapur was particularly common.

Tropical Timber Trees

A few small experimental areas carefully tended over many years gave some hope that almost pure crops of kapur could be raised without resorting to planting, but the main kapur-bearing forests have been logged over and at least partly destroyed in the last few years. Planting trials of kapur have been promising for the very early years but neither growth nor survival have been sustained.

Calophyllum spp. The genus *Calophyllum* is widely distributed in the tropics and several species produce a good medium-weight utility timber. The trees can usually be recognized easily by the bright yellow or orange sap characteristic of the family Guttiferae, by the more or less strongly fissured grey bark with the fissures interlocking like a fleet of canoes. And by the close parallel venation of the leaves (a character shared by the completely unrelated *Dryobalanops*). In Central America the timber is called Santa Maria, and in Brazil it is called jacareuba. Colour varies from pink to brick red and there are brown gum streaks on the tangential surfaces. The grain is interlocked and the texture is medium, somewhat woolly. The timber dries slowly and needs to be weighted, like obeche, to prevent distortion while seasoning. Santa Maria tends to have a moderate or severe blunting effect on tools. The heartwood is durable and can be used outdoors without need of preservatives.

Mahogany

Inevitably, and rightly, no account however brief of tropical trees and timbers can omit a mention of mahogany and some reference to its close relatives. The excellence of *Swietenia mahagoni* was recognized early on by the Spanish colonists of the New World. The natural historian Don Gonzalo Fernandez de Oviedo y Valdez noted that, in all parts of the world this timber would be esteemed' in 1535. The earliest record of use is in the cathedral of Santo Domingo, begun in 1514 and completed in 1540. The first major use in Europe was in furniture and interior trim for the royal monastery of the Escorial for Philip II of Spain. The timber was probably shipped from Cuba through Seville in 1579 and subsequent years. The larger ships of the Spanish Armada sent against England in 1588 were built of mahogany. The main shipbuilding

Above: Light red tropical hardwoods. From left: (1) Light red meranti (*Shorea* spp.), (2) Kapur (*Dryobalanops* spp.), (3) African mahogany (*Khaya ivorensis*), (4) Sapele (*Entandophragma utile*), and centre (5) Santa Maria (*Calophyllum brasiliense*).

Right: An avenue of big-leaf mahogany (*Swietenia macrophylla*) in Malaysia. The popularity of this wood is due to its appealing colour variations, stability and ease of working by hand.

centre in the New World was the Havana Arsenal in Cuba; operational in about 1626, over one hundred large naval vessels were built between 1724 and 1796. Fortunately for England, many of these ships were captured and continued to sail under the British flag as privateers or in the Royal Navy. The superiority of mahogany over European oaks was quickly noted. Shipwrights commented on its ease of working, good bending properties, buoyancy, resistence to dry rot and exceptional dimensional stability after seasoning. Of importance to the sailors were its slowness to ignite and that it does not splinter badly when struck by cannon balls.

Naval demand soon reduced Cuban supplies and from early on one of the log supply centres for Havana was the depot at Mina-titlan on the Rio Coatzacoalcos in Mexico. Differences between the mainland timber from *Swietenia macrophylla* and Cuban mahogany from *S. mahagoni* were quickly noted. The darker, harder and more close-grained island mahogany was used for the main structural beams and outside planking while the mainland timber, available in larger sizes and being somewhat easier to work, was used for inside planking. Mexican timber from the Isthmus of Tehuantepec was used in Havana to build the eighty-gun *Juan de Cordoba* in about 1750. After capture by Lord Rodney in 1780 she continued as HMS *Gibraltar*

until 1836. On being broken up in Pembroke dockyard, her timbers were still sound.

Although mahogany panelling was used in Nottingham Castle in 1680, the great period for mahogany furniture in England did not come until after 1715. For a hundred years between 1725 and 1825 mahogany was the cabinet maker's favourite wood. Three characteristics in particular are the reasons for mahogany's popularity. First, the colour variations are considerable. Different growing conditions seem to produce trees with different amounts of colouring chemicals in the timber. It is possible to include a variety of shades in the finished article by careful selection of pieces of wood from a variety of exporting regions. The colour variations are most marked in freshly sawn lumber, from yellow to dark red. Brazilian mahogany from the Araguaia river in southern Amazonia is bright orange when fresh from the saw; Florida mahogany is said to be the darkest red. Nearly all pieces tend to mature with time to a rich dark

and now supply the bulk of mahogany in that market.

After heavy cutting for the last four centuries, the remaining supply areas for mahogany are increasingly small, scarce and remote. Hardly any natural stands of small-leaf mahogany remain unlogged and very nearly all the *Swietenia* on the world market now comes from the mainland of the Americas. A very small 'gene bank' was established with great forethought by the US Forest Service in Puerto Rico in the 1960s and now represents the only source of genetic material from a number of previously well known mahogany areas in Central America which have since been cleared completely for farming. The collection includes both the *Swietenia* species already mentioned and *S. humilis*, which grows in drier areas than the other two.

Unfortunately attempts to cultivate mahoganies have met with little success. Indeed this applies to the mahogany family in general. A major and as yet unsolved problem is the persistent and heavy destruction of the growing shoots by the larvae of pyralid moths in the genus *Hypsipyla*. Mahogany plantations in those few areas completely free of the *Hypsipyla* pest have been initially promising; perhaps the best known are the line plantings of *Swietenia macrophylla* in Fiji. However in the last few years ambrosia beetle attack has appeared and further planting has been suspended.

The Future

The reader would be correct to conclude that the long-term supply of fine tropical timbers is far from assured. Only a miniscule fraction of the wealth derived from timber export has been put into safeguarding the forest areas and into research into domestication of the preferred species. Even areas set aside by governments as biological reserves for scientific and cultural studies and as national parks are, in many countries, under constant threat of the axe and uncontrolled farming. Only, it seems, when a country is on the verge of becoming a net importer of forest products will most governments really apply themselves to improving and caring for their forests. The speed with which previously major exporters of tropical woods have passed into timber deficits is quite startling. If trees had votes, it might have been another story.

Above: Natural stand of *Shorea glauca* in a forest in Malaysia. Known as light red meranti, this wood plays an immensely important role in the commerce of peninsular Malaysia.

nor doors jam in the wet. The third characteristic is the ease of working by hand or machine tools. So famous is mahogany in this respect that it is the standard for comparison with all other timbers. It is also strong for its weight (specific gravity 0.40 to 0.70). For fine cabinet work with curved surfaces and delicate carving mahogany is unsurpassed.

The two botanical species *Swietenia macrophylla* (big-leaf mahogany) and *S. mahagoni* (small-leaf mahogany) produce timbers which are not always distinguishable from each other. When both species were planted together in Java only minor differences in the wood were noted. Further, on well watered lowland soils in the Caribbean, the wood of *S. mahagoni* may look like big-leaf mahogany, while *S. macrophylla* grown on dry sites may resemble the small-leaf species. To add to the difficulty, the timbers of the *Khaya* species of West African mahogany are very similar to those of *Swietenia*. West African mahoganies entered European trade from about 1850

red-brown. The fine warm colour is enhanced by the natural lustre and brought out by polishing to produce an excellent finish. The second characteristic favouring mahogany is its exceptional dimensional stability. Intricate furniture made of seasoned wood can be constructed to close tolerances with a high expectation that thin panels will not split in dry weather

Tropical Flower and Fruit Trees

Those of us who live in a temperate climate are inclined to take for granted the tropical fruits and spices so readily available in the shops, and seldom think of their countries of origin or the types of plant on which they grow. They are so much a part of our daily lives as to be considered normal items of food. Indeed, it is hard to imagine life without oranges, lemons, bananas, cloves and a host of similar tasty things.

Yet there was a time when all these were either totally unavailable in Europe or so costly as to be delicacies known only to the very rich. Many of our most popular fruits and spices originate in the Near or Far East, where they have been cultivated for many hundreds or even thousands of years. Over the centuries they have worked their way westward by way of the great trade routes from China and elsewhere. In bygone times many of the merchants of

northern Europe had agents in the trading centres of the Mediterranean and the Near East who kept them sparsely supplied with spices and fruits which they could ship home and sell at enormous prices.

It was not until the era of colonial expansion in the 16th and 17th centuries that the major European powers were able to create their own supplies of tropical products by obtaining seeds and plants and taking them to newly founded colonies. Old monopolies were then broken and new ones created, often causing difficult problems for the governments of the day but enabling the average European householder to purchase commodities which had hitherto been far beyond his reach.

This chapter describes some of the more important groups of tropical fruit trees, spices, and flowering trees, briefly surveying their history and cultivation and

Above: A view of the highly-coloured frangipani (*Plumeria rubra*), greatly valued in tropical gardens for a variety of qualities such as fragrance, form and appearance.

giving some idea of their botanical relationships to other plants—some of which may come as a surprise to many readers.

Figs
(*Ficus* spp.)
The merchants of classical times who lived in the countries bordering the Mediterranean, particularly Greece and Turkey, would have been quite familiar with one of the most delicious fruits of the area, the common fig, *Ficus carica*, belonging to the family Moraceae. It has been grown since the dawn of civilization in Egypt and Asia Minor, and has now spread to many parts of the world. Although it is better known to us in its dried form, the fresh fruit is becoming increasingly popular owing to im-

Above: The common fig (*Ficus carica*) is one of the best-known members of the family Moraceae. Its curious flask-shaped fruits, known as synconia, are prized throughout the Mediterranean.

proved methods of transporting it from the lands where it grows. It is but one member of a genus of some 600 species, mostly occurring in the tropical Indo-Malaysian regions. Belonging to the same family but to a different genus are the mulberries, *Morus* spp., used in China to feed the larvae of the silk moths.

The genus *Ficus* exhibits great variation in size and shape of foliage and fruit and also in the habits of the plants themselves. The flowers of the fig are of great interest botanically, being of three types: male, with three to five stamens; female, with an ovary setting one seed; and gallflowers, similar to the females but containing a fig wasp. These three types of flower, borne in a cup- or flask-shaped receptacle, can occur all on one tree, or they can be separated, with the males and gallflowers together on one tree and the females on another. The gall wasps, which are specific to the genus *Ficus*, are essential for the pollination of the female flowers. The fleshy fruits, known as synconia, can take several months to mature and are normally found in the leaf axils or on twigs behind the leaves. They can, however, be found directly on the branches or trunks —a habit known as *cauliflory*— or even underground.

A characteristic of the genus *Ficus* is the presence of latex in the wood. This has frequently been used as a source of rubber—particularly from the indiarubber tree, *Ficus elastica*. This is probably the best known of the rubber-producing figs, and is, of course, common in Europe and America as a house plant. Certain *Ficus* species are known as strangling figs. These start life as seedlings growing on other trees and ultimately develop aerial roots of such magnitude that the host tree dies and the fig remains growing on its own roots. One such strangling fig is the banyan, *Ficus benghalensis*, which spreads outwards on large pillar roots to reach an enormous size. One, near Poona in India, is said to have had a circumference of about 300m (984ft). Certain figs have great religious significance in the East. The most important is probably *Ficus religiosa*, the Pipal tree of the Hindus and the Bodh tree of the Buddhists.

Jakfruit
(Artocarpus heterophyllus)
In the hot, humid lowlands of Asia, far away from the Mediterranean, another important member of the fig family occurs in the form of the jakfruit, *Artocarpus heterophyllus*. It has been cultivated in India and Sri Lanka since ancient times, but like the fig it has now spread throughout much of the tropical world.

It is a very striking tree standing some 20m (65½ft) high with attractive oval or elliptical leaves 10–15cm (4–6in) long and deep glossy green in colour. The flowers are minute and occur in male and female inflorescences on the same tree, the females appearing directly on the trunk or larger branches and the males on branches above them. The fruit is gigantic, probably the largest of all cultivated fruits, averaging 10–25kg (22–55 lb) each. These huge fruits are generally oval or pear-shaped, yellow in colour, and with sharp spines on the skin. They have a very distinct smell, and contain a sweet or acid brown pulp which can be eaten fresh or cooked in a variety of ways. The seeds of the jakfruit are either boiled or roasted.

Above: The mango (*Mangifera indica*) is one of the most widespread and important of all tropical fruits. It is used both as a dessert fruit and in the making of chutnies.

Mango
(Mangifera indica)
Totally unrelated to the jakfruit or fig but again originating in Asia is the mango, *Mangifera indica*, belonging to the Anacardiaceae family. This family contains among others the cashew nut, which is so popular as a cocktail snack. The mango probably originated in the forests of India and Burma, but is now one of the most widespread of all tropical fruits, having become naturalized in many countries. In its best forms it is among the most sought after fruits in the tropics; it can, however, taste distinctly of turpentine and be very stringy if good clones are not chosen. It is eaten as a dessert fruit, made into jams and juices, and used in chutnies and

pickles. The kernels of the seeds are a source of starch and the leaves can be used as animal feed in times of shortage. The timber is much used for boatbuilding, and the trees themselves are of special importance to Hindus.

The mango forms an attractive evergreen tree reaching 30–40m (98–131ft) high, with a dense canopy of foliage. The individual leaves are dark green and leathery, with a pointed apex and prominent veins, and can be up to 40cm (16in) long. The flowers, minute and cream coloured, occur in large inflorescences containing many thousands of individuals. The proportion of fruits that reach maturity is very small and can be less than 0.25 per cent. The size of the fruits depends on the variety, but the best can be up to 25–30cm (10–12in) long with a sweet, juicy, fibre-free flesh. The mango is of great commercial importance in India, some five million tons being produced annually. In the West mangoes are slowly gaining in popularity, but importing them in good condition is still a problem.

Citrus fruits
(Citrus spp.)

Almost all the popular tropical fruits of today have spread far from their countries of origin. Taken in many cases by early travellers and colonists from the tropics of the Old World to the tropics of the New World and vice versa, they have frequently succeeded in their new homes to a far greater extent than one would have believed. The success of the citrus fruits in almost all countries with a Mediterranean type of climate is a good example.

The genus *Citrus* is very small, consisting of only 16 species, which are believed to have originated in the tropical and subtropical parts of Southeast Asia. It belongs to the family Rutaceae which contains the well-known herb rue, *Ruta graveolens*. Various species of *Citrus* have been cultivated in their homelands since remote times, where they have long been highly esteemed for the dessert fruits they yield and as sources of essential oils. Nowadays, in addition to the enormous quantities of citrus fruits eaten fresh, they are canned, made into fruit juices, and their oils used in perfumery and as flavourings.

Although there are considerable differences between species of *Citrus*, they are in general small

Above: The lemon (*Citrus limon*) has been in cultivation since the 11th century. It is one of the best-known citrus fruits, having long been used for the production of oils and juices, or as fresh fruit.

evergreen trees attaining 10m (33ft) or more in height. They usually grow on a single trunk and frequently have thorns adjacent to the buds in the leaf axils. The foliage is variable in size but is normally ovate to lanceolate in shape and dark green in colour. The flowers are white and sweetly scented, appearing singly or in small clusters in the axils of the leaves in the new growth. The fruit is known as an hespiridium, the outer covering being a green leathery peel ripening to yellow or orange. Inside there is a colourless peel, the mesocarp, and finally the endocarp, composed of transparent membranes surrounding the carpels which fill with juice containing sugars and acids.

The Seville orange, *Citrus aurantium*, which is used to make essential oils, liqueurs, and marmalade, has been in cultivation in Europe since the 11th century and is now widespread throughout the world. Another species well known in Europe for many centuries is the lemon, *C. limon*. Its uses are many and include the production of juice and oils. It was taken to the New World by Columbus, and to

East and Central Africa by the Arabs. There are now large commercial plantations in Spain, Italy and California. *Citrus sinensis*, the sweet orange, is a native of southern China but no longer known there in the wild state. It arrived in Europe in the second half of the 15th century, where it became very popular as an ornamental plant, being cultivated throughout Europe in specially constructed orangeries. It was taken to the New World by Columbus in 1493 and reached Florida in 1565. The seedless cultivar 'Washington Navel' originated in Brazil and was subsequently taken to Washington—hence its name.

A fruit which has become very popular as a breakfast dish is the grapefruit, *Citrus paradisi*. Its origins are not known for certain but it probably originated in the West Indies. Commercial production did not develop in America until the 1880s. Satsumas, mandarins, and tangerines are all cultivars of *C. reticulata*, and are very widely used as dessert fruits. *C. reticulata* is hardier than most citrus species, surviving in more difficult climates than the others. It is a small tree from 2–8m (6½–26ft) high, with small leaves and spines. The curious 'ugli' or 'tangelo' are hybrids between this species and the grapefruit.

Probably the most important

juice-producing species is the lime, *Citrus aurantifolia*. It is a very distinct species, now widely spread throughout the tropics, but particularly cultivated in Mexico and the West Indies.

Guava
(Psidium guajava)
While the majority of plant introductions seem to have been from east to west there has, in fact, been two-way traffic, and the American tropics have provided us with many important vegetable products. Although most frequently seen in Europe as a tinned fruit, the guava, *Psidium guajava,* is very widely grown in tropical regions. It belongs to the Myrtaceae and is therefore related to the myrtles and eucalyptus trees. It is a native of tropical America and has been known ever since the Spanish and Portuguese arrived there. It is now so widespread as to be considered a noxious weed in some countries.

The guava is a small tree growing up to 10m (33ft) high with opposite leaves, elliptical or oblong in shape and reaching 15cm (6in) long. The flowers, 2.5–3cm (1–1⅙in) across, are rather attractive, with white petals and many stamens as is characteristic of the myrtle family. The fruit is a berry, rather variable in size but up to 15cm (6in) long in the best varieties. It has an extremely strong smell, and the flesh can be deep pink, yellow or white. It is used principally for jams, jellies and canning, but in its best forms it is also a rather popular dessert fruit.

Cocoa
(Theobroma cacao)
Besides fruits such as the guava, Central and South America have given us one of our most important beverages, in the form of cocoa. Botanically, cocoa is called *Theobroma cacao,* and it has been known to Europeans since the days of Hernan Cortes. It was cultivated by the Aztecs in Central America for many hundreds of years, where it was highly prized and considered to be of divine origin. The Spanish were almost certainly the first Europeans to make use of cocoa as a beverage and as chocolate. A substantial export trade from the New World to Spain was built up during the 16th and 17th centuries, during which period cocoa became extremely popular in many European countries. Chocolate houses sprang up in

Above: The guava (*Psidium guajava*), though rarely seen as a fresh fruit outside the tropics, is so widespread there it is often treated as a weed.

most major cities and were used as clubs by the more prosperous citizens. At this time it was an extremely expensive product.

The plant originates on the eastern slopes of the equatorial Andes, where it grows in the tropical rain forests as an under storey tree. It favours very wet conditions, often actually standing in water. It is a small tree in the wild, standing only 6–8m (20–26ft) high, but in cultivation it can in some cases grow almost twice as tall. The leaves are large, simple, and dark green when mature. The young growth occurs in flushes and is then an attractive red colour. The flowers are small, pink or whitish in colour, and occur in cymes directly on the main stem and branches of the tree—another example of cauliflory. The fruit is referred to as a pod and can be up to 30cm (1ft) long. It takes about six months to mature on the tree and is by then yellow or red. It contains up to 60 seeds, surrounded by a sweetish pulp which has to

Above: Cocoa (*Theobroma cacao*) was first brought to Europe in the 16th century. Today, most supplies come from West Africa.

be removed by fermenting and then drying. The seeds are then roasted and finally ground into a mass from which the cocoa powder is made.

Cocoa was spread throughout South America and the West Indies by the Spaniards and taken by them to the Gulf of Guinea and the Philippines in the 17th century. The large West African industry stems from its introduction to Ghana in the 1870s.

Nutmegs
(Myristica fragrans)
At the same time as the Spaniards were developing cocoa in South America, the Portuguese had discovered nutmeg trees on the Indonesian islands of Banda and Amboina. The discovery was of great economic importance to Portugal because up to this time

Below: *Myristica fragrans* provides us with two spices; mace, which is the red netlike aril covering the seed, and nutmeg, which is the seed itself.

nutmeg had been a precious and costly item in Europe and its exact source had never before been revealed. It had been known in Europe since the 12th century but on its way there—via Java, India and the Near East—it had changed hands so many times that its place of origin was virtually untraceable. Once the Portuguese found the source, they monopolized the nutmeg trade until the Dutch ousted them from the area in the 17th century. The Dutch, in turn, hoarded or even destroyed supplies to maintain high prices. Their monopoly remained intact until the late 18th century when the East India Company's botanist, Christopher Smith, managed to collect plants and have them sent to Malaya and elsewhere, initiating many large plantations. Present-day supplies come from Indonesia and the West Indies.

Botanically, the nutmeg is *Myristica fragrans,* a spreading tree growing from 5 to 13m (16½ to 42½ft) high, with dark shiny green leaves up to 15cm (6in) long. The flowers are pale yellow, fragrant, and have a waxy texture. The fruits that provide the nutmegs of commerce are yellow and plum shaped. They are pendulous, and when ripe split longitudinally to reveal the purplish brown seed and the striking red aril spreading over it like a net. The nutmeg tree in fact provides two spices: mace from the aril covering the seed, and nutmeg from the seed itself. In western countries nutmeg is used as a flavouring in milk dishes, and mace for savoury dishes.

Cloves
(Eugenia caryophyllus)
Another spice of great economic importance and coming from the same islands is the clove, *Eugenia caryophyllus*, belonging to the family Myrtaceae. Cloves are the dried unopened flower buds of the tree, and have been used in the East for centuries to combat tooth decay, as food flavourings, and in curry powders. In Indonesia they are mixed with tobacco in cigarettes, and an oil of cloves is obtained by distillation.

Cloves were an extremely valuable commodity in the Middle Ages, having reached Europe via Java and the Near East as early as the 8th century. The Portuguese and Dutch monopolized the trade until the French managed to acquire plants in the 1770s and take

Above: Clove flower buds drying in sun. Right: Cloves (*Eugenia caryophyllus*) are always associated with the islands of Zanzibar and Pemba off the African coast, to which they were introduced by the Arabs in the 19th century.

them to their possessions in the Indian Ocean and the West Indies. In 1819 the Arabs introduced cloves into Zanzibar and Pemba and these islands have since become the world's major producers.

Cloves flourish in the same conditions as the nutmeg. The tree is a small evergreen, some 14m (46ft) high, with elliptical leaves about 13cm (5in) long. The leaves are attractively tinged with pink when young and darken when mature. The inflorescences are terminal, containing from three to 20 flowers which are reddish with yellow anthers. As the flowers open the petals fall, giving the impression that they consist only of a mass of stamens. The fruits are red, oval and fleshy, and contain one or two seeds. The buds are generally harvested about six months after they first begin to develop.

Flamboyant
(Delonix regia)

Apart from trees of economic importance, the tropics also contain a great number of beautiful flowering trees. Most of these are unknown to gardeners living in colder climates, but a few are so widely grown that they can be deemed truly international. The most striking is probably the flamboyant, or flame of the forest. Botanically, it is called *Delonix regia*, and belongs to the family Leguminosae.

The flamboyant is a native of Madagascar and since it was first discovered, in 1824, it has spread throughout the tropics, becoming one of the most popular of all ornamental trees, though it is now extremely rare in the wild. In monsoon countries it sheds its leaves during the dry season, and at the onset of the rains new shoots appear, bringing with them inflorescences 30cm (1ft) or more across. The individual flowers are a brilliant flame colour with yellow streaks on the lower petals. The trees can reach a height of 30m (98ft) when fully grown, forming an umbrella shaped crown and a slightly buttressed trunk with grey, rather smooth bark. The trees grow very quickly from seed, reaching 8m (26ft) in about four years. The leaves, which develop fully when the flowers have passed, are pinnate up to 60cm (2ft) long. The pods, which remain on the trees for some considerable time before fully ripening, are over 30cm (1ft) long, dark brown in colour, and very woody. They can each contain up to 40 seeds.

In tropical towns, flamboyants are frequently planted as street trees, and when in full bloom they are indeed a spectacle. Although the main flowering season is rather brief, there are always some in bloom to attract the visitor.

Above and left: The flamboyant (*Delonix regia*), one of the finest of all tropical flowering trees. It is known throughout the tropics, even though it is now rare in its native island of Madagascar. The brilliantly coloured inflorescences appear at the onset of the rains and provide a spectacular display. They are followed by large seed pods 30cm (12in) long.

Frangipani
(Plumeria acuminata)

Another well loved plant in the tropics is the frangipani, *Plumeria acuminata*. While it lacks the striking colours of the flamboyant it makes up for any shortcomings by its very fragrant flowers and attractive form. It is often called the temple tree, owing to the fact that it is frequently planted around Buddhist and other temples in the East. *Plumeria acuminata* is characterized by its white or pale yellow trumpet-shaped flowers with yellow centres, occurring in inflorescences from 15–20cm (6–8in) across. Those frangipanis with highly coloured flowers—reds, oranges and purples—are probably forms of *P. rubra,* but whether they are true species or a group of hybrids is somewhat in doubt. Nevertheless they are all most attractive plants worthy of a place in any tropical garden, providing as they do pleasing colour, fragrance and form. The frangipanis are small much branched trees ultimately reaching about 10m (33ft) in height. Their twigs are very thick and fragile, each piece growing with little trouble when planted. The leaves are elliptical, from 10 to 20cm (4 to 8in) long with a pointed apex and prominent veins. If any leaves or branches are broken a white latex exudes, which is one of the distinguishing characters of the Apocynaceae family, to which the frangipani belongs.

Jacaranda
(Jacaranda mimosifolia)

The family Bignoniaceae provides a number of magnificent ornamental trees and climbers which are widely grown throughout the world. Perhaps the best known of these is the jacaranda, *Jacaranda mimosifolia*, with its beautiful blue flowers and feathery foliage. Like the flamboyant, it is frequently planted as a street tree, creating a wonderful effect when in full bloom. It is a native of tropical America but is now widespread—preferring, however, a climate with a distinct dry season. It is a medium sized tree attaining 15m (49ft) or so on maturity. The foliage is bipinnate and not unlike that of a member of the Leguminosae, while the flowers are blue, bell-shaped, and 5cm (2in) long.

This brief chapter can do no more than touch the fringe of a subject as vast as that of tropical trees of economic and ornamental importance. Nevertheless it has achieved its purpose if it has added even a little to the reader's knowledge and stirred him into further reading—or better still, inspired an ambition to visit the tropics and see their wealth of magnificent trees with his own eyes.

Below: The jacaranda (*Jacaranda mimosifolia*) belongs to the family Bignoniaceae, which is noted for its many beautiful trees and climbers.

Trees of Swamps and Deserts

Trees growing in the sea! It might seem impossible but it is true, at least along the coasts. Such trees are called mangroves and they occur on tropical and subtropical shores right round the world. There are different species in various genera, and even in several quite different plant families, the most famous being the red mangrove, *Rhizophora,* and the white mangrove, *Avicennia.*

Living in water

How do mangroves manage to survive in salt water? How can they breathe? These and other questions can now be answered satisfactorily to show how well adapted mangroves are to their extreme environment. Actually these trees grow in estuaries and muddy or sandy shores where the water is not too deep and wave action is limited. They are completely exposed to the air when the tide goes out, but at high tide the lower leaves may be at water level. *Rhizophora* has no main trunk at ground level as the whole tree is supported by a mass of arching stilt-roots which hold it in the unstable wet mud. The stilt-roots have large airspaces inside them and the oxygen enters through corky breathing pores *(lenticels)* and diffuses downwards to enable the roots to breathe in the very badly aerated mud in which they grow. In *Avicennia* there are special breathing roots (or *pneumatophores)* with the same function, which stick up from the wet sand around the trees. An aquatic palm *Nypa,* which is common as inland thicket mangroves along Far Eastern rivers, is also adapted to the habitat by having highly aerated tissue at the base of the leaves; from there the oxygen can diffuse down to the submerged roots. Local people actually use these spongy leaf-bases as floats.

When the tide is out a mangrove swamp is a mysterious, eerie place unlike anywhere else. The hot humid atmosphere, charged with the smell of rotting, salty silt—the silence broken only by the plop of crabs into mud—the uniformity of the laurel-like leathery leaves—

and the curious arching stilt-roots or pencil-like pneumatophores—all combine to make it a curious experience.

Although mangroves belong to several families, as already mentioned, none of them has particularly striking flowers. Several species possess reasonably sized flowers but most are inconspicuous, white or rather hidden away among the leaves. In fact the flowers of *Sonneratia* open at night and very little is known about their pollinators or pollination mechanism. When fully grown many mangroves are sizeable trees up to 30m (98ft) high, but one often sees them much smaller, especially those on the seaward edge where they are little more than bushes. Even while young they have the ability to flower and reproduce themselves.

The ecology of mangroves

Most species of mangroves grow in very clearly separated zones. This zonation is closely related to the lie of the shore, which also determines the pattern of tidal

Below: The white mangrove, *Avicennia,* usually grows well up the beach where the salt concentration is high at low tide. Other genera show a preference for different conditions, resulting in well-defined zonation of species.

flooding, how salty the soil is and the fluctuation in the water table. *Rhizophora* usually grows on muddy shores, while *Avicennia* prefers sand. In the Far East *R. mucronata* and *Sonneratia alba* usually colonize soft new mud, but they are soon replaced by the taller *R. apiculata* and *Avicennia alba.* There are also four species of *Bruguiera*—one of which may reach a height of 25m (82ft) and these are usually buttressed at the base and surrounded by stout tree-like pneumatophores. In Sarawak as many as 47 trees and shrubs have been recorded from the mangrove swamps, although only a few of them may be considered to be actual mangroves.

It is not always clear precisely why each species grows in such well defined zones, since a combination of factors affects them in complicated ways. The degree of salinity in the water and soil varies according to the position on the shore since there will be more evaporation, and hence greater concentration of salt, near high tide mark than lower down the shore where the concentration of soil water will differ little from the sea itself. On the other hand, in estuaries where fresh water is diluting the salty sea-water the conditions will be very

different. There is no doubt that *Avicennia* can tolerate saltier conditions than *Rhizophora*. In fact *Avicennia*, unlike *Rhizophora*, has glands on the upper surface of the leaves through which it can get rid of excess salt that has been taken up by the roots. On the other hand, species of *Lumnitzera* can tolerate only brackish water.

An interesting adaptation to the environment is the possession of seeds that germinate while still on the parent plant (a condition known as *vivipary*). Although the mangrove trees belong to several unrelated plant families the same feature occurs in all of them. The most spectacular growth is that of *Rhizophora* which parts with its seedling when it is about 30cm (1ft) long. The long torpedo-like root is said to plummet into the soft, oozing mud where it is anchored, instead of being washed away by the incoming tide. However, there is little evidence that this simple explanation is the correct one since it is unlikely that all the seedlings would fall while the tide is out. Actually one does see groups of young *Rhizophora* seedlings around a tree that may be assumed to be its parent. There is no doubt that many are washed away but, as they float easily, they may be washed up on a suitable shore. The long rootlet (or strictly the *hypocotyl* region between the root and the leaves) enables the leaves to develop above the water level. Of the other mangroves, for example *Avicennia*, *Aegiceras* and *Bruguiera*, all have the same characteristic, though less well developed. This ability for the seeds to be distributed by the ocean currents accounts for the very wide occurrence of the same species on both sides of the Atlantic, and others from the East coast of Africa across the Indian Ocean to the Far East. The cooler waters of southern Africa prevents them mixing and limits *Ceriops* and *Lumnitzera* to the eastern oceans.

It is often said that mangroves help to build up the coast by encouraging silting. However, there are conflicting opinions. It may be argued that the mangroves grow where they do because the shore is suitable and is being silted up anyway, or, on the other hand, that they cause the accumulation rather than follow it. Research in Mexico and Malaya shows that there is evidence for both points of view. Certainly the presence of the tangled growth of mangrove must calm the water, which will cause the silt to be deposited, and this can be seen around the pneumatophores of *Avicennia* growing on sand. The roots and pneumatophores also hold back debris of one sort and another which rots and forms humus mixed with silt and sand to the mangrove, a rich source of nutrients.

The commercial uses of mangroves

Unfortunately piecemeal chopping for firewood and charcoal is ruining much of the world's mangrove forests. If they are not totally destroyed, at least their composition is being changed since the more valuable *Rhizophora* is cut out and is naturally replaced by *Avicennia* of which the timber is useless. An official report has estimated that the huge mangrove forests of the Niger Delta in West Africa could yield 600,000 tons annually in perpetuity without diminishing the total timber. In other words these forests need to be managed and cropped skilfully, otherwise uncontrolled cutting will waste them away—and this is especially true where mangroves form a narrow belt along the coast and they may easily be wiped out. In Nigeria mangrove forest reserves are now proposed in order to conserve a valuable resource, the potential of which is not yet fully appreciated, but since the dry-land forests are being cleared so rapidly mangroves may soon be in great demand. In spite of *Rhizophora* timber not being available as large logs, it has the advantage of being durable in water and is not easily attacked by hole-boring molluscs. It is hard, close-grained, heavy and dark reddish-brown. Apart from small pieces of timber, poles can be used for fences and pit props, and the bark from the timber does yield tannin, albeit of a low quality. However, modern developments of chipboard and the demand for wood-pulp for paper manufacture are likely to make mangroves a valuable resource that must be carefully managed or it will be lost. In any case land

cleared of *Rhizophora* has been found to be too acid for successful rice cultivation unless the soil can be washed and leached before sowing. On the other hand, the landward side of *Avicennia* mangroves in Sierra Leone yields excellent ground for the cultivation of rice and such conflicting interests of land-use need to be resolved.

The above comments describe the mangroves in brackish water, but in many parts of the tropics there are afforested inland fresh-water swamps. For example, in West Africa there are stilt-rooted *Uapaca* trees and large *Mitragyna* with buttresses, which are all basically adapted to a watery environment short of oxygen.

Trees of the desert

As much as a quarter—some estimate it nearer one half—of the earth's land surface is arid. In this section we are looking at some of the trees that grow in the deserts and semi-deserts in the tropics where the daytime temperature is high and at night it is quite low. Some trees grow naturally in these conditions providing they have sufficient moisture. However, much of the arid land occurs in cooler and harsher regions where few trees are able to survive.

Tropical deserts occur in Australia, the Indian Peninsula, southern Arabia, much of Africa and in both North and South America. A desert absolutely devoid of vegetation shows that there is no

water available, but most deserts have rain at some time or other, although it is usually irregular and insufficient to sustain continued plant growth. All plants need water and some are better adapted to these conditions than others. Desert trees need quite a lot of water, which they obtain by having either an enormously spreading root system or a deeper one that can reach lower reservoirs of moisture.

Deserts are not necessarily rolling sand dunes where trees are unable to grow, for they are often rocky and mountainous with some trees in the dry valleys. As there is little ground vegetation or even soil to trap the rain such as it is, the water runs off rapidly, and accumulates in normally dry river

Above: This deep-rooting African *Acacia raddiana* subspecies *tortilis* can survive with little moisture, but it often lines wadis where water collects in pools after rain.

beds *(wadis)* which for a short time become dangerous raging torrents. Much of the water sinks into these water courses and the smaller streams that feed them so that long after the surrounding land has dried out in the baking sunshine there is underground moisture enabling the trees to flourish. A plane flight across a desert reveals these crooked finger wadis lined with little trees and shrubs, their dark foliage showing up against the sun-reflecting sand and stones. Even a few millimetres of rainfall can produce a great volume of water when collected

Above: *Acacia albida* has the unusual characteristic of becoming leafy during the dry season and then actually losing all of its leaves with the onset of the rainy season.

Below: Many dry country trees are armed, like this East African whistling thorn, *Acacia drepanolobium*, which has stipular thorns. The galls are inhabited by ants.

from a large surface area. So, in many deserts there is a considerable reserve of underground water, but the problem for tree seedlings is how to reach it before their roots dry up. Very few do. Only along the water courses does the soil stay moist enough for the roots to grow down into the permanently moist soil. However, if man would conserve or establish sapling trees in desert places where the water table is not too far below the surface we would eventually see large areas converted into woodland.

Perhaps the tree par excellence of the Old World arid zones is the

Acacia, of which there are many species. Like most dry country trees they grow as scattered individuals unless, as we have seen, they are limited to water courses where there is plenty of underground water. Being spaced out the trees' roots can obtain a little moisture from a large surface area. *Acacia raddiana* in Africa has a deeper rooting system but as the dry season advances it slowly sheds some of its leaves thus allowing its normal functions to continue as long as possible with a minimal loss of water. Different species of acacia have different requirements, which accounts for the presence of *A. nilotica* only along permanent rivers or beside pools, while *A. raddiana* subspecies *tortilis* in the Sudan can manage to grow in sandy soil with between 50 and 250mm (2–10in) of rainfall. In clayey soil, however, which dries out like concrete, 400mm (16in) is said to be required and *A. mellifera* needs nearly as much in sandy conditions. Experiments to compare the composition of the sap of desert acacias with that of trees from moister habitats have shown that, contrary to popular opinion, there was no difference. It had been expected that the acacia sap would be able to hold moisture better but this was not so, which means that the tree is adapted to survive in its harsh environment in other ways. Such slow-growing trees yield very hard, reddish wood, famous as the biblical 'shittim' used by the Israelites for making the Ark and Tabernacle in the Sinai Wilderness.

Since many acacias possess finely divided leaves, they have a very small surface area from which water may be lost. The ratio of water-gathering roots to water-losing leaves is therefore high for the size of the tree. In the Australian acacias the leaves are usually only present at the seedling stage and the food-manufacturing process of photosynthesis is carried on by a flattened leaf-like leaf stalk! These leaf stalks are known as phyllodes. The mulga of Australia, *A. aneura,* is well adapted to avoid drought by having its phyllodes reduced to narrow leathery strips, almost thorn-like. However, one might say that owing to the absence of browsing animals, Australian acacias did not need to become adapted to survive both browsing and drought, unlike their African counterparts, which are usually fiercely armed and effectively deter many a soft-mouthed creature anxious for fodder in arid country.

Also very characteristic of the Australian dry country are different kinds of eucalypts, which are described in more detail in a later chapter. The blue mallee, *Eucalyptus gamophylla,* like most of its cousins, has a blue-green foliage which is effective in reflecting much of the heat of the sun's rays; it is also thick enough to hold moisture and the waxy bloom on the surface of the leaves also helps to prevent water loss.

Fire is a hazard for trees in semi-desert where grass, which has

Above: A succulent tree spurge, *Euphorbia ammak,* that grows in rocky places in the Yemen. It is similar to other cactus-like spurges that live in the dry areas of tropical Africa.

Above: A specimen of *Pachycereus pringlei,* one of many tree-like cacti that gives the deserts of southwestern USA and Mexico their characteristic cactus country' appearance; made famous by countless Hollywood films.

grown rapidly after the rains have fallen, becomes tinder dry equally quickly. If the fire sweeps across country every year it is very difficult for tree seedlings to become established. However, some species of African *Terminalia* can exist with a perennial root, although the slender stems above ground are burnt off each year. Gradually the roots increase in size and woodiness until one year there is no fire. During the following season tremendous growth of the stems carries the leaves above any likely fire damage and the young tree is established.

One of the most remarkable trees of the semi-desert in Somalia is the frankincense tree, *Boswellia car-*

teri. It attaches itself firmly to large boulders by a sucker-like bulge at the base of the trunk. Actually, the root penetrates a crack in the rock where the small seed must have germinated and grown before drying up. As the sapling develops into a tree up to 12m (39ft) high, the base swells up around the crack and prevents the trunk breaking off during a storm at this point of weakness. The bark of this tree is very thin and papery, but when the inner bark is punctured a resin exudes like whitish tear drops. This resin is the famous frankincense which has been collected since ancient times for the sake of the fragrance produced when it burns.

The New World deserts are typified by an enormous variety of cacti. Tree cacti are conspicuous in some of these arid regions and they are especially adapted in the warm deserts of Mexico and the southwestern USA. They are well developed in the Sonoran Desert where *Carnegiea gigantea* reaches 11m (36ft) and *Pachycereus pringlei* may be up to 18m (59ft) high and weigh ten tons. These extraordinary cacti with great column-like stems, and the smaller *Opuntia,* are so striking that one can speak of 'cactus country', notably in Arizona, which has 'cactus forests'. They grow in regions that receive a fair amount of summer rainfall, which benefits them during their growing season and enables full development of their roots and stems to take place. In fact, the rootlets actually die off during rainless periods but within 24 hours after rain has fallen they have grown again from the extensive system of main roots only a few centimetres below the surface. These new absorbing roots enable the water-storage tissues to fill up.

Further south in Mexico some hillsides are covered with so many giant cacti that they form a curious kind of forest. Especially important there is *Pachycereus columnatrajani* which is locally called 'tetetzo', a name that also applies to another tall cactus *Cephalocereus tetetzo*. An arborescent cactus of southern Mexico, *Escontria chiotilla,* looks more like one of the African candelabra *Euphorbia* with numerous erect branches spreading from a short stout trunk. Its fruit is sold by the Mexicans, who appreciate its gooseberry-like flavour.

Near the equator in Brazil the catinga country takes its name from the abundance of prickly plants, especially members of the pineapple and cactus families. Many of them are tall column-like cacti, such as *Cephalocereus pentaedrophorus* which reaches 10m (33ft) in height and occurs as scattered trees in this very dry country. The rain storms are so erratic that the plants growing there are adapted to irregular growth whenever sufficient moisture is available. Perhaps the largest and most conspicuous tree-cactus is one the Brazilians call 'mandacaru' *(Cereus jamacaru)*. It branches from near the base of its stout trunk and has numerous four-ribbed stems growing up to 12m (39ft) high, which carry the large yellowish flowers and elongated succulent fruits.

Cacti are almost always armed with extremely sharp spines that occur in clusters. These clusters are called areoles and they are believed to represent a reduced branching system. Leaves are lacking in all the tree cacti, except *Pereskia* in Mexico, thereby reducing the surface area through which water might be lost. Water is actually stored most efficiently in the succulent cells of the stems for

Above: The grotesque baobab (*Adansonia digitata*) is famous throughout the drier parts of tropical Africa. Its soft trunk is often damaged by elephants (as here), and the fibres are used for string.

long periods during which water-use and water-loss is reduced to a minimum. Even the breathing pores (stomata) open only at night when the loss is likely to be at a minimum—which shows how well adapted cacti are to their desert environment.

Often confused with true cacti are the tropical African tree spurges, such as the familiar *Euphorbia candelabrum*. This tree has a heavy crown of numerous erect branches which can reach a

Above: A 'kokerboom forest' in southern Africa made up of the tree-like succulents *Aloe dichotoma*. These unusual plants are restricted to the very arid areas of Namaqualand and southern Namibia.

height of 10m (33ft). Although *Euphorbia* species may look remarkably cactus-like, they are easily distinguished by the presence of pairs of spines, and not clusters. They also yield milky latex when punctured and the flowers are totally different. As they inhabit arid country and semi-desert, they are adapted for the conservation of water in their succulent, usually four-angled branches.

Another well-known succulent genus is *Aloe*, some of the species being trees. One example is *Aloe dichotoma* which inhabits very arid areas of Africa, principally the northern part of Namaqualand and southern Namibia where it grows in the rocky hills that one would hardly expect to be able to support trees with such dense crowns. The paired forking branching habit of this tree is curious and characteristic. Perhaps the strangest tree of the drier parts of Africa is the baobab *(Adansonia digitata),* a giant that can only be called grotesque! Its huge trunk is bottle-shaped and serves to store water for periods of drought.

The Palm Family

True palms, 'the princes of the plant kingdom', belonging to the family Palmae, are of great economic importance, but remain largely unfamiliar in their richness and diversity to people of temperate countries. Of the 2,700 species of palms, very few are to be found in temperate lands, and palms are always popularly associated with the tropics. Most of the species are to be found in the rich tropical rain forests of Southeast Asia, the Malay Archipelago and Central and South America. Africa has remarkably few species, though what species do occur in that vast continent are often botanically rather peculiar. A few species can be found in temperate countries such as the Chusan or Chinese windmill palm, *Trachycarpus fortunei,* native of the temperate Far East, which can be grown out of doors in Britain even as far north as northwest Scotland. Two palms are native in Europe— the dwarf fan palm, *Chamaerops humilis,* which grows along the Mediterranean and Atlantic coasts of southern Europe, and a wild date palm, *Phoenix theophrasti,* which grows on the island of Crete. One would have thought *Chamaerops* an ideal temperate garden plant, but in fact it seems to be more frost sensitive than the Chusan palm. The true palms remain botanically very isolated and are one of the most interesting yet little studied groups of plants.

What is a palm?

Though many palms are tall and have well-defined hard trunks, they differ markedly from most other trees in the general inability of their trunks to increase in diameter—that is they show no secondary thickening, the process by which wood is built up by a cambium. Palmwood consists of compactions of very hard fibres— it is not like conventional wood and is usually difficult to work. Furthermore palms can hardly be said to have bark in the way most trees have. One perhaps surprising effect of this lack of cambium is that damaging the outer surface of the palm trunk does not necessarily

Above: The doum palm (*Hyphaene thebaica*) growing near dwellings in the Yemen. Note how the trunks branch by repeated equal forking (known as dichotomy), a rare condition in the palm family.

kill the tree. Slash and burning to produce farmlands in tropical countries often results in a landscape dominated by relict palm trees, which, with no cambium to be damaged, have survived the fires, even with some of the outer trunk burnt. The farmer may continue to harvest palm products even after the rest of the forest is destroyed, but such relict palms are often reproductively dead; that is they cannot regenerate, because their seedlings cannot survive in the open, and ultimately the palms, too, will follow the forest into extinction. Palm stems can be immensely tall—one of the species of South American wax palms, *Ceroxylon quindiuense,* the national tree of Colombia, may reach 60m (197ft) tall, and *Pigafetta filaris* of New Guinea and Celebes may reach 50m (164ft) tall. Some palms like the coconut may have single stems; others like the European fan palm may be tufted. More rarely the stem may be subterranean or creeping. Members of one group of great local significance in

some parts of Asia have climbing stems, sometimes exceeding 100m (328ft) in length; these are the rattans, important as the source of cane for cane furniture, and for innumerable local uses. Though the rattan habitat is best developed in Asia, a few species can be found in Africa, and species of *Desmoncus,* relatives of the spiny peach palm, *Bactris gasipaes,* climb in the forests of America. Mostly, branching of palm stems occurs at ground level to give clusters, but more rarely they branch above ground. The most famous example of branching in palms is the doum palm, *Hyphaene thebaica,* which is native to Egypt and the Sudan; it has a trunk which branches by equal forking or dichotomy. Closely related *Hyphaene compressa,* frequent along the coasts of Kenya and Tanzania, may branch in this way five times to give a head of 32 separate crowns— an extraordinary sight. Branching in coconuts is rare and almost always occurs because the apex of the stem is damaged in some way. Some palm stems such as those of *Verschaffeltia splendida* of the Seychelles are supported off the ground on a great mass of stilt roots and in this way tend to resemble many of the screw-pines or *Pandanus*

Left: Looking up into the crown of a coconut palm (*Cocos nucifera*), with feather leaves and fruit clearly visible. Note the clean trunk and the uniform leaf stalks.

Below: The coconut (*Cocos nucifera*), one of the most important of all tropical trees. Note the single trunk of almost even diameter and the massive pinnate leaves with evenly-spaced leaflets.

Palm Leaf Shapes

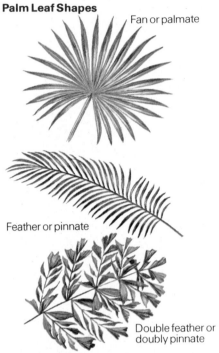

Fan or palmate

Feather or pinnate

Double feather or doubly pinnate

Above: The three basic leaf shapes in palms. Top: Fan or palmate (such as *Trachycarpus*). Middle: Feather or pinnate (coconut palm). Bottom: The double feather or doubly pinnate shape (*Caryota*).

Leaves

There are three basic leaf shapes in the palms, and though superficially very different in appearance they are built up in the same strange way, which is almost unique to the palms. Unlike the compound fan and feather leaves of other plants, in which the leaflets develop from the elongation of separate growth points, the leaflets of palms develop by the splitting of a folded leaf blade—this is quite easy to see in a growing palm where the leaf is expanding, splitting along its folds and then opening out to give the mature leaf shape. Though easy to see, it is very difficult to understand this process—a problem which has taxed botanists for over a century. The three basic leaf types are fan (palmate) (eg the Chusan, and dwarf fan palms), feather (pinnate) (eg the coconut, the parlour palm, *Chamaedorea elegans*—frequently incorrectly called *Neanthe bella*—and the oil palm *Elaeis guineensis*), and double feather (doubly pinnate) (only known in the fish-

233

Above: Majestic royal palms (*Roystonea regia*) with immense columnar trunks, each topped by a smooth green crownshaft and a head of plumose pinnate leaves.

tailed palms, *Caryota*). Palm leaves develop tightly enclosed within an apical bud. This is the 'palm heart' or 'palm cabbage', sometimes also called 'millionaire's salad'; it is often delicious to eat and a regular canning industry, producing canned palm hearts from *Euterpe edulis* in Brazil, has decimated wild palm populations of this species, as removal of any palm cabbage causes death of that stem, and if the palm is a solitary trunked species, of that tree too.

In palms such as the oil palm, the leaves do not fall neatly from the trunk, and the leaf base remains for a long time on the trunk. In the coconut the leaves fall off in their entirety and hence the trunk is clean. In *Washingtonia* the whole leaves remain on the trunk forming a gigantic column or skirt completely hiding the trunk. In many palms the trunk is surmounted by a column of leaf sheaths known as the crownshaft, which appears stem-like but is in fact analogous to the 'pseudostem' of the bananas. The royal palms, *Roystonea*, have huge crownshafts which are light green in colour. In the sealing-wax palm, *Cyrtostachys lakka*, a native of Sumatra, Malaya and Borneo, the crownshaft is brilliant red, hence making this species one of the most beautiful and desirable tropical ornamental plants. Where there is a crownshaft, the leaves always fall from the trunk cleanly.

Above: The true sago palm (*Metroxylon sagu*), native to Moluccas and New Guinea, showing terminal inflorescence; after flowering the trunk dies. Sago is obtained from starch stored in the trunk.

Flowers

Flowers of palms are extraordinarily varied but nearly always small; what they lack in size they make up for in abundance, for palm inflorescences may be huge affairs of thousands of flowers. The inflorescences usually occur in the axils of leaves but in a few palms they are crowded together at the apex of the stem forming a huge terminal mass of flowers. Palm stems with such aggregations of inflorescences usually pass through a long period of vegetative growth, come into flowering, fruit spectacularly and then die. Perhaps the most magnificent example of this type of flowering is the talipot palm of Ceylon, *Corypha umbraculifera*, which, incidentally, has huge fan leaves which have been used for thatch, umbrellas and as instant pages for writing. The true sago palms (*Metroxylon*) native to New Guinea

and the West Pacific islands (not to be confused with the sago palm of horticulturalists, which is the cycad *Cycas rumphii*) also flower in this way and it is the long period of vegetative growth preceding flowering with consequent laying down of food reserves in the stem pith which accounts for the accumulation of sago; the sago is extracted by beating the pith in water, and then removing and concentrating the starch suspension.

Fruits and seeds

Palm fruits range from tiny drupes only 5mm ($\frac{1}{5}$in) in diameter to large fruits like the coconut and huge fruit like the double coconut, *Lodoicea maldivica*, of the Seychelles. This last is frequently referred to as bearing the biggest fruit in the world but this is not so — that pride of place belongs to the pumpkin, but *Lodoicea* certainly has the biggest seed, inside an extraordinary bilobed nut, the shape of which has prompted fantastic tales and semi-magical uses. One group of palms to which *Raphia*, the sago palms *Metroxy-*

lon, and the rattans belong, has fruits covered with exquisitely neat vertical rows of scales quite reminiscent of the appearance of a pine cone, but structurally totally different. These fruits are much in demand for making necklaces and for use in flower arrangement.

The kernel of palm seeds is sometimes homogeneous, as in the coconut and the oil palm, or sometimes deeply penetrated by very fine lines called ruminations as in the betel palm and *Raphia*. The kernel may be extremely hard in which case if it is sufficiently large it may be used as a substitute for ivory in the making of buttons and *objets d'art*. Such vegetable ivory comes mainly from the *Hyphaene*, the doum palms, and the ivory palm itself (appropriately called *Phytelephas*). The ivory palm is Central and South American in origin and with a few closely related genera represents an extraordinary group botanically in almost every respect; from the female flowers with parts in fives to nines to the male flowers with up to 1,000 stamens, the ivory palms are weird and unlike any other palms.

Coconut palm
(Cocos nucifera)
'Coco' in Portuguese means a bugbear, or something to frighten children. It is thought that the first Portuguese seamen to see coconuts saw a fancied resemblance to a devil face in the three eyes of the coconut shell, and this is perhaps the best explanation of how the coconut got its name. The history of the coconut is so inextricably entwined with that of man in the tropics that it is still not known with certainty where this most useful of palms originated. Nowhere at the present time is the coconut unquestionably wild; trees on uninhabited coral islands may appear wild but almost certainly originate from nuts left behind by fishermen. The coconut can be distributed by sea—its thick husk, which is normally removed (and used in coir production) before reaching shops in Europe, acts as a float. Nuts floating in the sea for only a short period can germinate—coconuts reached the new-formed islands of the Krakatau group in the Sunda Straits by sea dispersal and grew there. So there is much to suggest that the coconut is a seashore plant. Its closest relatives are found in South Africa *(Jubaeopsis caffra)* and Chile *(Jubaea chilensis)*

Above: Fruit of the coco-de-mer (*Lodoicea maldivica*). Each of the massive rounded fruits contains a bilobed nut, inside of which is a seed larger than any other found in the plant kingdom.

Above right: Fruit of *Pigafetta filaris*, the tallest palm in Southeast Asia and a relative of the sago palm; each fruit is covered in rows of scales to protect the sweet pulp around the seed.

Right: The sugar palm (*Arenga pinnata*), a useful palm of Southeast Asia. Note the downwards sequence of flowering.

though most of the other members of the cocosoid group to which the coconut belongs are South American. The most reasonable theory suggests an origin in the East Indian Ocean area or the West Pacific.

Almost every part of the coconut is used in some way; in Indonesia roots of coconuts were even sometimes used as tooth brushes. Most especially the cuisine of coconut-growing countries requires the use of coconut oil, coconut milk (not the water of the central nut cavity but a creamy emulsion of kernel oil in water made by squeezing ground kernel with water many times) and sometimes of coconut sugar, though in areas where the Nypa and sugar palms grow these are often used as a source of sugar instead.

Sugar palm
(Arenga pinnata)
The sugar palm is a familiar tree of villages in Southeast Asia, parts of India and Ceylon and Malaysia. Like the coconut, almost every part of it is used in some way. It is a

rather massive palm with dark green, sombre, untidy leaves and a trunk, when allowed to grow naturally, densely covered with coarse black fibres. The sugar palm flowers once only and then dies; in flowering behaviour it is like many common temperate annual weeds such as shepherd's purse, except that it may grow for up to 15 years before flowering and then takes four years to flower—flowering on such a superbly massive scale makes the monocarpic or once flowering habit much more spectacular and remarkable in the big trees than in a lowly weed. This is not the only peculiarity of the flowering process in the sugar palm—the talipot (*Corypha*), sago (*Metroxylon*) palm and several other palms only flower once, and the stem produces a huge terminal mass of inflorescences. In *Arenga pinnata*, however, the first flower mass emerges at the top of the stem and then successive nodes downwards produce, one by one, a flower mass. The upper inflorescences are usually female and the lower male;

when the plant has exhausted its reserves or the bottom-most node has been reached, the palm dies.

The reserves built up in the stem of the sugar palm are in the form of starch and accumulate in abundance in the soft stem pith. This starch can be extracted as in the true sago palm, *Metroxylon,* to form sago. After the onset of flowering, the starch is mobilized into sugars for the developing inflorescences and fruit, and this abundance of sugar can be utilized by tapping the young inflorescences to give a sweet sap, quickly fermenting in the tropical heat to toddy or palm wine. If the sap is boiled soon after it has been collected, and before it ferments, it can produce sugar. Palm sugar is delicious, red-brown, aromatic and fudge-like and in the countries where it is produced often costs more than white cane sugar, because of the high demand for it for traditional recipes.

The fruit of the sugar palm can also be eaten, when it is still young, but it is fiercely protected by fearfully irritant needle-crystals (raphides) in the fruit wall. There is a story of how the town of Surabaya in Java in the sixteenth century fell after a long siege when the besieging army pounded up the young fruit of the sugar palm (and hence the needle crystals) and put it into the town water supply. The outer wood of the trunk is used for handles for axes and many other tools, and the

Right: *Elaeis guineensis,* the African oil palm, now the most important of oil-producing plants, cultivated in millions throughout the humid tropics.

Below: Nuts of the betel palm (*Areca catechu*). They are chewed by millions of Asians for the stimulating properties of arecine, contained in the seeds.

young developing leaves are often used, stripped from their midribs, as cigarette papers. The black stem fibre makes excellent rope, brushes, thatch and even a base resistant to burrowing-crabs for roads in mangrove forest.

In fact, the uses of the sugar palm are legion and the palm is a splendid example of the multiplicity of products palms supply. Yet this palm is little known outside Southeast Asia and Indonesia.

Betel palm
(*Areca catechu*)

The betel palm, *Areca catechu,* is a familiar pinnate leaved palm found throughout the more humid parts of Asia and the Malay Archipelago; it has also been introduced to parts of Africa where it is used as in Asia, and to other parts of the world where Asiatic people have settled. This palm is solitary-stemmed and rarely exceeds about 15m (49ft) tall; the lower part of the trunk is grey, but the upper part is shiny

dark green; there is a well-defined green or yellowish crownshaft which often appears swollen or almost pregnant with developing flowers inside. The flowers open when the leaf sheath surrounding the inflorescence falls and releases the pressure on the inflorescence; the flowers are intensely lemon-scented and because of this are frequently used in ceremonies in Asia. The fruit is dirty brick red in colour and contains a single seed, which is white and bony like coconut flesh but solid and deeply penetrated by fine brown lines (ruminations) like a nutmeg.

Though many parts of betel palm are used casually (such as the sheaths used folded into buckets), the reason for the palm's cultivation is that the seed contains a stimulant, arecine. Betel nut is chewed; as a masticatory it is found throughout Asia, but nowadays it is often only the older people who still chew betel. The preparation of betel for chewing

is extraordinarily complex and one wonders how and where the curious combination of ingredients evolved. First a leaf of betel pepper (*Piper betle*) is taken; on it is dabbed some lime (not the citrus fruit but mineral lime), a touch of gambir, and then thin slices of betel nut. These are the essential ingredients, but added to them may be tobacco and spices. Elegantly, the packet of betel may be pinned with a clove. The packet is chewed and quickly the saliva becomes brick red and the chewer is stimulated. Chewing certainly blackens the teeth, but it is thought to strengthen them—in fact areca nut tooth powder used to be sold in Britain in the last century. Novice chewers experience dizziness and constriction of the throat—it feels also much like chewing lumps of wood. But literally millions of people are addicted to betel chewing.

Oil palm
(Elaeis guineensis)

The oil palm, *Elaeis guineensis,* is native to the wetter parts of tropical Africa, but it has in the last 20 years become one of the most important oil-producing plants in the tropics. It is the most productive of all tropical oil-producing crops and huge plantations have been established in the Americas, Africa and Southeast Asia, especially in Malaya, which is now the major exporter of palm oil. The palm is single trunked, with rather large untidy pinnate leaves which do not fall off cleanly but leave ragged leaf bases adhering to the trunk. The inflorescences are either male or female (though occasional mixed inflorescences occur), and they are borne on the same tree. Usually the tree grows through periods of maleness producing male inflorescences only, followed by periods of femaleness. The fruiting bunch is a squat affair tucked in the leaf axil, and somewhat inaccessible. It consists of branches ending in rigid points, bearing numerous fruit up to about 5cm long by 3cm wide (2 by 1⅙in), blackish in the exposed areas but usually a glorious orange red where hidden by bracts or other fruit. The fruit wall (or pericarp) produces an orange oil (pericarp oil) and the kernel produces a colourless oil (kernel oil). The

Right: Fruiting tree of the date palm (*Phoenix dactylifera*); the old leaf bases have been removed. The fruit-bearing branches are borne at the end of a long stalk.

oils, after being decoloured and purified, are used in industry as lubricants, in margarine manufacture, in soap production and many other ways. The stone containing the kernel is so hard that occasionally the stone fragments, after the kernels have been removed, are used as road gravel.

A second species of the genus *Elaeis, E. melanococca,* is found in eastern South America and is gaining importance in the breeding of elite strains of oil palm as a source by hybridization of important characteristics such as disease and pest resistance.

Date palm
(Phoenix dactylifera)

The date has been associated with man in the Middle East and Egypt for millennia. Like the coconut and the betel palm, this association has been so close, that now nowhere can the date be said to be truly wild. It belongs to the genus *Phoenix*, which consists of about 17 species found from the Canary Islands and Africa through the Indian subcontinent to Ceylon, the Malay Peninsula and Sumatra, Laos and Hongkong. The species are all extremely difficult to identify because of their close similarity and also because many of the plants in cultivation seem to be of hybrid origin. All the date species are dioecious and in the cultivated date man frequently assists pollination by dusting the female inflorescences with branches of male flowers, a practice carried out by the Ancient Egyptians. In India *Phoenix sylvestris* is used as a source of palm wine and palm sugar and in Africa *Ph. reclinata* is used as a source of material for weaving into baskets which find their way to almost all the countries of the world on tourists' shoulders. *Phoenix roebelinii,* perhaps the smallest and most beautiful of the dates, is native to Laos, and is a much esteemed house plant.

Southern Hemisphere Trees

The eucalypts dominate the forests of Australia, and by a combination of unique characters at once mark out the Australian scene as distinct from that of other continents with broad-leaved trees. Leaves and bark especially contribute to the distinctive appearance of the trees. The leaves are generally of a narrow scimitar shape and they hang vertically downwards from the branchlets, allowing the brilliant sunshine to pass between without overheating them. The leathery texture of the leaves adds to their resistance to heat, as does a thin coating of wax over the surface, which is responsible for their grey-green or blue-green appearance. The pendent leaves and the open branching of the crown allows much light to reach the forest floor. This favours the growth of under-storey trees and numerous shrubs and herbs which contribute to the rich flora of these sclerophyll ('hard-leaf') forests.

Eucalypts

There are over 500 kinds of eucalypts in Australia and the different types of bark provide a convenient rough and ready means of classifying them into groups. Smooth-barked trees are called 'gums', a term which is sometimes applied popularly to eucalypts in general. Strictly, a gum sheds some of its bark every season, casting it off in thin strips which may be 5m by 5cm (16½ft. by 2in). The newly exposed bark is smooth and uniform in texture and may be mottled in shades of grey or dull green. In the salmon gum *(Eucalyptus salmonophloia)* the fresh bark is salmon pink and in the ghost gum *(E. papuana)* it looks like white vellum. It may appear strange that these smooth-barked trees are called gums, but the name goes back to colonial days. No eucalypt produces a true gum, but a number of species exude a reddish brown secretion when the bark is damaged and this hardens into a resinous substance, rich in tannin, known as kino or gum kino. A century ago eucalyptus kino was imported into the drug markets of Europe for use as an astringent in medicine. The best qualities were glassy in appearance and ruby red in colour, like that provided by the river red gum *(E. camaldulensis),* a valuable timber tree along the lower reaches of the Murray River. In the course of time kino fell into disfavour and the term gum was transferred to trees with smooth bark. With equal reason it could have been given to the bloodwoods, some of which also produce kino, as the name implies. The bloodwood bark is hard and dark grey and fissured into irregular plates.

At the other extreme of softness lie the stringy-barks with thick fibrous spongy bark, which can easily be pulled away in long strips as in the messmate *(E. obliqua).* In between lie the peppermints with harder interwoven fibres and the boxbarks with brown bark shallowly fissured and broken up into small tesserae like the bark of the European box tree *(Buxus sempervirens).* Hardest of all are the ironbarks with iron grey bark deeply fissured and transversely furrowed, as in the mugga *(E. sideroxylon).*

In the more humid forests of Victoria and Tasmania eucalypts develop into giant trees. Crowning them all is the mountain ash *(E. regnans)* which may exceed 100m (328ft) and so rival the Californian redwood *(Sequoia sempervirens)* for pride of place as the world's tallest tree. As we move into dryer areas and finally to the fringe of the desert different species take over. They dwindle in size and change their habit to something between a bush and a tree. These semi-desert trees are called mallees and are peculiar to Australia. They have adapted to arid conditions by producing a large woody underground rootstock or lignotuber, which sends up six or more stems to a height of 3–6m (10–20ft). Years of drought gradually prune off the lower branches, so old mallees finish with small flat tops on a spreading array of slender trunks. The secret of their survival in the desert resides in their far-flung roots, which tap the scanty

Above: The manna or ribbon gum, *Eucalyptus viminalis,* sheds its bark in long narrow strips. The leaves are a favourite food of the Australian marsupial possum, the koala.

water supply over a large area and retain it as a watery sap through the dry season. The Aborigines were aware of this water supply and used it on their journeys across the desert. Many early travellers died of thirst in their efforts to cross the country. Eyre was the first to learn from the Aborigines the trick of cutting a mallee root, pulling up a long section of it and cutting it into pieces which were held erect to allow the sap to drip into the mouth. By this means, Eyre was able to complete his journey across the continent in 1841. The giant mallee *(E. oleosa),* the congoo mallee *(E. dumosa)* and the lerp mallee *(E. incrassata)* were among the common species tapped for water. The Aborigines found many other uses for the eucalypts. The seeds were finely ground for food and the

Left: The dome-shaped crown of the red flowered gum (*Eucalyptus ficifolia*) casts a grateful shade and delights the eye with masses of scarlet blossoms.

Below: The river red gum (*Eucalyptus camaldulensis*) grows to perfection along the lower Murray River. Here an isolated tree stands out against a sunset sky.

Below: The bark of the river red gum is shed in irregularly shaped flakes, year by year, creating a harmony in shades of grey, a pattern which is common to many of the gums.

abundant nectar sucked off the blossoms, one Western Australian mallee, the mottlecah (*E. macrocarpa*), producing as much as a coffee spoonful of nectar from its 7.5cm (3in) blossoms. The sugary exudation of a scale insect living on the leaves was also gathered as a delicacy called 'lerp', giving its name to the lerp mallee.

The early colonists found a variety of timbers at hand to choose from for constructing their houses and furniture and for tools and fence posts. They tended to give familiar names of northern hemisphere timbers to those they resembled in their new homeland. Pale-coloured, straight-grained timbers recalling ash (*Fraxinus*) were dubbed mountain ash or alpine ash (*E. gigantea*). The reddish timbers of *E. resinifera* and *E. botryoides* were called mahogany. The native names were sometimes adopted as for jarrah (*E. marginata*) and karri (*E. diversicolor*), two of the most important timber trees of Western Australia. Karri reaches an immense size sometimes growing to 85m (279ft), and often having a straight bole 3m (10ft) in diameter clothed in a smooth blue-grey bark and clear of branches for 30m (98ft). The timber is reddish brown and harder than oak, which it can replace for furniture or parquet floors. Huge as the karri can be, it was overtopped by the mountain ash. Original stands in Victoria and Tasmania reaching 100m (328ft) were an inspiring sight, rising like cathedral columns from a base of 4m (13ft) diameter and covered with a whitish gum bark.

The mountain ash is one of the most rapid growing of all the eucalypts. Under favourable conditions it will reach a height of 18m (59ft) in 10 years. Some of the Tasmanian giants, when felled, were found to have produced annual growth rings 2.5cm (1in) wide for the first 30 years of their lives. They had increased 5cm (2in) in diameter each season over this period. The rapid growth results in a rather light, but strong and easily worked timber, which has many uses. The rapid growth of eucalypts like the mountain ash, river red gum and the Tasmanian blue gum (*E. globulus*) has caused them to be widely planted throughout the tropics and subtropics, both for timber and for fuel. In Brazil the river red gum, the Sydney blue gum (*E. saligna*) and other species have been grown extensively to

Above: The pleasant reddish-brown colour of karri combines with strength and durability to make it an attractive timber for a wide variety of interior furniture, panelling and flooring.

Above: The crimson flowers of the mottlecah (*Eucalyptus macrocarpa*), largest in the genus, make a striking and spectacular contrast with the broad silver-grey foliage of this drought-resistant shrub.

Above: The fuchsia gum (*Eucalyptus forrestiana*) is a small tree named for its fuchsia-like buds and in honour of Sir John Forrest, the first premier of Western Australia.

Above: The large urn-shaped gum nuts of the marri (*Eucalyptus calophylla*) follow clusters of creamy white flowers. The marri has been crossed with many species of gum to produce a great range of colours from red through to apricot.

provide fuel for the railways. South Africa favours the Sydney blue gum both for timber and for paper pulp. The pioneer work on conversion of eucalypt timber into paper pulp was carried out in Australia and commercial production of good quality writing and printing papers began in 1938 in Tasmania using predominantly mountain ash and messmate.

Gum buds and gum nuts

The fruits of the eucalypts are woody capsules popularly called 'gum nuts'. They are often bell shaped or half round and contain three to five chambers packed with tiny seeds. The whole gum nut of the mountain ash is only 5mm ($\frac{1}{5}$in) across and the seeds less than 1mm ($\frac{1}{25}$in) so the giant tree springs from 'a grain of mustard seed'. Many of the smaller trees and mallees have much larger gum nuts often sculptured into strange

and beautiful shapes. The gum buds that precede them may be brilliantly coloured and are always covered by a lid or operculum, variously shaped, which replaces the petals in other flowers. As the lid falls off it reveals a cluster of white pink or crimson stamens. The red flowered gum (*E. ficifolia*) produces masses of blossom which cover the tree and make it a favourite for street planting. By crossing with the marri (*E. calophylla*) a range of shades through pink to scarlet and apricot has been produced. The gum nuts of these trees are like monkey pots 2cm ($\frac{4}{5}$in) across but the largest gum nuts in the mottlecah (*E. macrocarpa*) are flat topped bowls 5cm (2in) in diameter. This is a mallee with large crimson blossoms displayed against broad silver grey leaves. Some species are most beautiful before the flower buds burst. The coral gum (*E.*

torquata) has clusters of coral coloured buds with pointed fluted caps and the bases similarly fluted. The *Fuchsia* gum *(E. forrestiana)* has pendulous scarlet buds like four-angled bells ending in slender tapering yellow caps, which decorate the tree for some time before they flower. In the yate *(E. cornuta)* the buds are clustered with caps like apricot-coloured horns, which become reddish yellow fingerstalls in the bushy yate *(E. lehmannii)*. Then one can pass to the grotesque in the warted yate *(E. megacornuta)* where the fingerstalls are bright green and covered with warts. There are endless beautiful and striking variants of these features in other species, many of which deserve to be more widely planted in parks and gardens.

Wattles

Everywhere in the Australian bush, springtime is heralded by the appearance of masses of yellow or golden mimosalike blossom on the wattles. They belong to the widespread genus *Acacia* found in India, Africa and South America as well as in Australia. Outside

Above: Spotted gum (*Eucalyptus maculata*), with characteristic flaking bark. Below: The snow gum (*Eucalyptus pauciflora*) edges the tree-line in the Snowy Mountains of New South Wales.

Above: Karri (*Eucalyptus diversicolor*), largest tree of Western Australia, raises its smooth grey boles for 30m (98ft) without a branch. Honey of the best quality is obtained from the flowers of this tree.

Australia the leaves always have numerous leaflets attached on either side of a stalk (pinnate), or a number of pinnae of this kind may be attached to a major axis (compound pinnate) and the leaf is then reminiscent of a fern frond. The silver wattle *(Acacia dealbata)* is one of the species to retain these fern-like leaves, but in the great majority the leaves are replaced by flattened leaf stalks (phyllodes) which are tough and thick skinned and much more resistant to damage by drought. The change over was probably a response to desert conditions and is repeated in the seedlings, the first leaves of which are compound. In the red-leaved wattle *(A. rubida)* the passage from compound leaves to red tinged 10cm (4in) long lance-shaped phyllodes is more protracted than usual and often adult branches revert to the juvenile kind of leaf.

The blackwood *(A. melanoxylon)* is one of the largest of the wattles and grows to 30m (98ft) high as an understorey tree in the forests of giant mountain ash in Victoria and Tasmania. The blackwood, in turn gives protection to a ground cover of tree ferns *(Dicksonia antarctica)* 5–10m (16½–33ft) tall. In this setting the creamy yellow blossoms are set off against its dark green foliage and are followed by twisted brown pods. When the pods split open they reveal shining black seeds surrounded by a fleshy pink seed stalk which winds itself back and forth twice round the seed. This striking colour contrast attracts birds to eat the fleshy bait and scatter the seeds. The timber of the blackwood is one of the best of all the Australian timbers. The heartwood varies from reddish brown to nearly black and, with bands of golden brown and a curly grain, it makes a beautiful wood for furniture and decorative panelling or hard wearing wood block floors. The willow wattle *(A. salicina)* is a smaller tree reaching only to 15m (49ft) in height, but with pendulous branches and phyllodes recalling a willow in appearance. Like the blackwood, its timber is hard and durable. From Western Australia comes the raspberry jam wood *(A. acuminata)* a small tree frequenting granite outcrops and rarely more than 10m (33ft) high. The heartwood is hard and lustrous and varies in colour from crimson to violet with a perfume likened by some to violets and by others to crushed raspberries. It is

Above: The silver wattle *(Acacia dealbata)*, beautiful in flower, is grown for its bark which contains up to 30 per cent of tannins, which are used in the leather industry.

a decorative timber for turnery and inlay work. The timbers of the mulga *(A. aneura)* and the myall *(A. pendula)*, abundant small trees of the dry inland, can be put to similar uses.

Mulga and myall are aboriginal names taken over by the white colonists but 'wattle' was bestowed by the colonists themselves. They soon found that young saplings of many acacias were strong and pliable and resistant to decay. This made them ideal for weaving the wicker work of wattle and daub houses familiar to the colonists in their English homeland. So in time, the name wattle was transferred to the trees that provided this useful house building material.

Many of the wattles combine decorative foliage with the beauty of abundant blossom and this has made them favourites for garden planting, not only in Australia but generally in subtropical countries. Cootamundra wattle *(A. baileyana)*, named after the locality in New South Wales where it originated, has brilliantly blue-silvery fernlike leaves. The leaves of the black wattle *(A. mearnsii)* are larger, but less silvery and the flowers are of a deeper yellow. The Queensland silver wattle *(A. podalyriifolia)*, which has curiously shaped silver-white phyllodes, completes a trio much grown for the cut flower trade. The black wattle has more mundane uses for the bark may contain up to half its weight of tannin and is an important raw product for the leather industry. Some other fern-leaved wattles are also rich in tannin, notably the silver wattle *(A. dealbata)* and the green wattle *(A. decurrens)* and among the phyllodic species the golden wattle *(A. pycnantha)* is widely cultivated for its tan bark.

Silky oaks, bull oaks and bottle trees

Sir Joseph Banks, naturalist and gentleman scientist, who accompanied Captain James Cook on his first voyage of discovery around the world, was fascinated by the many strange and beautiful flowers they observed around Botany Bay when first they reached the eastern coast of Australia in April 1770. Among the most curious were the *Grevilleas* which commonly have their flowers arranged in one-sided toothbrush-like groups. Individual flowers in bud have a long tube ending in a rounded head that conceals the stamens. The flower opens by the bursting of the wiry style through the side of the tube to form a springy arch, like a watch spring, before it finally separates the petals and straightens up. Coupled with this strange behaviour is a range of colours from white and cream to yellow orange and red, the petals often being a different shade from the tube and the tip of the style occasionally a brilliant green. Most of the grevilleas are shrubs, many like the rosemary grevillea *(G. rosmarmifolia)* with rose red flowers make beautiful ornaments for a garden, but a few are forest trees. Of these, the silky oak *(G. robusta)* is the largest, reaching a height of 30m (98ft). The timber is reddish brown with a silky lustre and a bold and handsome grain reminiscent of the true oaks *(Quercus)* and like them is used for quality furniture and panelling. With its finely cut leaves and large trusses of yellow and orange blossoms it is an excellent shade tree and is now planted in cities throughout the tropics and subtropics.

Among the trees seen by Banks at Botany Bay, later to be named in his honour, was the saw banksia *(Banksia serrata)*. It is a small tree with gnarled trunk and saw-edged leaves. The flowers are produced in dense lemon yellow bottle brushes which contrast with the silver grey of the buds. The timbers of this and the coast banksia *(B. integrifolia)* are reddish in colour and are known as beefwood. Like the silky oak they have a bold and decorative grain which is characteristic of this family (Proteaceae). White beefwood comes from a Queensland tree generally known as the wheel of fire tree *(Stenocarpus sinuatus)*. The brilliant scarlet flowers are arranged like the spokes of a wheel and are followed by brown pods 5–10cm (2–4in) long which enclose thin winged seeds in parallel rows. Seeds and fruits in the Proteacae vary as much as the flowers and leaves. The Queensland nut *(Macadamia ternifolia)* has the distinction of being the only Australian

Above: Isolated trees of bull oak (*Casuarina* sp) develop a picturesque habit; with seeds in cones the foliage makes the tree look more like a cypress than an oak.

Below: The silver-grey buds of the saw banksia (*Banksia serrata*), open into yellow flowers filled with nectar in order to attract the birds that come to pollinate them.

tree to provide a commercial food crop. The leaves are borne three together on the branches and the yellow flowers arranged in long strings give rise to hard woody globular pods which need a hammer to crack them. The labour is well rewarded for the kernels inside are 10–15mm ($\frac{2}{5}$–$\frac{3}{5}$in) across and of a delicious flavour.

The casuarinas (family Casuarinaceae) are another group of Australian trees to which the name oak has been transferred. Nothing could be less like an oak in appearance for the leaves are reduced to tiny scales on slender grooved branches, more like a cypress than an oak. The bull oak *(Casuarina luehmannii)* from eastern Australia has reddish brown timber with a bold oak like grain. The she oak *(C. fraseriana)* from western Australia is similar, but paler in colour. How these names suggesting different sexes came to be applied is uncertain for there are female bull oaks and male she oaks, flowers of the two sexes being on different trees. The male flowers are in slender yellow catkins which shed their pollen into the wind which bears it to the feathery red stigmas of the female. The fruits are woody cones made up of two-valved capsules which split open to shed a pair of delicately winged seeds. Bull oaks make excellent windbreaks and the branches provide emergency fodder in drought years.

Among the curiosities of Australia is the Queensland bottle tree *(Brachychiton rupestris)*. Imagine a wine bottle 7m (23ft) high and 2m (6½ft) diameter covered with a smooth grey bark, crown it with a spreading head of branches clothed in narrow dark green leaves and that is the bottle tree. The wood is soft and pithy, of no value as timber, but wood and foliage are relished by cattle. The flowers of the bottle tree are an inconspicuous greenish white, unlike those of the flame kurrajong *(B. acerifolius)*, which are bell-shaped and bright red. As they are produced in abundance on the bare branches they make a brilliant display which is followed by handsome maple-like leaves. Although the timber is of little value, it is a splendid ornamental shade tree.

Southern beeches

The southern beeches *(Nothofagus)* are closely related to the beeches *(Fagus)* of the northern hemisphere, but their buds are plump and rounded and the leaves are much smaller and often evergreen. Like their northern relatives, they prefer the mountains, where they ascend to the tree line and become more stunted as they spread out into a park-like landscape. On the slopes below, they form dense stands and cast such a deep shade that little else can grow below them. Such is mountain beech *(N. solandri* var. *cliffortioides)* which casts a deep green mantle over the mountains of New Zealand. The oval pointed leaves are evergreen and only 10–15mm ($\frac{2}{5}-\frac{3}{5}$in) long; in the silver beech *(N. menziesii)* they are similar, but distinctly toothed and in the red beech *(N. fusca)* they are up to 3cm (1$\frac{1}{6}$in) long. When first cut the heartwood of the red beech is of a deep red colour but this fades to a reddish brown. The timber of all of these New Zealand trees is smooth and fine grained and can replace beech in its traditional uses for brush backs, chairs and fine furniture.

Other southern beeches are scattered across the southern hemisphere from Australia and Tasmania to Chile and Patagonia and northwards into New Caledonia and New Guinea. The myrtle beech *(N. cunninghamii)* of Victoria is a magnificent timber tree equalled by the roble beech *(N. obliqua)* and raoul *(N. procera)* both of Chile. Antarctic beech *(N. antarctica)* reaches down to Tierra del Fuego.

Above: A typical dense stand of mountain beech *(Nothofagus solandri)*. Like beech woodland in the northern hemisphere, only meagre amounts of light reach the forest floor and thus little undergrowth develops.

Below: Flame kurrajong *(Brachychiton acerifolius)*, is a magnificent sight of bare branches covered with large red flowers and, in leaf, a fine shade tree.

Like its relative the dwarf beech *(N. pumilio)* of Chile it drops its leaves in the autumn. Although separated by the entire breadth of the Pacific Ocean, the closest relative of the dwarf beech is gunn's beech *(N. gunnii)* of the mountains of Tasmania. They share a number of characters including leaves with rounded teeth and veins which run, not as usual to the tips of the teeth, but to the base of the indentations between them. This remarkable distribution is not due to seeds drifting across the ocean to start new colonies on a distant shore, for the nuts sink in water and are soon killed by salt. It is known from fossil pollens that the southern beeches date back to the chalk period (Cretaceous) a hundred million years ago. Evidence is growing to support the belief that during the Cretaceous period all the countries where *Nothofagus* now grows were united into a single land mass, which has since been broken up and scattered by continental drift. Normal seed scattering on continuous land would allow the intricate pattern of relationships to be built which now exists. Many crossings and recrossings of the ocean would be necessary to achieve the same result, but for this evidence is scanty.

Ratas, tea trees and kowhais

As one drops down from the mountains of New Zealand into the valleys and plains the nature of the forest changes completely. The beeches are replaced by a great variety of broadleaved trees interspersed with pine-like trees of another southern group, the podocarps. There are no native eucalypts in New Zealand and other members of the myrtle family take their place. The most striking of these are the ratas *(Metrosideros)* which range in size from woody vines up to large trees. The northern rata *(M. robusta)* starts life as a vine clambering up other trees by means of short sucker roots like the ivy. Having gained height above its competitors in this way, the vine expands into a large irregular trunk and finally reaches a height of 20m (65½ft). Other ratas, among them the southern rata *(M. umbellata)* and the pohutukawa *(M. excelsa)*, start from the ground like ordinary trees. The pohutukawa prefers the coastal forests where it makes a spreading tree with a massive trunk. The silvery grey leaves are felted white below and provide the background for a magnificent display of crimson blossom along the sea cliffs about Christmas time. The flowers of other species range from orange red to scarlet and on some of the vines they are white.

The timber of the ratas is strong, hard and heavy and of a reddish brown colour. It has many uses where strength and hardwearing qualities are needed, as for parquet flooring. The natural bends of the branches of pohutukawa are taken advantage of in boat building. Like the oak, they provide the 'knees' on which the hull is built.

Tea-trees *(Leptospermum)* are common to both Australia and New Zealand. Captain Cook is reputed to have brewed tea from the leaves at Botany Bay and although the name has persisted the practice of making tea from them has not. The small (1cm; ⅖in) pointed elliptical leaves bear no resemblance to those of commercial tea *(Camellia thea)*. The common or red tea-tree *(L. scoparium)* ranges from the coast to the mountain tops in New Zealand, where it is known as manuka. On

Above: Spring time in New Zealand is enlivened by the kowhai *(Sophora microphylla)*, with its masses of golden blossom seen to advantage against the delicate foliage.

the coast it is a small tree up to 10m (33ft) tall, but the mountain form is prostrate. The white tea-tree or kanuka *(L. ericoides)* reaches a larger size, up to 15m (49ft), and early settlers soon found that the wood made shock-resistant handles for axes and other tools. It is also one of the best firewoods, easily kindled to make a hot fire. The traveller arriving at a New Zealand mountain hut is always gratified to find inside a pile of dry manuka branches with which to brew his camellia tea. His last chore on leaving is to replenish the store of manuka branches.

Unlike the forests of Australia, which are so liberally sprinkled with blossoms of many colours, those of New Zealand present a wall of green enlivened here and there by ratas, tea-trees and kowhais. While the southern alps are still capped with snow, on the plains the small-leaved kowhai *(Sophora microphylla)* covers its bare branches with golden pea-shaped blossoms about 4cm (1½in) long. Then the dainty leaves unroll like a fern with about thirty pairs of rounded leaflets. The pods that follow the flowers are narrowed between the seeds and provided with four wing-like ridges so that they look like a curious string of

Below: The white tea-tree *(Leptospermum ericoides)* enlivens the bush with its abundant white blossom but is better for making fires than for brewing tea.

beads. The bright yellow seeds develop into a shrub which forks again and again until it makes an impenetrable hummock 2m (6½ft) tall. Thus it remains for a number of years until, without warning, a straight shoot springs out of the centre and grows into a trunk 10m (33ft) high. This strange growth habit is not confined to the kowhais, for it turns up again in the lacebark *(Hoheria angustifolia)* and the ribbonwood *(Plagianthus betulinus)* in the hibiscus family, in several coprosmas (Rubiaceae) and in the putaputaweta *(Carpodetus serratus)*. There must be some common explanation for this reaction in many different families and the answer may be on the following lines. For millions

Above: The broad spine-tipped leaves of the monkey puzzle (*Araucaria araucana*) protect the large starchy seeds from the depredations of various marauding animals.

of years before man came on the scene the moas were the only large animals in New Zealand. These flightless birds browsed upon the vegetation. Recalling how the barnyard fowl picks out the shoot tips of plants and the plant, if it survives at all, does so by branching in all directions, the reaction to browsing by the moa may have been similar. So the seedlings survived by branching until they had formed a thicket and then were able to grow up and flower.

The southern gymnosperms

Kauris and monkey puzzles The true pines *(Pinus)* never reached further south than Sumatra before man carried them to the countries of the southern hemisphere. There they are replaced by other cone-bearing trees, chief among which are the kauris *(Agathis)* and the monkey puzzle *(Araucaria araucana)* and its relatives, which are placed together in a family of their own (Araucariaceae). Unlike the pines and spruces they rarely form extensive forests, but occur as single trees or small groves inter-mingled with broadleaved trees. The kauris tower above the other trees in these mixed forests, reaching 20–40m (65½–131ft) in height, their massive crowns supported on smooth grey cylindrical trunks which may be unbranched up to a height of 15–30m (49–98ft).

Above: A young tree of the Norfolk Island pine (*Araucaria heterophylla*) makes a formal pyramid with evenly spaced horizontal branches and close-pressed arching leaves.

Kauris are distributed from Malaya to Queensland, New Guinea, New Caledonia, New Zea-land and Fiji, each country or island group having its own special kind. The New Zealand kauri *(Agathis australis)* is confined to the North Island. Young trees have the narrow symmetrical shape of a pine, but the flat oblong leaves 4–8cm (1½–3⅛in) long are very different. Few large trees can be found now except in forest re-serves for they have all been felled for their timber. Some splendid mature trees can be seen in the Waipoua Reserve where a few ancient giants have also survived. The Maoris have given individual

names to these, such as Tanema-huta, meaning 'King of the Forest'. Tanemahuta dwarfs everything around it. The trunk is 4m (13ft) in diameter and rises straight up to 14m (46ft) to the first branches, the silver grey bark dimpled where it has flaked away. About ten huge limbs make up the massive crown, each one as big as an oak tree and decked here and there with tree lilies (*Collospermum hastatum*), the long sword-shaped leaves look-ing like giant birds' nests.

From colonial days, kauri timber has been prized for house building; a single tree would provide enough material to build a complete house with all of its furniture and fittings. The biscuit-coloured wood is strong and light and its easy work-ing qualities make it ideal for many purposes. The demand for the timber has been so great that everywhere the kauris have been over exploited to the point of extinction. Now, a search is being made for quick growing varieties able to compete with the introduced Monterey pine *(Pinus radiata).*

When the bark of a kauri is damaged it gives out a milky fluid which dries and hardens into a resin. Considerable quantities of this resin, or 'gum' as it was often inappropriately called, were produced and used for the manufacture of linoleum and varnishes. The resin was collected from living trees and also from the ground where it may have remained for hundreds of years in old kauri forests. After the trees had been felled gum prospectors would prod the ground with iron rods to locate masses of resin and dig them up.

The monkey puzzle or Chile pine was discovered in the eighteenth century, but it was not until 1844 when William Lobb sent a quantity of seed back that its remarkable habit caught the imagination of people in Victorian England and it became fashionable to plant it. The arching branches arranged in regular whorls give it a rather stiff habit and the broad, leathery 5cm (2in)-long leaves ending in a spiny tip and closely arranged along the branches produced an effect quite unparalleled. The globular cones with sharp pointed scales are 10–15cm (4–6in) long and fall to pieces when ripe. The seeds are 3cm ($1\frac{1}{6}$in) long with starchy kernels tasting like chestnuts, and were a regular article of diet of the Araucarian Indians of the coastal ranges of Chile where the tree is native.

The bunya pine *(Araucaria bidwillii)* of Queensland is not so bizarre as the monkey puzzle. The leaves are smaller, 2–3cm ($\frac{4}{5}$–$1\frac{1}{6}$in), packed closely on the branches which make a broad columnar crown with a rounded top. The cones weigh up to 4kg (9 lb) with seeds 5cm (2in) long. These seeds were much prized as food by the local tribes; each tribe had its own grove of trees and each family its own tree, which was passed on from generation to generation. The hoop pine *(A. cunninghamii)* of Queensland and New South Wales and the Norfolk Island pine *(A. heterophylla)* are again different in habit for they have wide-spaced branches on which the small (1cm; $\frac{2}{5}$in) leaves are closely packed and incurved giving a whipcord appearance. When Captain Cook discovered Norfolk

Above: Rimu *(Dacrydium cupressinum)* a dominant tree in the podocarp forests of New Zealand, has pendulous branchlets with short spreading leaves that are triangular in section.

Island on his second voyage in 1774, he noted the splendid forests of the pine which were duly reported to the Admiralty. Four years later when the first colony in Australia was founded at Port Jackson (now Sydney), the ships were immediately sent on to Norfolk Island to start another colony there. In the days of sailing ships this was a wise move to ensure a supply of good naval timber. All of the araucarias mentioned here produce a range of good quality softwoods equal to any of the pines and spruces of the northern hemisphere.

Podocarps The podocarps are another group of conifers almost confined to the southern hemisphere. They vary greatly in habit and appearance for the leaves may be small and scale-like, flat like those of the firs *(Abies)* or larger and strap shaped. The pollen-bearing catkins are not unlike those of pines *(Pinus),* but the cones are very different as they consist of two to four small scales, only two of which bear a seed and only one of these matures. The seed coat may be leathery or fleshy and brightly coloured. In North Island, New Zealand podocarps mingle with the kauri but South Island is too cold for the kauri and matai *(Podocarpus spicatus)* and miro *(P. ferrugineus)* are some of the largest forest trees, up to 25m

Above: A fine kahikatea *(Podocarpus dacrydioides)* silhouetted against the snow-clad Southern Alps, is a relict from swamp forest growing formerly on the low ground.

(82ft) tall. Their pine-like timber is of excellent quality and is put to a great variety of uses. The seeds of matai are black with a thin flesh and on the miro they are larger (2cm; $\frac{4}{5}$in) and purplish with a bloom like a plum. In lowland swampy areas the kahikatea *(P. dacrydioides)* may take over completely and form pure stands of tall mast-like trees. Young trees are graceful with slender drooping branches covered with scale-like leaves and the dark green seeds are perched on fleshy scarlet stalks. Rimu *(Dacrydium cupressinum)* is in many ways similar but the leaves are more spreading and triangular in section.

The celery-top pines *(Phyllocladus)* are a remarkable group of podocarps, for their leaves are reduced to functionless scales and the work of the leaves is performed by flattened wedge-shaped branches (phylloclades) which mimic leaves in appearance. The male catkins are placed on the tips of these phylloclades and the seeds in the indentations along the side. The celery-top pine of Tasmania *(P. aspleniifolius)* grows in lowland and mountain forests and the two tree species of New Zealand, the toatoa *(P. glaucus)* and the tanekaha *(P. trichomanoides),* are members of the mixed podocarp forests. The bark of the tanekaha is rich in tannin from which the Maoris used to obtain a red dye.

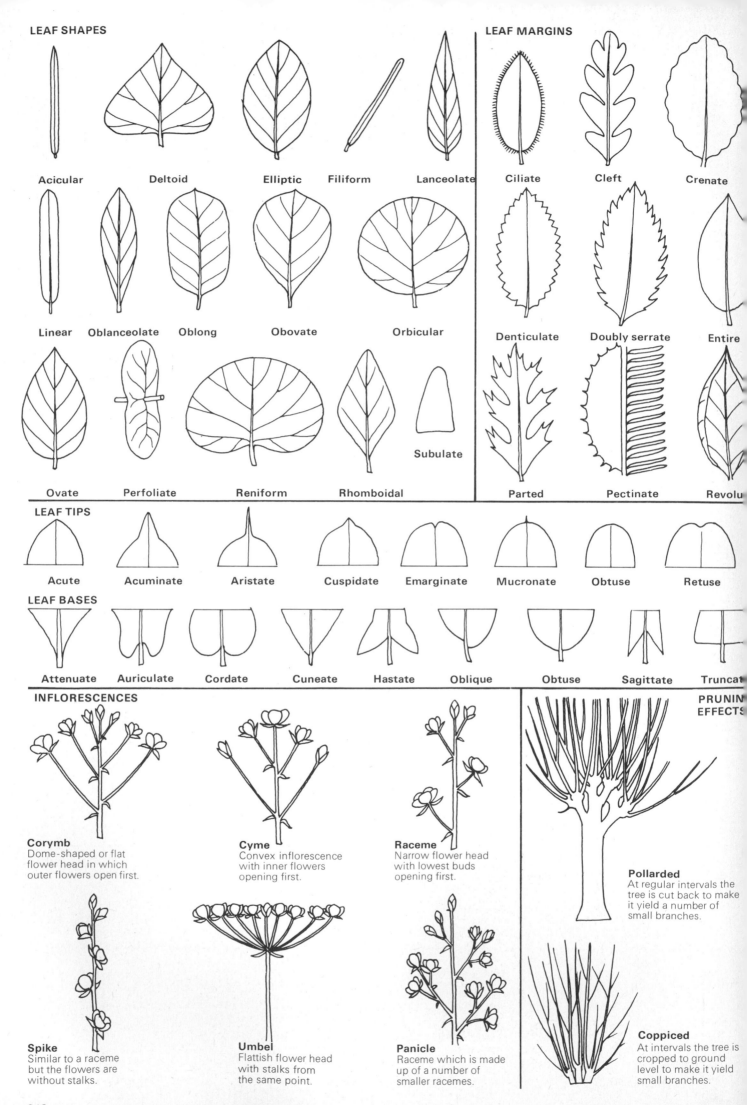

LEAF SHAPES

Acicular · Deltoid · Elliptic · Filiform · Lanceolate

Linear · Oblanceolate · Oblong · Obovate · Orbicular

Subulate

Ovate · Perfoliate · Reniform · Rhomboidal

LEAF MARGINS

Ciliate · Cleft · Crenate

Denticulate · Doubly serrate · Entire

Parted · Pectinate · Revolu

LEAF TIPS

Acute · Acuminate · Aristate · Cuspidate · Emarginate · Mucronate · Obtuse · Retuse

LEAF BASES

Attenuate · Auriculate · Cordate · Cuneate · Hastate · Oblique · Obtuse · Sagittate · Truncat

INFLORESCENCES

Corymb
Dome-shaped or flat flower head in which outer flowers open first.

Cyme
Convex inflorescence with inner flowers opening first.

Raceme
Narrow flower head with lowest buds opening first.

Spike
Similar to a raceme but the flowers are without stalks.

Umbel
Flattish flower head with stalks from the same point.

Panicle
Raceme which is made up of a number of smaller racemes.

PRUNIN EFFECTS

Pollarded
At regular intervals the tree is cut back to make it yield a number of small branches.

Coppiced
At intervals the tree is cropped to ground level to make it yield small branches.

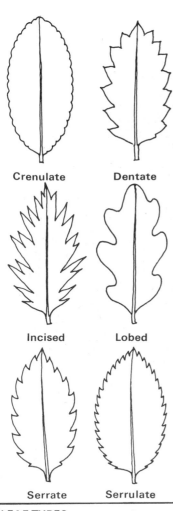

Crenulate   Dentate

Incised   Lobed

Serrate   Serrulate

LEAF TYPES

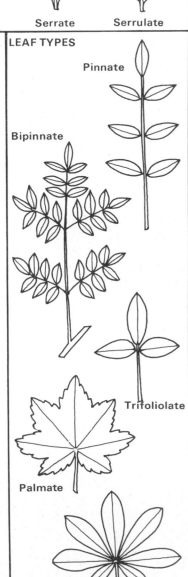

Pinnate

Bipinnate

Trifoliolate

Palmate

Compound
palmate (digitate)

Glossary

Afforestation To cover land with trees, usually to yield timber but sometimes to give shelter, conserve moisture or stop erosion.

Angiosperm A class of plants whose seeds are borne within the walls of an ovary.

Adpressed/Appressed Closely pressed to an adjoining member, such as bud to a twig.

Axil The upper angle between a leaf stalk and a twig, a twig and a branch or a leaf vein and the midrib.

Axillary Within that angle.

Bark The outer layer of a tree that protects the inner tissues from damage and disease.

Bast The soft, often fibrous, layer of phloem tissue between the bark and the inner cells.

Bole The trunk of a tree, usually the lower section.

Bract A leaf-like structure beneath a flower or at the base of a stalk. Often seen on conifer cones.

Broadleaved tree Often called hardwoods and usually with broader leaves than conifers, this large group, mostly dicotyledons, all belong to the group of plants called Angiosperms.

Cambium A layer of active cell division that produces new tissues, such as the vascular cambium that gives rise to new xylem and phloem tissue.

Catkin A dense spike of scaly-bracted, stalkless flowers. Usually drooping.

Coniferous tree Often called softwoods and usually with needle-like leaves, these trees belong to the primitive group of plants called Gymnosperms ('naked seeded'). They have woody fruit bodies called cones.

Copse A small wood.

Cork A layer of dead cells on the outside of a stem or root that guards the inner tissues against damage and desiccation. Well developed in the cork oak.

Cotyledon The first leaves that emerge from the seed.

Cultivar Cultivated varieties that are propagated, not by seeds, but by cuttings or grafting.

Cuticle The varnish-like impervious coating of an epidermis that prevents damage and water loss.

Deciduous Losing leaves in winter.

Deflexed Bent markedly outwards and downwards.

Defoliation Loss of leaves due to abnormal causes.

Dicotyledon A plant having two cotyledons. One of two major subdivisions of flowering plants.

Dioecious Having male and female flowers on separate plants.

Epidermis The surface layer of cells just below the cuticle.

Epiphyte A plant growing upon another for support only.

Exserted Projecting visibly from between other parts.

Glabrous Without hairs.

Glaucous Silvery or bluish-grey. Also, with a waxy bloom.

Growth ring The annual ring of growth by which a tree increases its diameter.

Gymnosperm A class of primitive plants that are 'naked seeded', their seeds being exposed on a scale and not concealed in an ovary.

Heartwood The darker, drier central core of wood in a tree. It contains no living cells and is more durable than the outer sapwood.

Hybrid A cross between two different species.

Lamina The blade of a leaf.

Layering The establishment of a new plant when a branch makes contact with the ground and sends roots into the soil.

Leaflet A single member of a compound or pinnate leaf.

Lenticel A breathing pore that shows as a corky or white mark on trunks and branches.

Liana A woody climbing plant with long, rope-like stems.

Lignin The chemical substance impregnated in the cell walls of xylem tissue and giving wood its basic characteristics.

Medullary ray A sheet of tissue running radially through a stem or root and responsible for food storage and transport of materials across the stem. Seen as silvery lines in some timbers. Very clear in oak timber.

Mesophyll The inner tissue of a leaf.

Monocotyledon A plant having one cotyledon. One of two major subdivisions of flowering plants.

Monoecious Having separate male and female flowers on the same plant.

Parasite A plant living at the expense of another organism.

Petiole A leaf stalk.

Phloem Vascular tissue that transports food materials made by the plant. Often called bast.

Photosynthesis The process by which carbohydrates are synthesized from carbon dioxide and water in the presence of sunlight and chlorophyll.

Phyllode A flattened stem that looks and functions like a leaf.

Pneumatophore An aerial root that grows vertically upwards to provide roots submerged in water or mud with essential air.

Podocarps A family of evergreen conifers occurring mainly in the southern hemisphere. They have male and female flowers usually on separate trees and characteristic stalked fruits.

Pollination The transfer of pollen from the male parts of a flower (anther) to the female part (stigma).

Pubescent Hairy.

Radicle The first root developing from a seed.

Reflexed Turned back sharply.

Relict A primitive survivor from earlier times; a 'living fossil'.

Resin The sticky 'sap' exuded by many conifers.

Respiration The reverse of photosynthesis, whereby some organic matter is broken down to carbon dioxide and water, with the release of energy.

Roundwood Timber in the form of logs before being sawn into boards.

Rubber The elastic substance made from the sap or 'latex' of rubber trees.

Sapling A young tree.

Sapwood The newly formed, light-coloured wood that forms the outer region of a tree trunk. It is composed of living xylem cells that transport water throughout the tree.

Scale A small leaf or bract. The term is loosely applied to many structures, such as bud scale, cone scale, and so on.

Sessile Without a stalk.

Silviculture The care of woods, usually for the production of timber. Arboriculture is the care of individual trees.

Springwood The paler and less dense wood formed in spring and early summer. Also called earlywood.

Stand A continuous growth or plantation of trees. Usually applied to one species.

Stave One of a number of curved strips of wood that make up a barrel.

Stomata Breathing pores, found mainly on the under-surface of leaves.

Stratification The grouping of vegetation into well defined layers, such as trees, shrubs and ground vegetation.

Sucker A shoot arising from below soil level close to the parent plant.

Summerwood Wood formed during the summer, usually recognizable as the darker and denser portion of the annual growth ring. Also called latewood.

Sustained yield A term used in forestry for the ideal situation in which timber can be produced in commercially useful quantities year after year.

Taiga Primeval Siberian forest. The term is also used in a general sense for the coniferous forest that stretches across the northern hemisphere.

Tannin An acidic substance distilled from the bark of oak and some other trees and used for converting hide into leather.

Taproot A stout, vertical, anchoring root developed from the radicle. A strong taproot gives a tree great stability.

Transpiration The loss of water from a plant by evaporation, especially through the stomata.

Tree line The line at which tree growth ceases at high elevations. Most clearly seen where coniferous forest clothes mountainsides.

Uniform stand A plantation of trees of similar size and age.

Unisexual Of one sex only.

Variety A subdivision of a species. The term is used mainly for natural variation within a species rather than for new plants produced by cultivation, for which cultivar is more appropriate.

Vascular tissue The tissue system in plants that conducts water and food substances and gives mechanical support. It is composed mainly of xylem (wood) and phloem (bast).

Veneer A very thin sheet of wood cut from a rotating log. Veneers are used as surface decoration on a wide variety of board products.

Vivipary The production of seeds that germinate while still on the parent plant.

Wane The rough edge of a timber board remaining after a log has been cut but before it is trimmed. Fences made of such untrimmed boards are often called wany lap.

Whorl A ring of structures, such as leaves or flowers, arising from the same level.

Xerophyte A plant adapted to living in very dry conditions.

Xylem The basic tissue of wood, consisting of long cells with thickened walls and responsible for transporting water and mineral salts throughout the tree.

Index

Encyclopedia of TREES

Credits

Picture Credits
The publishers wish to thank the following photographers and organizations who have supplied photographs for this book. Photographs have been credited by page number and position on the page: (B) Bottom, (T) Top, (BL) Bottom left, etc.

Photographs
American Forest Institute: 58(T).

American Plywood Association: 64(B).

Heather Angel: Half-title (L). Copyright page. 13, 16, 18(TL), 25(TR), 28(B), 29(BR), 31(BR,TR), 34–5, 40–1(T), 41(BR), 42(BR,CR), 43, 91(L), 95(TL,BR), 97(B), 98(BL), 115(TR,BC), 116–7, 120, 121(BR), 123(TR), 128, 132(TR), 133(TR), 136, 139, 145(BL,BR), 148(BR), 156, 164(L), 181, 190–1(BR), 192(L), 197, 201, 203, 221(R), 223(TL,BR), 226(TL,B), 229(B), 232(TL), 233, 234(TL), 235(TL), 237, 238–9, 241(BR,BL), 244(T), 245(B), 246(R), 247;

Animal Photography Ltd.;
(Sally Anne Thompson): Back endpaper;

A–Z Botanical Collection: 89, 103(T), 132(BL,BR), 157(BR), 167(R), 169(Maurice Nimmo), 187(CR), 210–1, 220(B), 221(TL), 222, 223(TR), 224(TL,TR), 233(TR,L), 238, 240(TR), 242;

Pat Brindley: 171(L);

Camera Press: 73, 74(L);

Michael Chinery: 46(B), 49(T,B), 52(B), and 204;

Eric Crichton: 12(TL), 20(T), 21(T), 22(T), 25(B), 35(R), 38–9(T), 53(B), 82(TR), 116, 124, 137(BL), 148(TL,TR), 149, 152(BL), 165(T), 174(TL), 175, 178(L), 187(TR), 224(B), 225(L), 235(BR), 239(BL,R), 240(BL,BR), 241(TR), 243, 244(B);

Bruce Coleman Ltd.: Title page, 29(BL), 231(B, Jane Burton), 236(BL);

Crown Zellerbach: 70(B);

Adrian Davies: 22(B), 26(T), 205(TR);

Dr John Dransfield: 234(TR), 235(TR);

Dunlop Sports Co Ltd.: 79(TR,CR);

Herbert Edlin: 70(T), 132(TL), 140, 200;

Elisabeth Photo Library: 32–3;

Robin Fletcher: Front endpaper, Half-title (R), Contents page, 14, 15, 17(T), 20–1(B), 38–9(B), 39(CL,CR), 48, 50(T), 51(B), 53(T), 55, 70–1, 76(BL), 80–1, 112, 146, 148(BL), 153;

Hugh Fraser: 12(CR);

Michael Freeman: 46–7(T), 64(T);

Govt. of British Columbia/MacMillan Bloedel: 40–1(B).

Cover Photographs: Robin Fletcher 'VISION INTERNATIONAL'

Gunn and Moore Ltd.: 79(TL);

Brian Hawkes: 24(TL), 78(B), 82(B);

F. Nigel Hepper: 28(TL), 68–9(B), 76(TL), 82(TL), 228, 229(T), 230(L), 232(TR);

Anthony Huxley: 30(T), 47(BL), 246(TL);

Irvine Development Corporation: 68(B);

London College of Furniture: 75;

Bob Marchant © Salamander Books Ltd.: 87(L), 101(B), 102, 105(TR), 106, 108, 113(L), 115(CL), 121(BL,TR), 123(TL), 133(BR), 137(TR), 147(BR), 152(BC), 174(BR), 189, 205(BL), 212, 217(B), 218(T), 240(TL);

Dr Pat Morris: 12(BR), 18–9, 26(B), 31(TL), 36–7, 52(T), 59, 60, 99(BR), 216, 217(T), 220(TL), 236(BR);

Natural History Photographic Agency: 29(T, James Carmichael), 37(B, Stephen Dalton), 39(TL, Stephen Dalton), 42 (L, N. Morcombe), 45 (Ivan Polunin), 47(TR, Stephen Dalton), 67(T, W. Perrie), 157(BL, Stephen Dalton), 227 (Ivan Polunin);

Natural Science Photos: 30(B, C A Walker), 33(TR), 41(TR, C A Walker), 44(TL, C Banks, BR, P H Ward), 50(B, P H Ward), 51(T, P H Ward), 52(B, Michael Chinery), 66(T, J M Hobday), 67(T), 68–9(T, J M Hobday), 80(TL), 83(L), 84, 95(TR, Isobel Bennett), 109, 154;

New Zealand Logging Industry Research Association Inc: 56–7;

Maurice Nimmo: 10, 24–5, 87(R), 97(TL), 96(TR), 98(BR), 99(T), 103(B), 104, 105(BL), 111, 113(R), 115(TL, BL), 118, 119, 121(TL), 123(BR,BL), 127(L,R), 131, 132(TC), 133(TL,C), 145(TR,TL), 147(BL), 150, 151, 152(BR), 155, 157(TR), 158, 161, 162, 163, 164(R), 165(B), 166, 167(L), 171(R), 173, 174(TC,TR,BL), 177, 178(R), 179, 187(BL), 191(TR), 192, 193(R);

Dr. Francis Ng: 208–9, 218, 219;

Robert Andrew Paterson: 213;

Rainham Timber Engineering Ltd.: 72(CR);

Rentokil Ltd.: 71(TR);

Rijksmuseum voor Volkskunde het Nederlands, Arnhem: 66–7(B), 76–7;

G. R. Roberts: 17(B), 27, 58(B), 61(TR), 65(B), 67(B), 208(TL), 211;

Dr Edward S. Ross: 230(R), 231(T);

Rothamsted Experimental Station: 32(L);

Bruce Scott © Salamander Books Ltd.: 6, 61(TL,BL), 63, 72(TL), 91(R);

Scottish Tourist Board: 74(R);

Harry Smith Photographic Collection: 245(T);

Sodra Skogsagarna: 54(TL);

Spectrum Colour Library: Foreword, 83(TR), 225(R);

Svenska Cellulosa UK Ltd.: 62;

Timber Research and Development Association (TRADA): 72(B);

M. W. Tweedie: 34(TL);

United African Company (Timber) Ltd.: 214–5;

Wales Tourist Board: 78(T);

A. W. Westall/Malcolm Scott: 101(T);

Trevor Wood: 79(B);

Jon Wyand: 77(TR), 79.

Artists
Copyright of the drawings on the pages following the artists' names is the property of Salamander Books Ltd.

Henry Barnett: 223;

Olivia Beasley: 23, 88–107 inclusive;

Caroline Dewing: 119, 121 (BW details);

Ian Garrard (Linden Artists): 18, 19, 35, 36, 37, 39, 41, 44, 46, 55, 60, 61, 130–205 inclusive;

David Nockels: 86–87, 108–127 inclusive.

Display titles designed by David Beard.

Acknowledgments
In addition to the credits on this page the publishers would like to thank the following organizations for their help: The Princes Risborough Laboratory of The Building Research Establishment, The Forestry Commission, the Council of Forest Industries of British Columbia, Phoenix Timber/Boards Ltd., Royal Botanic Gardens, Kew, Timber Trades Journal, Weyroc Ltd.

We would also like to thank Ms. Penny Bould for undertaking the picture research, Maurice Chandler, David Lambert and Peter Schofield for their editorial help, Nicolette Shawyer and Vernon Robinson for proof reading and copy editing, Sue McSwiney for typing much of the manuscript, and Martin Schultz for his invaluable help with many aspects of the project.

We are indebted to Mr. A. W. Westall of the Bedgebury National Pinetum, Kent for providing samples of most of the species featured in the Guide to Conifers, and to Mr. Archie Skinner, Head Gardener of Sheffield Park Garden, Sussex for providing a sample of the elusive Montezuma pine.

PRINTED IN BELGIUM BY
proost
INTERNATIONAL BOOK PRODUCTION